MW01027535

SANGER

TOLEDO-LUCAS COUNTY PUBLIC LIBRARY
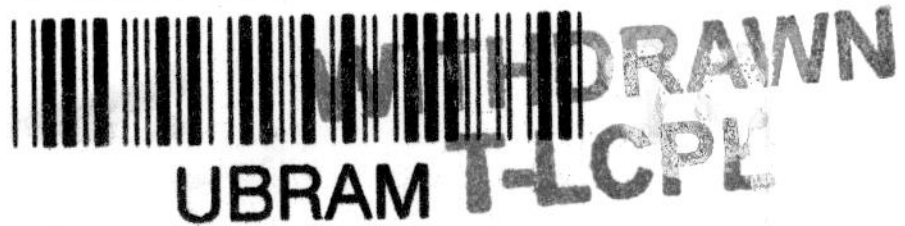
WITHDRAWN
UBRAM T-LCPL

92 G983 Kap
Kapr, Albert.
Johann Gutenberg #31655691
MAR - 1 1997

JOHANN GUTENBERG: THE MAN AND HIS INVENTION

Portrait of Johann Gutenberg.
Copper engraving by A. Thevet, Paris, 1584.
As all the other depictions of Gutenberg, this one
is pure invention.

ALBERT KAPR

Johann Gutenberg

The Man and his Invention

TRANSLATED FROM THE GERMAN BY

DOUGLAS MARTIN

SCOLAR PRESS

The German text © Albert Kapr, 1996
The English translation © Douglas Martin, 1996

All rights reserved. No part of this publication may be reproduced, stored in a retrieval system, or transmitted in any form or by any means, electronic, mechanical, photocopying, recording, or otherwise without the prior permission of the publisher.

The English edition published 1996 by

SCOLAR PRESS
Gower House
Croft Road
Aldershot
Hants GU11 3HR

ASHGATE PUBLISHING COMPANY
Old Post Road
Brookfield
Vermont 05036–9704

Albert Kapr has asserted his right to be identified as author of this work

Douglas Martin has asserted his right to be identified as translator of this work

This book was first published in German in 1986 under the title *Johannes Gutenberg: Persönlichkeit und Leistung* by Urania-Verlag, Leipzig, Jena and Berlin and under licence by C. H. Beck, Munich
Second revised German edition, 1988
This is the third edition, revised by the author for
first publication in English translation

British Library Cataloguing-in-Publication Data.
Kapr, Albert
Johann Gutenberg: the Man and His Invention –
3Rev.ed
I. Title II. Martin, Douglas
686.2092

Library of Congress Cataloging-in-Publication Data
Kapr, Albert.
[Johann Gutenberg. English]
Johann Gutenberg: the man and his invention / Albert Kapr:
translated from the German by Douglas Martin.
Includes bibliographical references and index.
ISBN 1-85928-114-1
1. Gutenberg, Johann, c. 1400–1468. 2. Printers—Germany—
Biography. 3. Printing—History—Origin and antecedents.
I. Martin, Douglas, 1939-. II. Title.
Z126.Z7K2813. 1995
886.2' 092—dc20
[B] 94-42062
CIP

The publisher acknowledges a grant for the translation from Inter-Nationes, Bonn

ISBN 1 85928 114 1

Typeset in Poliphilus/Blado by Poole Typesetting (Wessex) Limited and printed in Great Britain by Biddles Ltd, Guildford.

Contents

Contents

Translator's introduction

THERE IS NO GOOD BIOGRAPHY OF GUTENBERG IN ENGLISH, as Janet Ing states in her recent study, *Johann Gutenberg and His Bible*, which sets out to answer the question: 'What we do know about Gutenberg, and how and when did we know it?' Her book provides a map to the maze, and places in context the significant contributions made by scholars as various as Harry Carter, T. L. De Vinne, Otto Fuhrmann, Lotte Hellinga, J. H. Hessels, Hellmut Lehmann-Haupt, Douglas C. McMurtrie, Sir Irvine Masson, Paul Needham, George D. Painter, Robert Proctor, Richard N. Schwab, Victor Scholderer, Allan Stevenson and others writing in English.

Let Janet Ing continue to formulate this problem, and list the formidable qualifications any candidate must bring to the task of presenting all the facets of Gutenberg's personality and achievement in the light of our current state of knowledge:

> No fully satisfactory English-language biography has yet appeared; too often, writers have tended to follow the lead of earlier scholars in preference to examining the primary evidence and coming to their own conclusions. This is not surprising, for to understand the details of Gutenberg's life and work, one must have a practical knowledge of the social structure, political and religious institutions, and legal conventions of Gutenberg's time and place. Ideally, one should not only read Latin and modern German, but also understand the nuances of the Mainz and Strasbourg dialects of the mid-fifteenth century. Finally one must be capable of undertaking detailed bibliographical research involving (among other things) the identification of type, the dating of paper, and the critical study of early printed texts (Ing, 1988: 26–7).

I had encountered these hurdles and handicaps some years earlier, and concluded that the obvious answer must be to find and translate the best German-language biography: for only a writer to whom much of this cultural, linguistic and typographic background came naturally would be left with enough enthusiasm and energy for Gutenberg himself; and thus be able to command the interest of a worldwide and general English-language readership.

As might be expected, the German reader is confronted with successive scholarly strata dating from the late nineteenth century to the present – where detailed observations of enduring worth often mix with long-overturned conclusions – and a vast sub-literature of popular biography with epic, commemorative and novelistic sideshoots. The standard biography is Aloys Ruppel: *Johannes Gutenberg: Sein Leben und sein Werk,* not revised since 1947 or reprinted since 1967. An editorial overhaul of the original at different hands would be a precondition for translation into English. There is also a useful portrait in pictures and documents with text by Helmut Presser in the invaluable Rowohlt paperback series of monographs, and, more recently, a brilliant but lengthy study has appeared in French, Guy Bechtel's *Gutenberg et l'invention de l'imprimerie: Une enquête* (Paris, Fayard 1992), and a biography in German, Andreas Venzke's *Johannes Gutenberg: Der Erfinder des Buchdrucks* (Zurich, Benzinger 1993), which has been unfavourably reviewed (Kapr, 1994; Koppitz, 1994).

There the matter rested until Albert Kapr's book came into my hands, and it soon became clear that his would be by far the most suitable biography of Gutenberg to bring out in English. Expecting to be able to work with a regular translator and simply help with technical issues, I found that in the event Albert Kapr was keen for me to take on the actual translation, and for a reason quite different from any given by Janet Ing above: 'We have both handled type, and that is what counts'. In other words, those of us who started our working lives handling metal types could have been taken on as Gutenberg's journeymen – should a time-shift take place – and would quickly grasp in detail what was happening and what was expected of us. Current developments in information technology may move in parallel with the principles of typography and the book, but do not displace them. Designing and working with letter forms has remained in essence unchanged from Gutenberg's day to ours.

As well as this present full-length Gutenberg monograph, Albert Kapr published *Johannes Gutenberg: Tatsachen und Thesen* (Insel-Bücherei, 1977) and many papers in the *Gutenberg-Jahrbuch, Beiträge zur Inkunabelkunde* and elsewhere. He is also internationally renowned for his work as a calligrapher and designer of typefaces, and as a book designer, and for his many books on those subjects. For many years he was Professor and Rector of the *Hochschule für Grafik und Buchkunst* in Leipzig and Head of its Institute for Book Design.

Albert Kapr was writing this work in retirement during the last difficult years of the GDR, and accordingly had restricted access to recent books and journals in English and French – languages which in any case he read only with difficulty. He thus welcomed that his assertions and hypotheses should be compared with the latest work in these languages, and found the general consensus heartening. Several hypotheses first advanced by Professor Dr Kapr have in fact received independent corroboration as work proceeded, most strikingly, perhaps, that concerning the role of Nicholas of Cues and the Bursfeld Congregation in the diffusion of printing (Hellinga, 1993; Röll, 1994). Conversely, Kapr's extensive contacts and travel both within the former socialist bloc and in the West, and earlier to China as well, permitted him to take a global view of Gutenberg and the origins of printing in this volume.

It was the author's aim for this translation to incorporate as many as possible of the revisions which will eventually need to appear in a third German edition – such as the state of progress in the *Catholicon* debate, and the discovery of the Leipzig copies of the *42-line Bible* missing since the war (the vellum copy from the German Book and Script Museum has been found in excellent condition in the Lenin Library in Moscow, and the Leipzig University Library copy on paper is presently stored by the Moscow Lomonosov University Library) – and he was also anxious to include recent publications in English in the bibliography. Albert Kapr contributed to the English version of this book until a few days before his death, at the age of 76, on 31 March 1995. It is sad that he was unable to see it in proof or in print.

Dr H. J. Cohn, Department of History, University of Warwick, was kind enough to draw attention to several interpretational weaknesses, and to make suggestions for which both author and translator would like to thank him. I am also grateful to the Mainz-born librarian, Hans Eckert (Hattersheim), for kindly reading this translation in typescript, advising on and verifying a host of queries and spotting errors in translation. The translator's enthusiasm for Gutenberg dates from his first visit to the Gutenberg Museum in Mainz – which is to have a major extension to its exhibition complex in time for 2000. The inventor's birth is traditionally celebrated at the opening of each new century, and thus Gutenberg's achievement and influence will continue to be projected into the next millennium.

Douglas Martin
Oadby, May 1995

In memoriam

ALBERT KAPR
20 July 1918 – 31 March 1995

SUSAN CLARE MARTIN
29 August 1943 – 30 June 1995

Introduction to the first German edition

UNQUESTIONABLY GUTENBERG was one of the greatest figures in the history of mankind: his invention became the almost exclusive basis for the subsequent transmission of learning and literature. No amount of speculation about the 'Gutenberg Galaxy' coming to an end can diminish his achievements (McLuhan, 1962); neither has the progression through photosetting to digital composition altered the way in which, by his method, identical single characters are combined into words, lines and pages, from which prints are then taken in a relatively large edition.

Each generation has its own image of Gutenberg; one reason for this is that there are always new research findings to be assimilated, another is that the historical standpoint of the observer is necessarily also undergoing change. It is true that Gutenberg research in recent decades has brought fewer important discoveries to light than in the first half of the twentieth century, but there are still a number of significant new findings to be made known. Furthermore, it should not be overlooked today that the field of vision of some earlier Gutenberg experts was often narrowed down – through local patriotism or the national pattern of scholarship – to a specialized interest in some abstract, technical issue or specific artistic problem. Their fundamental scepticism opposed to speculation led to this concentration on problems of detail, and has hampered any broader attempt to draw conclusions about the achievement as a whole and the personality behind it, as well as on certain periods of time for which no facts can be presented.

Vital sections are still missing from a comprehensive and scholarly picture of Gutenberg. For instance, from the time of his childhood and youth up until his residence in Strasbourg there are no documents available; and there are contradictory views on the attribution of various items of Mainz printing. But even if we have only the fragments of a Gutenberg picture, it seems to me legitimate at least to sketch in the outlines for a complete portrait. It must be possible to reach close to the character of the inventor and his work from the reactions and reverberations of the world around him; and by moving on from his milieu to his commercial motivation, from the enterprise to the person, from the state of technology to the opportunities for discovery, from the known conduct of the master craftsman to his behaviour during the missing years and his upbringing. We have to view the problems surrounding Gutenberg and his invention in the widest possible cultural and historical context.

Gutenberg can only be understood as a man of his age – caught up in the tensions between the Middle Ages and the Renaissance. His personality brings together the devout yet superstitious representative of the old established order, and the inventive, steadfast seeker and striver after more knowledge typical of a new, middle-class and mercantile society.

The author's aim was to write a lively account accessible to the general reader, which will take into consideration all the essential scholarly findings. He did not have in mind a totally new biographical study, for the facts known about Gutenberg the man are insufficient for that. Rather, like a criminologist, he will present the Gutenberg files before the reader once more and also offer his personal interpretation of this historic case. To this end a wide area has been searched for clues, accomplices and witnesses questioned, and previously overlooked matters re-examined – knowing full well that there may be little to be found in this way which has a direct bearing on the master printer's life and work, and yet trusting to this as the most reliable procedure when it comes to elucidating people's attitudes in any age. Interesting parallel developments have been described even where they do not necessarily impinge directly on Gutenberg's life and the history of his invention. Above all the author poses questions, some of them fresh ones, to which, in the current state of knowledge, no answers can yet be given.

The last comprehensive monograph on Gutenberg in German, *Johannes Gutenberg: Sein Leben und sein Werk* by Aloys Ruppel, was printed in 1939; a second edition with only minor revisions appeared in 1947 and this was reprinted unchanged in 1967 (Ruppel, 1967). A collection appeared in 1972 under Hans Widmann's editorship, in which various challenges to Ruppel's explanations were reported together with the findings of more recent research (Widmann, 1972a). Further titles are included in the bibliography. Whereas Ruppel arranged his material under subject headings, the present volume will follow the course of Gutenberg's life, so that the description of inventions and printed works can be related to contemporary stages in his biography. Only through such an historical sequence can changes in the surrounding social fabric, in particular the inner conflicts within the cities of Mainz and Strasbourg as they affect our central figure, be illuminated in order to reveal information to the historical detective.

A high value has been set on reproducing the documents and references in which Gutenberg's life and work has come down to us; all the essential ones, even the extensive Strasbourg court records, have been fully quoted. All those pieces of printing believed to have been produced by Gutenberg in his own workshops, as well as some that may be linked to him only indirectly, have been represented. Where controversy prevails, the alternative opinions have been set out and the author's standpoint indicated. In such cases it has always been made clear whether we are dealing with a guess or a thesis, a belief or an assured statement.

For the specialist reader, who wishes to probe more deeply into a particular aspect, a comprehensive index and bibliography have been provided. Source references in the text are to this bibliography, so that the reading flow should not be impeded by footnotes; since it is intended that this book should fall into the hands of those who work in printing, publishing, bookselling or librarianship – in the making and dissemination of the printed book – as well as serve all who enjoy books and regard them as something important in their lives.

I am much indebted to the German Book and Script Museum at the Deutsche Bücherei in Leipzig, to Leipzig University Library, the Gutenberg-Museum in Mainz and the Mainz City Library. I have received friendly encouragement and critical advice from Prof. Dr Severin Corsten, Cologne; Prof. Dr Karl Czok, Leipzig; Dr Dietmar Debes, Leipzig; Dr Ferdinand Geldner, Munich; Dr Claus W. Gerhardt, Darmstadt, Prof. Dr Hans Halbey, Mainz; Dr Leonhard Hoffmann, Berlin; Helma Schaefer, Leipzig; and Prof. Dr Hans Widmann, Mainz; to all of whom I would like to express grateful thanks. I would also like to thank Urania-Verlag, and Helmut Selle and Horst Hering in particular, as well as the printers for the care they have brought to their work.

I have always found this inventor, technologist and artist, Johann Gutenberg, a fascinating personality, and hope that something of the excitement and pleasure I have experienced in writing this book may communicate itself to the reader.

Albert Kapr
Leipzig, 1986

Textura. Page from a Latin Bible in two volumes, written in the region of Leipzig in the mid fifteenth-century. Leipzig University Library. Reduced.

CHAPTER ONE

Gutenberg's origins, birth and early years

The arts of writing and the book before Gutenberg

THE WORLD SEEMED TO BE FLYING WILDLY OFF COURSE. Philosophers and theologians saw the happenings of the fourteenth and fifteenth centuries as a manifestation of God's predestination or the configuration of the stars. Every aspect of human life was being revolutionized. New technologies were being discovered or adopted from distant lands: the water-wheel for driving forge-hammers, flour-mills and mechanical saws; the crane, the wood-plane, the weight-regulated clock, the rudder, the compass, gunpowder and papermaking. Returning crusaders and merchants brought back unheard-of works of astronomy, geography, medicine, mathematics and philosophy which they had acquired from the infidels, and these were eagerly translated and copied in humanist circles. Writing and books were the custodians and mediators of this growing body of knowledge. And here too great changes were afoot.

The book arts of the Middle Ages remained settled in the monasteries, which had acted as centres for the preservation of culture since the fall of the Roman empire. St Benedict of Nursia had introduced the copying of church texts into the monastery which he founded in AD529 at Monte Cassino, and had defined this as suitable divine work. After Charlemagne (724–814) ordered the adoption of the Benedictine Rule by all monastic foundations within his empire, scriptoria sprang up in all the new cloisters of central and western Europe, in which not only religious manuscripts but also those of the Greek and Roman classics could be copied.

The shape of scripts can also be considered as an expression of inner attitude or religious creed. At Charlemagne's behest, a reform of handwriting had been carried out by the English theologian Alcuin of York. The resultant new model, the Carolingian minuscule, became the standard hand which prevailed throughout the realms of the Roman Catholic Church (Kapr, 1983: 39ff). It remained alive over the centuries, and still provides the basis for our present lower-case alphabet. In the eleventh and twelfth centuries this style became narrower and the characters were fitted closer together, and from the thirteenth century the upright shafts of letters begin to exhibit angular breaks. Also the thin 'pick-up' strokes received contrasting emphasis. The first appearances of this early Gothic style – just as in architecture – are to be observed in northern France. Whether calligraphy was stimulated or influenced by architecture or whether the same stylistic tendencies occurred in both arts at the same time is not really understood even today. Whatever the causes, a more expressive and innovatory style had arisen: curves were replaced by sharp angular transitions; lower-case letters massed yet closer together; the entire text page became darker. Gothic lettering had a spirituality and intensity resembling Gothic architecture. The distance between lines and consequently the space available for ascenders and descenders was reduced. Eventually the text area as a whole came to resemble a woven tapestry. As a result the term 'textura' was adopted to describe the fully developed Gothic book hand, which was primarily used for writing liturgical works in Latin, such as missals, psalters, bibles, gospels and lectionaries. Gutenberg would later return to the textura for printing his *42-line Bible*.

Monastic scriptoria, in which a division of labour between scribes, rubricators and illuminators had developed quite early, now experienced growing competition from the urban book trades and from university writing workshops. The universities, which had been endowed by princes and cities under papal licence, needed books for the study of the Latin language, theological and philosophical works, and medical and legal texts. Many of the larger and dearer books were being copied out by teachers and scholars for their own use. In this situation each university set up a stationer's, or writing workshop, in which textbooks approved by the rector could be copied, bound and offered for sale. Stationers, scribes and bookbinders were entered in the rolls of the university so that their status could be regulated (Lülfing, 1972: 48–9).

In parallel to this, writing workshops sprang up in many of the larger cities during the fourteenth and fifteenth centuries, where at times several scribes were at work. They mainly took on commissions for legal and commercial documents, but apart from that would usually copy books to order. In addition, there were industrial scriptoria in Italy, the Netherlands, France and Germany, where stocks of books were produced, as goods, to be sold subsequently by manuscript dealers or book distributors; some Italian workshops which were already using manufacturing methods grew into huge concerns. Rubricators later entered the headings and initials in the right places in red pigment; and illuminators completed the work in the case of expensive codices by painting in elaborately ornamented initials, decoration at the heads or frames to the pages, or miniatures. Some writing work was placed out of house from time to time and paid for according to the putting-out system. Towards the end of the fifteenth century the Florentine manuscript producer Vespasiano da Bisticci must have been keeping up to 200 calligraphers and illuminators occupied. He procured vellum and paper in bulk lots. The distribution of his manuscripts extended far beyond the Alps. Foremost among his clients was Matthias Corvinus, king of Hungary, who ordered more than a hundred codices from him. France's rulers, however, preferred the books of the Flemish and Brabantine illuminators, whose miniatures were considered more ostentatious and richer in detail than those of the Italian school.

Textura was not suitable for the books of the humanists because of its religious character, nor for secular literature in general, and least of all for written transactions between tradesmen and merchants or the records of civic jurisdiction. For everyday use in the languages of the respective countries, an informal hand was called for that would be practical and quicker to write. From this need stemmed both the Gothic bastarda and Gothic cursive scripts. The Gothic bastarda was the more handsome, and was customarily used for books in the vernacular and set aside for important occasions, while the Gothic current or cursive served the commonplace writing needs of notaries and merchants. Both scripts were susceptible to much provincial and individual variation (Crous and Kirchner, 1928).

In Italy, where Gothic never felt really at home, a separate modified form – the rounded Gothic or rotunda – emerged as a script for sacred and Latin literature, and later served early Italian and German printers as a model for similar purposes. Yet the Italian humanists from Petrarch onwards had censured all these writing styles as hard to read and even described them as barbarian.

genib9 flexis, cum cunctis tenetal
gius lacrimis ⁊ suspiriis. et ꝯpli
cans pectus suum orat. Tu c

Rotunda. Italian manuscript of the late fourteenth century. Detail, original size.

Through study of the Roman and Greek classics that had been preserved in copies dating from Carolingian times, the Carolingian minuscule itself began to be accurately imitated and refined. It was as a result of this that humanistic lower-case letterforms became the written

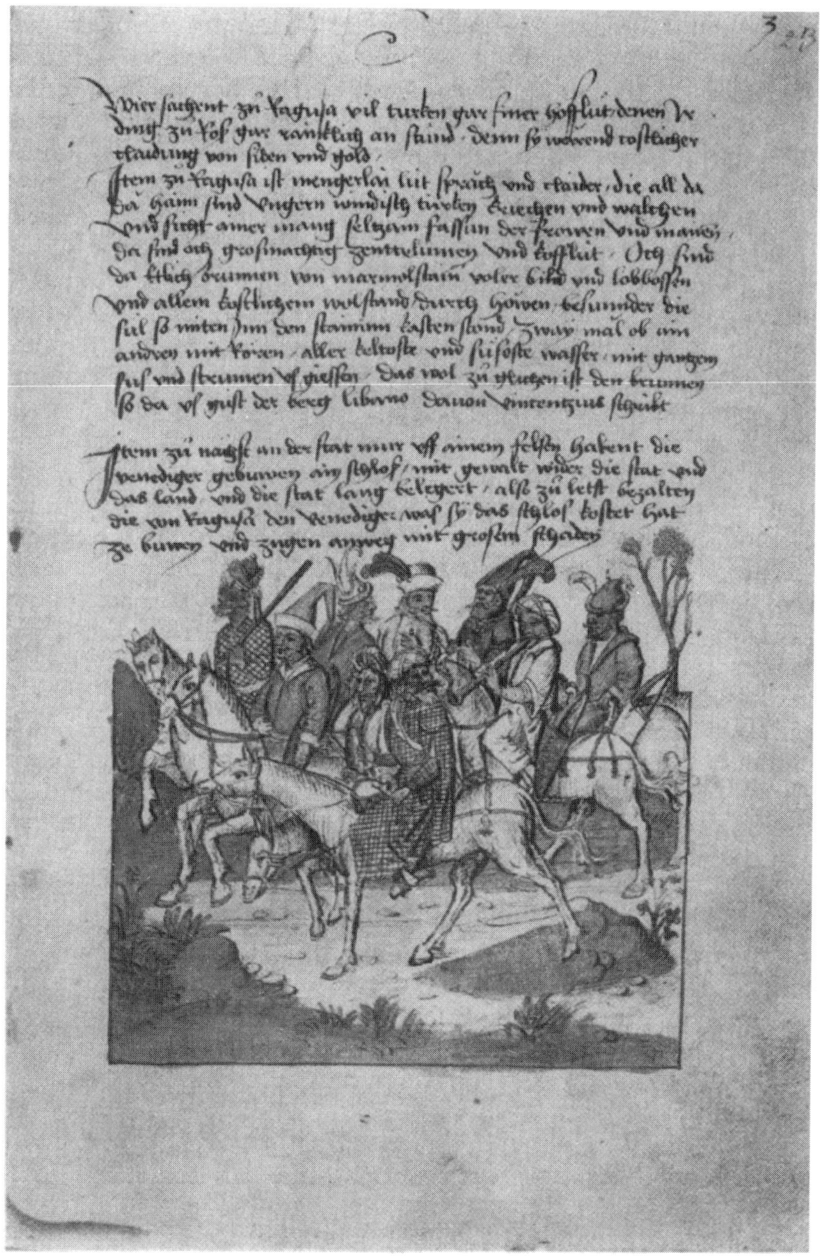

Gothic bastarda. Konrad von Grunemberg Pilgrimage from Constance to Jerusalem, *written in 1487. Gotha Research Library. Reduced.*

point of departure for the roman types in use today. Naturally within the context of the humanistic or Renaissance minuscule, numerous vari-ations were generated, of which at least one, the Gothic-roman, merits special mention. This was not a fully-developed Renaissance roman, since it still clung to certain Gothic impedimenta. All the same it suited

V i superum saeuae memorem iunonis ob
M ulta quoque & bello passus dum conde
I nferret q; deos latio: genus unde latin
A lbaniq; patres atque altae moenia ro

Humanistic minuscule. Florence 1480. Detail, original size.

the prevailing cultural climate and found its way through German students who had been at Italian universities, back to Germany, and was later adapted by Gutenberg as a typeface for printing indulgences and other small items as well as a large Latin dictionary.

Gothic-roman. Petrarch's own handwriting, 1368. Detail, original size.

As we have seen, by Gutenberg's time there was a host of scripts, each of which could be assigned to particular kinds of literature or writing tasks. This diversity of hands embodied at the same time a reflection of social attitudes, in other words graphological self-portraits of what motivated the world of the scribe or his patron. Furthermore, this variety of letterforms expresses after a fashion the confusion in economic, political, social and cultural aspirations as the Middle Ages made way for the Renaissance.

Above all, the arts of writing had assumed special prominence in the towns. Intra-urban conflicts, and disputes between cities, rulers and clergy, were often recorded by notaries. Armed warfare was frequently heralded by paper warfare, whereby both parties threw into battle university-trained lawyers conversant with not only Latin but also canon law and Roman law. Once again Italy was in the forefront: the new city fathers had attained a higher level of education, and were better read and spoken than the landed aristocracy. Information derived from the study of classical and arabic sources laid the foundations for the immense advances of the fifteenth century in technological, astronomical, medical and geographical fields. The book became a source of productive energy for a new breed of merchants and entrepreneurs; this information sped over the Alps and gave rise to an increasing demand for books in the larger German towns.

An important educational role in the towns was likewise performed by the more recently founded orders – the Franciscans, Dominicans, Augustinians and Brethren of the Common Life – all of whose domestic missionary work had an urban focus. Priests in town churches required at least a missal, and wherever possible further books intended

Medieval scribe at the writing desk. Woodcut. Paris 1526.

for divine service. Such books were mostly written by the cloistered monks of each order. The Benedictine scriptoria in particular strove to produce books of high artistic quality. More will be said later about the special role of the Brethren of the Common Life and their close involvement with the writing and printing of books.

The growing demand for books provided a natural challenge to reflect on ways of producing them more efficiently. Paper was still being imported from Italy and Spain in the fourteenth century, for all that paper-mills had been set up in Germany as well by the turn of the century. In 1390 Ulman Stromer had begun to produce paper close to Nuremberg. Other mills followed at Ravensburg, Lübeck, Basle and in the neighbourhood of university towns. Ever more frequently paper was chosen as an alternative writing material to the more expensive parchment.

The woodcut, too, had become known through contact with the Arabs. It was used for overprinting fabrics from wooden blocks. From the first decades of the fifteenth century in Germany, playing cards and small devotional images had been printed from woodcuts and then coloured by hand. The earliest dated woodcut, the Brussels single-page print of a *Madonna*, bears the year 1418. We already find single words or lines of lettering cut as part of these earliest woodblocks, which were followed by the first blockbooks or sequences of illustrated and captioned woodcuts, probably originating in Holland, wherein each leaf always consists of two woodcuts with their backs pasted together. This back-to-back placement proved necessary since, in printing the single pages, the sheet of paper laid on the surface of the woodblock was rubbed with a burnisher to produce the relief impression, and this left heavy indentations on the other side of the sheet. Several such conjoined leaves were then sewn together into a thin book and coloured.

Yet this method of producing blockbooks remained complicated and only suitable for the briefest of texts. A calligrapher had first to write out this text, which was traced as a mirror-image reversal on to a planed limewood plank and then cut out with a knife in such a way that the lettering was left as a raised surface. The woodblock was next dabbed with ink, paper laid over it and lightly pressed into contact, and then firmly rubbed down area by area with a spoon-like wooden burnisher. This laborious process could yield many hundreds of prints. Blockbooks presumably took their name from the woodcuts, or more specifically the woodblocks, used.

In broad parallel to this development came that of the engraving, which was also perfected in the first half of the fifteenth century. Instead of cutting with a knife into plank, the soft metal of a plate had to be pierced with a graver and the white areas gouged away leaving the

The earliest dated woodcut. 'Mary with the Child' (The Brussels Madonna*),*
1418. Reduced.

letters in relief. The production of an engraving was certainly a slower business, but the letter shapes were more precise, and larger numbers of prints could be taken from the plate.

When it comes to establishing just when the earliest of these blockbooks appeared, the opinions of art experts differ widely, all the more so since the oldest dated blockbook is from as late as 1470 and

Engraving (riddled-with-shot-manner). Ecce homo, *second half of fifteenth century, probably Upper Rhine. Reduced.*

many blockbooks were produced only after the publication of small items set and printed from movable types. A few researchers even claim that all blockbooks postdate Gutenberg's invention. I believe, rather, that the oldest group of blockbooks, to which the Haarlem *Apocalypse* belongs, should be assigned to the decade between 1430 and 1440. Later the so-called 'Bible of the poor' (*Biblia pauperum*) – in which events of the New Testament were set against similar stories from the Old –

Blockbook. Biblia pauperum, *second half of fifteenth century. Reduced.*

appeared in Holland and South Germany. These were slender, richly illustrated and almost invariably hand-coloured booklets, that found a mass public on account of their popular woodcuts and relatively low price. Among early blockbooks we find recurrent titles such as the *Ars moriendi, Canticum canticorum* and *Speculum humanae salvationis* (Musper, 1961: 16; Mayer, 1983: 84). An interesting aspect might be revealed if it were possible to find out who commissioned or made use of these booklets. It seems to me most unlikely that the Roman Church would have had any interest whatever in seeing such interpretations of the Bible propagated, and it may be that several heretical lay organizations or assorted sects were behind the publication of individual titles.

These primitive prints could never of course have entered into competition with the precious handwritten book. That would require new ideas and a new beginning.

Mainz around 1400

MAINZ, STRASBOURG AND ELTVILLE were the known settings for Gutenberg's activities; all three places are on the Rhine. Gutenberg was born in Mainz; from here his invention spread to all countries of the world, and in this city he lies buried. In Mainz the essential traits of his character revealed themselves; he received his first schooling here, and developed his bent for research and discovery.

On the left bank of the Rhine, at the crossing point of long-distance routes and facing the influx of the Main, an important settlement had grown up in Celtic and in Romano-Germanic times. After the chaos of the migrations of tribes Mainz belonged to the heartland of the rapidly strengthening Frankish empire. Under Boniface in 746 it became an archbishopric. The diocesan church of St Martin was begun on the site of the erstwhile Roman forum, where the present cathedral stands. The well-defended city soon became a favoured stopping place for the German emperor and stood firmly on the side of the central power against the attacks of territorial rulers. Archbishop Willigis (975–1011) received from the pope the right to crown the German kings and to preside over all German and French councils; he obtained royal privileges for the Rheingau, the lands on the right bank of the Rhine around Eltville. Archbishop Gerhard II von Eppenstein (1288-1305) gained the Upper Eichsfeld, with territories near Erfurt, and procured for himself and his successors the title of arch-chancellor of the empire, with the right to convoke the imperial assemblies (*Reichstag* and *Fürstentag*).

View of Mainz. Woodcut from Johann Stöffler's Romischen Kalender, *Oppenheim, 1518, Detail, reduced.*

Mainz grew into one of the richest and most important of Rhineland cities. Benefiting from the orders which flooded into the centre of the archbishopric from a wide area, a flourishing cloth trade and thriving guild of goldsmiths arose. As in other German towns, well-organized guilds of craftsmen had formed, capable of standing up to the privileged patricians. In Gutenberg's century this marked antagonism between patricians and guilds led to opposition between the interests of the city and those of the archbishop.

The archbishop, like the emperor, princes and other bishops, was surrounded by his officials, courtiers or servants, who held the higher posts and who could in some cases hand these on to their offspring. In the course of the thirteenth and fourteenth centuries the station of each of these persons was assessed according to their master's rank; they shared the situation of the gently born and were classed with the nobility. When the castle at Eltville became the archbishop's residence, he still had to carry out his archiepiscopal duties in Mainz itself, and his officials were likewise expected to be equally at home in Eltville as in Mainz. (In my view, Gutenberg researchers have hitherto paid too little attention to this feature, especially since the inventor's ancestors belonged for the most part to this group of officials.)

At the head of the archiepiscopal administration was the *camerarius* or chancellor, who controlled the archbishop's entire goods and revenues and supervised the jurisdiction, customs and coinage, and the craftsmen in his employ. In Mainz the chancellor was at the same time the city governor, whom the mayor (*Schultheiss*) represented in all municipal affairs. At the mayor's side were the official (*Walpode*) who controlled the markets and policing; the *monetarius* as overseer of the mint; the *iudex* responsible for the legal system; and the *officiatus* in charge of administration. Although these servants of the archbishop could be dismissed at any time, the offices generally remained in the same families, and their holders formed a dynastic power, a privileged stratum in the city; they became the patricians, or the 'ancients', as they were dubbed in Mainz (*Mainz*, 1968: I, 90). They made up a commercial network which dominated the city through its many links. The patricians were the social elite, intermarried and closely related.

Gutenberg research is complicated by the fact that in the thirteenth and fourteenth centuries there were as yet no family names that could be handed down from father to son and grandson. The Mainz patricians called themselves after the houses they possessed, and so we find zur Laden, zum Fürstenberg, zum Krame, zum Silberberg, zum Rafit, zum Eselsweck, zum Humbert, zum Gensfleisch or zum Gutenberg. Anyone with two or three houses at his disposal could bear two or three names. Anyone not yet owning a house carried his father's house-name or official appellation. When in distant parts, the sons of patricians occasionally identified themselves by the name of their home town or village, as we know from the university rolls.

The other important social layer in the towns was represented by the organized guilds of craftsmen. Urban wealth was created through their skills and the industry of their apprentices, and yet they remained excluded from the conduct of city affairs. This led in all towns to strained relations and to battles over the participation of the guilds in local government. Gutenberg's entire career was to be lived out under the shadow of these conflicts.

In 1244 certain rights of self-government were wrested by the city of Mainz from its archbishop. In this matter the patricians played an important and positive role for Mainz, as they also did for the protection of shipping from the tolls exacted by 'robber barons' along the Rhine. It used to be said that 'there were more tolls to the Rhine than miles'. After the formation of the Confederation of the Rhine in 1254 trade flourished, and Mainz and Cologne jointly enforced the right of staple, which meant that all upstream and downstream ships had to unload their goods and offer them for sale in each city for several days. As the patricians became richer they continued to consolidate these privileges which they had won from the archbishop. Feudal law allowed them to pay few taxes or none at all; one privilege (the *Gadenrecht*) secured for them a monopoly for the entire cloth trade, and another (*Hausgenossenrecht*) conferred an exclusive right to trade in precious metals and to inspect the coinage. Moreover, the patricians used their control of the city council to grant one another life-annuities at favourable interest rates. Because we will have to deal repeatedly with these annuities later in Gutenberg's life, a closer look at the topic is appropriate here.

The upper crust of Mainz patricians succumbed to the enticing lure of interest-bearing capital; in fact they became lenders and borrowers at the same time. In order to acquire the interest, which the church at that time still forbade, they cultivated a profitable pension business. For a fixed sum a wealthy patrician could purchase a pension or life-annuity for his children or for younger relatives, which these beneficiaries would then be able to withdraw any year or at shorter notice against signature on a given day. Fellow-patricians on the council obtained comparatively easy terms, so that the lifetime value of contracts paid out was frequently substantially higher than the capital invested. New loans, which the city council received from the sale of pensions, were receipted in the entry books as real income, and in this way an intrinsic indebtedness accumulated. It was normal for five per cent of the loan fund to be paid out annually in the form of pensions. If the recipient died before 20 years had passed, then the city had made a profit from the 'expired' pension, but if he lived substantially longer, then huge additional sums had to be found from outside the fund. Hence the citizenry opposed to the patriciate demanded that representatives of the guilds should be consulted over all pension sales.

It may seem unusual to be delving into the account books for Mainz in a book about Gutenberg, but a glance is well worth the trouble, for they show that since about 1400 the city had faced financial decline and mounting internal and external indebtedness. Nevertheless, to the external observer Mainz still looked as flourishing as ever: a city of churches and commerce, the spiritual centre of the German nation. It is true that Vienna and Cologne with some 35,000 inhabitants apiece, Lübeck with 30,000, Strasbourg with 25,000, and Nuremberg and Erfurt each with 20,000, were all much larger communities; but Mainz, with its 6000 souls, was of at least equal political importance.

Gutenberg's birth and parentage

IT WAS ON ST JOHN THE BAPTIST'S DAY (24 June) in the year 1400 that a son, Johann, was born to Friele Gensfleisch and his wife Else at the Hof zum Gutenberg in Mainz – or so the world's printers have traditionally told us for centuries. Unfortunately this is not established fact, but merely a legend. Johann or Johannes was the commonest first name in Mainz, where it took the variant forms of Henne, Hengin or Henchen; and this particular small 'Henchen' in all probability was not named after the saint's day of his birth, but simply because his parents conformed to a current vogue in choosing the name (Schweinsberg, 1900: 65ff).

Johann's elder brother had been named Friele, a Mainz diminutive of Friedrich, after his father. It might also have been derived from 'Frieling' or free-born, as it can be traced back through the grandfather, who was also a Friele – more precisely, Friele Gensfleisch, known as zum Eselsweck zur Laden – as far as the ancestral great-great-grandfather, one Friele Rafit zum Gensfleisch. The elder sister of the newborn child was called Else after her mother.

The parents had married in 1386. The first of their children, Johann's brother Friele, may have been born about 1387. His sister Else married the patrician Claus Vitzthum as early as 1414, which suggests that she was probably born between 1390 and 1397. It was previously accepted that the future inventor must have been born between 1394 and 1400, since he had appeared without a guardian at the division of his father's estate in 1420, and so must have come of age by then. More recently, however, it has been established that the age of legal majority at the time was much lower than had been thought, namely 15. Taking into account all possible combinations we can arrive at no more reliable indication for the year of Gutenberg's birth than between 1394 and 1404. Nevertheless, on the grounds of what is known about his life as a whole, we may assume that Gutenberg probably first saw the light of day in Mainz in 1400 or shortly thereafter (Corsten, 1966: 70ff).

His father, Friele Gensfleisch zur Laden, was born about 1350 and is mentioned as a citizen from 1372 onwards. Of his first marriage, to a woman of whom nothing is known, a daughter, Patze, was born. It is likely that this daughter married at roughly the time that Johann was born, for her husband, Peter zum Jungen zum Blashof, mayor of Mainz, died on 24 February 1403. Her father Friele had already led home his second bride, Else Wirich, in 1386. He was a merchant or head of a firm and was probably in the cloth trade. In addition he belonged to the society of companions of the mint (*Münzerhausgenossenschaft*), although whether this involved him directly in its business or in the trade in precious metals is unclear. Similarly, the fact of his election in 1411 as one of the masters of accounts for the city does not necessarily mean that he was ever responsible for its budget. Gutenberg's father never actually called himself Friele zum Gutenberg, even though after his death was recorded in 1419 he was known by that name; certainly this points to his residence at the Hof zum Gutenberg, but it does not prove that he was the sole owner of that property.

Henchen's paternal grandfather, the Friele Gensfleisch zum Eselsweck zur Laden already mentioned, can be presumed to have owned not only the properties from which he took his names but also that part of the Hof zum Gutenberg which his son inherited, and a farm in Klein-Winternheim as well. The patricians invested their money abundantly in estates in the surrounding countryside and thereby made additional profits from the duty-free import of corn and wine for the Mainz market.

Gutenberg's paternal great-grandfather, Petermann zum Gensfleisch, a rich cloth merchant and sometime lay-assessor in the city's court, together with his brother-in-law Pedermann zum Jungen, became involved in 1357 in investing in the Rhine island near Ginsheim. The inventor's ancestors on his father's side all belonged to the wealthy patriciate of cloth merchants and long-distance traders. Gutenberg's relatives shared an interest in one-third of a total loan of 78,800 gulden which the Mainz patricians granted to the debt-encumbered town of Wetzlar in 1382. This well-to-do patriciate was on an equal footing with the minor nobility, vying with them even in terms of economic superiority, as those landed gentry repeatedly had to pledge their estates to the city financiers.

Gutenberg's mother Else was the daughter of a shopkeeper, Werner Wirich zum steinen Krame (of the stone-built store), who in turn was born into a shopkeeping family and belonged to the Mainz tradesmen's guild. Her grandmother on her father's side was the daughter of Leo Ottini, a Lombard moneychanger living in Bingen. The inventor's mother came, then, from a different social background from his father, which from the start ruled out young Johann from becoming a com-panion of the mint later on. Thus the social conflicts and contradictions between patricians and guilds which were so decisive for the history of Mainz in the fifteenth century were represented within the inventor's personality through his respective parents, and may possibly provide a key to understanding certain aspects of his character and behaviour.

Gutenberg's maternal grandmother, Ennechin zum Fürstenberg, had died long before his birth. She was a widow from her previous marriage to a young nobleman, Jeckel Rode zum Fürstenberg, and was thereby related to a line of wealthy ministerial officials who held considerable estates in Eltville as well. One of these zum Fürstenberg ancestors had purchased the ruined abbey of Astheim in 1346 from the entailed estate of another minor nobleman, Dietrich von Gudenberg. In studying Gutenberg's genealogy one is bound to wonder about the social status of his Wirich grandfather: how did it come about – at a time when class boundaries were rigorously observed – that the widow of a rich nobleman married a shopkeeper, and then that a patrician of the standing of Gutenberg's father should marry this same shopkeeper's daughter? In fact, the shopkeeper Werner Wirich zum steinen Krame's grandfather (and Else Wirich's great-grandfather), Burgrave Wirich, had been the governor of the fortress of Mainz until he was declared an outlaw in 1332.

After the death of Archbishop Matthias in 1328, it came to open conflict between the successor selected by the cathedral chapter, Balduin von Trier, and the papal nominee, Heinrich von Virneburg. The city council ranged itself on the side of the latter. As Balduin threatened to besiege Mainz, the citizenry and their fortress governor Wirich – wishing to deprive him of possible strongpoints in the south of the city – destroyed the church- and watch-towers of St Alban, St Viktor and St Jakob, in the course of which they were plundered. As punishment, Emperor Louis the Bavarian imposed an imperial ban on the city and on a number of the ringleaders, including Wirich, the burgrave of the time. In addition the city had to find a substantial sum for restoration, which led to a further uprising by the guilds against the patricians who had been responsible (*Mainz*, 1968: I, 7ff). The social fall of the house of Wirich followed from the imposition of the ban and the subsequent marriage of the deposed burgrave to the daughter of the Lombard moneychanger, Ottini of Bingen.

If one looks at the complicated network of Johann Gutenberg's relatives, it is apparent that on three sides his ancestors were patrician. But perhaps it was just the social tie to his shopkeeper grandfather with his guild affiliations which diverted Gutenberg from following pre-dictable patrician lines, caused him to consider his opportunities and thus led him on towards his 'adventure and art'.

The Hof zum Gutenberg

THE LONG-SINCE DESTROYED GOTHIC BUILDING which stood at the corner of Schustergasse and Christophstrasse was divided into two parts. The front block on the corner was lived in, and the part set a little back probably housed the first printing office in Mainz. Both wings had two storeys above the ground floor. The windows at ground level would have been small and narrow, for many of the Mainz patrician houses were built like little fortresses for defensive purposes, and these rooms would have been used for storage and warehousing. The first and second floors afforded living space for several families, and the first floor of the range at the back may well have accommodated the composing room (Kirnberger, 1952).

This town house had belonged to the archbishop's treasurers, Philipp and Eberhard de Gudenberg, towards the close of the thirteenth century. They sold it together with other properties in about 1300, and some time later retired to their country seat near Kreuznach. One of the inventor's ancestors, Pedermann zum Jungen zum Eselsweck, acquired the imposing house and left it to his daughter Nesa and her husband Petermann zum Gensfleisch. By further hereditary bequest the house came down to our Johann Gutenberg's grandfather and father, although part of the building appears to have passed into other hands through a division of the inheritance.

It seems strange that three generations of owners of the Hof zum Gutenberg did not take their name from it, and it has been suggested that this could have been because the house belonged only in part to the inventor's grandfather and father. It was not until 1427/8, when one of the annuities due to the brothers Friele and Johann Gutenberg was adjusted, that their deceased father is first named as Friele zu Guden-berg. It is possible that his widow might only have come into the full inheritance of the building a few years previously. As the inventor was not resident in Mainz from 1428 onwards, the Gutenberg house would have been occupied by his mother, the family of his elder brother Friele, and the family of his elder sister Else and her husband Claus Vitzthum. Johann did not move back into his birthplace until his return from Strasbourg in 1448 or 1449.

In the meantime a legend had arisen, long since disproved, according to which the Gutenberg house had been brought in by his mother upon her marriage. Else Wirich would certainly have received a handsome dowry, as her father owned several houses. The Hof zum Gutenberg, or at least part of it, had, however, belonged for generations to the Gensfleisch forefathers. Nevertheless it may still have been his mother who, through acquiring the building in its entirety, made it possible for the inventor to take his name from the house where he was born.

One problem has particularly occupied the author's thoughts: the first known occupants of the Hof, the archiepiscopal treasurers Philipp and Eberhard, called themselves de Gudenberg. Might not the house have retained their name after its change of hands? Naturally the Johann Gutenberg born much later in this same house was quite unrelated to that old knightly lineage: it is simply that the prevailing custom among the Mainz patricians, of taking their names from the houses they possessed, gave rise to the paradox that the inventor's name is not the same as his father's but rather leads us back to that of some ancient householder. But I would like to leave these ideas explicitly as a mere hypothesis.

Yet another question must be raised in this connection: is it possible that the Hof zum Gutenberg may once in earlier times have been a Jewish property? Terrible Jewish pogroms took place in Mainz in 1096, 1146 and 1282. It was the city treasurers who were responsible for the money and the goods of those Jews who were killed. After the pogrom of 1282, a dispute ensued between the council and the archbishop over the 'Jewish inheritance', which was only resolved through a settlement of 1295 (Schaab, 1969: 9, 35, 51). In a chronicle of Mainz, 54 houses are cited as the 'Jewish inheritance'; among them was one on the corner entering Schustergasse, the granary facing the Gutenberg courtyard – although the house zum Gutenberg itself is not mentioned. Yet in its immediate neighbourhood were also to be found the old synagogue and the Jewish bake-house (Schaab, 1969: 60). It is accordingly possible that the city treasurers de Gudenberg were already in possession of the property before the settlement of 1295, and described it under their own names so that it could be sold on.

Again in 1349 an *auto-da-fé* took place in Mainz, as it was sought to hold the Jews answerable for the spread of the Black Death (bubonic plague) from Asia. On St Bartholomew's Day, 24 August, some hundred Jews were burned in a square by the church of St Quintin. Could it be because of these atrocious and, for the inhabitants of Mainz, shameful facts that this site became tainted, giving its occupants reason to shun naming themselves after the Hof zum Gutenberg for as long as these events remained in living memory? Future researches into local history ought at least to take this possibility into account.

Gutenberg's coat of arms

As FAMILY NAMES WERE STILL IN THE MAKING during the late Middle Ages and the patricians of Mainz frequently changed their names with their houses or the functions they exercised, it is sensible to follow the genealogy of the Gensfleisch family through its coat of arms which does not change. For this reason Gutenberg researchers have paid particular attention to the Gensfleisch arms.

The earliest traceable bearer of the arms was Frilo Rafit, who purchased the house zum Rafit on the corner of Dominikanerstrasse and Fuststrasse in 1298, and at some date before 1330 the house zum Gensfleisch in Emmeranstrasse as well. In 1330 he also became a councillor, and his name and seal carrying the coat of arms are repeatedly found appended to weighty civic documents. In addition he may have led the patricians in their battle against the guilds (*Mainz*, 1968: I, 26n.). This ancestor was twice married. He had three sons by his first wife Grede, from whom the main line of the Gensfleisch family is derived. From a later marriage, to the widow of a certain von Oppenheim, born a Sorgenloch, came a further three children of the Sorgenloch line (this part of the family comes from Sörgenloch, a village 10 miles southwest of Mainz). The descendants of both lines used the same arms and seal, with only minor differences.

The arms show a figure on foot, clad in a travelling cloak, who supports himself upon a stick held in the left hand, and with the right extends a bowl. On his head he wears a peculiar pointed hood and on his back is a moderately full sack or bundle, which is covered by the cloak.

For centuries scholars have disputed the meaning of these arms. There have been six different interpretations: there are those who see the figure as a pilgrim, but in that case he ought to have a long pilgrim's staff and broad-brimmed hat. Others suggest that he may be a beggar, who with outstretched bowl solicits food or alms. Whereas the beggar image seems to me rather paradoxical and far-fetched for the rich Gensfleisch [goose-meat] branch of the family, it might pass as more apt for the Sorgenlochs [hole of cares]. A third reading suggests that the cap could be a fool's cap. In fact such caps are still worn at the Mainz carnival, but the bundle on the back and the extended bowl are no part of the clown's accoutrements. A widely held view is that the figure shows a mendicant friar or hawker carrying his wares on his back, and symbolizes the occupation of the bearer of the arms as a merchant, clothier and long-distance trader. It is natural to ask what the pedlar can be offering for sale in his bowl – perhaps small objects such as buckles or bracelets? But the whole attitude of the figure suggests to me a demand rather than an offer.

Coat of arms of the Gensfleisch-Gutenberg family.
From the Register of Fiefs *of Frederick I, elector palatine of the Rhine, 1461.*

Finally, a few years ago I came across an astonishingly novel interpretation, according to which Gutenberg's ancestors were Sephardic Jews who had fled Spain around 1300 and converted to Christianity in Mainz. The author of this view was stimulated by the strange form of the headgear, which he saw as a Jewish hat; and then by the name Rafit, which has an arabic origin meaning war-horse; and further by eight crosses which he perceived on the ground to the shield, which he took to symbolize the number of Jews converted with Frilo Rafit, namely the parents and six children of his ancestor (Haemmerle, 1971: 31ff). I shall not go into a detailed refutation of this theory; it is based – among other matters – on the fact that a Jew who had transferred to Christendom could never have become a leader of the patriciate. Moreover, Hellmut Rosenfeld has drawn fresh attention to the religious-ideological significance of this coat of arms. In his view, the figure shows one of the Irish or Scottish wandering friars, who, since the foundation of the so-called 'Scottish cloisters', customarily roved from place to place, taking along whatever small wares or commissions were on offer. But the beggar-pilgrim at the same time symbolizes a medieval world-view, as 'never reaching one's goal', – a Christ-oriented wandering until death, which was still represented in modified form in the fifteenth century by the mendicant orders and notably by the Franciscans (Rosenfeld, 1974: 35ff).

This interpretation seems to be highly attractive, all the more so since the bearers of these arms were not just well-to-do burghers, but also included monks and nuns such as Frilo Rafit's eldest son, one Frilo Gensfleisch, who can be shown to have been in 1333 a canon of St Peter, and a daughter from his second marriage, Clara Gensfleisch, who became a nun in the convent at Dalen.

Childhood and schooldays

MOST BOOKS ON GUTENBERG pass over this period with the remark that not a single fact is known. In truth the surviving Mainz records contain nothing about little Henchen; instead one learns, for example, about a resplendent tournament held in the city in 1406, in which the duke of Austria and the counts of Berg, Württemberg, Kleve, Moers, Nassau, Katzenelnbogen, Leiningen and Veldenz all took part. It is possible, though, that Henchen could have been there too as a spectator. How might the early years of one who was to become an inventor have been passed? From what source did he derive the power for a creative achievement which was to outlast the centuries? It seems that many people are born with similar talents, but from their earliest childhood are weaned away from flights of imagination, composition and inventiveness, whereas Gutenberg incorporated them into a precise formula.

It seems to me that Gutenberg scholars have up to now taken insufficient notice of the role of Gutenberg's mother. Elsgen Wirich was much younger than her husband Friele, who was practically 50 by the time his youngest was born – while Henchen was still in nappies, his sister Patze was already married. In such circumstances the child's emotional structure must have been strongly conditioned by his mother.

It is yet a further shot in the dark to try to reconstruct Henchen's schooldays, but we are in general well informed about education in the cities of the Rhineland at the beginning of the fifteenth century. As a merchant, Gutenberg's father would have recognized the importance of number and literacy. As the daughter of a shopkeeper and of a mother who was related to the distinguished Fürstenberg family, Henchen's mother would almost certainly have been skilled at reading and writing – which could by no means have been expected of all the city's burghers at that time. Therefore it is reasonable to assume that the boy would have learned to read, write and do some sums at home.

He would probably not have begun to study Latin at home, although a knowledge of the rudiments of this language gave access to university or other higher learning. Most patrician families in Mainz steered the youngest son towards a religious career, which secured good prospects of a solid livelihood from the presence of so many rich foundations and stipends in the city and surrounding area.

With this in mind, Henchen's parents may have sought to send him to one of the town schools which were gaining ground at the time, in which private writing and arithmetic masters brought together the local children for instruction. These schools taught arithmetic with the new arabic numerals, which Christian churches and monasteries mistrustfully opposed, not just because they came from the infidels, but equally because of the use of the nought, which, although signifying nothing, could nevertheless, when placed behind another figure, multiply it tenfold. The private town schools were predominantly attended by children of guild craftsmen. The more conservative patricians sent their children to monastic schools.

In the Middle Ages the most important route to education lay through a cloister school. The Gensfleisch family had always maintained good connections with the Mainz foundations. Many family members left substantial endowments to churches and monasteries, others became priests and canons. In return, church and cloister upheld the privileges of the patricians.

Mainz had a whole string of such day schools, established at the churches of Our Lady, St Christoph – to which parish the Gutenberghof belonged – St Quintin, St Johann, the Carmelites and St Viktor, among others. There is some basis for the assumption that Henchen may have gone to school at the monastery of St Viktor (Geldner, 1976: 72ff). The office of *scolasticus* or schoolmaster was exercised from 1433 to 1439 by one Jakob Gensfleisch, called Sorgenloch, but he had already been there as a prebendary since 1422. Whether this Brother Jakob was a distant relative, and might even have been an ordinary monk there during Gutenberg's time at school, remains one of several arguments in favour of a connection between the future inventor and this particular foundation. At an advanced age Gutenberg was to become a member of the Brotherhood of St Viktor, a lay organization which was bound to the monastery and whose members had for the most part close relatives within the cloister. As we do not know of any close relation of Gutenberg who could have lived in the monastery as a priest or monk, this may increase the likelihood that his close connection was that of an old boy of the school. The abbey of St Viktor was situated on a hill south of the city near the village of Weisenau. It is just possible that Henchen may have spent some of his childhood years inside the monastery; although it seems unlikely that he would have become a boarder when the three-mile walk – from the Gutenberghof, through the Südtor, to learn Latin from the monks of St Viktor – could be made so easily. He might well have set out some days in company with his cousins, Friele and Ruleman (or Ulman), sons of his uncle Ortlieb, who would have begun to study there a year or so ahead of him.

However, we do know that on 15 August 1411 Gutenberg's father Friele was forced to leave his home town. To grasp the situation at that time, it helps to know something of the history of political conflict within the city. Renewed discord had broken out on 2 February between the burghers, or 'ancients' as they were called, and the 'young' power represented by the guilds. The elders had chosen Johann Swalbach as one of the new mayors, but the guilds would not accept his appointment, doubtless because of his reactionary conservativism. A group of 16 masters from the guilds confronted the ancients with their demands. Matters came to a showdown and it was threatened that some of the ancients might actually lose their heads. Just like their grandfathers and great-grandfathers before them back in 1332, many patricians fled the city in order to escape threats of taxation (Fischer, 1958: 11ff).

At the head of a surviving list which names all those who left the city in 1411, it states that Henne Gelthus went to nearby Oppenheim with his wife and child, and Hermann Fürstenberg to the Rheingau with his wife and children. The names of Friele zur Laden (this probably refers to the inventor's father), Ortlieb zur Laden and Petermann zur Laden (probably his uncles) are on the list as well. Whether they left the city alone or with their families, and where they went to, is unspecified; but presumably they would have taken their wives and younger children along just like those named first on the roll (Richter, 1902: 125). It can be assumed that the 117 patricians who made up this exodus all had houses or properties in the close neighbourhood and so were able to avoid paying taxes by living off the land for a time.

If his father decided that Henchen should be taken away with the rest of the family – which seems most probable – then this experience would have had a disturbing effect on the child's feelings and might have influenced his later political outlook. In any case these events would have united him with the exiles and their élitist attitudes.

It is probable that the family would have turned to the small town of Eltville on the Rhine, where Gutenberg's mother had inherited a property, presumably from her mother, Ennechin von Fürstenberg. This was the house on the town walls next to that of Gretgen Swalbach. (We shall hear more of this same house later on.) It also seems apparent that the family would have had other relatives and political allies in Eltville from whom they could expect support. It was here that the archbishop had his riverside castle and that the officers of his administration, who worked hand in glove with the burghers, were partly based.

In the autumn of 1411 the warring parties came to terms through the mediation of their archbishop. The family was able to return home to the Gutenberghof, and no doubt Henchen was able to go back to school. But the underlying political tensions remained unresolved. The winter of 1412/13 brought hunger riots. The guilds insisted that all those patricians who had temporarily left Mainz to get out of paying taxes should become guild members and pay the appropriate taxes. Furthermore, they required guild representatives to be consulted over all future sales of annuities. Finally it was declared that the council could no longer negotiate with individual guilds directly, but only through an opposition committee of 12 guild members.

Early in January 1413 Gutenberg's father Friele had to leave the city again, and once more it seems likely that his wife and younger children went with him. Although another letter of alliance was signed by the two parties to the dispute as early as 1 February, it could be foreseen that their quarrel would drag on for years. In fact there were fresh outbreaks in 1415 and 1416, in which King Sigismund had to intervene. There is much to suggest that Henchen might have stayed on in

Eltville with relatives and attended the community school which was held in the chaplain's house at the local church of St Peter. The Fürstenberg family is known to have made appreciable bequests to St Peter's in just those years from 1411 onwards, and Henchen's step-uncle Henne Leheymer – as one of the archbishop's courtiers – might well have been supporting his nephew (Kratz, 1962: II, 144ff).

Education in the Rheingau region at that time was more advanced than in the rest of Germany. Even village schools close to Eltville taught Latin, to encourage participation in the Gregorian chant during services. (Today there is still one local village where Gregorian chant is practised: Kiedrich, three miles from Eltville.) Early records contain some details of the teaching materials provided for Eltville's pupils, their fees and the incomes of their teachers. We are told that each year it was necessary to pay eight *albi* [silver pence] for those learning the alphabet; twelve for students of the Latin grammar known simply as *Donatus*, after its author; and the same amount for readers of Virgil, Terence and other Latin writers (Kratz, 1962: I, 145).

The reasons for assuming a period of school attendance at Eltville will be elaborated below.

Did Gutenberg study at Erfurt University?

BIOGRAPHICAL ASSERTIONS do not always have to be based on written documents. With Gutenberg we can also let the character of his works lead us towards conclusions. The *42-line Bible* is recognized as his indisputable product; it announces the daring, vigour, skill, staying power, artistic perception and intellectual bearing of its creator. Further examination permits us to deduce that its printer must have had a thorough command of the Latin tongue. It would not have been enough to have taken a carefully edited Latin manuscript as exemplar, and to have had a good proofreader familiar with Latin at his side, to go through each page carefully for errors. The compositors too would have needed some Latin; but above all the master printer himself would have had to be an excellent Latinist, familiar with all the difficulties that arise in that language – for instance, he would have needed to understand and anticipate the need for all the contractions and ligatures that would yield uniform word spacing throughout the page, and to find solutions for their design and deployment. It almost goes without saying that the future inventor of printing must have learned Latin well in his youth.

Did Gutenberg study at Erfurt University?

There is evidence that many of the early printers were scholars. Gutenberg's later collaborator Peter Schöffer was enrolled at Erfurt University and is known to have been active as a scribe at the Sorbonne in Paris. Cologne's first printer, Ulrich Zell, studied at Erfurt in 1452; and there is similar information for Mentelin and Eggestein from Strasbourg and Amerbach at Basle.

It may be assumed that Gutenberg too would have studied somewhere. In the earlier Gutenberg literature, there is a pointer to an individual attending Erfurt University as Johannes de Alta villa, who could possibly be identical with our subject (Geldner, 1976: 73). Erfurt was the fifth German university to be founded, after those of Prague, Vienna, Heidelberg and Cologne, and was in those days the Alma Mater for the archdiocese of Mainz (Kapr, 1980: 21ff). For centuries matriculation registers of student's names have been kept by universities. An entry made during Joh. Scheubing's rectorate shows that, in the summer semester of 1418, which usually began on 1 or 2 May, one Johannes de Alta villa was enrolled and charged 15 groschen for the privilege (Weissenborn, 1881).

A leaf in this register from the year before Johannes de Alta villa's name appears identifies Gutenberg's two cousins, 'Frilo and Rulemandus zu der Laden'. In 1421 'Conrad Humereye', later to become Gutenberg's patron, was admitted to Erfurt, and it is known that he went on to study at Cologne and Bologna. In 1444 and 1448 we find the name Petrus Ginsheym, and there can be no doubt that this refers to Peter Schöffer of Gernsheim, Gutenberg's future associate. Diether von Isenburg, later Archbishop of Mainz, is entered as student and as rector at the same time in 1434. Konrad Sweynheym from Schwanheim near Frankfurt also studied at Erfurt in 1455; he and Arnold Pannartz were to become Italy's first printers when their edition of Lactantius appeared from Subiaco, near Rome, in 1465.

Although still more names from the Erfurt matriculation lists can be shown to have some connection with Gutenberg, this is beside the point until we have discussed why the student Johannes was not enrolled as Johannes Gutenberg or Johannes Gensfleisch or Johannes de Moguncia [Mainz]. The first thing to grasp is that in 1418 and 1419/20 there was still no one to answer to the name of Johannes Gutenberg. Neither his father and mother nor his brother and sister at that time called themselves after the Gutenberghof in the centre of Mainz, probably because, as has already been explained, only part of it belonged to the family. The father was known as Friele zum Gensfleisch or Friele zur Laden like his ancestors. Eventually young Henne may have developed a certain antipathy towards his home town, perhaps

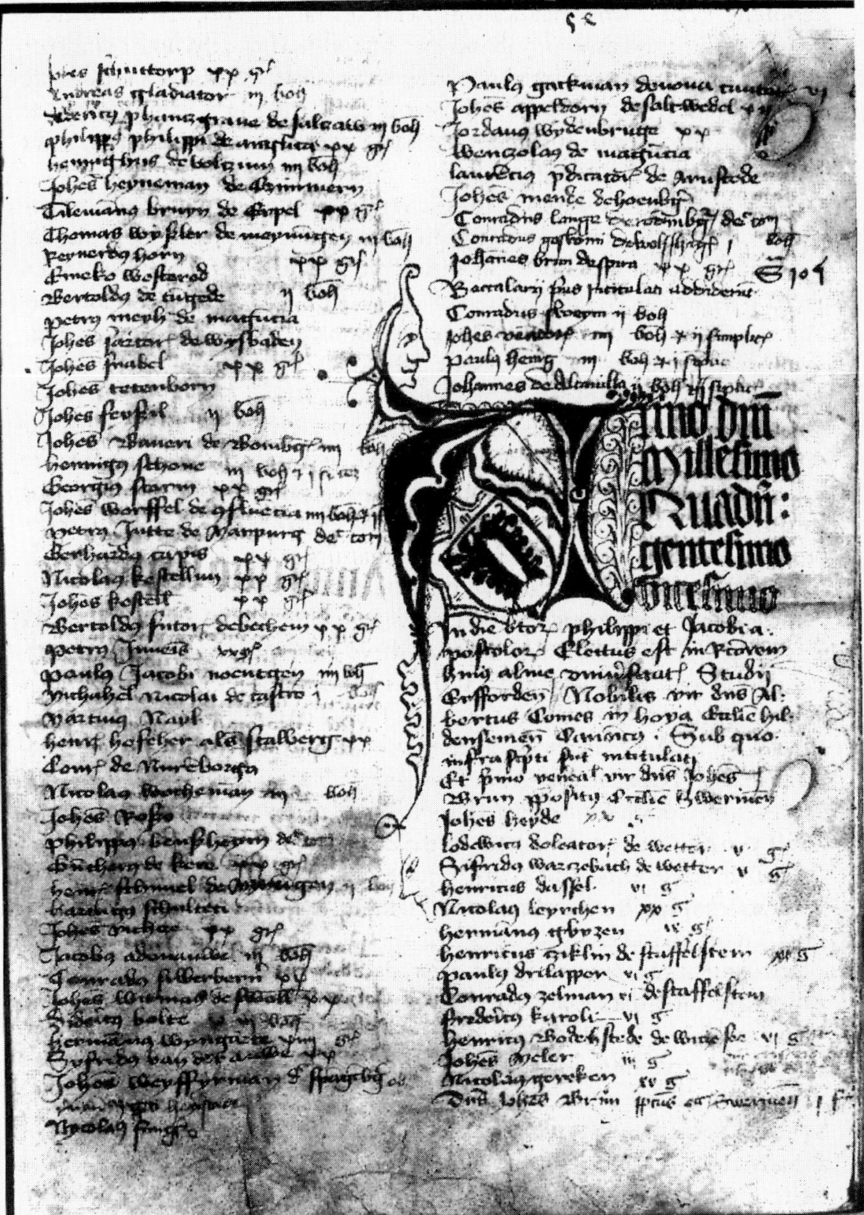

Page from Erfurt University register for the winter semester 1419/20. Johannes de Alta villa's name is 14 lines down in the right column. Reduced.

stemming from a tense relationship with his father, and this could have motivated him to enrol as Johann de Alta villa. Equally, most students at Erfurt were known by the places they came from, supporting the inference that – in the years before he began to study at Erfurt – the youngest son of Friele Gensfleisch zur Laden may have been resident in Eltville and not in Mainz at all.

My personal researches in Eltville centred on the question of whether there was perhaps someone else who might be identified as Johannes de Alta villa, and in fact one such candidate was found. According to the *Series praelatorum et canonicorum* of St Peter's religious foundation in Mainz, one Johannes de Eltvilt made an appearance there from their own Eltville chapter: 'Johannes de Eltvilt acceptit possesionem aò 1405 ita computu fabricae pag. 23 – obiit 1428.' [I am grateful to Hans Kremer, Eltville, for this information.] To have been a canon, he must have been at least 20 years old, and he was already dead by 1428. Someone born for certain before 1390 can scarcely be identified with our Erfurt scholar, Johannes de Eltville. There is no evidence for any other person with the common name of Johannes who came from Eltville and who could have studied at Erfurt at the time.

There are further weighty arguments in favour of Gutenberg's having studied at Erfurt: the inventor must have had close connections with Eltville, as has been accepted up to now. How else can it be explained how this little town of Eltville, which had so little to offer economically, has to be ranked alongside centres of early printing such as Mainz, Strasbourg, Basle, Bamberg, Cologne, Rome and Venice, if not because the elderly Gutenberg himself initiated his final printing venture there? And what can have been the nature of the 'agreeable and willing service that our dear and trusted Johann Gudenberg has done for us and our chapter' that archbishop Adolf II von Nassau refers to in his letter of appointment as courtier, if not the help afforded by the establishment of a printing works in the immediate vicinity of his court at Eltville? (Ruppel, 1967: 56–7).

At the time when Johannes de Alta villa studied there, Erfurt University would have been astir with the spirit of the Council of Constance and reform of the Church. Several of the professors driven from Prague by the Hussites had found an active base at Erfurt. In the curriculum of the arts faculty there was a programme of set lectures. Three semesters led up to the baccalaureate examination, which required proof of attendance at readings from various texts: on grammar – *Priscianus minor* and *Alexander, part ii*; in logic – the *summulae logicales* of Petrus Hispanus, the *ars vetus*, the first and second *analytica* and the *sophistici* of Aristotle; and in natural philosophy – the physics and psychology of Aristotle and spherical astronomy. Exercises were prescribed in ancient and modern logic, physics and psychology. Moreover, there were the faculty lectures to attend (Benary, 1919; Kleineidam, 1964: 229; Steiger and Flaschendräger, 1981: 20–21).

The lecture hall would have been a bare room, furnished only with benches. The reader stood or sat at a pulpit. Each listener had a booklet in which to take notes during the reading. Interruptions and questions were not expected; they were taken as signs of doubt and aroused distrust in the dogmatic system of teaching. The precepts of the Church fathers and of the Greek philosophers were held to be incontestable.

Three further years of study were required for a master's degree. During this time the high art of disputation and dialectical reasoning had to be acquired. Debates were held. Finally the candidate had to face half a dozen examiners for several hours of interrogation, before the master's gown was placed on his shoulders by the university rector at a festive convocation.

Most students lived together in one of the hostels; in Erfurt the most important of these stood in the Studentengasse close to the present scientific library. Some of the lectures were held in the small Gothic church of St Michael nearby. In that immediate neighbourhood, one can admire the fine town house in Allerheiligenstrasse of Johann Funke, subsequently master of the mint, who himself studied at Erfurt University some years later (Biereye, 1940: 9ff). Another name entered in the rolls (at the foot of the first column of the same page as Johannes de Alta villa) is that of a Nicolaus Fungke. He may have been the father or the elder brother of Johann Funke, who went on to become Erfurt's first printer. The fact that Johann Funke was a member of a coinmaking family, and similarly Johann Gutenberg and both his cousins Frilo and Rulemandus zur Laden were sons of companions of the mint at Mainz, gives a reason to infer that the parents would have been known to each other. There is a possibility that the three students from Mainz, one of whom describes himself as coming from Eltville, may have stayed at the house in Allerheiligenstrasse.

Conditions in the hostels were harsh. The senior students, who styled themselves 'Bacchants', were in charge of the regime. They made the younger students fag and keep house for them, wash clothing and scrub floors and even go out begging on the streets. Many students were compelled to find work in order to study, and most earned money through copying. There was a steady demand for essential textbooks, such as the *Donatus* and those of Durandus.

At one stage or another the future inventor must have learned all about copying books. It may well have been in Erfurt, where one of the most celebrated of Benedictine scriptoria flourished on the Petersberg. The type of the *42-line Bible* and its double-column arrangement resembles in a number of particulars those bibles that were written at the Erfurt monastery of St Peter.

If Gutenberg did indeed study at Erfurt then the lectures he attended there would have exerted an influence on his religious and ideological outlook. He recognized the boundaries of scholastic learning,

University lecturing in the Middle Ages. Woodcut belonging to Jena University.

experienced the new humanistic ideas that had pressed into Germany from Italy, and grasped the wider political implications. The German Franciscans stressed the individual rights of the German nation and defended themselves against the growing influence of the pope in internal German affairs. But they simplified the theological issues, reducing them to a strict rejection of the present life and to a disdain for every contact with reality. The Benedictines attracted Gutenberg with their higher educational standards: they spoke and wrote the finest Latin, although they supported the primacy of the Roman pope in all matters.

An effective voice at Erfurt University was that of the Augustinians, an order which took as its symbol a burning or arrow-pierced heart associated with book and cross. The Augustinians felt a particular attachment to the book. Whilst the Dominicans and especially their renowned Jean Gerson, one of the leading theologians at the Council of Constance, forbade the reading of the Holy Scripture by the laity, the Augustinians and Brethren of the Common Life were eager to promote the reading of the Bible and other religious texts. Even by that time, certain pre-Reformation stirrings were making their presence felt at Erfurt University, which later on were to inspire that monk of the Augustinian Eremites, Martin Luther. I suspect that the young 'Johannes de Alta villa' already knew of the necessity for a reform of the Church from the ground upwards, and, in common with most of his fellow-students, could observe his country's oppression under the Holy See, had at least heard of the heretical teachings of John Wyclif and Jan Hus, and felt the disadvantages of inadequate education for a wide circle and of illiteracy for the overwhelming majority of the population. He was able to expand his field of vision, had got to know masters and students from other lands, and took part in discussions about contemporary politics, above all what was happening at the Council of Constance.

We know that Gutenberg's father died in the autumn of 1419. On 1 July of that year Friele and his brother Ortlieb had both signed on receipt of an annuity, but on 27 December Ortlieb drew this annuity alone (Schweinsberg, 1900: 74). Presumably, Henne may have had to return to Mainz and support his mother for a while. In the winter semester of 1419/20, which began on 18 October, Johannes de Alta villa received his bachelor's degree from Rector Henr. de Moile, for which he was charged two Bohemian and two plain groschen. Soon after that he – if indeed this was the man we know as Johann Gutenberg – probably hiked back by way of Eisenach and Frankfurt-on-Main to Mainz.

WHEN HE CAME BACK TO HIS HOME TOWN Henchen had grown into a Henne, Hengin or Henchin; he was a young man, an aristocrat in all but name. As noted earlier, it was only having the one commoner grandparent that prevented him from being the minor nobleman that much about his demeanour at that time would have indicated.

Knights and burgesses would each have offered a different set of ideals as role models for a young patrician. Courage and honour were the cardinal virtues of a knight. Until the beginning of the fifteenth century the knightly ideal was paired with that of the crusader. The knight had to perform great deeds for the lady of his heart. His noblest task he regarded as defending the Holy Church against the infidel. From the way the nobles are depicted in contemporary sources, work was a burden reserved for the non-noble classes. According to this view, God had created peasants so that the lords could direct their labour in the fields, and merchants to exchange their produce for them. And the Church was there to show mankind the way to direct their souls to heaven, so that the order God had ordained on earth should remain undisturbed.

Diligence, respectability, thrift and the consolidation of profits were the dominant middle-class values. In this new dawn of commercialism and early capitalism, the entrepreneur still had something of the battle-hungry conqueror about him; investing speculatively to make quick profits from raised productivity, using science to devise novel production methods, and setting great store by new trade connections. This urban middle class, rich and self-assured, hankered after the status of the aristocracy. Although knights and burgesses feuded with each other, the impoverished sector of the nobility fell into the arms of the well-to-do citizenry, irresistibly drawn by the latter's brimming money-bags.

Both these ideals came together in Henne. As a child he was probably more taken with the knights; but the serious confrontations in Mainz may have brought out in him the self-reliant entrepreneur, who was never afraid to soil his hands with craftsman's work.

In 1420 his name occurs in a document for the first time: '*Anno Domini* 1420, an instrument was drawn up with regard to some legal disputes and errors concerning Friele zur Laden, his brother Henchen, and their brother-in-law, Claus Vitzthum, party of the first part, and Patze, Peter Blashoff's widow, party of the second part' (Schorbach, 1900: doc. I). Unfortunately this document does not continue, but we can safely infer that it dealt with some dispute over the inheritance left by Gutenberg's father, between Friele and Else (represented through her husband Claus Vitzthum) and Henne, and their stepsister Patze.

In the months and years following his father's death, Henne must frequently have been faced by the question of his personal future. What part could he best play at this stressful time? He took bearings from his surroundings, from his relations and from similarly placed contemporaries. Some of his forebears had exercised profitable offices for the archbishop or city council, others held livings as clergy at monasteries or churches, and nearly all enjoyed some kind of pension which parents or other relatives had purchased for them. All that was necessary was for them to put in an appearance on the right day each year at the town hall or wherever to draw these annuities. But the most important economic prop for the Gensfleisch clan was its longstanding affiliation to the society of the mint.

By this time it would already have become clear to Henne that – because of his shopkeeping grandfather – he could never hope to join this privileged club. It would have been natural for a young man to feel some frustration at finding himself barred from where he thought he rightfully belonged. He was just as gifted and at least as industrious as those patrician's sons, Frilo and Rulemandus zur Laden, his cousins, and eager to show the same zeal in opposing the guilds.

Henne had by now taken two educational strides forward; he had learned Latin and had achieved his bachelor's degree. Social and worldly inclinations may have made him decide against further study or making a career in the Church. It seems reasonable to assume that, by his twenties, Mainz had been his home for long enough for him to have journeyed to places nearby and further away; most likely to Frankfurt-on-Main, and possibly along the Rhine to the cities of Cologne and Strasbourg as well.

Once more the documents are deficient. His mother Else had apparently given up a house 'at the little high steps' in return for the house formerly occupied by Contz Frankenstein and Georg Wertheymer (Schweinsberg, 1900: 75). This barter of houses in 1425 may of course have been linked to the marriage of his elder brother, Friele, who was living at the Gutenberghof with his wife Else, née Hirtz, by not later than 1426. From then onwards the older brother called himself Friele zum Gudenberg, and was so named when he became a council member in 1430. Else, the elder sister, had married Claus Vitzthum back in 1414. Much leads us to guess that there may have been good relations between Gutenberg and his brother-in-law Vitzthum, but tensions with his own brother. The brothers espoused different political viewpoints in the fight against the guilds. It is hard to see otherwise why Henne would have moved with his mother into the house she had taken in exchange from Contz Frankenstein, while there was plenty of room for both of them to have lived at the Gutenberghof.

According to another source, we find during Henne's youth that besides his parental family there were other companions of the mint, namely Komoff and Reyse, already staying at the Gutenberghof. These may well, moreover, have been active as professional coinmakers. Certainly the coins themselves were struck in metal at the house called 'at the old mint', as would have been the silver coins which Emperor Sigismund ordered to be produced at Mainz in 1419. But part of the preliminary work, possibly even the skilful engraving of dies, may actually have taken place at the Gutenberghof.

In this way Gutenberg could have acquired the knowledge he later demonstrated of lapidary work and punchcutting as well as of metallurgy and casting techniques, in which Komoff and Reyse may well have been his instructors. He could thus have learned about a goldsmith's skills without needing to become a member of the goldsmith's guild. The departure of Komoff and Reyse – possibly even entailing the barter of living and working space at the Gutenberghof for the erstwhile Contz Frankenstein house – may be related to the point at which both brothers, Hengin as well as Friele, now call themselves zum Gutenberg. Hengin Gutenberg is named together with Heinz Reyse in the *Mainz Reconciliation* of 1430, a legal enactment of Archbishop Konrad III. This raises a number of questions: did Gutenberg continue to collaborate with Reyse after leaving Mainz? Did their work involve the decoration of fine bindings to handwritten codices with precious metals, silver clasps and finished with pearls? It should prove fruitful for Gutenberg research in the future to track down this Heinz Reyse and his activities. Hengin may have sought to test this coinmaker's skills and to accomplish something special.

It is also possible that he may have tried to distinguish himself through involvement in politics. It is known that political activists of the establishment met at the tap-room 'Zum Tiergarten', while those with progressive political interests gathered at the wine locale 'Zum Mombaselier' – the name is either a corruption of 'Mon plaisir' or refers to an earlier Jewish owner from Montpellier (*Mainz*, 1968: I, 40). Accordingly, Hengin would have found his friends at the 'Tiergarten' whenever he felt like spending an evening in discussion over a few glasses of wine or cider. He still remained bound to the views and way of life of the aristocracy. Certainly he must have joined in their social round and set himself up as a young nobleman. The famous Mainz carnival was already going strong by that time, and it can be assumed that he would have given comic 'barrel speeches' and been fond of the girls. His mother would have had to check up when her youngest occasionally lost half a gulden at the gaming-house on the Flax Market, or went on Saturdays with his aristocratic friends to the bath-house at Mill Gate to let the bathing women soap and scrub them. (The journeymen from the guilds used another bath-house, namely *hinter der Schweinemisten* ['behind the pigmuck'], to have their sweat washed off.)

To understand the thoughts and actions of people in the Middle Ages, one has to look at the painting and architecture of the fifteenth century and listen to the music and songs of that period. In the world-view of those living then it was an age of approaching apocalypse and for most a wretched time. War, hunger, plague and other illnesses, lice and fleas, tormented people. They saw three ways to a better life (Huizinga, 1965: 36). The surest way was to forsake the world, the monastic ideal, asceticism; but even this might not be foolproof, since the Antichrist was known to have infiltrated the cloisters and even threatened the papacy. The second way consisted in trying to improve life in this world. The Cathars and Waldensians, Hussites and many other sects and groups attempted to renew the Church and society. They took the life of Christ's disciples in a community of equals as their model, in order to distribute social burdens evenly through reform. Many chose a third way – that of achieving happiness in the present world – by recourse to eating and drinking, and to sexual love and consoling dreams. Painting and literature helped in this discovery of earthly beauty. Yet religiously oriented literature disapproved of these desires. In a manuscript book of that time, a *Mirror of Vanities*, next to interesting miniatures, can be found two stanzas that are spoken by a good and an evil angel:

[The evil angel speaks:]
'With cheerful eye this mirror scan,
thou fairest wife, thou noble man.
Observe, how fine are your proportions,
heed me and not the priests' distortions.
Deck out your body in fine dress,
that your youthful looks impress.
Take joy and pleasure in this time,
this world forsakes you in your prime.
For goods and honour daily strive,
that for long years you may survive.
To ponder death avails you nought,
should't come, it asks no further thought.'
[The good angel speaks thus:]
'O man, reflect when time has past,
you'll be a skeleton at last.

Just when you think, it's joy to be,
then death comes by and sucks up thee.
Whoever looks into this mirror,
will sin avoid and life discover.
His sight one day will God encapture,
O man, that will your soul enrapture.
Be not by vanities ensnared,
and hold your soul for God prepared.
Then may your heart with joy resound
and God grant you his heavn'ly crown' (Cosacchi, 1965: 495).

Human beings felt caught up in a great play between God and the devil, and the many religious and secular processions formed a chorus to this divine comedy. The figures that strutted and shambled past the observer somehow typified this outlook on life.

Many descriptions and book illustrations depict the *danse macabre* or Dance of Death, that had spread – especially during Gutenberg's lifetime – to nearly every country in Europe. Often such graveyard dances were combined with wild festivities. The Church attempted to give these old heathen practices a new content and to turn them into contemplations on death and the Last Judgment. In Mainz and the towns along the Rhine, a variety of carnival processions were held. At times a harlequin or devil danced or performed in front, followed to the cemetery by the maskers, often in pairs. All kinds of songs were sung along the way, which often had nothing to do with the coming spectacle in the graveyard:

Bovo rides through the wild and leafy wood –
he leads with him Kunigund, the fair ...

And if hold-ups occurred, then all sang the refrain: 'Why are we waiting here, why not let's go?', and took their partners for the dance.

A group of musicians would already be seated in the middle of the graveyard, and among them was Adam, who gripped his speech-roll and declaimed:

> You are all my children. You all came naked into this world. Who is peasant and who is knight? I see poverty and magnificence packed together. Why are you come? God created me from earth, you also came of earth and shall to earth return. Think on this, if you do wrong. Death holds the sceptre in his hand (Cosacchi, 1965: 285ff).

Then many dancers clad as skeletons strode out from the charnel house and mingled with the revellers by the graveyard wall. With courtly bows they invited the masker dressed as pope, then those playing king, queen, cardinal and all the other persons of state to dance. These hesitated at first, but were led or rather danced into the centre of the cemetery where they were laid out for dead (or equipped with an instrument and made to join the band). And so the canon, the townsman, the heathen and the peasant were similarly carried off by death. Whenever someone had been danced to the middle by a skeleton, the band struck up again, the skeletons bowed to left and right and took two steps forward in common time, and the dance went on. Finally a priest stepped forward and commanded everyone lying on the ground to arise, as Christ had triumphed over death and all should awake on the Day of Judgment. And then, by a different route than they had come – to return the same way would invite ill-fortune – the dancers went home, or more likely to carouse in the taverns.

The Dance of Death was supposed to work miracles against death and the plague. Non-participants were liable to be inflicted with boils or sickness by evil spirits, whereas those who joined in enjoyed a measure of protection against such ills. No wonder the homegoing revellers looked so merry. Some wore their breeches back to front and others had strung cow-bells between their legs. Bags were pulled over a few heads so that eyes peered from cut-out holes like Capuchin friars. Old cooking pots were beaten as drums (Cosacchi, 1965: 303).

This was all part of the life which went on around the young Johann Gutenberg; a part of the scenery of that theatre, of whose leading actor there is still little if any information available, unless one seizes on an obscure report – which looks quite good coming after a description of medieval carnival customs – into the business in Mainz life annuities.

In a collection of Mainz judicial formulae for the year 1427/28 a transcript is preserved of a document concerning a life annuity for the brothers Friele and Hengin Gutenberg, from which the salient points can be extracted as follows:

> Everybody shall know that Hans Gutlichter came before Johann Molsberg, Secular Judge at Mainz, to communicate, that the annuity of two persons called the brothers Friele and Hengin, sons of the late Friele zu Gudenberg, guaranteeing them 20 gulden a year for life, shall be transferred after their deaths to Johann Imgrase and his heirs. The said 20 gulden shall be paid to Johann [Imgrase] half and half on Twelfth Day [i.e. Epiphany] and St Margaret's Day. Hans Gutlichter has deposited as a security for Johann Imgrase one horn-strap with silver buckles and three goblets, together worth 36 marks, so that this contract is performed (Schorbach, 1900: doc. II).

No one has yet been able to say how this Hans Gutlichter came to have the life annuities of both the Gutenberg brothers (after their deaths) at his disposal. What is significant is that it is the sons of 'the late Friele zu Gudenberg' who are clearly spoken of here. It may be that the brothers had joined forces again to obtain financial support. This document also shows how closely the fate of the young Gutenberg was bound up with such pensions, with the economic practices of the city and their social consequences.

The civic conflicts in Mainz

MAINZ STILL SHONE WITH WEALTH. Between the Kaestrich – the Roman *castrum* or camp from which the quarter bordering the present old town takes its name – and the vineyard slopes to the south and the Rhine, the towers of over 40 churches pointed skyward. The city now exercised the right of staple on all goods travelling up or downstream by boat, and which had in any case to be unloaded, since boats could not pass the bridge between Mainz and Castell which was itself made of small boats. These goods now had to be exhibited for tender in the merchants' warehouse on the Brand. Two enormous floating cranes, for hoisting cargo from ship to land, rode at anchor on the river. Porters and barrow-men waited to unload sacks and barrels and convey them through the Mühlpforte to the warehouse. The Eisenturm, Mühlpforte and Fischtor were the points of access to the river. Near the Eisentor was the market where smiths and metalworkers offered their goods; the Fischtor led to the place where fish fresh from the Rhine was offered for sale on market days; and the Mühlpforte took its name from the milling ships which were anchored on the Rhine and ground grain more cheaply and conveniently than windmills. On the Flachsmarkt, near the Gutenberghof in the town centre, peasants offered the flax they had combed; and barge traders displayed there the fabrics which they had brought by river from Holland, Brabant and Burgundy, whenever the old families had not exercised their staple right of prior purchase. The town had yet more markets in which trades flourished. A great deal of hammering, fulling, sewing, kneading and polishing went on in numerous craft workshops. Mainz would have looked a prosperous place to the traveller; a city meriting the name *Aurea Moguntia*, golden Mainz, which it had adopted in rivalry with *Aurea Roma* itself.

But, for those in the know, its finances had by now reached a desperate state. When Henchen had been forced to leave Mainz on the first occasion with his father, back in 1411, the interest on the civic debt was eating up 40 per cent of income. Even when the guilds held power they had been unable to bring about any financial improvement, since the old families still got away with paying little or no tax, and the priests could still sell their wine free of duty as a result of holding written validation of their privileges. A Mainz council ordinance of 14 June 1422 called for an increase in taxation (*Mainz*, 1968: I, 53). Any dialogue with the patricians, who had again fled to their country estates, must have broken down, and no one dared seize their goods, for that would have been the only way that they could have been compelled to pay. In that same year the city found that it could no longer meet its interest charges when they fell due. A contract with Archbishop Konrad III dated 19 October 1422 made 8000 gulden available for the payment of the council's most pressing debts, in return for the surrender of some of its traditional privileges (*Mainz*, 1968: I, 55).

Bankruptcy threatened anew by the summer of 1428. Ten representatives were elected by the guilds, charged with working out a plan that would avert the danger. The ten demanded their own recognition as the highest civic governing body, and in the resultant confrontation the old families withdrew from the town yet again – and with them in all probability went Hengin Gutenberg.

On 1 October 1428 the moderates among the remaining patricians voted to carry the new tax proposals, and Hengin's older brother would have sided with this faction. The exiles had either to be persuaded to return or consider themselves permanently banned. Election results for the new council were declared on 1 February 1429: only seven out of 35 members were patricians, and they held on to just one of the four appointments as burgomasters made at that time. On 15 February 1429 the new council decree came into force, but by 18 March 1430 it had been overtaken by a reconciliation enacted by the archbishop (*Mainz*, 1968: I, 56ff).

According to this, 'Henchin zu Gudenberg' and some others 'who are at present not in town' were allowed to return home. Among these were Henne Fürstenberg – although he was known to be back in Mainz already – Henne Hircz, Peter Gensfleisch and Heinz Reyse. A certain Jorge Gensfleisch was expressly excluded from the benefits of this treaty of propitiation and reconciliation, and it can only be thought that he must have been a particularly hardline opponent of the guilds. Thereafter the patricians fell into two groups, one of which was formed by those who had stayed 'in town', and found it a lesser evil to live with the new levels of taxation and declare themselves ready to collaborate with the guilds. Henne's brother Friele belonged to this group, since an exile's lot probably struck him as being unnecessarily arduous for the father of a young family. The second group consisted of 'outcasts', those members of the old families who refused to pay their taxes and preferred to hold out on their country estates in the Rheingau and similar districts nearby until the guilds were financially ruined. The future inventor was a member of this company, as was his colleague at the mint, and Henne's former neighbour at the Gutenberghof, Heinz Reyse. (*Mainz*, 1968: I, 76–7 and Schorbach, 1900: doc. IV).

Evidence of the social shift that had occurred in the meantime in Mainz can be gathered from the tone of the opening lines of Archbishop Konrad III's act of reconciliation:

> We, Konrad, by God's grace archbishop of the Holy See at Mainz, archchancellor of the Holy Roman Empire in German lands, proclaim and make known through this document, that we have considered long enough such confusion and discord as are unfortunately now common in the German lands, and especially such dissension as has hitherto arisen, set in and taken place between the honourable members of the old families, on the one side, and the honourable burgomasters and council, municipality and common burghers at Mainz, on the other ...

This treaty of reconciliation goes on to detail the measures which have been agreed in the presence of representatives from Worms, Speyer and Frankfurt to prevent a further deterioration in the situation, and which may be paraphrased as follows:

> Henceforth, the council of Mainz shall have 36 members; of these, 12 shall be of the old families and 24 from the community [i.e. the guilds]. If a vacancy occurs through death or resignation, then it shall be filled by electing a new member from the ranks of the patricians or community, as the case may be. There shall be in future three burgomasters and three treasurers, one of each from the old families and two of each from the community. Each of the three treasurers shall hold one of the three keys to the vault wherein the register and money of the city are kept, so that only all three together may open the door. Likewise the keys of all three burgomasters shall be needed to remove the city seal from its casket. It has also been agreed that the citizens of the old families and their heirs shall for all time not be bound or pressed to become guild members unless they wish to do so of their own free will. The old families shall keep their rights of coinage and *gaden* [business premises], grants and privileges. It remains open for those named as absent to return to town on undertaking to observe this reconciliation.

A closely contemporary document – telling us about the halving and transfer of another of Gutenberg's pensions – can be related to these events and the parlous financial state of the city. This text of 16 January 1430 states:

> *Item*, whereas Katherine, daughter of Cuntze Schwartz of Delkenheim, has brought some time ago for the lifetime of Henne, son of the late Friele

> Gensfleisch, an annuity of 13 gulden, payable in weekly instalments, now then it has been agreed with Else zu Gudenberg, his mother, that she be given henceforth, as long as the said Henne is alive, not more than $6^1/_2$ gulden, namely every two weeks 6 shillings, and the remaining $6^1/_2$ gulden she leaves untouched till after the death of Henne, her son (Schorbach, 1900: doc. III).

Research has been unable to establish who this Katherine Schwartz of Delkenheim (a village three miles from Wiesbaden) may have been, nor why she should have bequeathed a life contract to Henne. It may be concluded that by the date on this document Gutenberg was no longer domiciled in Mainz, and so his mother needed to agree to transfer half this annuity into her own name to collect the income from the city.

Fresh negotiations were due to have taken place in Oppenheim at the end of 1430, yet the patricians did not despatch their representative until 1 May 1431. In the meantime the city could only pay two-thirds of its debt to its creditors in Frankfurt. As from 1433, the governing committee of ten guildsmen sought to tax the priesthood. In protest the priests took themselves off from the city and placed the matter before the Council of Basle. The upshot was that the clerics won back the right to sell their wine tax-free, and it even appears that they announced the licensed hours from the pulpit. Year by year the income of the town declined. Interest alone on the town's mountain of debt in 1436 reached 76 per cent of receipts. The city was only able to afford to maintain between six and ten mercenaries. Frankfurt, that thriving centre for trade fairs, made a small contribution by drawing business from Mainz (*Mainz*, 1968: II, 129–130).

By 1437 the insolvency of the town could no longer be concealed. Representatives of neighbouring towns, who were at the same time the major creditors, were asked in to inspect the account books. With the approval of the creditors, interest payments and life annuities were cut by half: but back in 1430, as we know, Gutenberg had been affected by this measure (*Mainz*, 1968: I, 92ff and compare Schorbach, 1900: doc. III).

The old families were heartened, and hailed the city's bankruptcy as a bankruptcy for the party of the guilds. The exiles too could resume the duty-free carriage and import of their goods – the wine, grain and hay produced on their country estates – into Mainz, for tax-free sale there. All their former privileges were restored, and the deputies of the guilds that had lately been so arrogant were now obliged to sign undertakings guaranteeing these rights to the old families. Here, in these original documents, are to be found the signatures or marks of gardeners, salters, cloth-shearers, vintners, chest-makers, coal-haulers, tanners, ferrymen, ship's carpenters, cobblers, fishsellers, anglers, porters, rope-makers, blacksmiths, furriers, butchers, house-painters, saddlers, linen-weavers, tinsmiths, wine-conners, grocers, iron-mixers, sheep-shearers, bathhouse-keepers, bakers, tailors, stonemasons and helmsmen (Fischer, 1958: 35). The old families had apparently won an overwhelming victory. But was it a victory? The community was approaching collapse as a city.

CHAPTER TWO

1429–1434: Years of apprenticeship and travel?

Five unaccounted years

WE CAN BE SURE THAT GUTENBERG did not stay long in Mainz after 1430, for otherwise the information blackout about him there between 1429 and 1434 would not be so total. Where can he have taken himself? Did he settle in the Rheingau region again, or in some large city like Frankfurt, Nuremberg, Erfurt, Cologne, Amsterdam, Ghent, Paris or Avignon? As an outsider and an aristocrat it would have been hard to set up as a goldsmith; the guilds in these places would hardly have given him a work permit. His social relationships were volatile, and drove him towards daring ventures. But it should not be ruled out that he may have entered a book workshop of the kind known at Hagenau and elsewhere in Alsace, or that he may have found somewhere to gather experience of metalworking techniques, in preparation for his later experimental work in Strasbourg.

Gutenberg research traditionally leapfrogs these five years, but the plan of this book at least allows for suppositions to be aired. In searching for Gutenberg's possible whereabouts it is necessary to remove later historical deposits before digging for what can be recovered from the fifteenth-century strata. The political and religious hub of Europe in those years was Basle. It was here that the finest minds of the age were gathered in council to debate the reform of the Church, the persecution of heresy, and reunification with those parts of the Church which had fallen away.

The years leading up to the Council of Basle had witnessed a strengthening of papal authority. This was not a smooth and continuous process – there were hard struggles with the Holy Roman Emperor, crises of papal succession and the Great Schism itself – but the overall consolidation of the centre of religious power went ahead nevertheless. The pope intervened ever more insistently in worldly politics. Each abbot, bishop or archbishop elected by a chapter was expected to pay the pope annates (a special tax, to put it kindly, which represented roughly half the first year's income from the benefice). A broad and unbroken stream of money flowed in from tithes, fees for nomination or investiture, and income from indulgences from Rome. The Church had grown into the largest financial organization on earth.

The Council of Constance, which met from 1414 to 1418, had ended the Great Schism – that terrible interlude during which there were two popes, one of Rome and the other at Avignon, each of whom had excommunicated the other. But the infamous burning of Jan Hus had ignited a popular uprising in Bohemia which brought the radical Taborites to power. The fathers of the Council of Constance had elected Martin V as pope, who, in the event, failed to come up to expectations. The Church still awaited reform 'in head and members'. At Constance it had been planned for new councils to take place every seven years to deal with the state of the Church. The synods convoked within this specified time in Pavia and Siena were limited in their authority by a mistrustful pope, as he feared a full council could curtail his privileges and his primacy. Taking advantage of the weakness of the Church during the Great Schism, the French had promulgated the so-called 'Gallican liberties' of 14 May 1408, which freed them from paying annates, taxes on inferior benefices and tithes to Rome. It goes without saying that German cities and princes were equally keen to see that such revenues stayed at home. To this end, the princes, who had strengthened their own standing compared to the emperor, sought to drive out foreign interference in internal affairs and stem the further flow of possessions and influence to the Roman Church.

Priests and prominent citizens from Mainz and its archbishopric joined in the pressure to hold a new council at which further reforms could be passed, but were equally conscious that Pope Martin V turned a deaf ear whenever a council was mentioned. Emperor Sigismund had exercised his pressure to bring about the Council at Constance; but now this German king had become older, and resided for the most part in Ofen, the Hungarian town which he had acquired through marriage. His troops fought against the Taborites in Bohemia, but the impassioned followers of Jan Hus were not to be vanquished on the battlefield, and their predatory reprisal raids through Saxony, Bavaria and Thuringia proved an embarrassment for royal prestige. The Mainzers hoped for a restoration of peace and an eradication of the deplorable state of affairs in the monasteries. The princes had already threatened to stage a German national council in the event that no agreement was reached to hold a universal one. By the middle of 1429, at roughly the same time as the internal conflicts reached their height, the first rumours surfaced in Mainz of the new council that was to be held in Basle.

The Mainzers glanced towards this Rhine city in the south with interest and a certain envy, for it was now assured a rich income through an influx of trade from the many princely visitors to the council. Many of Basle's churches and houses could now expect a face-lift; and painters, artist-craftsmen, tapestry-weavers, goldsmiths and scribes would be in great demand. Was there not an opportunity here for Johann Gutenberg, who wished to leave Mainz in any case after the guilds had decided to tax the establishment once again? He would certainly have come to hear early on, through the mint in Mainz, that the emperor and his treasurer, Konrad von Weinsberg, planned to equip Basle with a mint for the financial support of the council (Winterstein, 1977: 13).

Unfortunately my search for clues indicating the presence of Johann Gutenberg and his possible companion Hans Reyse in Basle has not met with any success. He cannot have been employed by the imperial mint at Basle; but he would have been more likely to have joined that 'Guild of Heaven', which, as an association of painters and skilled craftworkers, accepted commissions to be carried out by its members individually or in collaboration. The most celebrated member of the Guild of Heaven was the Swabian painter Konrad Witz, from whose paintings (see *The Miraculous Draught of Fishes*, Geneva Museum) the spirit of the council can be more closely discerned than through the mass of documents it generated. His artistic goal was no longer devotional emblems, but – influenced by the humanists – to depict reality and what could be known. The gold backgrounds of early Gothic icons yield to a portrayal of the visible world. The belief that God is omnipotent and to be found in all things continued to prevail; but the nature of this belief in God had changed. Whereas the figures of earlier paintings are bathed in a transcendental light, Konrad Witz and other fifteenth-century painters sought to ensure that their modelling and cast shadows corresponded to real light sources. He studied from nature and strove for a thorough realization of space by means of perspective and representation, as well as from vigorous natural colouring, clarity of form and intensity of spiritual expressiveness.

Whether the 'Mirror of Salvation' altarpiece at Basle, which Konrad Witz created about this time to represent subjects taken from the *Mirror of Human Salvation* – one of the favourite and most richly illustrated devotional manuscripts of the age – may be at least indirectly linked to the mirrors which Gutenberg was later to produce in Strasbourg, I would not claim with any certainty. But the kind of association that Gutenberg subsequently founded in Strasbourg, and the way in which it was organized, reveal certain resemblances to the Guild of Heaven which could lead one to assume that Gutenberg had visited Basle during the early years of the council.

Possible connections between Gutenberg and Nicholas of Cues

GUTENBERG RESEARCHERS devote too little attention to the inventor's motives. In general it is accepted that the need for books rose sharply during the fifteenth century as a result of the introduction of manufacturing, increased trade with the Orient, and an awakened interest in science and education. This is fine as far as it goes, and in this sense it follows that Gutenberg met this growing need by devising a rational way of producing quantities of books. But it has always seemed to me too obvious and over-simplified a conclusion, since scriptoria and individual scribes were keeping pace with the demand for their work. Requests for copies of standard texts could usually be satisfied off the shelf. The level of education and culture in Roman antiquity would have been far higher than in fifteenth-century Germany. This has led to the suggestion that, but for the cheap writing labour of slaves, the great need could easily have become evident there and then. The ancient Romans naturally lacked certain technical prerequisites such as a knowledge of papermaking. Nevertheless, I suggest that they would only have needed a push from a different direction to have discovered the printed book.

In support of this, I should like to refer back to observations of the historical roots of printing in the Far East. More than 2000 years ago in China, texts from Confucius were cut in great stone tablets and set up in public, so that unchanging impressions could be taken (by rubbing) for all time. Printing from blocks of wood in the Far East – by 770 one million copies of the *Dharani Charms* had been printed and placed in their miniature pagodas on the orders of the Japanese empress Shotoku – was motivated by Buddhist religious propaganda (Sohn, 1972: 217). State promotion of printing from movable letters in Korea at the beginning of the fifteenth century was again only intended for Confucian texts used in connection with the defence against Buddhism (Carter, 1925: 29). The possibility of a religious motivation for the discovery of printing in Europe as well has to be allowed.

When the Council of Basle (1431–1448) began, Nicholas of Cues (Cusanus), later a cardinal, was to be reckoned as one of the leading figures of the reform movement. In a work he dedicated to the presidents of the Council and representatives of the Holy See, *De concordantia Catholica*, he addressed the reasons for the Church's disintegration: the haughtiness of many priests and the pomp of some cloisters, which were often merely agencies to provide for the nobility. He took the view that priests should distinguish themselves by their humility, learning and straightforwardness (Kapr, 1972: 33ff). Furthermore he advocated a standardized procedure for the mass and a related reform of the missal, into which writing errors, modifications and partly intentional deviations from the text had found their way in the course of endless re-copying, and which could only be eradicated through editing and making copies from a new standardized text (Franz, 1902: 308). It is not known how these ideas of Nicholas of Cues were received by other Council participants, for as with his other demands – for example the inspection of monasteries – they may have appeared as unexceptional; but they would probably have made a lasting impression on one man, since much of what Gutenberg was later to strive for is encapsulated in this aim of producing a standard missal in many copies. And it is this, taken alongside much else, which inclines me to surmise that Gutenberg and Nicholas of Cues were known to each other.

The pair could already have met in Mainz as early as 1424, where Nicholas, as a doctor of canon law after studying at Padua University, took up his legal work. His profession as a young jurist has to be taken into account, and it is not simply possible but highly probable that, as educated contemporaries in an important but still small town of only 5700 inhabitants, they were acquainted (Kapr, 1972: 39).

During Gutenberg's later stay in Strasbourg – and here it is necessary to look ahead a little – there would be opportunities to renew any earlier acquaintance, and to talk about such matters as making copies of a revised missal that would be completely identical. By that time the future cardinal repeatedly stayed overnight in Strasbourg on his journeys between Rome and Germany. There would be even greater scope for dialogue after that in Mainz, when Gutenberg had returned to his native town in 1448 or 1449. It is significant that the patrician 'Johann Guldenschaph', at whose house Cusanus found temporary lodging when in Mainz, was later to set up a printing office in Cologne (Kapr, 1972: 40).

For those journeys throughout Germany, which Cusanus undertook as papal legate charged with implementing monastic and ecclesiastical reform, Mainz was one of his important bases. Seventy Benedictine abbots from the Mainz and Bamberg dioceses, congregating here in May 1451, took an oath in his presence to undertake reform of their houses. From 13 October to 7 November of that same year he again took part in the provincial council at Mainz (Kapr, 1972: 39 and see also Chronology, p. 291ff). As part of these monastic reforms, the libraries and their book collections came under review to ensure that at all events each monastery owned a properly edited copy of the Bible. It can scarcely be due to chance that preparations were in hand for printing the *42-line Bible* at precisely this time, and that recent research has revealed the first owners of several *Gutenberg Bibles* to have been just such reformed monasteries. Cusanus may have been the moving force behind Bible printing all along.

Moreover – as the Council of Basle proceeded – Cusanus had been sent to Constantinople by Pope Eugenius IV in 1437, to call for a high-level delegation from the Greek Orthodox Church, including the emperor, patriarch and 28 archbishops (to attend what became the Council of Florence). Among these was the celebrated humanist and bibliophile, Archbishop Bessarion of Nicaea, with whom Cusanus kept up a friendship. This eastward journey is mentioned because I should not like to rule out the interesting possibility that in Constantinople – by virtue of its position as gateway to the Orient – Cusanus might have heard news of the contemporary art of printing from metal letters in Korea and passed this information on to Gutenberg. This could hardly contain any technical details or direct knowledge of the process, but mere confirmation that this art existed somewhere else would have spurred on the future inventor at this juncture. After he became Bishop of Brixen, Cusanus made renewed efforts to promote his proposals for revising and standardizing missals at synods held in 1453, 1455 and 1457; and this leads to the further speculation that he was kept informed about the progress of the work at Mainz. (Kapr, 1972: 37).

Cusanus may possibly have proposed further subjects for Gutenberg to print later on. The great cardinal's church politics made him just the man to take charge of propaganda for a war against the Turks, who in 1453 had sacked Constantinople. At any rate Gutenberg printed the so-called *Turkish Calendar* and a *Bull Against the Turks*, as well as the *Indulgences for Cyprus*, to serve this same end. Even the printing of the *Catholicon* – a large Latin dictionary with a Latin grammar compiled by Johann Balbus in 1286 – must have resulted from many comments of the kind Nicholas would have made. Incidentally, the cardinal did have his own copy of the *Catholicon*, and it can still be seen today, together with the rest of his library, at Bernkastel-Kues on the Moselle (Kapr, 1972: 34). He would have got this book straight from Mainz, for he attached importance to seeing that the new art of printing was introduced in Italy.

In the Sweynheym and Pannartz edition of St Jerome, which appeared in 1470 in Rome, there is to be found a preface by Giovanni Andrea dei Bussi, addressed to the pope and relating that it was Cusanus who knew about printing and had transplanted it from Germany to Italy. Here are a few sentences in translation:

> ... In Your Reign among other signs of the bounteous grace of God is this gift of happiness for the Christian world, whereby for very little money even the poorest can acquire a library. Is it perhaps no slight glory for Your Holiness, that volumes which in former times could scarce be bought for a hundred gold pieces, are today to be had for reading in good versions and free of faults throughout for twenty? ... And thereto that which earlier talent brought forth and owing to the endless efforts and exorbitant prices of copyists lay almost concealed in dust and worms, but which under Your Dominion flows out from plentiful sources and has already begun to irrigate the whole globe. For such a work of art is that of our printers and creators of letters that one can hardly report inventions of like importance for mankind, whether in ancient or modern times. It is that which the soul, rich in honours and meriting heaven, of Nicholas of Cues, Cardinal of St Peter in Vinculis, so fervently desired; that this holy art, whose shoots became visible at that time in Germany, should be transplanted to Roman soil ...

From this it seems fairly certain that Cusanus, for whom the origins of printing 'became visible at that time in Germany', must also have known the inventor. This leads us to the assumption that Gutenberg was not only motivated by ambition and the pursuit of profit, but just as much – and increasingly as he grew older – from a religious-ethical commitment to education and learning. The dissemination of knowledge was not in the unqualified interest of the Holy See, since the Church based its existence on mediating between the word of God and the faithful. Only individual orders, such as the Augustinian Eremites and the Brethren of the Common Life, recognized the spreading of education as a religious duty.

It remains a mere hypothesis that Gutenberg was active in Basle in the years from 1429 to 1434; but I do maintain that a close acquaintance with Nicholas of Cues is extremely probable. It is easy to visualize these as years of wandering and instruction for Gutenberg, broadening his horizons and introducing him to new experiences; whereas it is scarcely credible that he would have simply sat back and lived on his annuities, which were themselves insecure in the Mainz of that period. He became involved in the technology of working with metals, and made himself into an outstanding expert in this field, as may be inferred from what was to take place in Strasbourg.

CHAPTER THREE

Gutenberg in Strasbourg

Clashes over annuities

AT LAST WE HAVE REACHED the end of one of those stretches in Gutenberg's life for which we have scant documentary evidence, but instead are forced to weigh probabilities and indulge in speculations to bridge gaps of years or even decades. No fewer than 18 documents survive for the 11 years which Gutenberg spent in Strasbourg, among them detailed evidence from a lawsuit. The Strasbourg documents frequently concern taxes and everyday matters, but even so they are cryptic and fascinating.

Why should Johann Gutenberg have chosen Strasbourg in particular as a centre for his activities? Strasbourg was an important city in the mid-fifteenth century and, with some 25,000 inhabitants, it was then – after Cologne, Vienna, Nuremberg and Lübeck – the fifth largest community in the German kingdom. Enea Silvio Piccolomini, later to become Pope Pius II, and himself a friend of Nicholas of Cues, wrote after a visit in the 1430s that: 'With its many canals, Strasbourg has a resemblance to Venice, except that its running waters are far more agreeable than the latter's salty and stinking lagoons. The town has mansions for gentlemen and priests which are fit for princes' (Piccolomini, 1962: 94).

Strasbourg was not situated directly on the Rhine at that time: although its boundaries approached the west arm of that river, it was in effect isolated from the plain of the Rhine on an island formed by the two branches of the river Ill. And in the centre of this oval formed by the river in Gutenberg's day, the cathedral already soared. This massive church, with aisles to the full height of the nave, had already been under construction for centuries. The building of the cathedral was begun in 1276 with the west front by the mason Erwin von Steinbach, and at about the time Gutenberg arrived in Strasbourg the northernmost of two planned towers was being finished at a height of 465 feet under the direction of the master builder Hans Hültz from Cologne.

The headquarters of the cathedral's architect or master builder was to be found at 'Unser Frauen Werk Hus' [Our Lady's House of the Works] on the Domplatz. Here, in a vast courtyard, statuary for the cathedral was carved by sculptors and stonemasons. The cathedral workshops at Strasbourg were the largest of their kind in south-west Germany, and their influence is still to be detected in many other towns. The magnificent relief carving for the arches of the cathedral's main entrance was carried out here, as well as the 'Rose of the West' window – that artistic symbol of medieval faith which still holds us enthralled.

Strasbourg was a hive of business activity, and the merchants' houses on the Ill – which served as a reloading point for transport by water and land – were its most characteristic edifices. Two substantial tower-cranes stood ready to load produce from Alsace on to shallow barges that plied between the Ill and the Rhine. Within the palace – a many-towered town hall with battlements and stepped gables – the self-assured expression of civic wealth and might prevailed. Opposite this stood the still earlier mint, probably the city's oldest public building, which had been erected when the monopoly for coinage was obtained in 1288. On the far side of the broad Kornmarkt was the Pfennigturm with its splendid crowning pinnacles, in which the civic treasures and archives were housed. Behind mighty town walls, the old town and the banks of the Ill were packed with decorated dwelling houses, the ground floors of which were mostly stone-built, while upper storeys of timber construction overhung the narrow lanes (Seyboth, 1890).

Strasbourg had experienced recent violent conflicts similar to those in Mainz. After an internal revolution against patricians, the guilds had attained participation on the council in 1332 and control of it shortly afterwards. The administration of the diocese and official appointments remained in the hands of the aristocracy. The monasteries were closed to the lower middle classes. In contrast to Mainz, all the monasteries were outside the city walls. As soon as its bishop could be gainsaid – as a consequence of the consolidation of Strasbourg's existing position as a free imperial city – the city fathers had prohibited urban monastic settlements. In 1390 the city was placed under an imperial ban because it had successfully prevailed against a siege imposed by the German king, its own bishop and patricians and a whole coalition of enemies; and had gone on to develop as a proud little city republic, able to absorb a whole series of surrounding villages into its sphere of influence and to strengthen its trade with the territory to the right of the Rhine. United with the Swabian League, Strasbourg afforded a rich and stable community in which the various social classes got along quite well, and an agreeable place to live. Alsatian hospitality, cuisine and wines had also begun to make a name for themselves in the world.

In looking for a direct reason why Gutenberg chose to stay in Strasbourg from 1434 onwards, there is a possibility that he may have had relatives on his mother's side in the town. His brother was still drawing an annuity in Strasbourg in 1433 (Geldner, 1976: 71). In that same year their mother died in Mainz. One of the Mainz documents is a memorandum on the division of her estate: '*Anno Domini* 1433, on Sunday after *Vincula Petri* [2 August], Claus Vitzthum and Else, his wife, divide with the brothers Friele and Henne Gensfleisch all the property which their late mother-in-law and mother, Else, has left.' The will was witnessed by Johann Leheymer (municipal judge and Gutenberg's step-uncle), Rudolf Humbrecht, Reinhard Weydenhoff and Peter Gelthus (Schorbach, 1900: doc. V). It is improbable that Henne journeyed to his home town either for the funeral of his mother or the division of her estate. If he were in either Basle or Strasbourg at the time, a message bearing the sad news would scarcely have reached him in sufficient time.

His share of the inheritance led the elder brother Friele to give up his sporadic office as one of the three Mainz burgomasters and withdraw to Eltville. Accordingly, it can safely be assumed that the apparently handsome property on the Ringmauer there had gone to him, since his sister Else and her husband Claus Vitzthum had spoken for the Gutenberghof. Henne, as equal claimant, would have taken his share in the form of annuities. He probably took over Friele's above-mentioned annuity of 26 Strasbourg denars as part of this fair division of estate, and this annuity in itself may have provided a good reason for his residing in Strasbourg.

The first document to give information about Gutenberg's stay in Strasbourg is in the first person, and announces his presence with some force:

> I, Johann Gensfleisch the younger, called Gutenberg, make known by this document: since the honourable and wise burgomasters and council of the city of Mainz are obliged annually to give me certain interest and fixed annuity payments, according to the contents of the sealed documents which I hold from them, with the provision that I may serve on them a writ of attachment, imprison them and seize their property should they not pay me ... Therefore have I, on account of my urgent necessity, served writ upon Niklaus Wörstadt, city clerk of Mainz, and he has sworn to pay 310 Rhenish gulden, owing to me, to my cousin, Ort Gelthus, at his house *Zum Lamparten* in Oppenheim by Pentecost next. I also make known by this document, that the master and council of the city of Strasbourg have urged me, as a favour to them, to release the said Niklaus, the city clerk, from such arrest and imprisonment and also from [personal liability for] the 310 gulden promised in the aforesaid manner. Given on the first Sunday after St Gregory's Day [14 March], *anno Domini* 1434 (Schorbach, 1990: doc. VI).

Gutenberg had defended himself vigorously and won his rights shrewdly in causing Mainz's civic envoy to be cast into a debtor's prison. With adroit diplomacy he avoided taking matters to extremes, but set the prisoner free again, at the request of the Strasbourg authorities and his friends, as soon as he had sworn secure payment of the debt. All the same, Niklaus von Wörstadt was a prominent leader of the party of the guilds. And so Gutenberg had first struck at one of his political opponents and had then offered him an olive branch. As Mainz sources confirm, the overdue annuities and the interest due on them were in fact paid, and, in consequence, Gutenberg came into possession of an appreciable capital sum. It is amazing that he was still on good terms with the Strasbourg authorities after this, since up to two-thirds of the Strasbourg council represented the guilds and were thus the political allies of Niklaus von Wörstadt. Gutenberg must accordingly have been quite well known in Strasbourg by the spring of 1434, which suggests either that he must in fact have been living there for a fair time already, or that he had good connections in Strasbourg society through his relatives or friends.

Some weeks later a further memorandum was drafted in Mainz with reference to financial documents:

> *Item*, an agreement has been reached with Hengin Gutenberg, son of the late Friele Gensfleisch, with regard to the 14 gulden which are registered for Friele, his brother, a resident of Eltville, which then became the share of the abovementioned Hengin. So that the same Hengin Gutenberg shall be given henceforth every year as long as he lives, 12 gulden, which shall be due half on St Catherine's Day, half on St Urban's Day. Dated [30 May], *anno Domini* 1434 (Schorbach, 1900: doc. VII).

This apparently refers to another annuity which Hengin had secured from his brother in order to equalize their inheritances. The discrepancy between the 14 gulden paid to the older brother and the 12 gulden which the younger one received is probably a reflection of the difference in their ages and life expectancies.

The following record in the Mainz archives confirms that the temporary detention of the city clerk, Niklaus von Wörstadt, had proved efficacious, and that annuities and arrears were apparently being paid on a regular basis: '*Item*, Hengin Gutenberg [at the time] of the Frankfurt Fair of last Lent on account of all annuities, 35 gulden in gold. Received by Claus Vitzthum who gave receipt for it. *Anno Domini* 1436' (Schorbach, 1900: doc. VIIIa).

And, from another entry in the city of Mainz account-books, it is clear that every 14 days a payment of 16 schillings was due to

Gutenberg from an annuity made over to him by his step-uncle Leheymer (Schorbach, 1900: doc. VIIIb).

Was Gutenberg married?

THE FOLLOWING ASSERTIONS are not textually underpinned; the document in question from the Strasbourg city archives went astray long ago. The eighteenth-century Strasbourg researcher Schöpflin had read in a memorandum that an action for breach of promise had been brought against Gutenberg in the ecclesiastical court by a certain Ellewibel zur Yserin Tür and her daughter Ennelin (Schöpflin, 1938). Such an Ennelin did in fact exist, and her ancestral house was at number 24 in the Stadelgasse. A document is still preserved in the city archive, which shows: '*Item*, Ellewibel zur Yserin Tür and Ennel her daughter on Weinmarkt', listed as contributors to the defence fund against the invasion by the Armagnacs. There is also a record of two donations by Ennelin zur Yserin Tür to the cathedral building fund (Schorbach, 1900: doc. X).

And then there is an apparently explosive entry in the 'Helbeling' tax register (*Helbeling* means a half-pfennig, which was the tax for a measure of wine): among a list of other names of members of chapters and convents for the year 1442, there appears: '*Ibi*: who serve with no one [i.e. who are not affiliated to any order]: Ennel Gutenberg' (Schorbach, 1900: 153). Was this the same Ennelin zur Yserin Tür whose mother had brought a suit against Gutenberg? Had she become his lawful wife in the meantime, and was now living apart from him? Why was her name to be found on file under the abbeys and convents if she was contributing at the same time to warding off an onslaught by the Armagnacs? Was she perhaps a totally different person who just happened to have the name of Gutenberg? Possibly, as has been suggested, she was a Beguine: that is to say a member of a lay sisterhood which, moreover, was persecuted by the Church from time to time for heretical views?

An extensive belletristic literature has grown up around the supposed relationship between Gutenberg and his Ennelin; one more notable for its sentimental imaginings than its literary merits.

Most Gutenberg scholars reasonably suppose that the action Ellewibel brought before the ecclesiastical court would have been dismissed. It seems likely that an acquaintance between Gutenberg and Ennelin must have revealed some weighty reason to have deterred him from wedding this young lady from Strasbourg. But not all Strasbourgers approved of Gutenberg's reluctance to marry Ennelin. In the trial before the Church court, the shoemaker Klaus Schott gave evidence, which Gutenberg contradicted and rejected. He went on to declare the deponent to be a miserable wretch who lived by cheating and lying. Klaus Schott, who was also known to his fellow citizens as Schotten Lawel, would not tolerate this defamatory language and took proceedings against Gutenberg before the Strasbourg council; they referred it back to the same ecclesiastical court where the breach of promise action had been brought. Finally, after long and costly delays, the parties laid the case before a civil arbitrator, who ordered Gutenberg to hand over to Schotten provisionally 15 Rhenish gulden until the principal case pending in the ecclesiastical court between Gutenberg and Ellewibel be brought to a decision (Ruppel, 1967: 40–41).

The verdicts are not known in either the Schotten vs Gutenberg or the Ellewibel vs Gutenberg case, apart from this 15 gulden fine paid by Gutenberg to Schotten; and no more is heard of marriage to Ennelin. The business with Schotten Lawel places any relationship between Gutenberg and Ennelin in an even less rosy light than before.

On the other hand, it is straightforward to prove that Gutenberg was not averse to a good glass of wine in his Strasbourg days. The following extract was copied from the Helbeling wine-tax register, before it was unfortunately destroyed:

> *Item*, Gutenberg one-and-a-half fuder and six ohm of wine laid in store. *Item*, his account has been settled on Thursday before St Margaret's Day [9 July) *anno* 1439, still owes 12 pfennigs and when he brings these in he will have paid up to St John's Day [24 June 1439] at last Solstice. *Item*, has brought 12 pfennigs on the same day [i.e. 9 July 1439] (Schorbach, 1900: doc. IX).

It touches us as sympathetic and human today to find that he had not enough money on his person when it came to paying wine tax, but that he went home to fetch or borrow the rest to settle up that same day. And although such details are of little importance in a scholarly work where conclusions demand space, and when one thinks that Gutenberg in the suburb of St Argobast had over 2000 litres of wine in store in 1439, and that tax was levied only on wine that was actually laid down, then the obvious conclusion is that he did a lot of entertaining and his guests must frequently have been in high spirits.

View of Strasbourg. Woodcut from Hartmann Schedel's Nuremberg Chronicle, *after drawings by Michael Wolgemut and Wilhelm Pleydenwurff. Nuremberg, 1493. Reduced.*

Holy mirrors for the Aachen pilgrimage

WHAT WAS GUTENBERG ENGAGED IN at Strasbourg? He had an address in the St Argobast suburb; probably a small house which he rented and where he lived together with his servant Lorenz Beildeck and his wife. Frau Beildeck would have run the household and cooked for both men.

From about 1437 onwards he had instructed the well-to-do citizen Andreas Dritzehn in the cutting and polishing of precious stones, and had also imparted special skills of his own for payment. This at least shows that he had at his disposal a knowledge of matters which others were keen to learn about. At the beginning of 1438 he entered into a common enterprise with Hans Riffe, governor of the Strasbourg exclave of Lichtenau on the right bank of the Rhine. Later the highly placed

Strasbourg citizens Andreas Dritzehn and Andreas Heilmann entered this association. Its object was to produce mirrors for sale to pilgrims travelling to see the sacred relics which were shown once every seven years at Aachen (Köster, 1973: 32). These holy mirrors were not intended simply to serve visitors as souvenirs of their journey to the shrine: believers were convinced that through such mirrors they could retain the miraculous power of the relics and take it home with them. Each convex mirror was fastened into a metal frame so that it could be held up towards a devotional object to capture its beneficial rays. It was believed that such mirrors, once they had been exposed to wonder-working relics, had to be carefully covered for the return journey and until needed in the healing of a sick loved one or an ailing cow. Early manuscript illuminations and woodcuts of the pilgrimage to Aachen show a bishop displaying the robes of the Blessed Virgin Mary – which had somehow ended their devious wanderings in Aachen – from the church balcony to the crowds below, who stretch upwards in their tens of thousands with mirrors raised high to try to capture the curative properties of the holy apparel.

The clothing already mentioned as belonging to the mother of God was the most imposing of these relics. It was followed by a display of Christ's swaddling clothes, the loincloth of the crucified Christ, and the cloth in which the severed head of John the Baptist had been wrapped. Those lucky enough to catch a glimpse of these sacred objects were reputedly immune from many ills.

The press of the masses at the parading of the relics was so immense that on many days the city gates had to be closed. It became necessary to exhibit the holy objects at long range. On a gallery between the towers of the cathedral stood bishops and prelates who in turn held up the cloths to view. A cantor or announcer described the significance of each relic. People pressed forward in the squares and streets, leaned from windows and took up position on the low hills facing the city. Almost everyone held a mirror which they angled aloft towards the towers in the hope of catching enough of the holy radiations (Köster, 1973: 37).

The production of these holy mirrors was a profitable business for Aachen's goldsmiths, but they alone could not keep pace with the gigantic demand. For this reason the customary privileges of the Aachen guilds were suspended between Easter and St Remigius (1 October) of those years in which the relics were exhibited to pilgrims. It was an adventurous idea of Gutenberg's – and one which probably fascinated his Strasbourg friends – that they should engage in the mass manufacture of mirrors of this kind. Unfortunately not one of the holy mirrors they produced has survived: but there are other museum pieces to be seen, as well as informative miniatures and woodcuts, which show us what these mirrors sold on the Aachen pilgrimage looked like.

A holy mirror was about four inches high by two-and-a-half inches wide and cast in an alloy of lead and tin. The design consisted of three rings fitted together. The lower ring contained a low relief depicting a Madonna and Child. A clerical figure appeared to either side, and these, between them, raised a relic behind the central pair. In the uppermost and mid-sized ring, the anguished face of the crucified Christ appeared within a halo. Between the upper and lower rings there was a circular frame about threequarters of an inch across, around which were metal tongues which could be bent forwards in order to keep a convex mirror in place. These fragile, lattice-work castings have mostly survived through the custom of soldering them on to bells (Köster, 1973: 57).

It was a rather unusual joint undertaking for productive ends that had been set up under Gutenberg's leadership in Strasbourg. Hans Riffe, who had introduced the largest sum into the business, was not able to participate in the actual work. Andreas Dritzehn and Andreas Heilmann contributed their working capacity as well as their capital. Gutenberg, who provided the ideas and technological know-how, was to receive half the proceeds, Hans Riffe a quarter, and the two Andreases an eighth apiece. All stood to become rich men in a year's time, if everything went to plan, for each mirror should sell for half a gulden. An estimated production of 32,000 mirrors would yield 16,000 gulden; which would have meant 2000 gulden for each Andreas, 4000 for Hans Riffe, and 8000 for the fertile inventor (Köster, 1973: 64). They were in a state of 'blissful expectation'.

But they had miscalculated – the pilgrimage was not to take place until 1440, a year later than had been thought – and so they had unwittingly locked up their working capital. It is not known where the already completed mirrors may have been stored; possibly with Andreas Heilmann's brother, Anton (deacon of the new church of St Peter), or at Hans Riffe's town house, or even by Gutenberg himself in St Argobast. Alternatively, the participants may have taken custody of the mirrors in proportion to their shares in the profits. Since these profits had been postponed for a year, what was to become of the business cooperative: could its members find a comparably profitable and far-reaching venture to embark upon?

In this situation, Johann Gutenberg set out on a new enterprise which was shrouded in secrecy and has remained so to this day. Both Andreases, who were eager to be instructed by him in secret arts, were expected to pay premiums for this teaching and to provide assistance as well. The 'chestmaker' Saspach built a press. The goldsmith Hans Dünne was commissioned to engrave 'forms'. Metal was purchased in some quantity. Gutenberg would have needed money for all this. But he must have been looking towards the year 1440, as soon as the Aachen pilgrimage was over, when his coffers would be replenished and his new undertaking, 'the adventure and art', would be on the road to success.

But first there came an unexpected setback, in the form of the Black Death, which spread from Constantinople, through Venice and into the valley of the Upper Rhine. On the second day of Christmas, St Stephen's Day 1438, Andreas Dritzehn died. His brother, Jörg Drit-

Three-ringed Aachen mirror-badge (158mm × 87mm). First half of fifteenth century. Casting from a bell of 1464 in Breithard (Köster, 1983).

zehn, proposed that he and his other brother, Claus, should take the departed's place in the cooperative. Gutenberg, aware above all things of the need to maintain secrecy, turned down their application. Jörg Dritzehn proceeded with a civil action in the Strasbourg court.

Three-ringed Aachen mirror-badge (105mm × 57mm), where the six retaining tongues around the mirror frame have never been used. First half of fifteenth century (Köster, 1983).

The documents in the Strasbourg case

A PROTOCOL of the great council of Strasbourg records the case brought by Jörg Dritzehn, brother of that Andreas who died of the plague, against one Johann of Mainz. Far more important than the immediate details of the trial or the merits of Jörg Dritzehn's action is the question of what is meant here by the 'adventure and art' or by 'the work'. This leads us straight to the heart of the problem of whether Gutenberg had already conceived his invention in Strasbourg and had gone on to experiment with printing there. It is probable that the generally accepted version, which has Gutenberg inventing printing in Mainz, may need to be revised. In order to afford the reader a full insight into what occurred during this trial, all the relevant surviving evidence is reproduced. The only passages which have been cut are those which are quite extraneous to the central issues. I have tried to make the German dialect spoken in Alsace in the Middle Ages more intelligible without losing its colour and character altogether.

These transcripts begin with the evidence of the witnesses for the plaintiff. Then follow the witnesses for the defendant. In conclusion we are given the judgment of the great council. To help in following the proceedings more easily the successive witnesses have been numbered.

WITNESS 1: *Item* Bärbel von Zabern said that one night she had the following conversation with Andreas Dritzehn: 'Are you never going to bed today?' He answered: 'I must finish this first.' This witness then said: 'But, God help me, how much money you are spending, you must have got through ten gulden by now.' He answered her again and said: 'You are a fool if you think it has only cost me ten gulden. Listen! If you had what this has cost me over 300 gulden in cash you would have enough for the rest of your life. And what it has cost me under 500 gulden thus far is so negligible that I've had to pledge my property and my inheritance.' But, this witness replied: 'For heaven's sake, if it doesn't work out, what will you do then?' He answered her: 'Nothing can go wrong; before a year is up, we shall have our capital back and then we shall all be happy.'

WITNESS 2: *Item* Frau Ennel, wife of Hans Schultheiss the timber dealer, said that on one occasion Lorenz Beildeck came to her house to see her cousin Claus Dritzehn, and said to him: Dear Claus Dritzehn, my master Johann Gutenberg has asked me to tell you that the late Andreas has left four pieces lying in a press. He requests that you shall take these out of the press and take them apart, so one cannot know what it is, for he does not wish anyone to see this yet.

WITNESS 3: *Item* Hans Sydenneger testified that the late Andreas had told him that he had needed to lay out a great deal of money for the common work.

WITNESS 4: *Item* Hans Schultheiss said that Lorenz Beildeck came to his house one day to Claus Dritzehn, after the latter's brother had died, and asked him on Johann Gutenberg's behalf to take out what was lying in the press and take it apart. Accordingly Claus Dritzehn went and looked for the pieces, but found nothing. The same witness had also heard Andreas Dritzehn say that the work had cost him more than 300 gulden.

WITNESS 5: *Item* Konrad Saspach said that at one time Andreas Heilmann came to him in the Krämergasse and had said: Dear Konrad, you made the press and know about the matter. So go in there, take the pieces from the press and separate them, then no one will know what it is. And when this witness went along with Heilmann to search – that was on last St Stephen's Day –

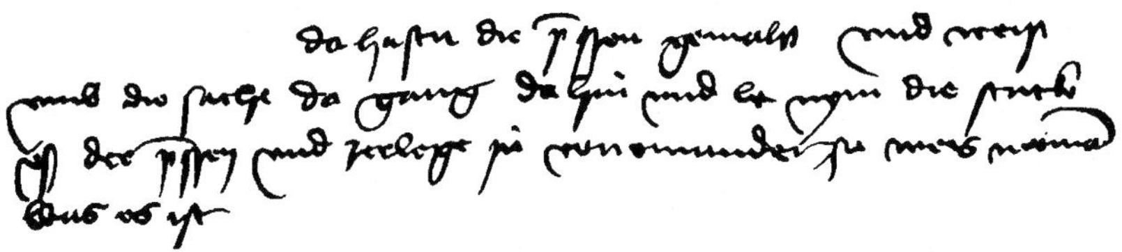

Evidence of the witness Konrad Saspach.
Facsimile extract from the Strasbourg documents of 1439.

the thing was gone. The witness also confirmed that the late Andreas had borrowed money from him for the work.
WITNESS 6: *Item* Werner Smalriem stated that he had made about three or four purchases. Among these was one for 113 gulden. Andreas Dritzehn had to get this money together for him. The money was at Anton Heilmann's house and the balance was then paid by Friedel von Seckingen.
WITNESS 7: *Item* Midehard Stocker said: When the late Andreas Dritzehn fell ill on St John's Day at Christmas, he was put to bed in the room of this witness, who, going to him, asked: 'How are you, Andreas?' He answered him: 'I truly know that I am mortally ill. If I am about to die, I could wish I had never joined that society, for I know well that my brothers can never come to an agreement with Gutenberg.' The witness asked him how the partnership had come about, whereupon he was told how Andreas Heilmann, Hans Riffe, Gutenberg and himself entered into an association, into which Andreas Heilmann and he [Dritzehn] had each paid 80 gulden. After a while Andreas Heilmann and he went to Gutenberg at St Argobast, where they learnt that Gutenberg was keeping some other art hidden from them. They therefore formed a new partnership, in which Heilmann and Dritzehn agreed to add as much to their first 80 gulden each as would raise the value of their joint share to 500 gulden, and similarly Gutenberg and Hans Riffe were each to contribute, separately, as much as the other two. An agreement covering all this was drawn up with this provision that on the death of any one of the partners the surviving partners should return to his heirs 100 gulden, but that the rest of the money should remain in the society.
WITNESS 8: *Item* Peter Eckart, secular priest at St Martin's, said that the late Andreas Dritzehn sent for him at Christmas time to hear his confession. When this had been freely completed, this witness had asked the dying man whether or not he had contracted any debt or made a loan to anyone; Andreas replied that he had put 200 to 300 gulden into a partnership with Andreas Heilmann and others, and that he did not have a penny left.
WITNESS 9: *Item* Thomas Steinbach testified that Hesse, the broker, came to him at one time and had asked him if he did not know someone to whom one could loan some money with little chance of loss, and that he then named Johann Gutenberg, Andreas Dritzehn and one Heilmann, by whom cash was needed for their work.
WITNESS 10: *Item* Lorenz Beildeck related that he had been sent by Johann Gutenberg to see Claus Dritzehn, shortly after the death of his brother Andreas, and to tell him not to show the press in his care to anyone. Further he should undo both screws so that the pieces fell apart. He should lay these separate pieces on the press, as nobody would then be able to see or work out

what they were for. After the funeral had taken place, he should go out to see Gutenberg who had something to talk over with him. The witness Beildeck well knew that Johann Gutenberg owed nothing to the deceased Andreas, but that on the contrary Andreas was in debt to Gutenberg. The witness had often seen Andreas sitting at table with Gutenberg, but had never seen him pay a penny for anything.

WITNESS 11: *Item* Reimbolt von Ehenheim said that, when he had gone to see him just before Christmas, he had asked Andreas how he was getting on with the troublesome problems which occupied him. The late Andreas had told him that the business had cost him over 500 gulden, but that, as soon as everything was finished, the money from it would relieve his great needs and debts. The same witness then said that he had loaned Andreas eight gulden at that time, because he had to have money. Andreas brought a ring to him, valued at 30 gulden, which the witness pawned for him among the Jews at Ehenheim for five gulden. The witness went on to say that at harvest-time last Andreas had made two half-ohms of brandy-wine in two barrels. One of these half-ohms he had presented to Gutenberg and the other to Midehart. In addition he had given Gutenberg a quantity of pears. Andreas had also begged the witness to buy two half-fuders [about 1000 litres in total] of wine for him. From this supply Andreas Heilmann and Andreas Dritzehn had then jointly given half a fuder to Gutenberg.

WITNESS 12: *Item* Hans Niger from Bischofsheim said that Andreas had come to him to say that he needed money, since he had work in hand for completion for which he could not raise enough money. When the witness asked him what he did, he answered that he was a mirror-maker. So when this witness had finished his threshing, he took his corn and sold it at Molsheim and Ehenheim, and paid the money to Andreas. He also said that Andreas and Reimbolt bought of him two half-fuders of wine which he, the witness, had taken by cart (together with the brandy-wine and pears) to St Argobast, where the late Andreas and Andreas Heilmann had presented one of the half-fuders of wine to Gutenberg as a gift.

WITNESS 13: *Item* Friedel von Seckingen said that Gutenberg, having made a purchase, had asked him to stand as surety for him; but that afterwards the debt incurred for the same purchase was repaid. He was then persuaded by Gutenberg, Andreas Heilmann and Andreas Dritzehn to guarantee a further 101 gulden advanced by Peter Stoltz's son-in-law. Gutenberg had repaid all this money as well during the last Lenten fair. He was quite ignorant of the partnership of these three, as he had never been invited to, nor been present at a meeting.

All the witnesses above gave evidence for the plaintiff. There now follows the evidence given by Gutenberg's witnesses:

WITNESS 14: *Item* Anton Heilmann said: When he found out that Gutenberg was willing to admit Andreas Dritzehn to a one-third share in the production of the mirrors for the Aachen pilgrimage, he earnestly begged him to admit his brother Andreas as well, if he wished to do him a special favour. Eventually an agreement was signed to the effect that Andreas Dritzehn and Andreas Heilmann should each pay 80 gulden to Gutenberg for the new art in which he was to instruct them. The partners began work on the enterprise in the belief that the next pilgrimage to see the relics displayed would be in 1439, but in fact the great pilgrimage was not due to take place until 1440. In the meantime they had learned that Gutenberg knew of other arts besides, and demanded to share this knowledge. After initial reluctance Gutenberg drew up a new contract with the pair, according to which they undertook to pay him a further 250 gulden in two stages. An immediate payment of 50 gulden each was stipulated, which Heilmann met in full, but of which Andreas Dritzehn paid only 40 gulden. They were to let Gutenberg have the remaining 150 gulden in three instalments at set intervals.

The new agreement was to last for five years. If one of them should die during this period then his investment, all things finished or unfinished, all forms and all the equipment and materials, should pass to the surviving partners, and the heirs of the deceased should only be entitled to receive back 100 gulden at the conclusion of the enterprise. The two Andreases had informed this witness in the Kürschnergasse, that they had come to an agreement with Gutenberg with regard to this contract.

This witness also testified that he well knew that Gutenberg a short time before Christmas sent his servant to the two Andreases to fetch all the forms to be melted down, so that no one saw it, although he felt regret for some of the forms. After the death of Andreas, Gutenberg feared that the objects in the press might be seen and recognized. So he sent his servant out again to take them apart. The witness stated furthermore that Andreas Heilmann and Andreas Dritzehn had given Gutenberg half a fuder of wine, half an ohm of brandy-wine and 1000 pears in return for what they had eaten and drunk at St Argobast. He likewise said, that he had afterwards asked his brother when they would begin to be taught, and had been told that Gutenberg was still awaiting the ten gulden with which Andreas was in arrears.

WITNESS 15: *Item* Hans Dünne, the goldsmith, testified that he had earned over the past three years from Gutenberg approximately 100 gulden: solely for that which pertains to the use of a press.

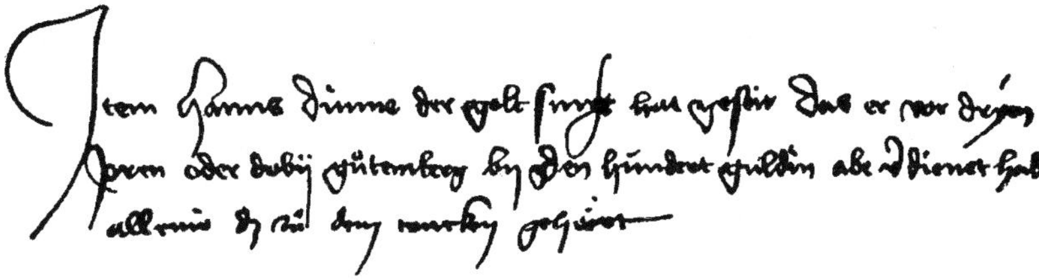

Evidence of the goldsmith Hans Dünne.
Facsimile extract from the Strasbourg documents of 1439.

WITNESS 16: [identical with witness 7 for the plaintiff]: *Item* Midehart Stocker said that Andreas had borrowed money and given it to his brother Claus. He had also heard Andreas say: God grant that the finished work of the society will find buyers, for thus I hope and believe to be released from all my hardships (Schorbach, 1900: 154ff, doc. XI).

Unfortunately all the originals of the Strasbourg documents were lost during the Napoleonic Wars and the Franco-Prussian War of 1870/71.

However, all the texts and quotations are based on authentic copies and facsimiles. In fact considerably more witnesses were called – 14 for Gutenberg and 22 for Jörg Dritzehn – but transcripts are lacking for the evidence of just over half of them. But we know the Strasbourg council's judgment of 12 December 1439 from a protocol of the chamber of contracts:

> We, Cune Nope, Burgomaster, and the Council of Strasbourg, make known, that before us came Jörg Dritzehn, in his own name and on behalf of his brother Claus Dritzehn, and summoned into court Hans Gensfleisch of Mainz, called Gutenberg, our resident, and said that: Andreas Dritzehn, his late brother, had mortgaged his paternal inheritance and paid such money into a society and partnership organised by Gutenberg. They had jointly practised their craft. Andreas Dritzehn had on many occasions stood surety and also paid for lead and other things which they needed for their work. Therefore, as Andreas was dead, he and his brother Claus wished to be taken into the partnership in place of their late brother.
>
> To this Hans Gutenberg answered that he considered such demands unjust, since the plaintiff must know from the many writings and documents how he [Gutenberg] and Andreas Dritzehn had been associated with each other. For Andreas Dritzehn had joined him some years ago and undertook to learn and master some art from him. Therefore he had taught him, in compliance with his request, to polish stones.
>
> Much later Hans Riffe, prefect of Lichtenau, and himself had taken up an art to be used on the occasion of the Aachen pilgrimage. They had agreed that Gutenberg should have a two-thirds share, and Hans Riffe a one-third share, of the profits. This became known to Andreas Dritzehn, who begged to be instructed, offering to become indebted to Gutenberg as he willed. In the same way Anton Heilmann had pleaded for his brother Andreas to be admitted. Gutenberg had considered and then promised to teach and instruct them, and let them have a partnership share in such art and enterprise so that these two should jointly own one quarter, Hans Riffe another quarter, and Gutenberg the remaining half-share of the proceeds. For this the two were to give him 160 gulden, and he had in fact collected 80 gulden from each at that time. All of them had it in mind that the pilgrimage was to be that same year (1439), for which they then prepared and made ready with their art.
>
> When, however, the pilgrimage was delayed a year longer, the two Andreases immediately requested and begged him to teach them all his arts and enterprises, and any he might further discover or know, and hide nothing from them. He agreed on condition they added between them 250 gulden to the former amount, making a total of 410 gulden, of which 100 gulden should be paid cash down. Thereupon he received 50 gulden from Heilmann, but only 40 gulden from Dritzehn. The remaining 75 gulden, due from each, was to be paid in three specified instalments. In the meantime Andreas Dritzehn had died and the money due from him was still outstanding. It was planned for work on the art and adventure to last a full five years, and that if one of the four partners should die within the five years, all the implements of the art and goods manufactured should remain with the others, who after five years should pay 100 gulden to the heirs of the deceased. A sealed contract was drawn up to this effect. Hans

Gutenberg had indeed taught and shown them all about the adventure and art, as Andreas Dritzehn had acknowledged on his death-bed. Therefore, as the contract concerning this matter which was found among Andreas's effects shows, Gutenberg demanded that Jörg Dritzehn and his brother Claus should deduct the 85 gulden which their deceased brother had never paid him from the 100 gulden, whereupon he would pay the estate the 15 gulden remaining in settlement despite the fact that there were several years to run under the contract before such a sum was due. And whatever Andreas Dritzehn may have mortgaged or sold was no concern of Gutenberg. He had not received anything more from him than he had declared, except for half an ohm of brandy-wine and a basket of pears. On one occasion the two Andreases had presented him with a half-fuder of wine. Moreover, Andreas Dritzehn had never stood surety for him, neither for lead nor for anything else, except one time against Friedel von Seckingen, from which Gutenberg had freed and released him after his death. And with that Gutenberg concluded his testimony and evidence.

Therefore, we, masters and council, after having listened to the abovementioned complaint and answer, plea and counter-plea, also testimony and evidence which both sides have put forth, and especially the content of the contract of which discussion has been held before us, now agree on a just verdict and accordingly pronounce it by law: Since there is a document that shows how the terms of agreement were made and should be carried out, be it required that Hans Riffe, Andreas Heilmann and Hans Gutenberg swear a sacred oath that things have been done according to the document aforesaid, and that it had been planned to turn this document into a sealed contract, if Andreas Dritzehn had remained alive, and that Hans Gutenberg must also swear that the 85 gulden had not been paid to him by Andreas Dritzehn, then he may deduct these 85 gulden from the aforesaid 100 gulden, and shall pay the remaining 15 gulden to Jörg and Claus Dritzehn and thus will the 100 gulden be paid according to the contract. And in the future Gutenberg shall have no further obligation arising from his work and partnership with Andreas Dritzehn. Hans Riffe, Andreas Heilmann and Hans Gutenberg have thereupon taken such oath between us, wherefore we order this decision to stand (Schorbach, 1900: 161, doc. XI).

The wording of this judgment of the Strasbourg council has only been abridged in non-essential matters and put into modern language, since it is the fullest report we have, and reveals – as if in a series of flashbacks – that the inventor had been engaged since 1436 in mysterious arts. But we still do not know today what to make of such vague terms as 'art and adventure', or 'art and invention' or 'enterprise'. Gutenberg and his associates have deliberately left us in the dark, for they were bent on telling the Strasbourg court only as much as was absolutely necessary in order to win their case. The Strasbourg financier Friedel von Seckingen must have been interested in the project – it appeared creditworthy to him – yet in court he emphasized that he did not know what was going on. All Gutenberg's collaborators patently had great faith in his venture. It must have appeared lucrative to Andreas

Dritzehn's brothers, if only because they wanted to be let in on it.

There is one more document that should be examined in this context. In a protocol book of the great council for the end of 1439 there is to be found a complaint of Lorenz Beildeck, Gutenberg's servant, against Jörg Dritzehn:

> I, Lorenz Beildeck, complain to you, lords and guildmasters, about Jörg Dritzehn. For he had summoned me before you to speak the truth, my learned lords, masters and council, and I have said under my sworn oath what I knew about the matter. Later, the aforementioned Jörg Dritzehn again came before you and sent a messenger to me demanding that I give testimony for him, and thereby has accused me of not speaking the truth before. In addition, he also shouted to me in public: 'Listen, soothsayer, you must tell the truth for me, even if I should get upon the gallows ladder with you'; and thus he maliciously accused me and charged me with being a perjured villain. He has done me injustice before the grace of God, and these are surely very serious and evil charges ...

Unfortunately this is the only fragment of the complaint to have survived (Schorbach, 1900: 160, doc. XI).

Our present purpose in studying the evidence of these witnesses and this judgment in minute detail is to find out what may have been going on behind the everyday occupations of these Strasbourg men and women. That these matters were momentous at the time can be seen from the scale of the sums in question, as well as from the excited feelings and conduct of those involved. The complaint of Lorenz Beildeck is additional testimony to this.

What was this 'adventure and art'?

THE STRASBOURG ENTERPRISE evidently revolved around three different activities, which need to be considered separately. Gutenberg describes the first of these occupations in his counter-plea, as relayed in the judgment. He taught Andreas Dritzehn how to cut jewels and polish semiprecious stones. It follows readily from this that Gutenberg may have been an experienced goldsmith who knew of skills not yet current in Strasbourg, the mastery of which seemed so advantageous to Andreas Dritzehn – and possibly to others as well – that Gutenberg was paid to impart them.

Likewise, the second undertaking is already described as an adventure and an art, but it is unlikely that this relates to that important art which had to be kept secret at all costs. It concerned the manufacture of mirrors for the Aachen pilgrimage, and Gutenberg had entered into a partnership for this purpose with Hans Riffe, the prefect of Lichtenau. Hans Riffe only put up the capital, for which he was to receive a one-third share of the proceeds as against Gutenberg's two-thirds. Later, two other partners made urgent pleas to be taken into association – Andreas Heilmann and Andreas Dritzehn – and as we have seen the profits were re-allocated in the ratio of one-eighth of the total to each of these, a quarter to Riffe, and half to Gutenberg. What is remarkable is the degree of trust and confidence shown by these prominent Strasbourg citizens in the newcomer from Mainz. This suggests that Gutenberg must have given his financiers and associates an impressive demonstration of his abilities.

The predominant view of modern Gutenberg scholarship is that this second enterprise entailed the physical production of mirrors. It was formerly thought that printed books rather than actual mirrors were the product of this venture: copies of *The Mirror of Human Salvation*, or in Latin *Speculum humanae salvationis* – a popular book that is known in numerous copies from the first half of the fifteenth century and later as a favourite subject for blockbooks and editions from movable types (Grabes, 1973: 246ff). Confirmation that Gutenberg was making actual mirrors is given by witness 14, the priest Anton Heilman; and also by witness 12, Hans Niger. But what can these mirrors and their production have to do with the subsequent invention?

Viewed from the standpoint of those days it is stretching the imagination to regard making mirrors as a preliminary step towards the invention of printing from movable types. And yet it results from a metal-casting or metal-pressing technique. Mirror frames are cast in an alloy of tin and lead from a soapstone or sand mould. It is improbable that Gutenberg would have worked with moulds of that kind, however, since having a background in the techniques of coinmaking it is much more likely that he would have engraved a dismantlable die in harder metal, from which castings could have been taken in a softer metal and removed when cool. Stamping in a specially constructed coining-press is another possibility. Thousands of identical mirror frames could be produced in this way, into which the employees of the company would only need to fit the round glass mirrors. Perhaps such a method of stamping was what was new about the mirrors in Strasbourg, compared to earlier castings from sand impressions or soapstone patterns (Köster, 1972: 146ff).

Another remarkable feature about this enterprise was its own institutional arrangements, which in some respects anticipate the later association formed with Fust, and may even have characterized the original

Mainz printing house at the Gutenberghof. This organizational model – which took the form of a cooperative with inputs for capital, productive labour and creative ideas – was relatively novel in Germany at that date. In Italy, where serial manufacture and the stockpiling of goods had developed earlier, comparable types of working cooperative had evolved. The Strasbourg court proceedings reveal Gutenberg as a man thoroughly at home with the financial and legal niceties of the day, an experienced businessman, articulate and well able to take care of himself.

The third undertaking was quite different in nature, and Gutenberg had been working on it at least since the late summer of 1438, in parallel to the project for the mirrors – and had shrouded it in the greatest secrecy. This new enterprise is repeatedly referred to as 'the adventure and art'; Andreas Dritzehn knew the same venture simply as 'the work', but these descriptions can have a variety of meanings. Names do not lead anywhere in any case, and even camouflaged descriptions cannot be ruled out; it is more productive to question whether the incidental details come together to make any sense. We hear of a press housed by Andreas Dritzehn and which was made by the chestmaker Konrad Saspach in the Krämergasse. We know moreover that Gutenberg sent his servant Beildeck to the house of Andreas Dritzehn just after he had died in order to undo two screws, so that four pieces, which were to be found in the press, should fall apart. There is talk of 'tackle and work made', of the 'thing made and unmade', of 'forms and many instruments'. 'Lead and suchlike, to do with it' was purchased. Shortly before Christmas 1439 Gutenberg had his colleagues fetch and melt down 'forms'. The goldsmith Hans Dünne sounds fairly explicit when he testifies that he had earned from Gutenberg 100 gulden, solely for 'that which pertains to the use of a press'. To be precise, his statement relates back as far as to 1436, that is to say, long before the partnerships for the second and third undertakings had been formed. This at least admits the possibility that Gutenberg may have made an early start on the third undertaking at that time, on his own and on a small scale, while conceiving the mirrors venture as a means of raising capital for his most important initiative: the adventure and art.

At all events, Gutenberg placed great importance on keeping the object in the press a secret. But, when Lorenz Beildeck and Claus Dritzehn went to take it apart, they found it was no longer there. Dishonest hands had made off with it earlier. Nor was it to be found when Konrad Saspach, the maker of the press, visited the house of the deceased in company with Andreas Heilmann. What can have been the purpose of this piece that came apart after two screws had been undone? Elsewhere it is equipment and tools which are mentioned; the word for tools or instruments (*Gezüge*) is one which makes a later appearance, in Dr Humery's affirmation concerning the printing equipment left at Gutenberg's death, where it is used to mean letters or characters in type. Forms (*Formen*) is a term, subsequently adopted for matrices, that occurs frequently in the evidence, and which also crops up in Latin in the Avignon documents, which we shall encounter later on, as *literae formatae* and *formae ferreae*.

Jörg Dritzehn, who eventually became a burgomaster of Strasbourg, appears to have been a quarrelsome and self-seeking man. According to the records, he later brought an action alleging that one Agnes Stösser had stolen cash and other property from Andreas Dritzehn's house after his death. Reimbolt from Ehenheim, who has already made an entry as witness 11 in the case against Gutenberg, was accused of taking part in the same theft (Schorbach, 1900: 244, n. 155). Further to this, part of a document from 1446 in the Strasbourg archive refers back to the events of December 1438:

> *Item* Jörg Dritzehn demands that he should now receive a half share or payment for what his brother Claus took after the death of their brother Andreas as undivided goods: namely 30½ pounds in pfennig coin, and also jewels, and large and small books that Andreas had left, and then 100 pounds in pfennigs that Hans Renner had given him. *Item* Claus Dritzehn demands of his brother Jörg, that he should give him one half part of what he, Jörg, had taken of their late brother Andreas's belongings and which had not yet been divided between them: namely three gold rings, a silver button, the '*Snytzel Gezug*', the press and other things (Schorbach, 1900: 244, n. 156).

One can visualize that among the books from this estate there would have been manuscripts and notebooks, and it is just conceivable that among the smaller books there may have been experimental attempts at printing. It is also apparent that Andreas Dritzehn had the use of the *Snytzel Gezug* (or 'cut[ting] instrument[s]', probably letters) and a press, and equally clear that these objects had not found their way back to Gutenberg. In consequence Jörg Dritzehn found himself the inactive proprietor of the first Strasbourg printing press.

Various theories have been put forward to account for the adventure and art, that third venture which Gutenberg and his business companions embarked upon in Strasbourg. One interpretation is that Gutenberg may have manufactured punches, impressed from engraved steel dies, for use by bookbinders in tooling letters on leather. The press in question would not have been a printing press at all, but a stamping press; and the two screws – which, when opened, allowed the whole object to fall into four parts – would have clamped a blank punch between two iron angle-pieces, which in turn were held in a wooden casing. (See the interesting conjectures in Gerhardt, 1970: 56ff). While this suggestion is technically perfectly feasible, the advantages of such an innovation would have been too inconsequential to have caused a furore like the Strasbourg court hearing.

I rather suspect that the two screws may have locked a chase or printing forme containing four very small pages of setting – an alphabet booklet, for example – and that loosening these screws would have caused the types to 'pie', or fall apart as single characters. And so the press would have been a printing press, and the forme would have been in its right place. Although this version is the prevailing interpretation in Gutenberg scholarship, it remains only a hypothesis.

If printing was in fact already under way, then a certain interest attaches to the way work was split up between Gutenberg's staff of colleagues. Andreas Dritzehn was apparently in charge of printing, at which Lorenz Beildeck and Konrad Saspach may have assisted from time to time. At Andreas Heilmann's house or that of his brother Anton, priest and deacon of the new church of St Peter, a composing room could have been established, since it was from there, shortly before the death of Andreas Dritzehn, that Gutenberg had the forms fetched and melted down before his eyes in order to keep the art and adventure secret. Anton Heilmann must have been deeply involved in the undertaking, because on several occasions it was at his house that sums advanced by financiers were repaid. He would have been useful in preparing copy and reading proofs. The typefoundry must have been at Gutenberg's own residence; where the master carried out his own typecasting, while Hans Dünne undertook the engraving of punches. And so everything necessary for printing books was already present at Strasbourg: typefounding, typesetting and a press. Only a bindery would not have been required, since printed books were bound in virtually the same way as manuscripts. Having separate workshops in different places doubtless complicated communications, but conferred the advantage of near-perfect security, in that only through observing the active interplay between the three parts could any outsider grasp the total significance of the operation and its productive goal.

The Strasbourg case marks a critical moment in Gutenberg's life. Without any doubt the work they had started will have continued. The new contract of association which had been concluded in 1439 had five years to run – until 1444 – which precisely matches Gutenberg's remaining stay in Strasbourg. The events which were triggered by Andreas Dritzehn's sudden death may also have wrought some long-term changes in Gutenberg's personality. Certainly, his political activities in

Mainz, the imprisonment of Niklaus von Wörstadt or the slandering of Schotten Lawel, combine together with his great consumption of wine to indicate an impetuous young man; but from now onwards he appears to mature and become more furtively absorbed in his work and increasingly obsessed with the need for secrecy.

A number of documents involving Gutenberg have been handed down from the years immediately following the court case, but none have anything to do with the invention or the further progress of the adventure and art. Next in sequence is the copy of a document to the effect that Johann Karle, knight, had taken out a loan of 100 gulden against an annual interest of five per cent from the St Thomas Chapter in Strasbourg on 25 March 1441; and that Johann called Gensfleisch alias Gutenberg and Lüthold de Ramstein, a soldier, are co-debtors and guarantors (Schorbach, 1900: 176, doc. XII). Should this knight, Karle, not discharge his debt on time, then Gutenberg and the soldier must step in for him and be taken as hostages or pay up.

This document is valuable for showing that Gutenberg was regarded as a credit-worthy guarantor by the St Thomas Chapter in Strasbourg, and that his contacts extended beyond his fellow-craftsmen to the aristocracy. It is likely that the mirrors for Aachen yielded a good profit when they were finally sold in 1440, and that he passed for a man of means. But, in the event that the contract for the adventure and art went ahead, a new printing shop would have had to be set up, for, as we have already learned, Jörg Dritzehn had taken away the press formerly belonging to his late brother. In any case, sufficient experience had probably been gained by now to enable a larger and improved press to be built. There would be additional outlay for large amounts of paper and vellum to be prepared and trimmed down; and lead, tin and antimony would be required to cast new letters.

A document of 17 November 1442 informs us that Gutenberg personally took out a loan of 80 denars from the St Thomas Chapter. Once again the customary interest rate of five per cent was incorporated in a thinly disguised way. Gutenberg pledged the annuity amounting to ten Rhenish gulden from his late step-uncle Johann Leheymer, and thus a higher sum than the interest amounted to (Schorbach, 1900: 181, doc. XIII). A natural explanation may well be that the strained financial situation in Mainz meant that these pensions were no longer paid out regularly or in full. The Strasbourg citizen Martin Brechter stood surety with Gutenberg in this matter, and he may well have been a new business partner admitted to the cooperative after the death of Andreas Dritzehn. As the account books show, Gutenberg regularly paid interest for several years in succession; but then no comments appear after his name, as was usual in the case of defaulters. According to such payment entries, he would appear at that time to have been living in the parish of St Thomas, as they are made under the heading for that church district. This suggests that he may have moved there from the suburb of St Argobast in connection with the setting up of the new printing house. It is more likely, however, that this came about because Martin Brechter, as a parishioner of St Thomas's, was making interest payment under Gutenberg's name on behalf of the association.

Whether or not the inventor enlarged his community through admitting more persons can only be conjectured. Later on, as one of Gutenberg's assistants in Mainz, we encounter a goldsmith called Götz von Schlettstadt (now Sélestat, 26 miles from Strasbourg). And finally, Johann Mentelin, also from Schlettstadt, later became Strasbourg's first typographer – unless we are inclined to reserve that distinction for Gutenberg himself. Mentelin had his printing office close to the Fronhof, while living at the house 'zum Dorn' in Dornengasse near St Thomas's. It has been suggested that Strasbourg's original printing house may likewise have been in this same neighbourhood (Schorbach, 1900: 16–17).

It is also possible to point to an acquaintance or collaboration with the priest and keeper of the archiepiscopal seal, Heinrich Eggestein, who ran a printing works in Strasbourg together with Mentelin in 1458 and 1459. Eggestein had given up his office with the archbishop in 1455, and it has been suggested that thereafter he may have gone to Mainz in order to find out all he could from Gutenberg about the latest state of the art of Bible printing. He went so far as to renounce his rights as a burgher of Strasbourg temporarily in 1457, but reacquired them in 1459 (Schorbach, 1932: 36; also 40, where we read that Eggestein and Gutenberg served together as constables in the Strasbourg civic guard).

It still remains open to question whether anything at all was actually printed in Strasbourg in those years from 1440 to 1444. I am quite convinced that the adventure and art did produce returns in Strasbourg; since that was the only way for Gutenberg to have retained the confidence of that city's distinguished burghers over all those years. This view is further strengthened by the fact that Mentelin and Eggestein were able to print in Strasbourg as early as 1458–9 (Geldner, 1970: I, 57ff). We should also reflect that it was possible to erect the first Mainz printing office in a relatively short time, and that printing on a smaller scale in Strasbourg would have paved the way for the impressive quality of Mainz printing. And, in conclusion, leaves from the oldest copies among the 12 editions of the *27-line Donatus* were retrieved from the bindings of Strasbourg books (Ruppel, 1967: 119). From this it follows that a small schoolbook in constant use, the Latin grammar of Aelius Donatus, may have provided a suitable subject for printing in Strasbourg. It was copied out countless times prior to Gutenberg's invention, since as a textbook it came in for heavy wear and tear. The typeface used for this little work is the so-called 'Donatus and *Kalender*' (or DK) type, Gutenberg's very first letter, a black letter or textura that will later be considered in greater detail. Perhaps these *Donatus* editions were preceded as the very first printing of all by single sheets: broadsides of the *Lord's Prayer* such as those which the future Cardinal Cusanus wished to see hanging in churches, for instance, or even small copies of the *Abecedarium* of the sort known from Holland. But none of this can be known; for no printed evidence survives from, or can be ascribed with confidence to, Strasbourg in these years.

To return to the documents: the Helbeling tax register contains a brief entry dated 12 March 1444, stating that Hans Gutenberg has paid one gulden in wine tax for two persons (Schorbach, 1900: 185, doc. XIV). Past attempts have been made to infer from this that Gutenberg must have married Ennelin after all, but this is a false conclusion as it is made clear elsewhere that no additional wine tax needed to be paid for a wife. It is more probable that Gutenberg still had his servant Beildeck living under the same roof, and that he had become a true and indispensable amanuensis. For each member of a household who was 'liable', the wine tax was eight schillings a year.

Gutenberg's name appears again in a list of persons obliged to supply the city with horses for its defence against the Armagnac hordes (Schorbach, 1900: 186–7, doc. XV). Although this record is undated, it can be assigned to 1443 or 1444. This assessment reveals that Gutenberg, who is entered as a constable (*Nachkonstofelern* would be drawn into any fighting in company with patricians and nobles), was due to contribute half the price of one horse.

The regulations afford a glimpse into his financial condition at that juncture, stating that: 'Those with a wealth of 400 gulden shall give the city one half of a horse, that is to say two together shall provide a horse at 20 gulden. Whoever is worth 800 gulden shall supply a horse. Those who have goods valued at 2000 gulden shall give a stallion' (Schorbach, 1900: 187). According to this yardstick, Gutenberg had not yet become a wealthy man through his adventure and art, but he was numbered among the *Nachkonstofelern*.

Gutenberg's name appears on another list of armed soldiery who could be deployed in battle against the Armagnacs, alongside those of goldsmiths, painters, saddlers and harness-makers. '*Item*, those listed here are affiliated members who do not have full standing in the guild: *item* Hans Gutenberg, *item* Andreas Heilmann, *item* Johann Roibel, a clerk, *item* Johann Slimpbecher, a clerk, etc.' (Schorbach, 1900: 187, doc. XVI). The early printers of other German towns are later found enlisted in the guild of goldsmiths, painters and clerks. Incidentally, this list is dated 22 January 1444.

Although Gutenberg's name appears alongside that of Andreas Heilmann, it is important to bear in mind that 1444 was the year in which the contract for the society was due to end. It is not known whether the inventor himself was in fact called upon to bear arms; surviving reports concerning the defence of the city mention Andreas Heilmann, the Dritzehn brothers, Martin Brechter and others from his circle of acquaintances, but Gutenberg's own name never appears.

The final dated report of Gutenberg's presence in Strasbourg is the entry in the Helbeling tax register of 12 March 1444, which has already been discussed. Not until four and a half years later, on 17 October 1448, does the next dated document show him back in his home town of Mainz. When did Gutenberg actually leave Strasbourg, and what were the reasons for his departure? Were there differences with his business associates? Or could it have been because of the Armagnacs who were then marching and plundering their way through Alsace?

'Die armen Gecken' [the poor fools]

THERE WAS SOME SUBSTANCE behind this current label for the Armagnacs [*Die Armagnaken*] in question; for they were 'fools and sinners' in the sense Sebastian Brant uses in his *Narrenschiff*, as well as being mercenaries and criminals driven to make an everyday living from violence. A monk is supposed to have greeted one of these mercenaries once: 'Peace be with you', to receive the indignant riposte: 'Why peace? The war brings me wages and bread. Do you wish for me to go hungry?'

We have to look at contemporary French history to understand the emergence of these Armagnac mercenaries. In the course of a decades-long struggle between the house of Orleans, which occupied the throne, and that of Burgundy, which had become even richer through the acquisition of territory in the Netherlands, a marriage took place in 1410 between Charles, son of Louis, that duke of Orleans who had been assassinated by the Burgundians, and the daughter of the count of

Armagnac. A long-lasting alliance ensued between the house of Orleans and the Armagnacs. This French civil unrest gave the English an opportunity to make a landing in the Seine Estuary. The fighting of the Armagnac adventurers during the Anglo-French wars was connected with the figure of Joan of Arc, who led the French troops to Rheims, where the Dauphin was anointed as Charles VII of France. The well-known story of the Maid of Orleans is only mentioned here in order to refer to the parallel historical course of events. Joan was imprisoned by the Burgundian forces at Compiègne in 1430, handed over to the English and burned in the market-place at Rouen on 30 May 1431. The Norman peasantry revolted against the English occupation in 1434; and in 1435 Philip, duke of Burgundy, came over to the French king. In 1436, the king's troops, supported by a civil uprising, were able to seize Paris back from English occupation. This strengthened the king's position, and in 1444 he was finally able to sign a truce with the English.

The Armagnacs, who were thus thrown out of employment, went on the rampage throughout France. Bands of Spanish and Lombard peasants swelled their ranks. This led the German king, Frederick III, and the pope, Eugenius IV, to consider a plan to deploy these undisciplined troops for their own political ends. Frederick III persuaded Charles VII to set the Armagnacs on the march against the Swiss uprising, and Eugenius IV hoped that this would disperse the Council of Basle. The French king seized the chance to shift these dissolute troops to German soil and extend his own influence as far as the Rhine (*German History*, 1983: II, 391).

About 20,000 Armagnacs gathered outside Basle. The cantons sent in a small force of 1650 men to aid the citizens. On 26 August 1444 the Armagnacs under Marshal Dammartin attacked the Swiss confederates under their commanders Anton Rüss, Heinrich Matter and Hermann Seevogel. The Swiss flung themselves courageously upon the superior enemy forces; killing many and forcing a retreat over the river Birs. The Swiss pursued them, unaware that a lethal ambush had been prepared for them by the Dauphin on the other side of the river. The Basle defenders, having spotted the danger from their watchtowers, were powerless to assist, for in the meantime enemies had burst into the suburbs and were already plundering the wealthy villas. Under fire from French cannon and an attack from 600 German knights, the Swiss battle-lines disintegrated, and they were forced into a meadow between the waters of the Birs and annihilated (Witte, 1890: 48ff). However, the Armagnacs and the Dauphin did not want another battle with such losses, which chroniclers at the time likened to Thermopylae. The battle at St Jakob-on-the-Birs saved the Swiss and the city of Basle from further attacks.

On turning back, the Armagnacs plundered the Sundgau and Breisgau regions, Alsace and especially the surroundings of Strasbourg. Contemporaries describe them as a half-naked horde of starving barbarians, inhuman in their lust for booty and bestial in their appetites. Frederick III, whose fault it was that they had been brought into the country, now appealed in vain for the German diet in Nuremberg to send an army against them. Strasbourg pressed for these Armagnacs to be unified with the Swiss. This situation eventually compelled Frederick to conclude the peace of Ensisheim with the Swiss, in which the independence of the free cantons was confirmed (Witte, 1890: 145, and Barthold, 1842, 119ff).

Strasbourg made a further stand in the so-called little war against the Armagnacs, until a settlement of 13 February 1445 finally required the French troops to withdraw from imperial lands. Over 20,000 lives had been lost in consequence of the Armagnac wars and their depredations. Hatred continued to rage in Alsace against Frederick III and those German knights who had fought on the same side as the mercenaries, for although the city of Strasbourg had been able to repulse the invading hordes, many of its surrounding villages had been destroyed.

What may Gutenberg have printed at Strasbourg?

THE ARMAGNAC CAMPAIGN, Gutenberg's departure from Strasbourg, and a recent work written in Russian by Natalia Vasilievna Varbanec – which, like this book, is very much occupied with the world Gutenberg inhabited – give rise to further reflections on whether it could in fact be shown that a book had been printed in Strasbourg by 1444 (Varbanec, 1980: 249). Varbanec also appears to be looking for a motivation on Gutenberg's part which transcended ambition and pursuit of profit.

However, Varbanec goes fundamentally beyond my own conjectures in assuming that Gutenberg may have joined one of the many heretical brotherhoods, closely related to the Cathars or Waldensians, which strove for religious enlightenment and separation from the Roman *curia*. Her thesis is supported by various deeds and attitudes of Gutenberg, which signify little enough in themselves, but together add up to a more impressive picture. These details range from his anonymity and the fact that his name never appeared on anything he printed, to his refusal to marry Ennelin zur Yserin Tür, and the strange anomaly that the later action with Fust over the credit transactions for the community printing house in Mainz was brought before a religious and not a civil court. (There is more to be said on this later.) The most significant evidence she presents, however, is drawn from Gutenberg's earliest printing, which in her view was unquestionably produced in Strasbourg. One argument demonstrates that the very early piece of printing known as the *Fragment vom Weltgericht* [Fragment of the World Judgment] or the *Sibyllenbuch* [Sibylline Prophecies] is connected with Frederick III's election as German king. This fascinating and hitherto neglected problem in Gutenberg research must now be presented in a little more detail.

When a small oblong scrap of paper – measuring about 5 inches × 3½ inches and printed on both front and back with 11 lines in Gutenberg's earliest typeface – was discovered in 1892 beneath the leather covering of an account book for Mainz University, it was immediately recognized as an extremely early printed item. The primitive state of the type, which is obvious from its uneven fitting and poor alignment, led scholars of the day to accept this as the earliest printing from movable types yet identified (Schröder *et al.*, 1904). Aloys Ruppel upheld this view in his celebrated biography of Gutenberg (Ruppel, 1967: 116). Evident difficulties had been experienced in casting this type. The height to paper of the types varied, so that some characters printed up heavily and others more weakly. It was observed that the same letters occurred in variant states, showing that the process of reworking the design had already begun (Zedler, 1904: 12). But there was and is no doubt that Gutenberg must have printed this piece, for, right up to the year 1457, only he used this typeface as it passed through its successive stages of revision and improvement.

A few difficulties arose in attempting to identify the literary source for this fragment of text. It consisted of a poem in Middle High German on the subject of the Last Judgment, and on account of this the print became known as the *Fragment vom Weltgericht*. Only later was the fragment recognized as a passage from a Thuringian version of the *Sibyllenweissagung*, that ran to 750 lines of verse. Gutenberg had not set this as poetry, but had instead run the text on in a kind of ragged setting so that it would have made some 570 lines. On the basis that there would have been 21 lines to each page, in a format of about 8½ inches × 6¼ inches, then this text would have occupied 27 or 28 pages. This matches the extent of the first *Donatus* editions, which Gutenberg probably had in mind when devising his first typeface. In any case the 'Donatus and *Kalender*' (or DK) type was prepared for setting Latin texts, since it lacks the capitals W, X, Y and Z, and a makeshift is called for when these letters crop up in vernacular composition. Gottfried Zedler, who made invaluable studies of all the editions printed from Gutenberg's first typeface, also found that no overlapping (i.e. kerned or morticed) char-acters had been used in the *Weltgericht*. Meticulous examination of the types led him to conclude that, whereas the *27-line Donatus* preserved at Darmstadt had been printed earlier than the *Weltgericht*, those distinct *27-line Donatus* editions known as the Berlin-Heiligenstadt a, Berlin-Heiligenstadt b, and the Paris, had followed it (Zedler, 1934: 36ff).

What can have been Gutenberg's reason for interrupting his succes-sive production of these *Donatus* editions to print this other title of which only a tiny fragment has come down to us? Gottfried Zedler spotted that the ancient legend of the return of the Emperor Frederick played an important role in the text of the *Sibyllenweissagung*; and raised the possibility that the inventor may have responded to the popular euphoria that greeted the election of Frederick III as the next German king and emperor: 'Gutenberg's edition should be taken as a sign that the inventor of printing was never far removed from popular life, and

lebē vñ nimmer do bien do got vrteil wil·
gebē Sie gene mit schreckē dobien Die
got nye erkante noch forchte en Niema
mag sich übergē nicht Vor dē gotlichē
angesiecht Cristus wil do urtel sprechen·
Vñ wil alle boszheit rechen Die nie ge=
dadē den willē iin Den wil er gebē ewige
pin Vñ wil den gudē gebē Hymmelfreude
vñ ewig lebē Siit die werlt vñ alle ding
Die in dē werlt geschaffē sint Czu gene
vñ werdē auch zu nicht Als man wol

The Fragment vom Weltgericht, *a piece of a* Sibyllenbuch.
The earliest printing in Gutenberg's very first type.
Probably produced in Strasbourg between 1440 and 1444. Front side.

knew what would engage the interest of the masses!' (Zedler, 1934: 41). A hint of speculation on a ready market for printed copies of the Sibylline legend may well be present here, although I think a political or religious motivation should not be overlooked.

As author of the *Sibyllenweissagung*, or, more accurately, simply of this rhymed version of what is best understood as a compilation of ancient Sibylline prophecies, we encounter the leader of a Thuringian sect of crypto-flagellants, Konrad Schmid, who had been burned as a heretic together with six of his companions in Nordhausen in 1369 (Haupt, 1890: 683). It is recorded that when 300 more followers of Konrad Schmid came to the stake in 1416, in the realms of the margraves of Meissen, the landgraves of Thuringia and the counts of Schwarzburg, some of the accused said before the Inquisition that the martyr Konrad Schmid would rise from the dead as the prophet Enoch, and the lay brother Gundolt, who had been burned in Erfurt, as the

er werde vō pine erlost · wā iii ix ypmu:
rich ist Der hat freude mit ihesu crist Der
von dē hȳmel her nidd ist kōmen Vnd
mentschlich natuer hat an sich gnōmē
Vñ an d mentscheit ist erstorbē Vñ mi
dem tode hat erworbē Dz wer do glaubi
hat an en Mynne vñ zuū siecht d sal zu
ym · wir sollē gantzē glaubē habē Da:
wir vō ihesu crist horē sagē Vnd sollen
alle vns werck vñ syne Czu xpō kerē yn
liebe vñ yn mȳne Vñ zu ym habē zu d:

Reverse side of the Fragment vom Weltgericht.
Actual size.

prophet Elijah (Förstemann, 1828: 171–2). The *Sibyllenweissagung* contains a passage to the same effect. Unfortunately there is no way of proving – and besides it seems improbable to me – that Johann Gutenberg knew anything about these connections or of Konrad Schmid's authorship.

The text of the *Sibyllenweissagung* begins with the creation myth, and the apostasy of Lucifer and his casting into hell. A description of paradise follows, with the temptation of Adam and Eve by the serpent and the expulsion of the first human pair from paradise. All this follows the Biblical account closely; particularly in the published text of the *Sybillen boich* of 1513 and 1515, in which Schmid has been rendered 'religiously correct' (Schade, 1853: 296ff).

It is then related how the 900-year-old Adam lay sick and close to death and asked his son Seth to fetch him a healing fruit from paradise. Seth met an angel at the gates of paradise, who handed him a twig, which Seth, learning on his return of his father's death, planted on his grave. From this grew a gigantic tree that was felled when King Solomon's temple was being built, and from its wood – which was found unsuitable for the temple – a bridge was constructed that led across a river.

A Sibyl foretold to King Solomon the birth of Jesus Christ, his persecution by the Jews, and his death on a cross that would be made from the wood of Adam's tree. She spoke of the victory of Christendom, of strife within the empire in the Middle Ages, as well as tribulations and years of famine. Then followed a diatribe against the rule of the popes: charging them with the mortal sins of oppressing the people, appropriating Christian property and perverting justice (Schade, 1854: lines 457ff).

In this era, so prophesied the Sibyl, the Emperor Frederick – whom God had preserved in his might and had vested with diverse powers – would return. He would unite Christian people in the honour of God and

> The Holy Tomb shall be regained,
> the glorious crown adorned.
> Then bliss on all descendeth,
> Sibyl foretells no dream,
> when Kaiser Friedrich hangeth
> his shield on withered beam:
> the prophecy will be fulfilled
> in heaven and here below ... (Schade, 1854: lines 514ff).

After the Emperor Frederick had hung his shield on the withered tree and this had once more broken into bud, he would convert all Jews, infidels and Tartars to Christianity, so that there would be only one faith in the whole world. He would attend to equity and peace, until the Antichrist should reappear for a short time to lead the people astray. Once again the faithful would be oppressed and persecuted. Then God would send his prophets Enoch and Elijah to preach truth to the people. The Antichrist would be overcome and despatched to hell. In conclusion Jesus Christ would conduct that Last Judgment of which the text fragment of the *Weltgericht* gives an account.

The Sibylline legend survives in a variety of fourteenth- and fifteenth-century copies. But there was a gap of nearly 50 years between Gutenberg's printing and the next appearance of the *Sibyllenweissagung*, from Hans Sporer of Bamberg in 1491. This was closely followed in 1492 by further reprints from Max Eyrer in Bamberg and Heinrich Knoblochtzer in Heidelberg, that heralded in a host of others containing many textual variations (Zedler, 1934: 34). Possibly the reappearance of these texts – down to a chap-book which appeared in Landshut in 1519 under the title *Kaiser Friedrich, der erst seines Namens mit einem langen rothen Bart* [Emperor Frederick, the First of his Name with a Long Red Beard, i.e. *Barbarossa*] – should be seen in the context of the Reformation.

Frederick III, a Habsburg, had been elected German king in Frankfurt on 2 February 1440. His election had been supported by Nicholas of Cues, acting on papal orders. The overwhelming majority of the populace had great expectations of his reign. Dissension had come to a head between the reform party, which drew its strength from the cities and from the nationally conscious nobility, and the papal adherents, who wished to grant unconditional precedence to the pope's demands. The pope declared the Council of Basle dissolved and called a fresh one in Ferrara. But the Council continued to sit; and ushered in a new schism by electing a counter-pope. King Frederick III now had his hands full in trying to achieve peace, to carry forward the reform of church and empire, and at the same time to repulse the Turks. In Strasbourg – which had opted for the politics of the Council and had only recently been visited by the Black Death – a fusion took place between the Emperor Frederick legend and the hopes which the citizens placed in the newly elected king, Frederick III (Stenzel, 1915). The text of the *Sibyllenweissagung*, with its censure of the priesthood's encroachments, desire for social justice, and hopes for freeing the Holy Sepulchre from the Turks, found a receptive audience at the time; and it seems probable that this was Gutenberg's reason for interrupting the series of *Donatus* impressions in order to print it.

But Frederick III disappointed his political supporters. He was neither adept nor interested in affairs of state and became known as 'the empire's day-dreamer'. His rule meant a set-back for those cities with free status (under the constitutional law of the Holy Roman Empire of the German nation which lasted until 1806, the *Reichsunmittelbar* were those free cities and persons over whom the Kaiser had direct power and influence without the intermediate rule of a regional government), for he chose to exploit them as 'imperial goods and property'. And he damaged the empire by exploiting specific conflicts to his own dynastic advantage (Stenzel, 1915: 180).

The expectations which had been aroused in Strasbourg by Frederick III's election in 1440 had died away by not later than the autumn of 1444, when it became clear that he had been responsible for bringing into Alsace the Armagnac hordes which had besieged Basle, Strasbourg, Worms and Mainz. Any later printing of the *Sibyllenweissagung* would have been injudicious having regard to public feeling in Strasbourg, and has to be excluded in the state of modern research. Consequently, I believe that the *Sibyllenweissagung* can only have been printed within a time-span of four years, between 1440 and 1444. I regard this as a legitimate and unbiased conclusion, although, as I am well aware, it may not be one shared by that Gutenberg scholarship which gives primacy to Mainz.

However, an unprejudiced examination of the historical sources supports my assumption. Hans Widmann offers an interesting survey in an essay called: 'On the sources for the dating of Gutenberg's invention' (Widmann, 1972c: 38ff). The *Chronik der Stadt Köln* reports that the invention of printing came about through Johann Gutenberg from Strasbourg in Mainz in 1440 and was brought to perfection by 1450 (Świerk, 1972a: 79ff). Matteo Palmiero asserted as early as 1483 that printing had been invented in 1440 by Johann Gutenberg zum Jungen in Mainz. Jacob Wimpheling wrote, in his *Epithoma Germanorum* of 1505, that Johann Gutenberg had invented printing in 1440 at Strasbourg and later perfected it in Mainz (Świerk, 1972a: 84). As Gutenberg was demonstrably still living in Strasbourg at this time, we can only regard this early dating of the invention in the closest connection with Strasbourg itself.

Whether Gutenberg printed the *Sibyllenweissagung* with any heretical intentions remains an open question. I do not agree with Varbanec's suppositions. Of course it is impossible to remove all political motivation from the piece, but on balance its text reflects views that came under discussion at the Council of Basle – where, not surprisingly, even the popes were frequently undecided – and it is probable that many prominent Strasbourg citizens and councillors would have seen it as a positive contribution in a wretched political situation. It would not have been known that the text came from the pen of a heretic, and besides the legend of Emperor Frederick had all the ingredients of a folk-tale or saga.

However, it should not be ruled out that a public reaction may have vented itself against the printing of the *Sibyllenweissagung*, following the incursion of the Armagnacs and the exposure of the king. Gutenberg's enemies – and he must have had to reckon with the fact that not everyone in Strasbourg can have wished him well after the court proceedings went against the Dritzehn brothers – may not have held back from publicly discrediting him for this political miscalculation. Since not a single copy of the Sibylline book has ever turned up in Strasbourg, it could be that many owners burned or destroyed their copies when the prophecies were shown to be so wide of the mark. The hatred against Frederick III may have rubbed off on the inventor and contributed to his departure from Strasbourg.

I believe that the conclusion to be drawn from these explanations is that anyone who considers the *Fragment vom Weltgericht*, not only with a skilled eye for its typography, but also in connection with the political happenings of the contemporary background, should be convinced that this piece of printing was produced between 1440 and 1444, and that at least one of the *27-line Donatus* editions preceded it. From this it follows that the technique of printing was invented in Strasbourg in about 1440. But it was from Mainz that the art of printing went on to conquer the world.

CHAPTER FOUR

Printing parallels

The Coster legend

LET US TURN NOW TO ANOTHER EVENT that may have taken place at this same time, an account of which has been for centuries a source of dispute between the partisans of Johann Gutenberg and those of Laurens Janszoon Coster.

A Dutch scholar called Adriaen de Jonghe wrote in Latin (identifying himself as Hadrianus Junius, *historicus publicus* to the States-General), a description of the Netherlands, which was printed and published at Leiden in 1588 under the title *Batavia.* This contains a report of the invention of printing in Haarlem as it had been related to him at the time his book was written – that is, in 1568, for it had to wait a further 20 years for publication (Linde, 1886). The writer's style may be inflated and pompous, but he does capture the graphic and naïve tone in which fairy-tales are generally told, and is worth quoting at length:

> I am not moved by either envy or ill-will to credit to one man that which I would deny to another's reputation. Nor shall I come to imitate the shamelessness of Crassus, who feigned the honesty and dignity of Scaevola, whilst at the same time he strove to win the public's favour through flattery ...
>
> I will recount then what I have learned from elderly and respected inhabitants who have held eminent office and who have sworn and assured me that they had heard it from their ancestors, to whose reputation in turn such weight must be attached that they are entitled to receive credence.
>
> There dwelt in Haarlem 128 years ago [i.e. in June 1440], in a grand house of which some buildings are still standing today, on the market-place opposite the royal palace, one Laurens Janszoon, surnamed Coster or Küster. It was for that age a profitable and respectable station which the family of that name held in the world. This is the man to whom should be restored the fame, at present usurped by another, of the invention of the whole art of printing; which entitles him to finer laurels than those of all other victors.
>
> It all began one day when, whilst walking in the woods near Haarlem – as everyone likes to who has time after lunch or on a feast-day – he cut some letters from the bark of a beech tree, from which, reversely impressed like seals one by one on paper, he composed one or two lines to serve as an example for the children of his son-in-law. When this succeeded, he began to contemplate greater things, since he was a man of keen mind, and, assisted by his son-in-

law Thomas Pieterszoon (who left behind him four children who nearly all went on to become burgomasters – I mention this so that everyone shall know that this art sprang up in a worthily married family and not in one of the baser sort), he first of all invented a more gluey and substantial kind of ink (as the ordinary ink was found to blot). With this he printed whole tablets with pictures, with the letters added. I have seen the beginnings of his labours of this nature; printed on the facing sides of the leaves only, not on both sides. The

Portrait of Laurens Janszoon Coster.
Copperplate after a picture of J. van Campen. Detail.

book in question was written, in Dutch, by an anonymous author and was entitled *Spieghel onzer behoudenisse* [The Mirror of our Salvation]. In these cradle pieces – for no art had yet been both found and perfected – the leaves were printed on one side only, with the blank reverse sides pasted together, so that they should not present any unsightliness.

Afterwards he exchanged the beechwood characters for leaden ones, and later still he made them of tin so that they might be less pliable and more hard-wearing. Wine-pots cast from these melted-down types are still shown as antiquities at the said Laurens Janszoon's house on the market-place. This house was later occupied by his great-grandson, Gerrit Thomaszoon, a prominent and excellent burgher who died of old age only a few years ago. And so the new art was greeted with enthusiasm, and its wares, of a kind never seen before, drew purchasers from all sides and brought in rich profits; for as skilfulness grows, so business flourishes. Assistants were taken on – the beginning of misfortune. For among these apprentices was a certain Johann, and it may be, as one would suspect from his ominous surname Faustus, that it was he who proved a faithless servant and bringer of misfortune to his master; or it could have been another of the same name. That is all the same to me, since I do not wish to trouble the shades of the dead, who during their lifetime were tormented enough by conscience.

This Johann, who was bound to the work of printing by oath, as soon as he thought he knew enough about the art of joining the letters and of casting the types – in fact, the whole trade – sought the first favourable opportunity to make off. This fell on Christmas Eve, and when everyone was at church, he took the entire apparatus of types and the tools and equipment which his master had prepared for the performance of his craft, and stole away from the house with it all. He hastened first to Amsterdam, thence to Cologne, until he finally found sanctuary in Mainz – where he was out of the range of fire, as they say – and could live in security and harvest the rich fruits of his theft by opening a printing workshop.

What is known for sure is that within the space of one year from that Christmas Eve, in the year 1442, he had printed and issued in the same types which Laurens had used at Haarlem: the *Doctrinale* of Alexander Gallus, a grammar at that time in general use, and the *Tractatus syncategorematum* of Petrus Hispanus.

This is roughly what I once learned from men advanced in years but credible; survivors, so to speak, of those who have relayed this blazing torch from hand to hand. But I have met with others since, who have reported and testified to the same. I recollect that Nikolaus Gaal, my tutor, a man of firm memory and venerable old age, told how as a boy he had heard more than once from a certain Cornelis, a bookbinder, who must by then have been at least 80 years old and who had been an apprentice in that same printing office, about the sequence of events in the course of that invention, as these had been related to him by his master. This Cornelis had spoken of the polishing and increase of the raw art, and other matters of this kind, with such involvement that he was close to tears when it came to describing the theft, and became so enraged about the misappropriated fame that – if he had been charged with that office – he would have executed the culprit on the spot. He cursed those nights, during several months, when he had been forced to sleep in the same bed with him.

This agrees with the words of the burgomaster, Quirinus Talesius, who admitted to me, that he had formerly heard the like from the mouth of the same bookbinder ...

If the truth is to be protected, then our city should retain the honour of this wonderful invention, and partake once more of the fame that was snatched away from it. For how futile are the presumptions of those who are not ashamed to appropriate a foreign heritage as their own, whilst arrogantly suppressing the rights of the legitimate heirs (Linde, 1886: I, 232ff).

One has to make allowances for Hadrianus Junius and accept a certain lack of focus in his account, for in any case he was writing down events nearly a century and a half after they had taken place. However, it is still little short of miraculous that Coster should have had the idea of cutting letters for his grandchildren, and should have gone on to make books and to print, first from wooden blocks (as did in fact happen in Holland and in Haarlem in particular), and then from lead and from tin, and all this in the same half-year leading up to the Christmas Eve on which his faithless apprentice was able to steal the types and the secret of printing. Such a sequence of events would in reality have extended over a number of years.

And how was it still possible for pots to be cast from the tin letters, after the dishonest assistant is supposed to have stolen all of them? Should one conclude that new types were cast with the same speed as before and that printing continued, particularly since the enterprise was evidently such a profitable business? The bookbinder Cornelis did indeed exist as a bookbinder, bookseller and calligrapher, dying in 1522 aged over 80, which means that he would still have been in his cradle at the time of the theft and in no position to have shared a bed with the villain responsible. Those typographic books, which earlier generations had attributed to Coster, are all now known to have been printed after 1470 and probably in Utrecht. Among this group there is certainly a *Spieghel onzer behoudenisse* to be found. In Holland, there is above all a tradition of the blockbook which stretches back; and to this day it is considered to have been proved that Coster was a not insignificant producer of blockbooks (Musper, 1961: 20). That part of Junius's account which concerns this aspect is still regarded as valid.

Some of these Dutch blockbooks were probably of an unusual kind. Before blocks could be cut, it was normal for the texts to be written out, and then traced down back-to-front onto the smooth planed wood. It may well be that some accomplished cutter hit upon an idea to simplify this task – particularly for those deficient in lettering skills – by carving right-reading wooden stamps, which could be used to mark out the text, letter by letter, on the surface of the block prior to cutting. Naturally the result would be a conventional woodcut; but with the peculiarity that, since the identical stamp had been used as a pattern for the cutter each time a particular letter appeared, and because of irregular alignment, the printed image could easily be mistaken for one where the text had been produced from movable types. The same method would have been equally practical on a lead or tin plate, for, as we know from the history of picture printing, metal-cutting is practically as old as the woodcut (Kristeller, 1921: 57ff).

Still another hypothesis haunts the literature surrounding Coster, according to which the earliest Dutch printing (Costeriana) was set from single types that were produced using a sand-casting technique

(Zedler, 1921: 19). One of the Dutch typefoundries even went through all the processes of producing a book composed from types which had been cast in sand. But, judging from this actual reconstruction, the method is extremely involved; for after each casting the matrix has to be abandoned and a new impression taken in fresh sand. Even if this process could in fact have been put into operation in the fifteenth century, then it would have remained a blind alley.

While my own attitude towards this technology remains sceptical, that indefatigable researcher, Gottfried Zedler, offers an explanation of the intricacies of the sand-casting process in his book *Von Coster zu Gutenberg*. According to him, this begins with wooden model letters that have been fashioned with a knife (!) and which the types to be cast will replicate. Thus each rectangular body carries a printing surface, and is accurately adjusted for height to paper, and in width for setting against other similar characters to build words. He continues:

> A number of these patterns are planted upright, and with the printing surface at the top, in moulding sand, which rests on a wooden base and is retained within an iron casting-box. Then sufficient of this sand is added and pressed down until only the top three millimetres of these patterns are visible. The sand surface is levelled off, and strewn with a layer of separating powder. An upper

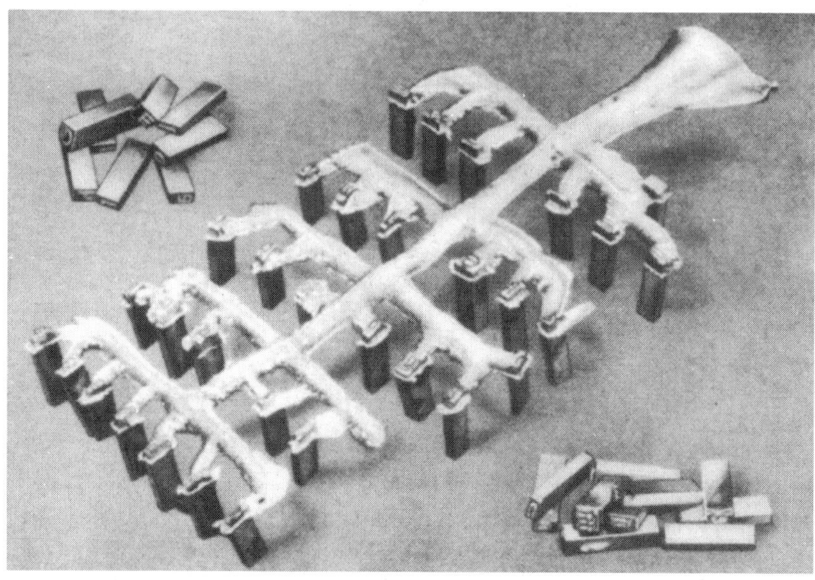

The sand-casting method.
Top left: wooden patterns, centre: crude casting, below right: dressed types.
from Bogeng: Geschichte des Buchdrucks. *Reduced.*

> frame is closely fitted to the casting-box, and filled with compressed sand until the patterns are as tightly embedded as possible. The top frame of the casting-box, containing all its sand and impressed with the heads of the characters, is then lifted clear; and the wooden models are removed, leaving voids for the bodies of the types in the sand of the lower frame. Channels are laid in the sand of the top frame: a main channel and as many branches as are needed to connect each individual type and allow the molten typemetal to reach all destinations before it can cool. Finally the two halves of the casting-box are fitted and held together with screws passing through the wooden top and base boards. Now the casting can proceed (Zedler, 1921: 18).

After considering the technology of the sand-casting method, I simply do not believe that Coster could have produced type by such tedious procedures. It seems unrealistic to expect to be able to carve letters from wood so precisely that different letters cast from such models would share the correct height. The tale that the Dutch inventor sawed apart the individual letters from a panel of woodcut text, and used them afterwards for setting as movable types, sounds equally far-fetched. It is true that a similar technology was used for a time in the Far East, but this was based on the underlying square shape of all Chinese letter forms (Zedler, 1921: 1).

If the Coster legend has remained alive over the centuries, then this is due above all to the observations concerning the invention of printing which appear in the already mentioned *Chronik der Stadt Köln* of 1499. The original text states:

> The first inventor of printing was a citizen of Mainz, and he was born in Strasbourg and called sire Johann Gutenberg. *Item* However, although the art was first invented in Mainz in the manner in which it has generally been practised from that time to this, the first stages of the development are to be found in Holland in the *Donatuses*, which were printed there earlier. From and out of these is derived the beginning of the Foremost Art, which is now much more skillfully and more cleverly invented than the earlier manner was, and which has been practised more and more dexterously with the passing of the years (Świerk, 1972a: 86–7).

The chronicler – who names as his informant Ulrich Zell, Cologne's first printer – not only confirms Gutenberg as the inventor of the art, but also states that books had been printed in Holland at some still earlier date. Some researchers have concluded from this that Gutenberg must have known about these Dutch blockbooks, and that they somehow provided him with both a starting-point and a stimulus for his invention. Of course it is perfectly possible that he may have come across such *Donatuses*, or that he could even have journeyed to Holland at some time or another between 1444 and 1448 and seen there for himself the technology involved in cutting, manufacturing inks for, and printing from these woodblocks. However, I remain convinced that Gutenberg the metallurgist would not have been deflected from his course by such woodblocks, or by the wooden pattern and sand-casting method for types.

A monument still stands in Haarlem's Grote Markt to the 'inventor of the art of printing'. The Franz-Hals-Museum in the Groot Heilig-land has a fine collection of blockbooks and prefigurations of printing from movable types; including copies of the *Biblia pauperum* and *Donatus*, an *Abecedarium*, a *Septem vitia mortalia* [Seven Deadly Sins], and the previously mentioned *Spieghel onzer behoudenisse*. In the Vleeshal, where the Enschedé Museum is housed, reposes an over-lifesize sculpture of Laurens Janszoon Coster, who holds a piece of type, and Hadrianus Junius, book in hand. The Coster legend lives on.

What took place in Avignon?

AVIGNON, A SIZEABLE TOWN IN SOUTHERN FRANCE, was the seat of the popes from 1309 to 1417, including the years of the Great Schism from 1378. It continued as a flourishing trading centre after the Schism was brought to an end by the Council of Constance in 1417. A number of documents testify to the appearance at Avignon in 1444 – and thus at precisely the time that news of Gutenberg in Strasbourg dries up – of a certain Procopius Waldvogel from Prague, who was there offering to teach a method of artificial writing (*ars artificialiter scribendi*). He had brought with him letters of iron, tin, brass and lead. According to a legal document of 4 July 1444, he had in his possession two alphabets of steel and 48 forms of tin, and other forms as well, which he had prepared for magister Manaudus Vitalis. There is further mention of one steel screw, two iron forms and other things (Ruppel, 1967: 195).

In a contract which is dated 26 August 1446, Waldvogel bound himself to instruct Georg de la Jardine of Avignon in the art of artificial writing. In return he was to receive a fee of ten gulden and thereafter eight gulden each month. Georg de la Jardine had to swear not to teach the new art to others (Ruppel, 1967: 196).

A further contract of 10 March 1466, this time with a Jewish textile printer from Avignon, Davin de Caderousse, committed Waldvogel to delivering a set of 27 letters for Hebrew. Once again the new art was to remain a secret for as long as Procopius Waldvogel should remain at Avignon (Ruppel, 1967: 196).

Finally, it is on record that Manaudus Vitalis, as his erstwhile business partner, had to take an oath that the art of artificial writing was 'a true and authentic one for any who tackled it with love', and that it could easily be mastered, and would be found to be useful. Vitalis had to return the instruments of iron, steel, copper, brass, tin and lead as well as wood with which he had been provided; and he then received back 12 gulden as his share on quitting the business (Ruppel, 1967: 196). Procopius Waldvogel disappears from view after April 1446; or at least we have no further news of his presence in Avignon, and he left behind no surviving printed books or other evidences of his work.

What can have been these secrets which Waldvogel offered to impart at Avignon? Clearly Manaudus, as a schoolmaster, would not have needed to seek mere instruction in the current hands. More is involved here than the making of books and manuscripts by conventional means, and it appears that these characters (*literae formatae*) and forms (*formae ferreae*) must have been used to reproduce material that hitherto would have been written in pen and ink, by means of this new kind of artificial writing. It would follow that these characters and forms always constituted an alphabet; for a set of 27 Hebrew letters would represent a complete alphabet for that language, and 48 letters of steel, or a corresponding number of forms in tin, would make up a roman fount of capitals and lower-case. But there is no way that one can set a book from a single alphabet, and, to argue against this ever having been the intention, there is the testimony of Manaudus Vitalis that the new art was easily acquired. Setting and printing books has always been a time-consuming and complex affair.

Yet several of the surviving references hint at typefounding; for the variety of metals – steel, iron, copper, tin, brass and lead – invites the conjecture that iron or steel punches may have been struck into copper or brass, so that letters could be cast from these in turn from lead or tin. The blind impression of lettering on leather from brass tools was quite familiar, for example, as was the taking of castings from impressions of metal letters in sand – a process which had long been practised by bellfounders. But nothing of this kind quite fits the description of 'artificial writing', in which Procopius Waldvogel claimed expertise. That is why I suggest that these punches, matrices and cast letters could have served to impress texts on woodblocks that were subsequently cut with a knife, for printing as blockbooks in the conventional woodcut technique. The *Abecedarium* and *Donatus* texts seem the most likely candidates, since magister Manaudus Vitalis would have known the needs of schoolchildren and students in this field. Even the wording of Vitalis's assessment, that the new art was:

'a true and authentic one for any who tackled it with love', makes more sense if one considers that the single characters would need to be positioned and impressed with precision and patience to achieve good fitting and alignment, so that an even and handsome printed page would result. Once again, this whole idea must remain unsubstantiated, for we know of no blockbooks from Avignon.

Now who was this Prokop or Procopius Waldvogel or Waldfoghel? Was he just a trickster or charlatan? His father lived as a maker of knives in Prague, and the family had been driven out of the city and robbed of their property by the Hussites. Procopius became a citizen of Lucerne in 1439. It is known that the Dritzehn brothers – who brought an action against Gutenberg in Strasbourg in 1439, and subsequently came into possession of his press – also had well-established business connections at Lucerne. The 'fines-book' of that city records the penalty for a brawl provoked by one Jörg Dritzehn from Strasbourg on a visit there in 1443 (Ruppel, 1967: 197). This opens up the vague possibility of an encounter between Jörg Dritzehn and Procopius Waldvogel in Lucerne. A knife-maker would require little time or practice to grasp the basics of engraving dies or casting letters from a mould. He may even have arranged to purchase punches, matrices or types from Dritzehn – and perhaps that iron screw which seems to represent the most important component of the press – and then have sought to set himself up in business at Avignon in a way that closely parallels Gutenberg's beginnings in Strasbourg, that is, by selling his technical expertise to others. But there is a still more direct link to be found between Strasbourg and Avignon. It is extraordinary to find, staying at Avignon at that time, a silversmith from Strasbourg named Walter Riffe. One of Gutenberg's Strasbourg partners was of course Hans Riffe, the prefect of Lichtenau (Ruppel, 1967: 197). Whether these two may have been related, and whether the silversmith Walter Riffe and the knife-maker Procopius Waldvogel found themselves in Avignon for similar ends, are questions that, like so many similar ones, must remain open.

Or could it be that Gutenberg himself may have been directly involved in the proceedings at Avignon, as has sometimes been suggested? Although there is nothing to establish his presence elsewhere at that particular time, I should like to rule out that possibility completely, on the grounds that a mere replay of what had already been accomplished in Strasbourg would not have been in character with his dynamic progress towards bringing his invention to fruition. To all appearances the art of artificial writing, as reported from Avignon, was a consequence of Gutenberg's activities in Strasbourg. Partial knowledge of the invention must have leaked out, and others were trying to turn it to profitable account. The Avignon episode should not be overrated; but the *ars artificialiter scribendi* (equally an expression in use by writing masters of the time to describe calligraphic virtuosity) is nevertheless of interest to the printing historian, for what it reveals of some of the technical details concerning Gutenberg's Strasbourg 'adventure and art' (Świerk, 1972b: 243ff).

Did printing in Asia influence Gutenberg's invention?

THE PARALLELS BETWEEN PRINTING from metal letters in Korea and Gutenberg's invention are striking. The notion that knowledge of printing in the Far East could have found its way to Strasbourg or Mainz becomes more insistent and persuasive. This theme has only begun to intrigue Gutenberg scholars comparatively recently. In his standard work on Gutenberg, first published in 1939, it was still possible for the then director of the Gutenberg-Museum, Aloys Ruppel, to say: 'The question of whether knowledge of early Korean printing technology can have reached Europe in Gutenberg's day and may have influenced his invention has to receive a negative answer, since up to now it has not proved possible to establish the slightest link between the Korean and the Mainz discoveries' (Ruppel, 1967: 188). This conclusion now calls for a careful and comprehensive reassessment.

European indebtedness to ancient Chinese science and culture is indisputable in many fields. Silk, the magnetic needle, gunpowder, paper and porcelain – these are just a few of the more significant of the discoveries that spread from China and were later found in Europe. The path taken by papermaking through Samarkand and the Islamic world can be followed and plotted intermittently over the centuries with reasonable accuracy. Woodcuts and blockbook printing were also introduced in the Far East some 600 years before they reached the West. Certainly the one million copies of the *Dharani Charms* ordered by the Japanese empress Shotoku had come into existence by 770, as previously mentioned, and several of these are to be found in the British Library, where the unique copy of the *Diamond Sutra* is also preserved. This last, with its known printing date of 868, had formerly been regarded as the oldest surviving blockbook in the world, but still earlier printing has since come to light in China and Korea. L.C. Goodrich concludes that 'we now have charms printed within a few years of each other – in Korea (751?), China (757), and Japan (764–770)' (Goodrich, 1972: 214). All researchers confirm the old tradition that printing in the Far East was from texts cut in woodblocks at this stage.

Chinese written characters played a role of comparable importance in spreading the teachings of Confucius and Buddha to that which the Latin language and alphabet performed for the Roman Catholic Church. The printing of blockbooks accompanies the diffusion of the language in those lands that fell under the influence of Buddha's teaching, and above all in Korea and Japan. Buddhist literature flourished in China and Korea during the tenth and eleventh centuries with the aid of woodblock printing. During the reign of the first Sung emperor, probably in the year 972, a monumental edition of the whole Buddhist canon (the *Tripitaka*) was published in 130,000 pages, which of course entailed cutting a corresponding number of woodblocks. Furthermore, paper money printed from woodblocks reached all strata of the Chinese population from the eleventh century onwards (Sohn, 1972: 211).

The Chinese statesman Shen Kua (1030–1093) recorded that in the years between 1041 and 1049, a smith named Pi Sheng made movable types of clay, which were then baked, and assembled and printed from. Shen Kua described the method as follows:

> He took sticky clay and cut in it characters as thin as the edge of a seal. Each character formed as it were a single type. He baked them in the fire to make them hard. He had previously prepared an iron plate and he had covered this plate with a mixture of pine resin, wax and paper ashes. When he wished to print, he took an iron frame and set it on the iron plate. In this he placed the type, set close together. When the frame was full, the whole made one solid block of type. He then placed it near the fire to warm it. When the paste [at the back] was slightly melted, he took a perfectly smooth board and rubbed over the surface, so that the block of type became as even as a whetstone (Carter, 1925: 160).

Shen Kua praised the economy of the invention and emphasized that the same types could be reprinted from repeatedly. Unfortunately his account is not altogether satisfactory. First of all it seems improbable that a smith, of all people, should choose to work in clay. Then it seems scarcely conceivable that Chinese characters, which are brush-drawn in origin, could be successfully cut directly into clay, especially when mirror-reversed as well. And finally, the economic advantages must have been slight if each type had to be individually carved in clay. It does seem to me that there are good grounds for taking a closer look into the technology of this smith, Pi Sheng.

On account of blurred edges to the type impression – and probably due also to this impractical method of type production – a changeover

Chinese ceramic types made by Pi Sheng's method.
Reconstruction prepared in China for display at the International Book Art Exhibition, Leipzig 1959.

was made at some later date from ceramic letters to wooden ones. T.F. Carter reprints in full a detailed description, written in 1314 by Wang Chen, of the oldest techniques for making, setting and printing from movable wooden types:

> A skilful calligrapher is chosen who picks some writing which shall serve as model for the type. In accordance with exact measurements as to size, he writes one copy of every character. These are pasted (in reverse) on the wooden block, and a workman is ordered to engrave them. A little space is left between the characters for sawing. For each auxiliary, numeral and other specially common word, there is a larger number of types made. In all, somewhat more than 30,000 types are needed. After the engraving of the characters on the wooden block, each single character is cut on all sides with a small fine-toothed saw. Next, the types are finished off with a small knife until they are alike and exact. After that they are subjected to careful measurement, and by this measurement are tested for exact uniformity in size and height. Finally the types are arranged and kept in wooden cases according to the official *Book of Rhymes* (Carter, 1925: 163ff).

The production technique for a book made with metal letters is mentioned in the foreword to the first such book to be published in

Korea, the 50-volume *Kogum Sangjong Yemun* [Detailed and Authentic Code of Etiquette] of 1234. Yi Kyu-Bo (1168–1241) wrote in the afterword to the statute-book for the state of Koryo: 'By good fortune the *Code of Statutes* was not lost. There were 28 copies of it printed from metal letters [!] and sent to the officials for safekeeping' (Hong, 1963: 193). The colophon of the *Song of the Monk Ch'uan Nan-Ming on the True Doctrine* states that it was: 'Printed for all time from newly prepared letters after the edition produced from minted letters, in the year Riha [1239], first decade of September'; i.e. from woodblocks recarved in 1239 from the original typographic edition of a few years earlier (Hong, 1963: 193). Printing from cast-type was evidently undertaken under difficult conditions while the government was in exile, but otherwise it has to be assumed that printing from movable metal letters

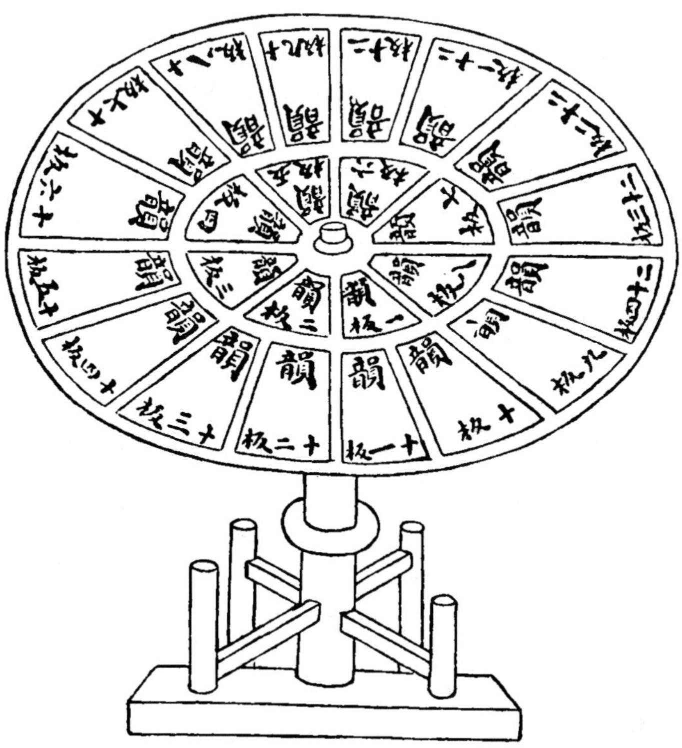

The Revolving Wheel.
Typesetting device described by Wang Chen in 1314.
The illustration (reproduced from Carter: 1925) is from an eighteenth-century edition, and may even go back to the original.

would not have been greatly affected by the Mongol invasion of 1231, particularly since we do not know much about the exact technology that was in use at that time. In any case the technique of type production seems to have been improving all the time. The best book on the history of early printing in Korea is Pow-Key Sohn's *Early Korean Typography*; he also produced an illustrated exhibition catalogue on that theme for the Gutenberg Museum in Mainz (Sohn, 1971 and 1983). King Tadchong set up a book factory in 1403, in which 14 woodcutters, 8 typecasters, 40 compositors and 20 printers were employed. Within a few months, hundreds of thousands of copper types had been cast. Calligraphers designed letters that were copied and carved in wood, impressed in clay and then hardened. Molten copper was poured into each clay mould, destroying it in the process (Funke, 1963: 54ff). Further improvement were made by the Korean inventor, Yi Chon. The developed state of the art for minting coins and seals in Korea must have contributed to this rapid advance (Hong, 1963: 191). Pow-Key Sohn reports on the manufacture of newer and larger types by these techniques.

Song Hyon (1436–1509) in his description of the 'cast-type' process, in his *Yongjae ch'onghwa*, gives us the following information:

> At first, one cuts letters in boxwood. One fills a trough level with fine sandy clay of the reed-growing seashore. Wood-cut letters are pressed into the sand, then the impressions become negative and form letters [moulds]. At this step, placing one trough together with another, one pours the molten bronze down into an opening. The fluid flows in, filling these negative moulds, one by one becoming type. Lastly, one scrapes and files off the irregularities, and piles them up to be arranged. These types are then spaced and held together by means of strips of bamboo and paper (Sohn, 1972: 224ff).

I suspect that the sense of this technical process may have become unclear through inadequate translation. It seems most likely that a single wooden punch was impressed in a rectangular block of clay, which was hardened and then used as a matrix at the base between two separable angle plates. The molten metal was poured through a special opening (that may be likened to Gutenberg's hand mould), and the angle pieces forming the walls of the mould taken apart to remove the finished piece of type after it had cooled. Filing and finishing the types would be simpler; given the uniform 'em' or square body for Chinese and Korean characters, in contrast to the varying character widths of the Latin alphabet. Uneven shrinkage of the clay during firing would have been a disadvantage of this Korean technique, so that the surface level and thickness of the moulds would call for adjustment before accurate castings could be taken.

From the Korean descriptions it is evident that letters of brass, copper, tin, iron, lead and a bronze-like alloy were in use (Funke, 1963: 54). The respective melting points of these metals – and the procedures for preparing punches of steel for striking into the softer copper, and thence to cast in lead from such copper moulds – would have been familiar in Korea at that time, and well within the capacity of the highly developed state of metallurgy in that country.

The most serious drawback to this oriental method came at the actual printing stage. No press of any kind was involved. A sheet of thin paper was simply laid over the inked type, and an impression taken by rubbing with a wooden spatula. This process was painfully slow, as the rubbing proceeded by strips or partial areas, with the paper lifted slightly from time to time to check the progress of the proofing and see whether more rubbing was called for. Consequently the technological potential of the process had a built-in limitation.

As noted at the outset of this chapter, Aloys Ruppel assumed that the Koreans, whose writing called for over 40,000 signs, had less to gain from access to setting from movable types than we in the West with our alphabet of 26 letters. Whereas this conclusion holds true for the Chinese, with the Koreans it is necessary to differentiate between their full-dress script and a more basic form of writing. A simplified form of syllabic script was in use in Korea as early as 690, which certainly resembled Chinese but drew on substantially fewer characters (Jensen, 1958: 197). King Sejong (1419–1450), the pre-eminent ruler of the Yi dynasty, ordered several measures for promoting the teachings of Confucius, the most significant of which was to introduce the phonetic *Unmun* script consisting of 11 vowels and 14 consonants, with 13 diphthongs (Jensen, 1958: 201). Unfortunately this excellent alphabet was withheld from widespread typographic printing at the crucial moment. Despite the recommendation of one of his ministers that 10,000 copies should be printed of every book then being published, as a direct means of financing movable typography and paper production, the king was determined to confine the benefits of his measures strictly to Confucian texts and official printing. The commercialization of book printing and the free sale of books were prohibited (Sohn, 1972: 226). In these politically and religiously motivated decrees are revealed not only a defensive suppression of Buddhism but also the innate conservatism of Confucian thought: 'I mediate, but I create nothing new. I believe in the ancient and cherish it' (Confucius, *Analects*: VII, 1). In my view, insufficient attention has been paid so far to this basic attitude of hostility towards progress, as a reason why the new technique of printing from movable types failed to permeate the East to the same extent that it did in Europe.

It must have been a matter of a few years at most after the Mongol occupation of Korea before printing from movable types was known in Karakorum, the capital of the Mongols, as well. The Mongol notoriety for cruelty in warfare was oddly balanced by a tolerance towards the religions of conquered peoples. In order to develop their own civil superstructure, the barbaric authorities of the nomadic and shamanistic Mongolian race needed the support of oppressed tribes like the Uighurs who were able to read and write. No obstacles were raised to spreading the teachings of Confucius and Buddha further or to continuing to print expressly religious books, since the Mongols themselves simply did not wish to know about the use of movable type for printing books. From their point of view it was simply a convenient means of printing paper currency, with which to pay the wages of the mounted Mongolian hordes. Millions of printed notes were circulated, and are described in detail by Marco Polo and other European travellers. Korean printed books were exported not only to China and Japan, but also to the home territories and capital of the Mongol empire, and so became familiar to merchants and artisans working in those places.

Now how can this knowledge of printing from movable letters have got from Karakorum to Europe, and to Strasbourg or Mainz? In this connection one immediately thinks of the Silk Road, much used at that period, running from the Mongolian capital by way of Turfan, Dzungaria, Tashkent, Samarkand, Bukhara and Khiva to the capital of the Golden Horde, to Sarai on the lower Volga, and thence on to the Crimea. As next-door neighbours bordering the Silk Road in Central Asia were to be found Christians of the Nestorian sect and Buddhist Uighurs, who shared the key positions as scribes and advisors to the Mongols in the thirteenth and fourteenth centuries. The alphabet of the Uighurs – which had been derived from the Aramaic [Syriac] alphabet – was now taken over in a modified form by the Mongols (Rachewiltz, 1971: 76ff); and so these Uighurs have in any case to be assigned a special role as intermediaries between Eastern and Western cultures.

After the Mongolian invasions, which reached as far as the Adriatic coast and into Bohemia, the Mongol empire attempted to consolidate itself. The new rulers detained scientists, merchants, craftsmen and artists at their court while extending trade outwards to the most distant lands. In the thirteenth and fourteenth centuries diplomatic encounters repeatedly took place in Central Asia between representatives of the Holy See and the Great Khan. The papal objective in this was to make an alliance with the Mongols against the Arabs, who still held on to the holy places in Palestine.

When the two Franciscan papal missionaries, Joannes de Plano Carpini and Benedict the Pole, finally reached Karakorum on 24 August 1246 after a long and arduous journey, they found there before them not only Nestorian Christians, Greek Alani, Christians of St Thomas and Manichaeans, but Buddhists, Taoists, Confucians and Mongolian Shamanists as well. In attendance for the designation of Kuyuk as the new Great Khan, they met with the ambassadors of Russia, Armenia and Georgia; the sultans or emirs of Syria, Iraq and Turkestan; the calif of Baghdad and representatives from China and Korea (Rachewiltz, 1971: 110). Books from Korea may have been among the gifts these visitors would have brought with them, and it cannot be ruled out that these Franciscan monks could have returned to Europe as early as that with intelligence of printing from movable types. In fact their homeward journey led the brothers to Cologne on 3 October 1247, and they stayed there long enough for Benedict to write his account of their mission. This demonstrates that there was indeed a bridge linking Korea and Europe at that date, once it is seen that one of its most important piers had been placed in Karakorum. On the other hand, it seems unlikely that any concrete knowledge of printing with movable letters would have been preserved for two centuries.

After visits by various other delegates, the Flemish friar, William of Rubrouck, arrived at Karakorum on 27 December 1253, and he stayed there for several months. He reported the presence of a colony of European artists and craftsmen at work in the Mongolian capital, comprising Germans, Russians, French, Hungarians and one Englishman. He thought that he had stumbled on some kind of centre for communicating handicrafts and technical skills. William declared himself impressed by the Chinese system of writing, by which he seems to have had in mind printed matter as well. But he does refer unambiguously to paper money, which was still unknown in Europe at the time. His travel writings were later exploited by Roger Bacon in the *Opus Majus* (Rachewiltz, 1971: 134–5). Whether anything that William of Rubrouck had learned of printing influenced the development of the blockbook in his native Flanders must remain a matter for conjecture.

Giovanni di Monte Corvino was created archbishop of Peking (Beijing), capital of the Great Khan, in 1307. Until his death in 1328 he was effective in strengthening the influence of the Roman Catholic Church over the Khan, and in expanding the work of the mission stations (Rachewiltz, 1971: 171). Italian merchants found that trade increased in volume and profitability by the sea route (Rachewiltz, 1971: 172). When Giovanni di Marignolli visited the port of Zhengzhou in 1346, he found a depot established there for European traders – who were predominantly Italian (Rachewiltz, 1971: 173). In the same sense Marco Polo had earlier written of the friendliness towards Europeans to be encountered in the Chinese cities (Forman and Burland, 1970).

With the end of Mongol rule in China in 1368, however, this situation was to change radically. The emperors of the Ming dynasty set out to persecute and banish from their country not only Roman Catholics but Orthodox and Nestorian Christians as well. Relations with the Holy See were broken off and trade with Europe discontinued. The channels of communication which had functioned under Mongol overlordship were closed down. In the meantime, though, knowledge of printing technology may have pressed further westwards and into the successor states of the Mongolian empire.

Excavations by Paul Pelliot at the turn of the twentieth century uncovered hundreds of small blocks of wood, dating in his view from about 1300, on the floor of a temple cave at Tunhuang – the place where the Silk Road divides into its northern and southern routes. These resemble the wooden types described earlier by Wang Chen, except that they show Uighur letters which are frequently placed as vertical pairs and cut in combination (Gabain, 1967: 16). This find

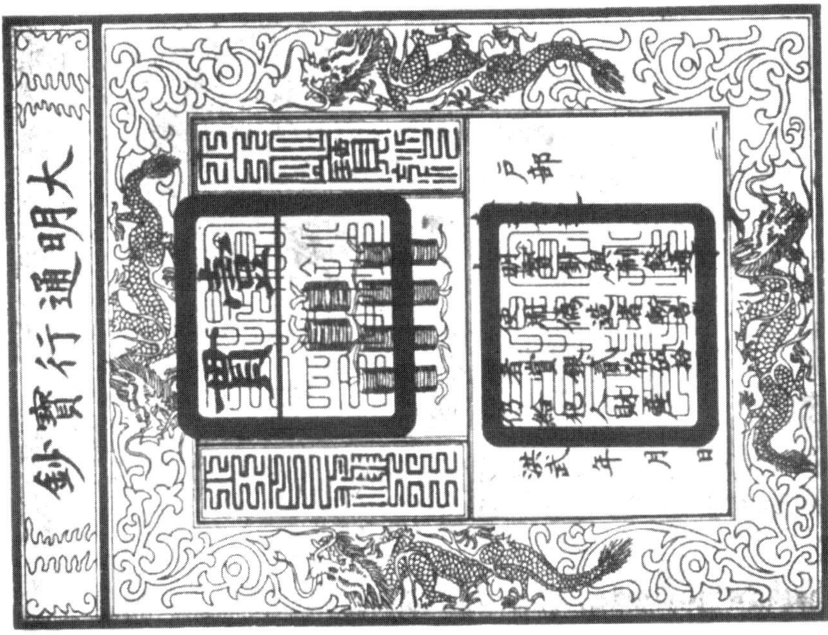

Note for 1000 Cash *issued between 1368 and 1399. Woodcut. (Carter, 1925). Reduced.*

proves that the Uighurs printed from movable types, and it is similarly intriguing to discover their use of logotypes, ligatures and other linked signs. These types are not square – like the Chinese and Korean ones – but rectangular blocks varying in length.

Finds made at Turfan – which is situated in the Turfan depression, to the west of 90°E, on the northerly route of the Silk Road – may prove more interesting yet for our purpose. The manuscripts and prints discovered there by the German scholar Grünewald, and transported to Berlin, have been examined in part for the first time quite recently by Annemarie von Gabain. Most of the blockprints are Buddhist texts in Chinese, Uighur, Mongol, Sanskrit, Tibetan or Tangut (Gabain, 1967: 26). As their faith entered an expansionist phase, Buddhists were encouraged to regard the copying, printing and distribution of sacred texts as meritorious. Carter even explained this development as follows: 'It can be said with equal truth that every advance into new territory made by printing has had as its motive an expanding religion' (Carter, 1925: 17) (which raises the question of whether we may relate this generalized observation to Gutenberg's invention and the contemporary struggle for religious reform).

Further investigation revealed that among the pieces of printing from Turfan were some produced from movable types. But perhaps the most surprising discovery made by Gabain rests on the interpretation of a mural painting from Turfan in which she claims to have found a representation of the smith Pi Sheng. Beneath this picture appear the words

The supposed smith Pi Sheng and his assistant. Wall painting from Turfan. (Gabain, 1967).

'*bo tämürcí*' [the smith] in the Uighur tongue. The rest of the inscription has been lost. Gabain offers this description of the scene:

> A man wearing a long gown and with official or scholarly head-dress is in a working position – i.e. crouching with one knee on the ground and the other bent – and appears to be instructing another person in front of him and handing him a thin stick or bar. This stick is apparently not the only object of its kind, for there is a similar one lying on the ground, and the person in front appears to be working a third piece of this kind with a hammer on an anvil. This person has adopted the same working stance as the man behind him. His hair is tied up in the style of a workman; but it so happens that he is also wearing, despite his manual work, not short jacket and trousers but the same long robe of rank and leisure. This unsuitable clothing as well as the headgear of the master appear to show that the illustrator is not depicting routine manual labour, but some pursuit of cultural significance. Perhaps the artist at Turfan sought to show an important master smith at work preparing letters of tin – which he drew here much enlarged for the sake of clarity. And so might Pi Sheng have been a smith after all? (Gabain, 1967: 16).

I surmise that a maker of coins or medals is shown here, and that he is striking an impression into a bar of relatively soft metal from a shallow

For comparison with the depiction of Pi Sheng.
'Master coinmakers', detail from plate 36 for Emperor Maximilian's Weisskunig.
Woodcut by Hans Burgkmair from the early sixteenth century. Reduced.

steel die which is placed beneath. The impression in the softer metal yields a matrix, from which, after dressing, a moulding could be taken in moist clay and subsequently fired. On this principle, familiar to any coinmaker or medallist, it would be possible to produce ceramic letters of the kind described by Shen Kua. This theory disposes of the apparent contradiction whereby a smith is supposed to have formed letters from clay. If this were indeed the case, then the smith in question would have been a goldsmith or coinmaker, and Pi Sheng moves closer to Johann Gutenberg in consequence. In fact, that decisive interplay between punches, matrices and types on which Gutenberg's invention ultimately rests, and which is poetically alluded to in the *Catholicon* colophon as: 'the wondrous agreement, proportion, and harmony of punches and types' (McMurtrie, 1943: 157), would already have been discovered in the eleventh century.

Resuming the Silk Road's trail to the West, printing could also have reached Samarkand, capital of the Mongol ruler Tamerlane (1333–1405). My own enquiries in Samarkand itself, and at Tashkent and Alma Ata, proved unproductive at the time; but the remarkable advancement of science under Tamerlane prompts the conclusion that he would have grasped the importance of printing as well. Perhaps relevant evidences will be found at a later date.

Moving further westward, we come to the kingdom of the Persian Ilkhanids, where we know that paper money was printed for a very short while. Because of adverse financial circumstances the state had to compel merchants to exchange their gold reserves for paper money. These payment certificates were oblong, with Chinese printing and the Muhammadan creed in Arabic script. Nine presses had to be set up in Tabris and the provincial capitals, but, as the population had no trust in the printed notes, this monetary reform led to economic collapse. Paper currency was only in circulation from October to November of 1294 (Spuler, 1968: 302). Nevertheless, knowledge of printing had reached thus far.

The Tartars or Golden Horde formed the westernmost remnant of the Mongol empire, and had their capital first at Sarai on the lower Volga, and later at New Sarai near what is now Volgograd. Repeated skirmishes have obliterated any possible traces from these sites. Nevertheless, the Golden Horde maintained good contacts with the Italians following the breakdown of relations between China and Europe. As early as 1303 the Dominican, Thaddeus, became Roman Catholic bishop to the Golden Horde; and in 1370 Cosmas of Trebizond was translated to the bishopric of New Sarai (Spuler, 1965: 234). A see was also founded at Cherson (later Sevastopol) in 1333. Italian – and particularly Genoese – merchants were allowed to establish themselves here and in other cities of the Crimea under Tartar overlordship, and trade with the Golden Horde and via the Silk Road to the Far East once again flourished (Spuler, 1965: 395). In this way, channels were kept open for news to pass between East and West.

Fragments of blockbooks have also been found in Egypt, and these have been assigned to a period between 900 and 1300, although such an early starting date seems implausible to me. Knowledge of blockbooks could have reached the Land of the Nile from Tabriz or Baghdad; but, again, it should not be discounted that such printing may have evolved out of the ancient mastery of fabric printing from wooden blocks in Egypt itself. Another use of woodblocks was for playing cards, which must have been introduced from the East by the crusaders – and although such cards surviving in Europe are all hand-painted ones, from the early fifteenth century onwards playing cards were printed from woodblocks, especially in southern Germany, where their production paralleled that of devotional images (Carter, 1925: 139ff, and Rosenfeld, 1975: 353ff).

There is one more rather unusual theory with which to conclude this chapter, which concerns how Gutenberg may have come to hear about the printing of books in the Far East. Could Nicholas of Cues perhaps have been the go-between, when a papal commission took him to Constantinople in order to collect the Greek emperor, the patriarch and 28 archbishops, and bring them to the Council of Ferrara? Among these papal guests was the renowned Greek scholar, Basilius Bessarion, the greatest authority on books of his day. Could it be that he, or another of these ecclesiastical potentates, had encountered the Korean technique of printing, or had even come by an example of printing from movable types? We know that Bessarion assembled the richest collection of books of his age in the West, which he later presented to Venice as the nucleus of the library of St Mark.

The permeability of the apparent wall between East and West has already been noted, and it is likely that one would have been far better informed in Constantinople than in Rome about cultural and technological developments in the Far East. The thesis that Nicholas of Cues could have been the intermediary is also supported by a contemporary sequence of events. The Council of Ferrara, to which Nicholas of Cues had accompanied his Greek guests, was opened by Pope Eugenius IV on 5 April 1438. While the Council was still in session, the pope sent Nicholas to Germany with letters to the Swabian League of Cities intended to avert a newly threatened schism (Lübke, 1968: 100). He betook himself first of all to Koblenz, and he would almost certainly have gone there by way of Strasbourg and Mainz. By the middle of 1438 in any case, Gutenberg must have been working intensively on his invention of printing from movable metal types for long enough to have practical solutions superior to anything that Nicholas may have had to suggest.

I have not raised the issue of whether Gutenberg may have been influenced by printing in the Far East in order to diminish his reputation in any way. Even if a comprehensive knowledge of this form of movable typography had been at his disposal, and he had been shown a printed sheet or book of this kind, he would still not have been spared any of the remaining work on his own trials and inventions.

CHAPTER FIVE

The technical problems of the invention

The typefounder's hand-mould

THE MYSTERIOUS HAPPENINGS IN AVIGNON provide confirmation of what may be gathered from the records of the Strasbourg lawsuit: Gutenberg had invented the hand-casting instrument at Strasbourg. With this device it was now simple to cast as many identical types as required in lead or a lead alloy from a matrix of a harder metal – probably copper. The hand-mould was the key to printing from movable letters, as De Vinne was the first to demonstrate (De Vinne, 1876). Admittedly, my submission that the *Fragment vom Weltgericht* was printed in Strasbourg cannot yet be substantiated beyond reasonable doubt; but the decisive factor for the birth of typography, the hand-mould, was unquestionably contrived in Strasbourg. (The various technical aspects are fully considered in Schmidt-Künsemüller, 1951; Gerhardt, 1976; and Corsten, 1979.)

Before describing the apparatus, I should elaborate on a creative idea that conditions my approach to this problem. This philosophical notion was familiar to the ancient Greeks, but one would not need to have read Democritus to have come across such thoughts in the Middle Ages. According to Democritus, the world consisted of many unchanging units (atoms) which, through constant rearrangement, gave things their appearance and nature. In a similar way, first the northern Semitic peoples, and then more decisively the Greeks, succeeded in splitting up the record of speech – writing – into alphabetical characters or graphemes corresponding to sounds, so that it was possible to reshuffle these single characters endlessly to build new words and texts. And to these two distinct sorts of letters – the phonemes which were spoken and heard, and the graphemes which were written and read – Gutenberg now sought to add a third class, namely physical letters or types which could be set and printed.

This in itself was a very ancient preoccupation, for the Greeks and Romans had stamped single characters into clay tablets, and medieval coinmakers, engravers and bookbinders produced dies of single motifs or letters for impressing into sealing wax or leather. Gutenberg's innovation in this context was to assemble numerous single characters into text columns and pages, from the surface of which impressions could be transferred in a press. The shape and size of his letters were determined by this purpose. Each letter had to be exactly rectangular and easy to pick up and place in order. The end-product of these considerations was a small rectangular block, on the top of which was an image in relief, with the printing surface – or 'face' of the type, as it was termed in the trade – in reverse. The ideal height for types works out in the region of one inch. This is confirmed by an early printing accident from which the lateral view of a piece of type may be inferred: this type was drawn out and fell across the printing surface, damaging a surviving sheet from Johann Nider's *De lepra morali*, printed in 1468 by Conrad Winters of Cologne.

The body size of a printing type accommodates the height of the letters including ascenders and descenders (see diagram on page 129); and in the case of his first type, the 'Donatus and *Kalender*' type, and later for that of the *42-line Bible*, Gutenberg matched the sizes customarily used in handwritten books of a similar kind. It would have been easier to master the initial technical difficulties with these relatively large or medium type sizes than with extremely small sizes. The width of the block on which each letter was set had to vary, since, in the contemporary textura writing which served as model, a lower-case 'i' was only half as thick as its neighbouring 'n' and only a third the thickness of the 'm'. Lastly, these 'soldiers of lead' all had to be precisely the same height, so that when printed, each made the same light and even impression in the paper. This stipulation could only be met after casting, when each character had to be placed face downwards on a smooth surface and the feet carefully dressed to the required height with a plane or file.

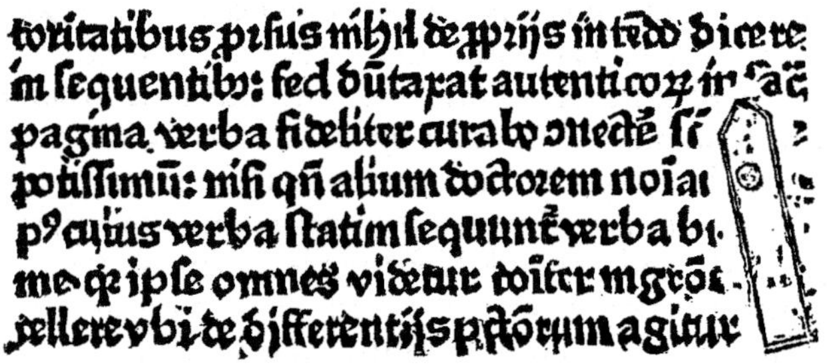
toritatibus prius nihil de proprijs intendo dicere
in sequentibus: sed dūtaxat autenticoꝝ in sac
pagina verba fideliter curabo conectē sic
potissimū: nisi qn̄ alium doctorem noiat
p9 cuius verba statim sequunt̄ verba bi
me qz ipse omnes videtur doctor mgrōs
pellere vbi de differentijs pctōrum agitur

A technical fault in the printing of Nider's De lepra morali *by the Cologne printer Conrad Winters in 1468, where a loose type left lying on the forme caused enough damage to indicate the rough shape and height of the type.*

Gutenberg had probably acquired his metalworking expertise through some of the privileged fraternity of patricians in control of the mint at Mainz, and conceivably from the archbishop's mint at Eltville as well. He was a master in this sphere, as his early enterprises at Strasbourg testify. He understood how dies were engraved and struck. His technology called for an ability to engrave relief images of letters in reverse on steel or other hard metal. To this end, he began with a short rectangular-sectioned length of metal, that could be held in a vice or clamp for the head to be filed and polished at right-angles to its shank. After that, from a manuscript which had previously been selected to serve as design reference for the new typeface, a particularly fine example of the letter in question was chosen and traced on thin paper. Oiling this paper made it translucent, so that when it was turned over, the reversed drawing would be visible to position for transfer to the polished surface of the metal. Instruction in all the techniques of engraving was widespread by the fifteenth century, and so there would be no problems in this department for the master (particularly since he could call upon the engraving skills of the Strasbourg goldsmith, Hans Dünne, when pressed for time). After the contours of the character had been established and the background, non-printing, areas had been sunk sufficiently, then the punch could be finished with regular filed edges, sloping away from the printing surface of the letter.

The prepared and tempered punch was then driven with a single, sure hammer-blow into a rectangular bar of copper, in order to yield a matrix. When the hardened steel punch was driven into copper it caused the displaced softer metal to bulge, and therefore the matrix had to be painstakingly corrected and adjusted with file and graver after being struck by the punch. At the end of this work a small plate had been produced in which a straight and true image was sunk. The verticals of this letter had to be absolutely parallel to, and fitted for position in relation to, the sides of the matrix; and the distance from the foot of each character – the so-called base line – to the edge of the matrix had to be standardized for all matrices, so that when the individual types were set into lines there would be no dancing up and down in alignment. Equally the depth to which the matrices were sunk required critical adjustment to ensure that all types were cast to an even height (Fuhrmann, 1950: 111ff, and Schmidt-Künsemüller, 1949: 343ff).

For the further development of the work, it is important to mention that several strikes can be made from the same punch, and therefore a number of matrices can be produced. There are theories which assert that a specific type could only have been set and printed from in a given place. However, a contrary view is perfectly tenable. By means of the technique of repeated strikes, ready-prepared matrices could be offered for further sale and letters cast from them elsewhere; or, equally, the quantities of types produced in the same workshop could easily be doubled as soon as a large edition made this necessary – provided only that the indispensable instrument, the hand-mould, was available.

It is quite hard to describe the hand-mould, and the earliest figurative representations – for instance, Jost Amman's woodcut of *The Type-founder* dating from 1568 – are inaccurate. The ladle shown in Amman's illustration for pouring in the molten lead is almost ten times larger than

The typefounder. Woodcut by Jost Amman
From Hartmann Schopper's Panoplia omnium artium, *Frankfurt 1568.*

it would have been in reality, and in practice an implement of this size would have led to the caster being constantly burned by splashing lead. For this reason I have had to turn to a much later source for an account of the hand-mould, a volume with the quaint title:

> *Die so nöthig als nützliche Buchdruckerkunst* ... The essential as well as useful art of printing and typefounding, with its typefaces, formats and all the instruments appertaining to it depicted, and also clearly described, together with a short relation of the origin and progress of the printer's art in general, and in particular concerning the foremost printers in Leipzig and other places in Germany in the three hundredth year after the invention itself was brought to light ... by Johann Friedrich Gessner in Leipzig 1740 (cf. Bigmore and Wyman, 1978: 265).

I have been unable to find any German book of earlier date which gives a good explanation of the hand-mould; although the subject is treated in detail in Moxon's *Mechanick Exercises* of 1683–4 (Davis and Carter, 1958). Allowance has to be made right away for the fact that Gutenberg's device would probably have been considerably simpler, although its casting principle and method of operation can scarcely have changed:

> The casting instrument consists of many pieces, which are precisely held together by iron screws, but in such a way that, each time an individual letter or other character is cast, the instrument can instantly be separated into two halves and as quickly reassembled. The two halves of this instrument generally each consist of, or come together to form: the jet or mouth-piece (for pouring-in the metal), the bottom pieces each with a sliding core on top (which form the void in which the body of a type is cast), the adjustable side pieces (for centring the matrix on its body), a movable back gauge, and the wire or spring which keeps the matrix in place. These pieces are all made from brass, but encased in an outer wooden shell, for otherwise the brass would soon get too hot to handle. In addition a couple of pointed iron hooks are fastened into this casing, with which to help pick and draw the cast letters out from the mould.
>
> This instrument forms an actual shank or body for the types in such a way that each one, except for its individual character design and width, will have precisely the same proportions as all the rest, so that the compositor can set these types together without difficulty. It is from the matrix, however, which is inserted at the base of the instrument and is thrust against it by the action of the wire or spring to close the casting space at one end, that the type receives its identifying face or character.
>
> The matrices must be very accurately finished, in such a manner that each and every character is recessed to the same depth, thus resulting in equal height to paper, and also that the striking into copper is exactly level and upright, which work is called justifying.
>
> The cores of this instrument are movable and may be pushed in and outwards. Accordingly, if the matrix in use is an 'm', for example, then these core walls need to be moved further apart. But if 'a' or an 'e' is the next to be cast, both being narrower characters than the 'm', then the cores are driven

inwards again, and in this way the letters acquire their proportional set widths.

Through adjustment of the walls of this casting void the body size of the type is likewise regulated; for the body needs to be at least deep enough to accommodate the required height of letters like the 'f' and 'g' (i.e. those having ascenders and descenders) in order for an entire typeface to be cast upon it.

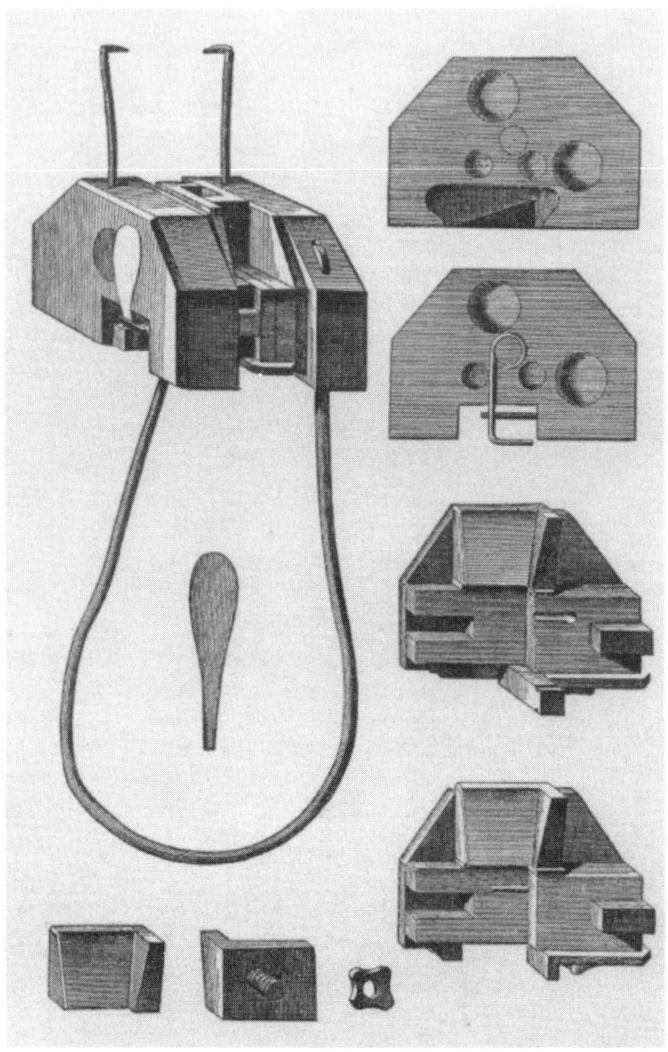

The typefounder's hand-mould and its parts. (Bogeng 1930-41). Reduced.

The most striking feature of the hand-mould is in fact this casting void – adjustable in both set width and body size – to the lower end of which the matrix is fastened, and which can be filled with molten lead from above. Skilled typefounders, equipped with a similar instrument in 1740, were capable of casting up to four types a minute. Even if this had taken four times as long in Gutenberg's day, a founder would still have been able to cast some 600 types in a working day. Compared to carving individual letters in wood, this represents a gigantic escalation in productivity, which in turn has to be multiplied, since, after printing, these same types could be distributed and set up again.

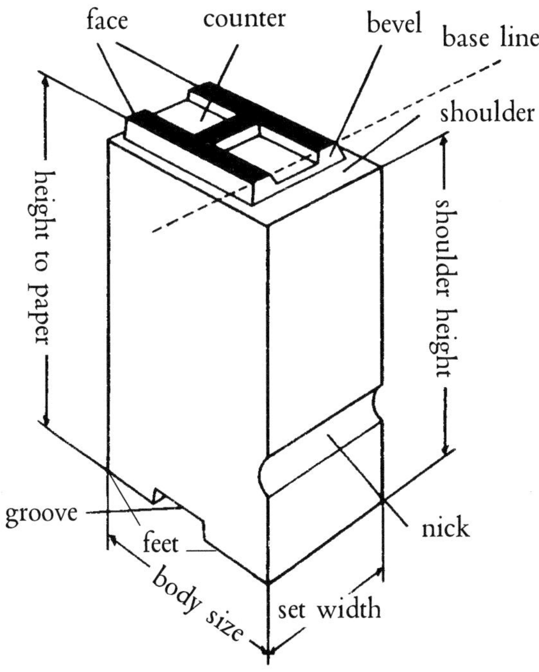

The parts of a type.

Even so, these types required further finishing after they had left the hand-mould. A so-called jet or tang had formed from the overspill after the casting opening had filled. When these jets had been broken off, the newly cast types were planed at the foot to bring them to standard type height, and carefully inspected again.

Types dating from 1580 have been assayed to determine the composition of the typemetal, which was found to consist of an alloy of 82 per cent lead, 9 per cent tin, 6 per cent antimony and traces of copper. It has been suggested that Gutenberg may have used rather more tin.

With the advent of movable type, there certainly must have been something corresponding to a 'bill of fount', or scheme setting out the relative frequency with which particular letters would recur in text setting. Larger numbers of letters such as e, n, s, t, i, m and a, would need to be cast than of b, c, v or the capitals. An inventory of type sorts clearly shows also that Gutenberg's first typeface was designed for setting Latin texts. Gutenberg's own sophisticated typographic system, as well as the range of special letter combinations (ligatures) and contraction signs (abbreviations) that it called for, will be considered later.

The literature about Gutenberg usually relays the statement that the first types already possessed nicks – those indentations that were cast or cut along the front edge of the body to help the compositor handle types easily, and prevent any letters from facing the wrong way round in the composing stick. However, I have never found any evidence for this, and indeed the accidental impression from a type on its side (illustrated on p. 124) shows no visible nick. Surely those printers who came along in the wake of Gutenberg must have found scope for a few improvements to his invention?

Furnishing a composing room

AS USUAL, most information about how the first composing rooms looked and were equipped comes from illustrations. Unfortunately we do not have a single example from the fifteenth century itself – perhaps a reflection of the great security with which the 'black art' surrounded itself. The earliest interior of a printing house appears in a woodcut *Totentanz* from the workshop of Mathias Hus in Lyon from the year 1500. A number of interesting details can also be recognized from the woodcut printer's marks of Jodocus Badius Ascensius in Paris from 1509 onwards, and Dirk van der Borne of Deventer's mark of 1515, and a whole series of other sixteenth-century woodcuts. After the press itself the most important object in all these pictures is the compositor's case, which is always shown more or less sloping. It looks just like the cases which were in regular use until quite recently, being some four feet wide by three feet high, with about a hundred shallow compartments for types and non-printing material (spaces used between words and to fill out line endings). The most frequently used characters are placed in larger compartments to the fore to be within the compositor's easy reach. Even though Aloys Ruppel maintained that Gutenberg's case for types must have had far more compartments, since the extended fount for the *42-line Bible* comprised 290 sorts, this is not borne out by these illustrations (Ruppel, 1967: 113). It seems more probable that those characters needed only infrequently would be kept in a special side case.

The compositor – who wears a cap or hat in contrast to the mostly bare-headed pressmen – sits on a stool, holding the composing stick in his left hand while with his right he reaches for a type. His eyes are directed towards the manuscript, which is held above the middle of the case in an upright copyholder having a horizontal wooden pointer.

The composing stick, in which types are set in a row and justified (or spaced out into lines of equal length and tightness), was probably made of wood and had a fixed line length. It is quite conceivable that a composing rule was used as early as this to help set several lines in the stick before transferring them together onto the galley, but this detail is not clear from any of the pictures.

The galley, on which the growing column of completed typesetting

The oldest representation of a printing office – note the bookshop adjoined.
Woodcut from a Dance of Death *issued at Lyon in 1500. Reduced.*

was placed, usually stood to the right of the compositor's case. This would have been a metal plate with low flanges at right angles on three sides, and with the left edge open. In those days, sometimes the finished pages of type – still on the galley itself – may have been set up on the bed of the press and printed. But in any case a foul proof would have to be taken first for the reader to correct. The customary use of Latin for so many kinds of text offered plenty of opportunities for errors to creep in. But the printer's devil should not be blamed for all the setting faults, for the copyist's devil had usually done greater mischief to the text long before.

It is not necessary to speculate here about other basic composing room equipment: a stone, or table for correcting and imposing the pages; chases and shelving for holding standing type; wood and metal furniture to constitute the non-printing areas of the forme. All these basic objects would have been needed, but none of the illustrators saw fit to include them.

The printing press and printer's ink

GUTENBERG'S INVENTION is strictly a bringing together of many inventions and the modified application of known working practices for printing from type. The hand-mould represents the central item in this cluster of discoveries, but the printing press shares almost equivalent importance. Printing in the Far East, whether from metal letters of the kind described earlier, or for blockbooks or woodcuts, always involved taking copies by rubbing and not with the use of a press. A sheet of slightly dampened paper was laid over the inked printing surface, and pressed into contact by hand before careful burnishing with a wooden tool, a small area at a time over the whole surface. In consequence, an indentation was created on the other side of the sheet, from which it could be judged which parts needed further pressure. While the left hand worked at rubbing down the paper onto the block, the completed corner of the sheet could be lifted with the right hand to check how well and evenly the impression of the text was progressing. This transfer of ink to paper by rubbing, also known as anopisthographic printing, remains unchanged as the rudimentary and time-consuming way in which an artist takes first proofs from a woodcut.

Presses came in domestic, medium and gigantic sizes according to the scale of wine production along the Rhine, and Gutenberg would have seen them from early childhood in Mainz itself or at the monastery of Eberbach near Eltville. His knowledge of everything to do with wine must have been fairly formidable by his Strasbourg years. Similarly, there were presses adapted for printing textiles from wooden patterns. Cloth would have been fed along the bed of the press, a coloured pattern block placed face downward on a predetermined spot, and then the platen forced down upon the woodblock with a single heave on a lever, impressing pigment deeply into the fabric. Bookbinders and paper-makers were also using their own presses by then. It simply came down to choosing, from a range of available models, the version most suitable for further development to print pages of type.

All the early views of printing presses show remarkable resemblances to each other, pointing to the conclusion that they must have been closely modelled on the one built by the Strasbourg chestmaker Konrad Saspach to Gutenberg's instructions (Ruppel, 1967: 114n.).

On the Parisian printer's mark of Josse Bade (Jodocus Badius Ascensius), we see his large wooden press projecting into the fore-ground. Its frame consists of two massive wooden side columns, held together with a crosspiece, or crown, which must be a good 18 inches thick. This colossal head has the important job of taking the strain of the lever from above. Lower down, the side walls were connected by a further balk of timber which supported the track on which the carriage of the press could be pushed in and out. It cannot be seen whether these early presses had a winding handle and straps to help accomplish this. This sliding carriage carried the bed, on which the type was positioned when the carriage was extended. A hinged tympan and frisket were attached to the carriage's outer edge. The sheet about to be printed was positioned on the open tympan or parchment-covered frame. The frisket which folded down over it was a cut-out mask, again held in an iron frame, and designed to hold the page in place and protect the non-printing areas from accidental smudging. After the type had been inked, the tympan was closed so that the paper was above the inked forme and the carriage could be slid once more into the press. Apropos of the very first presses, one authority argues for a kind of running-board or sledge with side guides as an early form of carriage (Wolf, 1974); whereas another thinks that there would have been no carriage as such and speaks of some 'forerunner of the carriage' (Gerhardt, 1975: 45).

Printing was effected by the platen, a thick and level plank of wood, linked by hooked bars at the corners to the lower end of a mighty screw, which was perhaps wooden in the first place but soon came to be made of iron. This was the spindle of the press, which ran in two joists between the side walls, the upper of which was resilient since it rested in pegged holes, while the lower one, known as the till, was held firm. A powerful nut or collar can be seen above a kind of square box which worked up and down in the till. Below, the press spindle operated a hardened steel toe, which fitted a centre stud in a metal plate above the platen, so that an accurate impression fanned out. From the centre of the spindle a horizontal sheath, probably of metal, ran out to take the wooden bar or lever of the press, which was about three feet long. A pull on this lever moved the platen down and printed the sheet from the inked type (Schmidt-Künsemüller, 1951: 71, and Schwab *et al.*, 1983).

The pressman had to heave the lever towards himself with both arms in order to exert sufficient pressure. He would then thrust the lever back into its starting position, withdraw the carriage from the press (possibly

An early printing shop, shown in a printer's mark of Jodocus Badius Ascensius. Paris, 1520.

with the aid of a crank?), lift the tympan up, and also raise the frisket, before the printed sheet could be taken out. While he checked the print for quality and cleanness, and laid it on a pile or – as other illustrations show – hung it up to dry like a piece of washing on a line, his team-mate would already be inking up the setting for the next print.

For this purpose an inking table stood close to the press. In each hand the workman held an ink ball, which was stuffed with horsehair and covered with dog-skin stretched over a round wooden pad, and provided with a handle. He dabbed both these mushroom-shaped heads in the stiff and sticky printing ink on the stone, distributing and smearing it evenly by rubbing and turning his ink balls together. Then he rocked these dabbers to and fro over the forme, covering all the types

Depiction of a printing house, showing an inking table.
Sixteenth century.
German Book and Script Museum, Deutsche Bücherei, Leipzig.

and ensuring that each page was evenly inked. Print quality depended upon the care taken in inking just as much as on the skill and sensitivity with which the pressman applied his lever.

The printer had a further task which called for the greatest exactitude. He was responsible for ensuring that all the paper or vellum copies of an edition were printed in the same position, so that the white margins as well as the printed areas remained constant throughout. To this end, register marks were incorporated into the tympan and frisket. At those points just inside where the edges of the sheet were to be laid, small pins were set. Thus the printer could see, after the front side of the sheets had been run, how to position the same sheets when they were turned over for backing-up, or printing on the other side. Everything printed by Gutenberg is distinguished by near-perfect register. Here it should be emphasized that Gutenberg was the first to confront this problem of printing on both sides of the sheet, for, as has been shown, this was quite out of the question for the blockbooks produced by hand burnishing, whether in the Far East or in Europe. The inventor sought – here as elsewhere – to emulate the model of the handwritten book, and through his principle for laying the sheets in the press he resolved all the attendant problems in an inspired way.

Making a suitable printing ink presented further challenges which were met with comparable mastery, for Gutenberg's printing exhibits the same velvety and gleaming black as it did over five centuries ago, and an intensity which only our finest modern inks can achieve (and we have no means of telling whether these will retain the same blackness in five hundred years' time). The inks used by the incunabula printers were mixed from soot from lamps and varnish, with albumen and human urine as probable additives. It seems likely that purchasers and mixers of inks would have taken care to use commonly available raw materials, so that an ink of consistent quality could be guaranteed.

Among numerous questions of technical detail surrounding the invention, most of which need not concern us here, is the anchoring of the press to the roof of the printing room. From all the historical views we see two upright beams – and frequently supplementary ones – which connect the upper cross-beam of the press to the roof. Occasionally this pair of upright beams even incorporate spindles and leverage holes for adjusting the tension between crown and roof. It follows from this observation that transporting a press – i.e. dismantling and reassembling it in another place – would have been only a qualified possibility.

Presses continued to be built on Gutenberg's pattern without significant change for centuries. Not until 1800 did Charles Stanhope construct a radically improved press where all the parts were made of iron.

Later came the toggle-action press, where an elbow-shaped lever joint reduced the force required; and around the middle of the nineteenth century the Koenig cylinder press was used to print books (Gerhardt, 1971: 43ff, and Moran, 1973). But let us get back to the beginnings!

CHAPTER SIX

The return to Mainz

Scene changes in Gutenberg's birthplace

GUTENBERG HAD LEFT MAINZ some 20 years previously – having been caught up while still a child in its whirl of civic infighting – as a convinced upholder of patrician ideals. In Strasbourg, he had got to know what happened under the leadership of the guilds and had come to terms with their system. He probably took an informed interest in similar social conflicts in other cities as well, and observed the general advancement of the guilds and nascent forms of capitalist production. He must have perceived that insistence on outmoded social privileges brought ever-decreasing returns.

Medieval folk were often absorbed into social groups; they were great joiners of orders, guilds, kindred interest societies and brotherhoods. Each of these groups had its own particular moral identity which marked it out from the rest. A craftsman was not allowed as a member of his guild to turn out any work below the prescribed standard, and yet at the same time he must shun new practices. In reality such guilds obstructed technical progress, and the economic and social developments which were underway had to take place outside these groupings.

The concepts of craftsmanship and art formed a predominant unity. The craftsman's ideal was that workmanship should be in demand and esteemed not by quantity, but rather for its quality. Quality was the basis of his calling and appertained to his status, and was regarded and valued for its own sake in wares that had not as yet become simply those of an anonymous producer. Gutenberg's achievement rested on the knowledge of handicrafts that he had gained in Mainz and Strasbourg. The stimulus for his invention was rooted in the religious controversies and other closely related needs of his age, and he must have been influenced by the more highly developed economies of Italy and the prospering Netherlands. Mainz was still a political centre of the Empire, but in economic terms it had already been overtaken by Frankfurt and other cities. Its political future hung in the balance.

A third force had entered the fray alongside the undiminished antagonism between the guilds and the ancient families. Archbishop Dietrich von Erbach had challenged Mainz's standing as a free imperial city, demanding that all its inhabitants should pay their taxes and customs duties and render military service directly to himself as their archbishop. Burgomasters and council had referred him to the existence of their rights of action in these matters for as long as anyone could remember, and to their customary confirmation by his predecessor, Archbishop Sigfrid. They were not prepared to accept him as lord and master, but only as archbishop of Mainz. He countered by conceding that, although it was true that Mainz was a free city, he was its supreme authority in all matters of spiritual and temporal law, interest levied on all market sales would be his and senior officials and judges must be appointed by himself (*Mainz*, 1968: II, 157ff).

The indebtedness of the city to surrounding towns was assuming yet more ominous proportions. The creditor towns had got together to avoid making the city bankrupt in 1438, on condition that a new council – predominantly made up from members of the old families – was installed. Nevertheless this regime put there by the 'friendly towns' was eyed by the guilds with increasing mistrust. After six years of government by this 'council of ancients', which was there to bring down a debt mountain of 373,184 gulden through parsimonious housekeeping, it had been reduced only by an insignificant sum. The committee of 20, or 'friends of the community', under the leadership of Dr Konrad Humery, accused the city rulers of incompetence and embezzlement. They called for disclosure of the accounts, and, with guild support, forced the resignation of the council of ancients (*Mainz*, 1968: II, 131ff).

On 30 November 1444, while the Armagnac mercenaries stood before Mainz, a fresh council was elected. It consisted of 29 members, all of whom came from the ranks of the guilds. The ancients were completely ousted from the council, but held on to their privileged sinecures at the mint and in the cloth trade. The council appointed the three burgomasters, four treasurers and other officers from its own midst. It embodied the highest authority in the city after the archbishop himself; who retained supreme judicial authority and continued to appoint the chancellor, mayor, judge and the magistrates and controllers of markets and policing. All 37 guilds affixed their seals to the new democratic constitution of the council on 23 December 1444 (*Mainz*, 1968: II, 180ff).

There were clashes for years after that, in which the new council blamed the ancients for misappropriating funds and in some cases confiscated the property of the guilty ones in the city. Many who belonged to the old families once again withdrew to their country estates, as new taxes were introduced and their traditional privileges abolished.

Renewed conflict broke out over the tax-free inns where the religious houses sold their wine. An earlier complaint to Emperor Sigismund had resulted in a prohibition of this tax-free competition. Since then the papal authorities had nevertheless renewed permission for the opening hours of these wine locales to be announced from the pulpit. When the burgomasters objected to this with a deputation of citizens to the cathedral chapter, they received the surprising explanation that as most abbeys and foundations were endowed through winegrowing, their ancestors had merely inherited a traditional right to sell wine everywhere over the counter without rates or duty. (*Mainz*, 1968: I, 326-7).

It appears that the new council ran a tighter budget than the former council of ancients. Under the four treasurers for the year 1449, Eberhard Diemenstein, Johann Apteker, Johann Nuwehusen and Jakob Fust – the last of whom we shall encounter again later – it was still possible to pay off debts of 6000 gulden; but by 1460 only 700 gulden were repaid, as interest had accumulated so steeply. The seemingly flourishing city was heading towards disaster.

The privileges of the clergy developed into the biggest obstacle to financial reform. The so-called 'priests' revenge' of 1435 once again set the seal on the tax exemption of clerics. But the clergy exceeded all bounds in enriching themselves, while the community sank more deeply into debt. The secretary of the council, Dr Humery, requested the religious authorities to contribute at least something towards reducing the civic deficit by not permitting any excessive supplementary profits to be made from the sale of wine. There were negotiations as well between the Mainzers and the not too distant towns of Speyer and Worms, which were experiencing similar problems. Despite expressing their regret at the plight of the city, the clergy did not feel disposed to relinquish their tax advantages.

Although the clergy finally came up with an offer of 14,000 gulden and the archbishop with 7000 gulden in aid, in 1448 the city had to declare itself bankrupt and seek the archbishop's protection against its urgent creditors. The council turned to its creditors to request their forbearance, on the expectation that the city would return to solvency as its annuity contracts were wound up, since these accounted for half the debt. But not all creditors were happy with this proposal. Speyer cathedral chapter extracted an unpaid demand with the help of papal excommunication, imperial proscription and their own archbishop's interdict. As a result of not paying interest to the clergy at Speyer, the Mainzers had to atone by doing without services, baptisms, masses and church burials for 21 weeks, until Archbishop Frederick eventually lifted his interdict in December 1450. (*Mainz*, 1968: I, 335, 342, and Fischer, 1958: 49ff).

The priests' revenge proved to be the last straw in this grave situation. The council's letter of 26 December 1451 to the abbey of St Stephan sounds like an outcry, bewailing the fact that the foundations are getting richer as the city becomes impoverished. All the same the clergy refused to go along with these requests, hanging on to their privileges and stressing their role as patrons for the city's many craftsmen. In many respects the clergy were taking the place of the politically discredited patriciate in opposition to the community.

There was a particularly active anti-clerical circle which behaved conspicuously. In the *Chronik von alten Dingen der Stadt Mainz*, which was presumably written by a member or sympathizer of the ancients, a satirical poem concerning the *Bruderschaft der leckerichten und viressigen Knaben* or 'federation of hearty *bon-viveurs*' appears (*Mainz*, 1968: I, 315–6). The writer describes the members of this drinking club as the instigators of the uproar which finally led to the takeover of power on the council by the guilds. These – for their time – relatively progressive representatives of the town's middle class were defamed in the pamphlet as oafish gluttons and boozers. It is possible that their federation not only prefigured the much-later Mainz carnival societies, but at the same time concealed a grouping with broadly defined political aims; although – at least at a later date – councillors from the ancients, the head of the cathedral's chapter and a chancellor became members. The most active brethren were opponents of the priest's revenge and spokesmen for the guilds. These sample verses have been left in medieval German for the colouring of the period. (The translation attempts the general drift, but the reader has the task of visualizing it in the English of Chaucer's day!)

It is said of the federation:
   There was a brotherhood existing
   Of hale and greedy lads consisting,
   Who ruled an order of their own,
   Carthusians wouldn't have liked or known.
Doctor Humery is known as Curly Whip,
   Eats finest food and lets the poor stuff slip,
   Makes short work and hurries to the pudding,
   Soon he's full and dashes to the closet
   And makes like haste his contents to deposit.
Henne Knauff is called the abbot.
   His other name is Hoglet Henne,
   This brother abbot, as I remember,
   He's for a sucking pig that's roasted well,
   And is so crisp and succulent in smell,
   He fancies that it must be Easter Day.
   All other dishes gladden him this way.

And so it goes on to describe everyone: Conrat Becherer, who loves tripe and brawn; Henrice Iseneck, who prefers butter, cheese and wine;

Hermann Wendeck, who relishes veal; Clas Gise, who enjoys game and fish; Canon Claus Gussel, who is fond of a good drink of wine; in all, 11 persons are named. And what has this company come together to talk about?

> And so they eat and turn to praising
> Good fare, that honest friendship brings,
> And discuss a few important things ...

Then follows an example of such tittle-tattle:

> Said Curly Whip to Hoglet Henne:
> 'Say there, where's the one you mention?'
> 'He's with you! But your nephew's own intention?',
> Asked Hoglet Henne, 'Pray tell me that.'
> Whilst in two groupings the others sat
> And went on boozing, each man like a cow;
> Who found his pasture quite pleasant for now. –
> This order foregathers frequently
> In mutual trust and amity,
> Whomsoever to membership aspires,
> Companionship and worth requires.

If any member got too drunk or revealed a confidential matter, then the abbot, Henne Knauff, sentenced him to some penalty for the amusement or benefit of the rest. For everything discussed within the federation was spoken *sub rosa*, a synonym for secrecy. Whether indeed the federation served as a cloak for substantive political ends, as the writer of this chronicle implies, we are hardly likely to discover after all this time.

A new beginning

THERE IS NO MEANS of establishing for sure when Johann Gutenberg may have returned to Mainz in the period between 1444 and 1448. He probably left Strasbourg right at the end of 1444. His sister Else is mentioned for the last time in 1443 and most probably died that same year (Ruppel, 1967: 49–50). Gutenberg's brother-in-law may be assumed to have stayed on alone at the Gutenberghof, since his grown-up daughter was by then married and living in Frankfurt. So as early as 1443, Vitzthum could have invited his brother-in-law still residing in Strasbourg to consider establishing his workshop at the Gutenberghof. Yet it is hard to see the inventor choosing to return to his native city at that very time in December 1444 when a new constitution for the council had been passed, finally depriving the patricians of any voice in civic affairs, and causing many to seek refuge outside the city once again. It is true that this erstwhile staunch upholder of the conservative cause had become a man who had learned to live alongside the guilds, but his reappearance in Mainz, just as his patrician cronies stood accused of incompetent administration and embezzlement of public resources, seems improbable. The standing aggression of the new council against the ancient families could not begin to lessen until further negotiations had been conducted with the creditors of neighbouring cities.

All thoughts about where the inventor may have spent his time and what he may have done in these years from 1444 to 1448 must of necessity remain speculative. Taking his experiences in Strasbourg as a starting point, and assuming that the production of holy mirrors for the Aachen pilgrimage had proved financially rewarding, then a possible repetition of his mirror enterprise has at least to be left on the cards, since the next pilgrimage was scheduled for 1447. The technological method for producing these mirrors was a known factor; even the moulds for making the metal castings may have been kept. Under the earlier partnership associations, the capital had been put up by Hans Riffe, prefect of the Strasbourg exclave of Lichtenau. So it is quite conceivable that Gutenberg moved his place of work for a few years to this small town in Baden, between Kehl and Rastatt, in order to manufacture a new supply of holy mirrors, accompanied perhaps by his servant, Lorenz Beildeck, and the experienced constructor of presses, Konrad Saspach, who can be shown to have been absent from Strasbourg for several years at that time. Territories to the right of the Rhine appear to have been safe from the Armagnacs, and the governor of Lichtenau would have been able to place not only capital, but also workrooms and accommodation, at the disposal of his business partners. Gutenberg's motive would have been that he needed to acquire vast new resources to last him through the next stage in the 'adventure and art'. Perhaps large numbers of mirrors were manufactured again in 1445 and 1446, sold in Aachen in 1447, and after that preparations made for the move to Mainz. This is a jigsaw piece which fits perfectly into place in Gutenberg's curriculum vitae – but it has to be stressed yet again that this is purely speculation.

It may in any case be supposed that, before the final removal, Gutenberg would have made one or more visits to Mainz to weigh up the working conditions there. At all events by some time in 1448 – the year of the great bankruptcy in his native city – Gutenberg had found his way back to Mainz. For on 17 October 1448 he took out a loan there, which his cousin and relative by marriage Arnold Gelthus zum Echtzeler had obtained for him. This is known from a certified transcript of the original, which sets out in detail those Mainz dwelling houses and other properties of Gelthus that were pledged to Reinhard Brumser and Henchen Rodenstein as security for a loan of 150 gulden at interest of five per cent, which the above-mentioned Arnold Gelthus had received from them.

This document ends by recording:

> Also was present here Henn Gensfleisch, who is called Gutenberg and has affirmed for himself and his heirs, that the afore-described one and a half hundred gulden have been handed over to him and that he has received the return and profit from them. He will pay and settle for the above-mentioned seven and a half gulden annually, without cost and expense arising for the said Arnold Gelthus and his heirs, and he guarantees, to observe this declaration firmly and steadily ... (Schorbach, 1900: 191ff, doc. XVIII).

What can be inferred from reading between the lines of this document? It is immediately clear that Gutenberg once again needed working capital and was able to obtain it. Arnold Gelthus, like the earlier partners in Strasbourg, must have had to be persuaded of the soundness of his relative's proposals. There may well have been pieces printed in Strasbourg for him to inspect. It is possible that by then Gutenberg with his brother-in-law Vitzthum may have begun to build a workshop. Konrad Saspach, who may either have accompanied Gutenberg or followed him on to Mainz, might have completed the construction of a new press. At least in Mainz the art would have appeared ready to be put into practice. Compared with the dispersed layout in Strasbourg, the Gutenberghof offered many advantages. Here there was room enough for a large workshop as well as plenty of storage space for paper, vellum, metal and ink.

The servant Lorenz Beildeck and presumably his wife would have accompanied his master to Mainz. Perhaps one or two other collaborators from the original Strasbourg 'adventure and art' may have followed him there; the association with Heinrich Keffer and Berthold Ruppel from Hanau may have dated back to the Strasbourg venture, and the early Strasbourg printer Johann Mentelin may have worked in Mainz for a time. Certainly all these assistants could have found board and lodging at the Gutenberghof.

Another question mark hangs over the circumstances of ownership of this first Mainz printing shop. It turns out, that in no single item of work is Gutenberg cited as the printer; whereas most later printers, from Fust and Schöffer onwards, identified themselves in the colophon. This has often been put down to a religious world outlook on Gutenberg's part, which will be examined later. Another explanation offered is that the original workshop was never Gutenberg's personal property, but represented a collective undertaking, in which there were several investors and perhaps even worker-owners. This recalls the model of the Strasbourg partnership, in which shares in future profits had been set and where too a communal hostel was planned or provided. Perhaps Claus Vitzthum may have been involved in this partnership as well until his death in 1449 or 1450.

It should not be ruled out that Gutenberg may have visited Holland at some time or other between 1444 and 1447 to inform himself on methods of relief printing from woodblocks or metal plates, and above all about the production of blockbooks in Haarlem. It has already been explained that he did not get the original idea of printing from types from that source, but he may have wished to see which texts were being printed in Holland, how paper stocks were organized and how these books were sold. The notion that the inventor may have cribbed his art from the Haarlem blockbook printers must be discounted, but, conversely, it is unlikely that their techniques would have escaped his notice or that he would have neglected the opportunity to make the relatively effortless journey down the Rhine to find out for himself. Whatever he may have seen can only have strengthened his resolve to press ahead with his own superior process.

Undoubtedly, when the Mainz press was set up in the Gutenberghof, much would have been improved in comparison with the Strasbourg workshop. But for Gutenberg it would have brought the wonder and excitement of starting something new, which grips every creative person, when all options remain open and even the unforeseen can be turned to good account. This path into the unknown constituted for him part of the quality of life itself. He was never harassed by lost time and the consequent absence of material profit; he wanted to achieve the best possible at each new step in the adventure and art.

The 'Donatus and Kalender' *type*

IT HAS PROVED EXPEDIENT to arrange the printed works of Gutenberg and the other early printers according to the types used in their production. Gutenberg's original typeface, insofar as this can ever be conclusively demonstrated, was the one now known as the 'Donatus and *Kalender*' type – or DK-type for short – after its primary use for setting *Donatuses* and calendars; only much later, and in a greatly improved state, did it become the fount used for printing the *36-line*

Bible. It is a fairly large black letter, a textura in fact, a name which refers to the visual resemblance between a page of text closely set in such types and a tapestry or woven textile sample. It takes as its model the letterforms in which missals were written in the Gothic scriptoria of France or Germany. This typeface is dark and heavy, and dominated by a fairly evenly spaced lattice of parallel upright strokes. This massed effect is accentuated through the lower-case height being relatively large and the ascenders and descenders correspondingly short. For the DK-type, this lower-case 'x-height' is 5mm, with ascenders of 2mm and descenders of about 1mm.

Gutenberg's type system contained not only the capital and lower-case alphabets, but an additional range of narrower and wider alternatives for most letters, as well as ligatures (letter combinations cast together as single pieces of type), not to mention further signs for abbreviations and contractions, and punctuation marks. The narrower letters were used to contract the length of a line and the wider ones to expand it. The space separating words remained constant, in order not to disturb the even texture and overall tonal value of each page. The products of the original printing shop in the Gutenberghof almost all have lines of slightly varying length, that is to say, the right-hand column edge is a little ragged, rather than with lines ending beneath each other in exact vertical alignment as is the case with typesetting from the communal printing house established later. There, the narrower or wider alternative characters were skilfully deployed to yield lines of identical optical width, so that columns and pages of text had straight edges on the right as well.

The number of types in this first fount fluctuates. Gottfried Zedler, who made the most thoroughgoing study of the DK-type, found that, after a decade-long evolution (and including the works later printed from it at Bamberg), it totalled 202 different characters. There are no fewer than ten variants of the lower-case 'a' for a start (Zedler, 1934: 13ff). Although these newly introduced characters may not supply exact dates of printing, they do at least confirm a chronological order for pieces printed in the DK-types. These series of recuttings of fresh characters reveal quite a lot about changing trends in the work.

The manuscript page provided Gutenberg with his aesthetic model. He was striving for a *nova forma scribendi*, a new method of writing, and not looking for any special set of artistic standards which applied to his way of setting and printing text. Viewed in this way, the uneven line lengths in these early printed examples came about quite naturally, since for a scribe it would have been pointlessly demanding if not downright impossible to try to keep the right edge of his text lined up or 'justified'. Again, to approximate as closely as possible to the handwritten ideal,

Gutenberg devised 'kerned' or overhanging letters, whereby parts of some letters could overlap the bodies of adjoining characters to left or right, since the scribe made such flourishes without thought of confining each character within a notional rectangle. The characteristic beauty of typography evolved slowly at first, and found expression as the special properties and artistic potential of the new technology became more familiar.

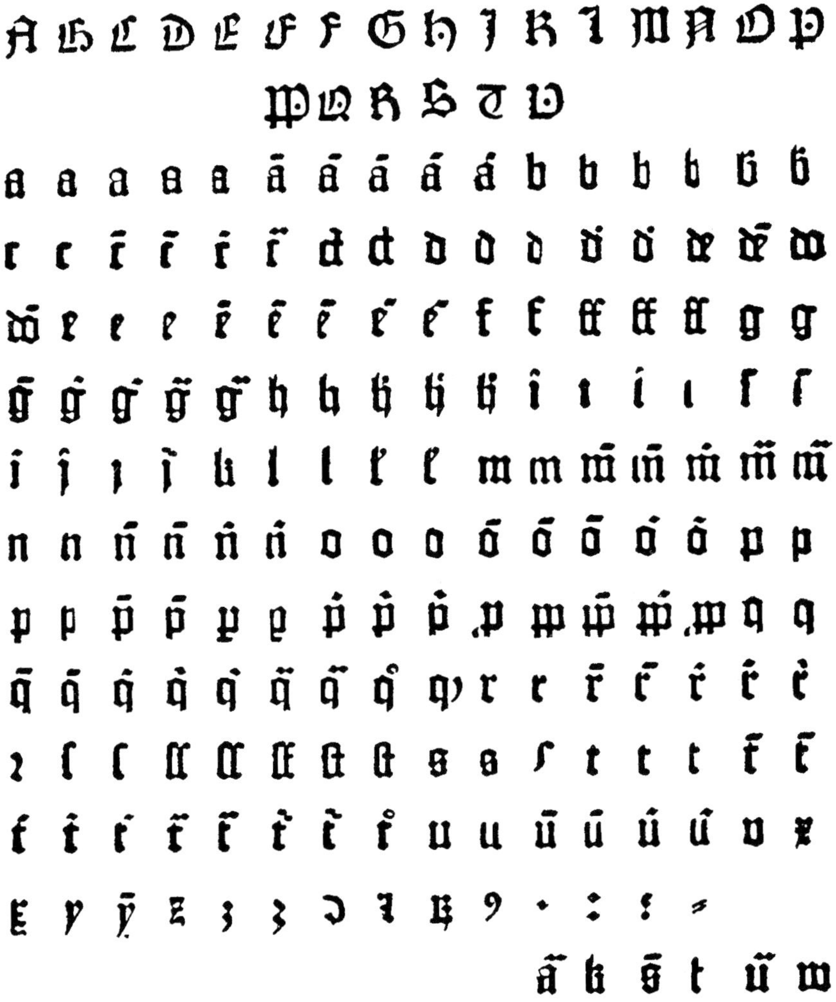

The DK-type fount with the types of the 36-line Bible *together with those characters added later (bottom line). Reduced. Reconstructed by Gottfried Zedler.*

The Donatuses

GUTENBERG WAS TO CONTINUE in Mainz what he had started at Strasbourg. He had already invented the typefounder's hand-mould there by 1440. The phrase 'adventure and art' had been coined to camouflage the new and still-secret process of printing. Eminent Strasbourg citizens, such as the merchant and banker, Friedel von Seckingen, had been business associates of his. In the period between 1440 and 1444, the *Sibyllenweissagung* had been printed, in which the interwoven Emperor Frederick legend had gained political topicality through the election of Frederick III as German king. As Gottfried Zedler proved, whereas the *27-line Donatus* preserved at Darmstadt was printed before the *Sibyllenweissagung*, the Berlin-Heiligenstadt *Donatus a*, Berlin-Heiligenstadt *Donatus b*, and Paris *Donatus* were printed later, although presumably still at Strasbourg. Zedler also showed conclusively that the DK-type had been intended for setting Latin texts in the first place, since certain ligatures only make sense for Latin, and capitals for W, X, Y and Z were missing (Zedler, 1934: 23).

On printing these *Donatuses*, with which Gutenberg brought his work in Strasbourg to a conclusion, he would then have had to make a new start in Mainz, first by constructing a new press and by casting fresh types from the old matrices. Presumably the very first attempts at printing in Strasbourg and Mainz have been lost, but it is likely that the DK-type was planned with the printing of *Donatuses* in mind. '*Donatus*' is a short form for the *Ars Minor* of the Roman grammarian, Aelius Donatus, which was the standard introduction to Latin throughout the Middle Ages. As all roads to education led through the Roman tongue, this made *Donatus* the most important of all schoolbooks, and the most widely distributed book of the fifteenth century. The DK-type was used for producing 24 different printed *Donatus* editions at the very least. Every single copy which has come down to us is incomplete; some are known only from a single leaf or fragment of a leaf. It is safe to assume from this that yet more editions must have gone missing, one or two of which could still come to light by chance.

So the first books to be printed from type in Europe would have been schoolbooks. The wear and tear of constant use called for their continual replacement, and their relatively short extent of 14 leaves or 28 pages would have suited the capacity of the original Mainz printshop. All these *Donatuses* were printed on vellum for the sound reason that this material would stand up to rough treatment much better than paper. It is interesting that probably only one page could have been printed at a

Xylographic Donatus – *a woodcut rendering of handwritten characters. Printed in the region of the upper or middle Rhine around the mid-fifteenth century. Munich, Bavarian State Library. Reduced.*

27-line Donatus, *fragment, set in Gutenberg's original type. Paris, Bibliothèque Nationale. (Zedler, 1902). Reduced.*

time, since the platen size, and thus the effective printing area and force of the press, was so limited. This factor would not preclude having several or all of the pages set up in type ready for printing. The quantities of vellum available and the degree of wear to which the type – which did not as yet have the hardness of later alloys – was subject, kept the size of editions small.

In view of the evident demand, I would estimate that from 200 to 400 copies were printed for each of the 24 known editions of *26-line*, *27-line*, *28-line* and *30-line Donatuses*. On this basis, then, somewhere between 4800 and 9600 *Donatuses* would have left Gutenberg's workshop over the years. Maybe this business was slow to develop, and only later provided steady work for the printing shop in the Gutenberghof, but certainly it would have more than paid its way in the longer term. It is likely that representatives would have been sent to university cities to sell these *Donatuses*; but apart from Erfurt, Heidelberg, Cologne, Leipzig and Paris, there would have been a sure demand from college towns in closer proximity, and monastic and municipal schools must have offered just as big a market. The new trade, when compared to the existing one in manuscripts, held out excellent chances of earning money to stationers or travelling book salesmen. It is even possible that Johann Fust, who is said to have had good connections with the University of Paris, was an agent for that first Mainz printing shop and in this way gained an insight into the far-reaching potential of the new art, for no one could be better placed than a salesman to identify the marketing advantages of the printed book over the codex. It would have been a slower process for the customer to get used to the novelties and differences of print and to weigh up the pros and cons of the new form of writing in relation to the old. This *nova forma scribendi* had at least one immediate advantage in that there were fewer spelling mistakes. Before an edition was printed, correction proofs were taken and read through for errors which could be rectified in the typesetting. In view of the frequent complaints about faulty texts they were accustomed to, this must have counted greatly in favour of the new system in the eyes of schoolmasters and professors.

Gutenberg research has delved deeply into the chronological order of the *Donatuses* printed in the DK-type. The earliest *Donatus* editions are considered to be those fragments of *27-line Donatuses*, which have mostly been recovered as waste used in the covers of bindings of Basle and Strasbourg incunabula printers. They could have been printed in Strasbourg between 1440 and 1444 and in Mainz from 1448 to about 1452. Here it is possible to distinguish between no fewer than 12 editions (Zedler, 1934: 30). The three editions of *28-line Donatuses* have been dated between 1452 and 1456, because the state of the DK-type corresponds to that of the *Türkenkalender*, which can be assigned to that period. It can generally be assumed that the printer, by introducing extra lines to the page, is trying to reduce the number of pages that will be needed. However, it is altogether more difficult to provide a dating for the *26-line Donatuses*. Two different editions of these have so far been found, and a further two leaves printed on one side only, but which are apparently *cancellans* or correction leaves. In the *26-line Donatuses*, question marks add a new feature and the meticulous execution recalls the *42-line Bible*; moreover the right edge of the setting is straight, and the lines have all been equalized in length, which likewise points to a relationship with the *42-line Bible* (Wehmer, 1948). I accept that from the time the printshop at the Gutenberghof opened its doors in 1448 or 1449 until 1458, a sequence of *Donatuses* was regularly produced.

As to the calendars and other works printed in the DK-type, these will be considered later in their historical order.

CHAPTER SEVEN

The 'work of the books'

The invention crowned by success

IT HAS LONG BEEN DEBATED whether it was in Strasbourg or in Mainz that the decisive historic moment occurred at which printing from movable types was discovered in Europe. My own view is that the inventor lived in a constant state of creative ferment throughout the entire span from about 1440 to 1454. At least a decade must have elapsed between the conception and the realization of his invention. With the Strasbourg *Sibyllenweissagung*, and the *Donatuses* which must have been produced both there and in the Mainz printing shop, it was demonstrated that books could be made and multiplied more quickly and cheaply through letterpress than by handwriting.

But there had as yet been no crowning achievement, and there was still no conclusive evidence, to show that the printed book could also be quite as beautiful as any manuscript. Gutenberg did not see printing as a cheap substitute for handwriting, but as a craft that needed to be perfected on its own terms. The handwritten book was enjoying a heyday in the fifteenth century. In France, and Burgundy in particular, exceptional skills were lavished on producing Books of Hours, and renowned artists were attracted to the arts of the book as miniature painters. The merchant bankers and princes of Italian cities had begun to furnish their libraries with copies of great literary and artistic value. Gothic or black letter had reached its apogee in the monastic scriptoria of Germany, France, Spain and Italy. In order to merit aesthetic comparison with contemporary calligraphy, the new method of writing had to take on more ambitious and sophisticated tasks.

The most essential book in the Middle Ages was the missal or mass-book. At mass, the priest transformed bread and wine into Christ's body and blood and offered them for the living and the dead, and this stood as a symbol of Christ's sacrifice and the eucharist at the heart of the Roman Catholic liturgy. The mass-book was indispensable for celebrating mass, indeed the whole ritual was also referred to as a 'reading of the mass'. Every church had to have a mass-book, which contained the fixed canon of the mass with its rubrics and ritual directions for the priest, together with the ecclesiastical calendar and the psalms and antiphons, lessons and prayers proper to the various Sundays and festivals.

Handwritten medieval mass-books may have been richly decorated with initials and miniatures, but as a result of continual copying they were full of mistakes and even varied in content when derived from different sources. In connection with the planned major reform of the Church, which Nicholas of Cues supported at the Council of Basle, and wrote about in his *De concordantia catholica* during his stay at Basle in 1432, Cues advocated a uniform procedure for the liturgy and in consequence the preparation of a standard text for mass-books to be used throughout the realm of the Catholic Church (Blum, 1954: 98). When he became bishop of Brixen he repeatedly raised these same issues. There are various indications that Gutenberg may have had in mind the conditions which the standardized 'copying' of so vast a number of mass-books would create for a new technology (Franz, 1902: 308). The four textura typefaces in existence by 1457, all of which were at the very least initiated by Gutenberg, provided the exact range of sizes required for setting a missal. It follows that it is reasonable to assume that printing mass-books was Gutenberg's long-term objective. Nicholas of Cues, who was made cardinal in 1448, may well have stimulated and supported him in this (Kapr, 1972: 32ff, and König, 1984: 101ff). (König here confirms a connection between the copy of B42 now in Vienna and Nicholas of Cues. A previously misread entry has revealed Brixen cathedral church as the original owner, and it can be assumed that Nicholas, then bishop of the Tyrol, brought about this purchase. König also points out that several copies of the *Gutenberg Bible* were illuminated in reform monasteries such as Melk, Tegernsee and Augsburg, or those of the Bursfeld Congregation such as St Jakob in Mainz or the Petersberg at Erfurt.)

But for the time being the Gutenberghof printing house had only the DK-type at its disposal, which would have been designated as the text size of a missal. The choral-type, the smallest in the series, as well as the small-canon and large-canon sizes, had yet to be added. Several years would elapse before these missing types could be cut and cast in sufficient quantities. Any plan for a missal would accordingly have had to be shelved, and another work selected instead, for which only the single typesize would be needed.

Another thought may have been to print a psalter, since divine service likewise required this collection of psalms of praise, thanksgiving and lamentation. But that too would have called for the cutting of two new sizes of larger type, and had the further disadvantage of a text which differed from one church province to the next, so that only as many copies could be printed as could be sold within a particular province.

It is only if the issue is approached from a purely modern viewpoint that the choice of the Bible – in the Vulgate or Latin translation made by St Jerome – as a prime candidate for printing will seem an obvious one. In the mid-fifteenth century the Holy Scriptures had not yet come

The four textura typefaces in use by 1457. Actual sizes.

Timor dñi principiũ sapiẽtie. Sapien-
tiam atq; doctrinam stulti despiciũt.
Audi fili mi disciplinã pr̃is tui et ne
dimittas legem mr̃is tue: ut addatur

B42-type.

es factus esset apparuit iudas
in campo cũ trib; milib; viroꝝ
tantũ: qui tegumẽta ⁊ gladio

DK-type.

ĩpmendi ac caracterizandi·
ne sic effigiatus ,Et ad euse-

Small psalter-type.

oris eius iniquit
ligere ut bene age

Large psalter-type.

to occupy nearly so central a position in religious life as they now do. Catholic theologians took the view that the Bible needed to be explained to the populace through the interpretation of the church fathers and by priests. It lay in the interests of the church hierarchy to restrain access to the Bible, and vernacular translations were proscribed by successive councils. Although the church as a whole could scarcely be expected to encourage bible printing, there were nevertheless pre-Reformation endeavours, and powerful figures, such as Nicholas of Cues, within its ranks who were in favour of the wider dissemination of bibles. It would be a mistake, however, to assume that an assured market existed for bibles from the outset. Students and priests could not have afforded a printed Bible for their own use. Potential buyers would have to be sought among the monasteries and universities, rich clerical or secular nobles, and princes of the church.

Gutenberg and his associates would have considered the selection of the major book they were about to print with care. Their decision to print bibles may have been influenced by Nicholas of Cues and his current involvement with monastic reform. He had received, as papal legate, the oaths of 70 Benedictine abbots meeting in Mainz in May 1451 to reform their houses, and on that occasion he had placed great emphasis on the need for the libraries of all these monasteries to possess a well-translated and edited Bible. The inventor must have recognized the opportunity this presented to match his new technology to the needs of the reform monasteries.

At this juncture, we have to introduce a man who had an important role to play in the history of printing. Johann Fust was a merchant and money-lender in Mainz. His brother, the goldsmith Jakob Fust, belonged to the new council of 29 members that had governed Mainz since 1444, and was subsequently elected one of its burgomasters. It appears that Johann Fust also dealt in manuscripts and travelled the university towns to offer *Donatuses* and other volumes. So it is quite conceivable that he may have had a loose business relationship with Gutenberg from as early as 1449, since the printing office in the Gutenberghof would have needed a dealer to sell its completed *Donatuses*. This would have afforded Johann Fust first-hand experience of the new art's commercial prospects. The earliest stockists of the new-fangled printing would not have evaluated it as such, but would have mixed it up with the manuscripts they were used to handling. And, as tradesmen, they would have been keen to learn that prices were substantially lower without wishing to go into the detail of production methods. As a matter of course an awareness of this special kind of writing would have filtered through, and it would have become a matter of concern to book distributors and sellers that printing

Portrait of Johann Fust.
From Petrus Opmeer: Opus chronologicum, *1611. Reduced.*

should not come to be regarded as an inferior product.

Gutenberg has usually been represented as the 'inventor', with his head in the clouds and ignorant of business and commercial matters. In contrast, Johann Fust is supposed to have been the ruthless business-man, unconcerned with whatever technical or artistic problems arose, but to have staked his capital in the venture as a cold-blooded calculation and then waited for the right moment to pull the rug out from under the inventor's feet. This picture is exaggerated, to say the least, since Gutenberg's own financial transactions in Strasbourg could scarcely be described as naïve or kid-gloved. He had brought about the imprisonment of Mainz's civic envoy for debt and imposed unfavourable conditions on his partners in both the 'mirrors' and the 'adventure and art' ventures; with craft and success he fought off the action brought by the Dritzehn brothers. Another of his Strasbourg guarantors, Martin Brechter, later had to spend two terms in a debtor's prison on his account (Ruppel, 1967: 53). We know relatively little concerning Johann Fust, and only recently has he received much scholarly attention. This has shown that Johann Fust was not merely a financier, but a goldsmith as well, and belonged to their guild, just like his brother. The decades of feuding between guilds and patricians cannot fail to have conditioned his attitude towards Gutenberg. In all probability, Gutenberg would still have struck him as an aristocrat; a commendable and imaginative man admittedly, but at the same time one of those privileged and self-assured persons in dealing with whom prudence and cunning are the order of the day to avoid being outsmarted. The duration and nature of their work together is reported in the so-called *Helmaspergersche Notariatsinstrument*, a document set down by the notary Helmasperger at Johann Fust's request in the course of legal proceedings (Geldner, 1972a: 113). This document is the keystone in the edifice of Gutenberg research, and consequently the full text is given below (pp. 173–5). However, the archaic German in which it is written is often difficult to follow and interpret precisely, and for this reason the principal events it deals with are narrated first.

As early as the summer of 1449 Gutenberg received from Fust an initial loan of money for the production of *geczuge*, or equipment to print with. In the *Chronik der Stadt Köln*, printed in 1499, we are told on the basis of information supplied by Ulrich Zell, Cologne's earliest printer, that in 1450 a start was made on printing a Latin Bible in Mainz. The merchant Fust, convinced by the results from the first printing house of the profits to be made from printing, enabled a new and larger workshop to be equipped through his loan of 800 gulden (Świerk, 1972a: 86). As a suitable building for this purpose, the Hof zum Humbrecht was chosen, which belonged to a distant relative of Gutenberg's, Henne Salman, then living in Frankfurt (Ruppel, 1967: 60–1). So far as is known, the Humbrechthof stood empty in 1450 and there would have been little difficulty in renting it, particularly at a time when so many patricians had once again fled the city.

It would have been the second time that Gutenberg had faced the task of setting up a new printing office in Mainz. Once again it was probably Konrad Saspach who built his presses, and there would have been four to begin with – insofar as one can work back from the evidence available – and six at the height of production; while at the Gutenberghof it seems unlikely that more than a single press was ever installed. A composing room large enough for no fewer than six work stations would have been required, and storage lofts for vellum and paper that were correspondingly generous in layout. Gutenberg may have intended all along for the two printing works to continue in operation side by side, but producing clearly differentiated wares: the one in the Gutenberghof largely for *Donatuses* and jobbing printing in the DK-type; and the new office in the Humbrechthof for books, of which the Bible was to be the first.

It was agreed that the printing equipment to be produced with the money should serve Fust as security against this loan of 800 gulden. In the later dispute between the two partners and contracting parties, it also arose whether payment of interest had been agreed on this loan. Gutenberg affirmed that any interest had been waived, and further, that he did not immediately receive the full sum according to the contract. He maintained that he had gained possession of less than 800 gulden. Fust swore on oath that he himself had needed to borrow this 800 gulden against six per cent interest. However, what is not in question is that Gutenberg and Fust entered into a contract in 1450 to set up a new printing establishment.

The type and printing of the 42-line Bible

GUTENBERG DESIGNED A NEW TYPEFACE for the planned Bible, or to be more exact, he selected in consultation with his colleagues a manuscript Bible, which for its accuracy of text and beauty of handwriting could serve both as setting copy and exemplar for the printing. From this manuscript the best examples of each letter were chosen and traced out, until the complete alphabet with all its combined letters and abbreviations existed as a set of traced designs. After that – just as in the case of the DK-type – the punches would be engraved, then the matrices struck, justified and finally fitted into the typefounder's hand-mould, so that printing types could be cast from them. Gutenberg and his fellow craftsmen produced in this way 290 assorted types for the new Bible: 47 capital letters and 243 lower-case letters, including narrower and wider alternatives and punctuation marks (Ruppel, 1967: 139). How long did this work take?

Subsequent detective work has established that at first four and later six compositors would have worked simultaneously at typesetting the Bible. Each compositor would have needed enough material for three pages: that is to say for the page he was working on, a second that was on the printing press, and a third awaiting distribution back into the case. A simple count shows that 2600 characters go into a page of Bible setting; thus each of the six compositors needs 7800 types at his disposal, so that no fewer than 46,000 types must be kept available, and continually renewed as they become worn through repeated use. I estimate that it would take not less than half a year's work to prepare sufficient quantities of type for Bible printing to commence. (Later on we shall consider what might have been set up in type during this interval.)

The height of the B42-type works out at 7.2 mm. Of this, 4.2 mm is allotted to the average height of the lower case (the so-called x-height), with 2 mm for the ascenders and 1 mm for the descenders.

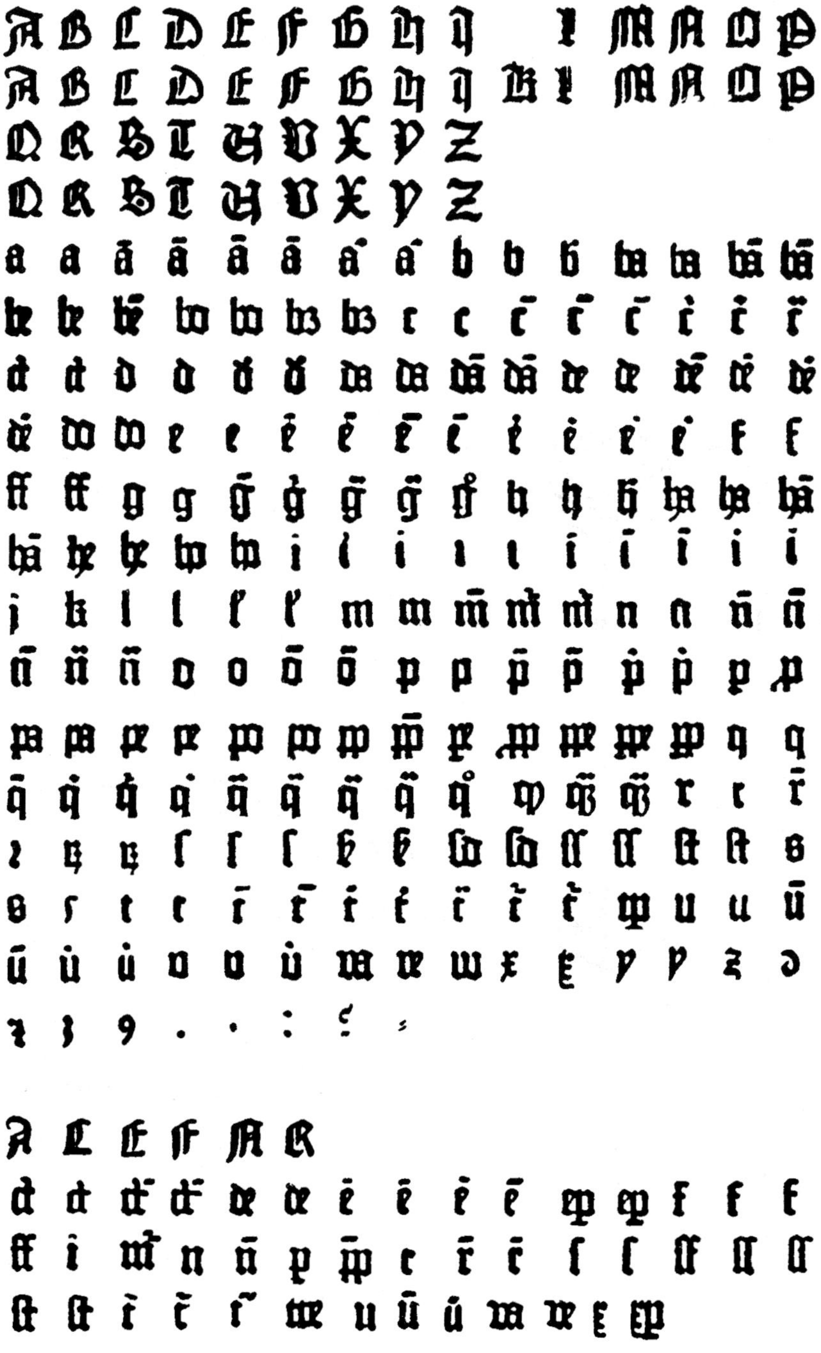

This new, smaller size of type produces a closer and more elegant effect than the DK-type. While the lower-case letter forms are strikingly similar, the capitals have greater calligraphic sureness and invention. But the overall impression is that the B42-type and the DK-type are cut in the same spirit and so at least under Gutenberg's influence – though this does not mean to say that the master inventor would have cut the punches personally, for he had at that same time to supervise the installation of a new printing works, the purchase of vellum and paper, and the engagement of suitable workmen. He had to work out the technology and logistics for printing so massive a work, consider how to train his employees, and ponder the typographic page design in detail. New recruits had to learn their crafts as compositors and pressmen; probably from more experienced men like Heinrich Keffer and Berthold Ruppel. Heinrich Günther, sometime parish cleric of St Christoph's, appears to have been persuaded to act as corrector for the press, and may also have acted as theological advisor for the project as a whole (Stöwesand, 1956: 62ff). Keffer and Ruppel, his associates at the first printing works, must have spent much time advising and assisting at the Humbrechthof, particularly in the run-up to continuous production. However, I have never found a convincing argument for Gutenberg to have abandoned the printing works in the Gutenberghof. He and his new collaborators presumably lived some distance away at the Gutenberghof, while the Humbrechthof provided a hostel for the compositors, pressmen and typefounders who worked there.

We should never lose sight of the fact that for Gutenberg the most important thing was to prove the new technique capable of creating something of supreme artistic quality, and these strivings after synthesis at an uncompromising level consumed his constant attention. The page size of the new Bible, 420 mm deep × 320 mm wide, is typical of handwritten bibles from the finest scriptoria (Rosarivo, 1955: 70ff). The noble and harmonious proportions of the printed columns and their surrounding white margins, which later generations of printers have admired, results not so much from Gutenberg's personal design as from correspondence to the golden mean, a proportional canon applied in monasteries throughout the Middle Ages (Corsten, 1979: 37).

The B42-type.
Above: the original range of characters; below: characters added later.
Reconstructed by Gottfried Zedler. Reduced.

GUTENBERG RECEIVED a further 800 gulden from Fust, spread over the years 1452 and 1453, for the 'work to their common profit' or for the 'work of the books'. According to Gutenberg's later declaration, this was an interest-free investment for the production of the work; whereas Fust attested that it was a new loan at six per cent interest against the security of the work (see the full text of the Helmasperger Instrument: 173ff). The point at issue in the dispute between Gutenberg and Fust, and equally in the scholarly debate between differing interpretations of the Helmasperger Instrument, is the question: What was the 'work of the books' or the 'work to their common profit'? We shall return to this later.

Introducing the investment of 800 gulden enabled a start to be made on setting and printing the Bible. The Bible itself provides the best evidence for how it was actually made. If you turn the leaves of the Bible already knowing a little about its production, you go first to pages 9, 10 and 11 and count the number of lines on each, just to confirm, as others long ago discovered, that there are only 40 lines of text on pages 1–9 (ff. 1–5r) and on the first 7 pages of *I* Samuel (ff. 129–132r) which were printed concurrently. Page 10 alone has 41 lines, but from page 11 onwards the remaining pages in both volumes are standard at 42 lines (Ruppel, 1967: 142). By merely glancing at the pages this can be overlooked. Why did the compositors apparently change their minds in midstream and increase the number of lines to the page? The decisive factor can only have been an economy of about five per cent in the quantities of vellum and paper required. Closing up the lines further enhances the visual look of the page, and it is characteristic of Gutenberg that he should still be seeking aesthetic improvements even while work was in progress (Scheide, 1973: 129).

Far-reaching insights can be reached through the meticulous study of individual pages. At first Gutenberg set out to insert red-printed headings at the start of each prologue or book. This red printing was shortly abandoned and corresponding spaces left for these rubrics to be added by hand, because a separate second-colour printing and the complicated register did not warrant the time involved. As a result of this decision an eight-page table was printed, of which only two copies have chanced to survive (in Munich and Vienna), showing which headings were to be entered by the rubricators.

Since a pattern of tiny discrepancies in typesetting practice can be detected between the opening leaf onwards and leaf 129 onwards, it

The golden mean or section.
Drawing by Maria Kapr.

Incipit epistola sancti iheronimi ad
paulinum presbiterum de omnibus
divine historie libris. capitulū pmū.

F Rater ambrosius
tua michi munus-
cula pferens. detulit
sil' et suavissimas
lrās. q̄ a principio
amiciciaꝝ. fidē pba-
te iam fidei ⁊ veteris amicicie nova:
pferebant. Vera enī illa necessitudo ē.
⁊ xp̄i glutino copulata. q̄m non utili-
tas rei familiaris. nō p̄ncia tantum
corpoꝝ. nō subdola ⁊ palpās adulacō.
sed dei timor. et divinaꝝ scripturarū
studia conciliant. Legim⁹ in veteribꝫ
historiis. quosdā lustrasse pvincias.
novos adiisse pplos. maria trāsisse.
ut eos quos ex libris noverant: corā
q̃ viderēt. Sicut pitagoras memphi-
ticos vates. sic plato egiptū. ⁊ architā

shows us that two different craftsmen were involved; one starting work on the opening leaf and the other at f. 129. And when the second volume was reached a similar division of labour took place: a third compositor was added to start again from the first leaf, and a fourth at f. 161. Soon after they were joined by yet another pair of compositors. One can differentiate between passages set by all of them, primarily through their different habits in setting recurrent Latin words and contractions. It has even been calculated that compositor number two was the most industrious, for he began work at f. 129 of the first volume and completed 140 folio leaves, or 280 pages.

For the first time a special strategy is found in use, which book designers and printers have returned to from time to time over the centuries. All lines of text in the Bible are brought out to equal length, but this way each column has a very narrow additional provision to the right, reserved exclusively for word-division and punctuation marks so that these may overhang into the margin, thus improving the optical edge to the column. Through such details, Gutenberg set the new style of typesetting which emerged as a hallmark of the Humbrechthof printing house, where the aesthetic qualities of book printing were cultivated – whereas at the first printing works in the Gutenberghof lines of type were never brought out to uniform length, for this ragged or unjustified setting was probably considered quite adequate for the jobbing printing carried out there. Here we have the first demonstration, albeit in one area only, of the superiority of the printed book over the manuscript, as it is virtually impossible for a scribe to write out a whole book in lines of equal length.

It still appears miraculous that this first typographic book in Europe – and I prefer to describe the *Donatuses* and the *Sibyllenweissagung* as jobbing printing rather than bookwork – should be of such sublime beauty and mastery that later generations up to our own day have rarely matched and never excelled it in quality. For regularity of setting, uniform silky blackness of impression, harmony of layout and many other respects, it is magisterial in a way to which we can rarely aspire under modern conditions. Behind such an achievement can only have stood a personality inspired by a passionate commitment to excellence, and able to communicate this drive and enthusiasm to his fellow workers.

The Bible, known to incunabulists as the *42-line Bible* or B42, may also be cross-examined to discover the approximate size of the workforce engaged in its production. We have seen that there were six compositors,

Part of a single column from the B42.
Gutenberg-Museum, Mainz. Actual size.

who would have supplied six presses – i.e. 12 printers, as each press had an inker and a pressman to lay the sheets, move the carriage and operate the press lever. To these we need to add the typecaster, engraver, distributor of types, inkmaker and other assistants. Altogether there can never have been a staff of fewer than 20 assistants involved in the production of the Bible at the Humbrechthof. Only a few of these craftsmen's names are known to us, and we have simply no information concerning their dates of engagement. We come to hear of Götz von Schlettstadt and Hans von Speyer by chance in Mainz documents dated 14 November 1461 and 26 January 1462 which record: 'Present were Clas gotz and Hans von spyre the goldsmiths.' Both could have helped Gutenberg as engravers. We further encounter the names of Numeister, Spiess, Krantz, Peter Drach (of Speyer), Johann von Stein, Remboldt, Johann Renner, Jans von Koblenz, Hans Reinhard and Clas Wolff; as well as Peter Schöffer of Gernsheim and Nicholas Jenson, of whom we shall hear in more detail later (Geldner, 1970: I, 56). A colleague from the Strasbourg cooperative days, Heinrich Eggestein, apparently came to Mainz rather later, both to contribute to the further development of the 'adventure and art' and to learn about it. Perhaps Konrad Sweynheym from Schwanheim, later to become Italy's first printer, may also have been a member of Gutenberg's staff for a time. Many of these names are to be met with again in the 1470s as the first printers in all sorts of places. It seems that the Humbrechthof became a kind of training school for incunabula printers (Geldner, 1970: I, 60).

Ahead of printing came the tedious labour of cutting out the best broadside sheet from each skin of parchment, leaving offcuts wherever possible to be used for indulgences and single-sheet printing. (It is true that sheets cut to format were on the market, but with such an exceptionally large demand the workshop would almost certainly have done its own trimming to size on economic grounds.) Then the sheets of vellum or paper would have to be dampened. For paper, it would suffice for every sixth sheet or so to be drawn through a bath of water and then interleaved with five dry ones, so that over several days dampness would penetrate equally through the pile. Finally, the sheets had to be folded exactly and pricked through with a needle or pointed awl, using a master sheet as template, so that the text area and margin proportions were transferred. This painstaking preliminary work allowed the printer to lay each sheet in a precisely standard position.

Printing proceeded page by page. Each of the pre-folded double leaves, i.e. each sheet about to be printed, would have been pressed flat again and then printed with its first page, and probably after that with the conjugate (fourth) page. Then the sheets had to be hung up to dry before the reverse sides could be printed. After further drying, the finished sheets were inspected and stacked; from time to time they were made up into gatherings of five sheets placed one within the other to form quinternions, or 20-page sections. (To have printed page by page in numerical sequence, as some Gutenberg scholars have suggested, would have been infinitely more complicated and time-consuming.) Any slur or imperfection in the inking of one page naturally ruined the sheet as a whole and meant that it had to be replaced. However much care was taken, a spoilage margin must have been added to the planned edition (Schmidt-Künsemüller, 1951: 71).

It has been calculated that with the presses of that time two printers could take between 8 and 16 impressions in an hour. The printing of 1282 pages to yield 180 finished copies may be reckoned as 237,170 operations of the press. If six presses were working flat out for an average daily shift of ten hours, then this would call for 333 clear working days. But a plethora of religious festivals reduced the effective working year to a mere 188 days at that period. If further allowances are made for the fact that only four presses were in service to begin with, and for errors and breakdowns and the need to transfer workmen to other duties, then an estimate of roughly two years seems reasonable for this work (Ruppel, 1967: 144).

A probable size for the edition has already been mentioned above. Today there are in existence 12 copies on vellum and 37 on paper, though not all of these are complete. These totals include a vellum example and one on paper, both missing from Leipzig since the end of the war in 1945, which have been rediscovered very recently in Moscow. (Negotiations for their return were instituted in 1994.) These surviving numbers support estimates that about 30 to 35 vellum copies may have been printed, besides 145 to 150 copies on paper. Some 5000 calfskins, all tanned and prepared in a uniform manner, would have been needed for printing the vellum copies. A great deal of labour would have gone into the production of handmade paper as well, and in the end the selection of papers involved crucial aesthetic decisions. The bill for paper alone, including the carriage from Italy, has been put at between 300 and 900 gulden by experts, and that for the vellum estimated at 400 gulden (Ruppel, 1967: 145–6). To this must be added expenditure for metal, ink, wages, rent and much else besides. A hypothetical balance-sheet will be ventured later.

Producing books for a group of unidentified buyers presupposed

Following pages:
a double-page from the The Shuckburgh copy of B42,
with kind permission of the Gutenberg-Museum, Mainz.

[L]Ucas syrus · natõe anthi-
ocensis · arte medic⁹ · disci-
pulus apostoloꝝ · postea
paulū secut⁹ usq; ad con-
fessionē ei⁹ seruiens dño sine crimine:
nam neq; vxorem unq̄ habuit neq; filios: septuaginta et quatuor annorū
obijt in bithinia · plen⁹ spiritu sancto.
Qui cū iam scripta essent euāgelia · ꝑ
matheū quidē in iudea · ꝑ marcū aūt
in italia: sancto instigante spiritu in
achaie partibȝ hoc scripsit euangeliū:
significans etiā ipse in principio ante
suū alia esse descripta . Cui extra ea q̄
ordo euāgelice dispositionis exposcit-
ea maxime necessitas laboris fuit: ut
primū grecis fidelibȝ omni ꝓphetati-
one venturi in carnē dei cristi manife-
stata humanitate ne iudaicis fabulis
attenti : in solo legis desiderio tenere-
tur : uel ne hereticis fabulis et stultis
solicitationibȝ seducti exciderent a ve-
ritate elaboraret : dehinc · ut in principio euangelij iohānis natiuitate pre-
sumpta · cui euangelium scriberet et in
quo elect⁹ scriberet indicaret : cõtestās ī
se cõpleta esse · q̄ essent ab alijs incho-
ata . Cui ideo post baptismū filij dei a
ꝑfectione generatõnis ī cristo implete-
repetēde a pricipio natiuitatis huma-
ne potestas ꝑmissa ē : ut requirentibȝ
demonstraret in quo apprehendēs e-
rat per nathan filiū dauid introitu re-
currentis ī deū generationis admisso-
indisparabilis dei ꝑdicās in homini-
bus cristū suū · ꝑfecti opus hoīs redire
in se ꝑ filiū faceret : qui per dauid patrē
venientibus iter ꝑbebat in cristo . Cui
luce non immerito etiā scribēdorum
actuū apostoloꝝ potestas ī ministerio
datur : ut deo in deū pleno et filio ꝑdi-
tionis extincto · oratõne ab apostolis
facta · sorte domini electionis numer⁹
compleretur : sicq; paulus cõsummatio-
nē apostolicis actibȝ daret · quē diu
cõtra stimulū recalcitrantē dñs elegis-
set . Quod et legentibȝ ac requirentibȝ
deū · et si per singula expediri a nobis
utile fuerat : sciens tamē q̄ operātem
agricolā oporteat de suis fructibus e-
dere · vitauim⁹ publicā curiositatem :
ne nō tā volentibȝ deū demōstrare vide-
remur · quā fastidientibus prodidisse.
Explicit prefatio . Incipit euangeliū secundū lucam . Prohemiū ipsius
beati luce in euangelium suum .
[Q]Uoniā quidē multi co-
nati sūt ordinare nar-
ratõnes q̄ ī nobis com-
plete sūt reꝝ · sicut tradi-
derūt nobis q̄ ab inicio
ipsi viderūt · et ministri
fuerūt sermonis : visū ē et michi assecuto
oīa a pricipio diligēter ex ordīe tibi
scribere optīe theophile : ut cognoscas
eoꝝ verboꝝ de q̄bȝ erudit⁹ es veritatē . i.
[F]Uit in diebus herodis re-
gis iudee sacerdos quidam
nomine zacharias de vi-
ce abia · et uxor illi de filia-
bus aaron : et nomen eius elizabeth.
Erant autem iusti ambo ante deum :
incedentes in omnibus mandatis et
iustificationibus domini sine quere-
la . Et non erat illis filius · eo q̄ esset elizabeth sterilis : et ambo proces-
sissent ī diebȝ suis . Factū est aūt cū sa-
cerdotio fungeretur zacharias in ordine vicis sue ante deū : scdm cõsuetudi-
nem sacerdotij sorte exijt ut incensum
poneret ingressus in templū domini.
Et oīs multitudo ppli erat orās fo-
ris hora incensi . Apparuit autem illi
angelus dñi : stans a dextris altaris

incensi. Et zacharias turbatus est vi-
dens: et timor irruit sup eū. Ait autē
ad illū āgelus. Ne timeas zacharia:
quoniā exaudita est dp̄catio tua. Et
uxor tua elizabeth pariet tibi filiū · et
vocabis nomē eius iohannem: et erit
gaudium tibi et exultatio: et multi in
natiuitate eius gaudebūt. Erit enim
magn⁹ corā dn̄o: et vinū et siceā nō
bibet. Et spiritu sancto replebitur adhuc ex utero matris sue: ⁊ multos filio-
rū isrl' cōuertet ad dn̄m deum ipsoꝝ.
Et ipe p̄cedet ante ipm̄ i spiritu et vir-
tute helie: ut conuertat corda patrū in
filios · et incredibiles ad prudentiā iustoꝝ: parare dn̄o plebē pfectā. Et dixit
zacharias ad angelū. Unde hoc sciā?
Ego enī sum senex: et uxor mea pcessit
in dieb3 suis. Et respōdens angelus
dixit ei. Ego sum gabriel q̄ asto ante
deum: ⁊ missus sum loqui ad te: ⁊ hec
tibi euangelizare. Et ecce eris tacens
et non poteris loqui usq3 i diem quo
hec fiant: pro eo q non credidisti ver-
bis meis · que implebūtur in tempore
suo. Et erat plebs expectans zachariā:
et mirabātur q tardaret ipe i templo.
Egressus aūt non poterat loqui ad il-
los. Et cognouerūt q visionem vidis-
set i templo. Et ipe erat innuens illis:
et pmansit mutus. Et factū est ut im-
pleti sunt dies officij ei⁹: abijt i domū
suā. Post hos aūt dies cōcepit elizabeth uxor eius: ⁊ occultabat se mēsib3
quinq3 dicens. Quia sic fecit michi dominus · in diebus quibus respexit au-
ferre obprobriū meū inter homines.
In mense aūt sexto missus ē angelus
gabriel a deo in ciuitatem galilee cui
nomen nazareth · ad virginem despō-
satam viro cui nomē erat ioseph · de
domo dauid: et nomē virginis maria.
Et ingressus āgelus ad eā dixit. Aue
gratia plena: dn̄s tecū: benedicta tu in
mulierib3. Que cū audisset · turbata est
in sermone eius: et cogitabat qualis
esset ista salutatio. Et ait angelus ei.
Ne timeas maria: inuenisti enī grati-
am apud deū. Ecce concipies in utero
et paries filiū: ⁊ vocabis nomen eius
ihesum. Hic erit magnus: ⁊ fili⁹ altissimi vocabitur. Et dabit illi dn̄s de⁹ se-
dem dauid patris eius: ⁊ regnabit i
domo iacob in eternū: et regni ei⁹ nō
erit finis. Dixit aūt maria ad angelū.
Quomō fiet istud: quoniā virū non
cognosco? Et respōdens angelus dixit ei. Spiritus sanctus supueniet in
te: ⁊ virtus altissimi obumbrabit tibi.
Ideoq3 et qd̄ nascet̄ ex te sanctū: voca-
bit̄ fili⁹ dei. Et ecce elizabeth cognata tu-
a: ⁊ ipa cōcepit filiū i senectute sua. Et
hic mēsis est sext⁹ illi q̄ vocat̄ sterilis.
Quia nō erit impossibile apud deum
omne verbū. Dixit autē maria. Ecce
ancilla dn̄i: fiat michi secundū verbū
tuū. Et discessit ab illa āgelus. Exur-
gens aūt maria in diebus illis abijt
in mōtana cū festinatione in ciuitatē
iuda: et intrauit in domū zacharie: ⁊
salutauit elizabeth. Et factū est ut au-
diuit salutationem marie elizabeth:
exultauit infans in utero ei⁹. Et reple-
ta est spiritu sancto elizabeth: et excla-
mauit voce magna ⁊ dixit. Benedicta
tu inter mulieres: ⁊ benedictus fructus
ventris tui. Et unde hoc michi: ut veni-
at mater dn̄i mei ad me? Ecce enim ut
facta est vox salutationis tue i aurib3
meis: exultauit in gaudio infans in
utero meo. Et beata que credidit: quoniā pficientur ea q̄ dicta sunt ei a dn̄o.
Et ait maria. Magnificat anima me-
a dn̄m: et exultauit spiritus meus in

holding stocks and tying up invested capital for relatively long periods. Gutenberg was not simply a great inventor and important book artist; we encounter in him an entrepreneur who recognized the advantages of manufacture, far-reaching labour division and the rationalization of production, and who was not afraid of taking risks.

The close of 1455 has been generally accepted hitherto as the probable date of completion for B42, since the Bibliothèque Nationale, Paris, copy contains entries by Heinrich Cremer, vicar of St Stephan's in Mainz, which show that he finished the work of rubricating, illuminating and binding both folio volumes during August 1456. The rubrication of 1282 folio pages, painting 170 initials, and then binding could hardly have taken less than several months – say half a year. But recently a new find has led to surprising conclusions.

A contemporary report

ENEA SILVIO PICCOLOMINI, then bishop of Siena and legate to the Emperor Frederick III, visited Frankfurt from 5 to 31 October 1454 to attend the Diet, which was attempting to engage the support of the German princes for a war against the Turks. Later, in a letter dated 12 March 1455 to the Spanish cardinal, Juan de Carvajal, he gave a report of an interesting encounter:

> Everything that has been written to me about that remarkable man whom I met in Frankfurt is quite true. I did not see complete Bibles but sections in fives of various books thereof, the text of which was absolutely free from error and printed with extreme elegance and accuracy. Your Eminence would have read them with no difficulty and without the aid of spectacles. I learned from many witnesses that 158 copies have been completed, although some asserted that the total was 180. While I am not quite sure about the actual number, I do not have any doubt, if people are to be believed, about the perfection of the volumes. If I had known what you wanted, I would undoubtedly have purchased a copy for you.
>
> Some of the sections have been sent here to the Emperor. I will try, if it can be arranged, to have a complete Bible that is for sale brought here, and I will buy it on your account. I fear, however, that this may not be feasible, both because of the distance involved and because they say there have been ready buyers for the volumes, even before they are finished.
>
> That your Eminence was most anxious to receive reliable information about this matter, I infer from your having indicated this by sending a courier who goes faster than Pegasus! But enough of this levity (Meuthen, 1982: 108, and Hoffmann, 1983: 473ff). [Latin–English translation by A. S. Osley.]

This passage in a letter discovered quite recently caused a sensation when it was reported in Gutenberg circles in 1982. Apparently Piccolomini, later to become Pope Pius II, had written earlier about this 'astonishing man' and is here replying to a further enquiry from Carvajal. There can be no doubt that he is writing about the completion of the *42-line Bible*, and he tells us a number of previously unknown facts. The most important of these concerns the completion date: his letter sets this back to the autumn of 1454. A second issue resolved is the size of the edition: Piccolomini writes that he had received conflicting reports, of 158 and of 180 copies. Perhaps this discrepancy can be related to the fact that the edition was increased shortly after printing had begun, so that some copies contain variant leaves printed from new typesetting, those affected being ff. 1 to 32r and 129 to 158v of the first volume as well as ff. 1 to 16 and f. 162r of the second volume (Corsten, 1979: 53). It is quite conceivable, then, that the original edition was to have been 158 copies, later increased to 180. The third matter relates to its success: the entire edition had sold out by the time printing was complete; and even the emperor and his entourage in Vienna, as well as a cardinal in Rome, were not slow to learn of this outcome.

To be sure we are not told the price asked for the Bible, and equally we may never discover whether that 'astonishing man' whom Piccolomini saw in Frankfurt was Gutenberg or Fust. Gutenberg may have been in Frankfurt hoping to meet Nicholas of Cues, who was presumably kept in the picture throughout the undertaking. On the other hand it could have been the more commercially-minded Fust who needed to visit Frankfurt to promote Bible printing.

The Helmasperger Legal Instrument

THE ACCOUNT IN PICCOLOMINI'S LETTER compels a thorough reconsideration of all problems connected with selling the Bible and the fortunes of the shared Humbrechthof printing works. The letter makes clear that both partners in the venture had been able to sell the Bibles for a good price and establish a market. But the printing works had been left in financial straits, and it came to dividing up the property between the business partners. Fust demanded his capital back at compound interest, as he was himself paying interest on the money he had borrowed to invest. He asserted that Gutenberg had misappropriated some of the funds provided for their joint venture, and used it for his own projects. Gutenberg offered to render an account.

Fust brought a lawsuit before the secular court of the archbishop.

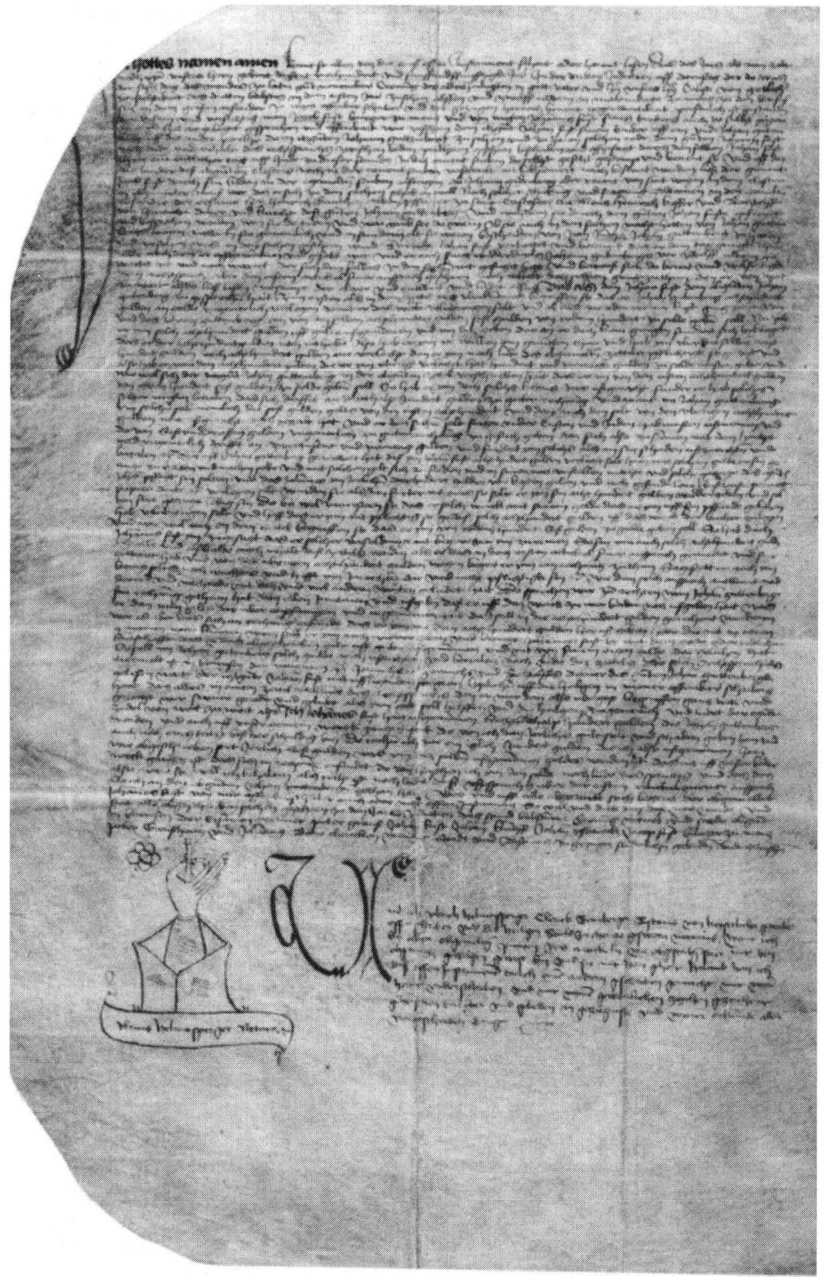

The Helmasperger Instrument. Reduced.

The fact that hearings were held in the refectory of the barefoot friars has occasionally led to the assumption that the matter came before an ecclesiastical court. In fact the negotiations took place under civil jurisdiction, presided over by the city treasurer and mayor. There is no documentary record of when proceedings were instituted, since the notary's instrument deals with a later stage of the case and was not drawn up until 6 November 1455. But it can be estimated that six months or so would have elapsed between these later proceedings and the original hearing in order to make the necessary enquiries, examine witnesses, and weigh up the claims and counterclaims of the two parties to the contract. The instrument deals with the background to the relevant transactions; Fust's plaint and Gutenberg's rejoinder, in which each man presents his somewhat different story; and the verbatim text of the court's verdict, stipulating an oath which Fust must make. Many questions arise while reading this document, but the really significant ones concern the actual subject matter referred to in the dispute. What distinguishes the 'work of the books' from 'his work', that is, Gutenberg's own work? The text of the Helmasperger Instrument which follows is a translation based on Ferdinand Geldner's accurate rendering into modern German, with only non-essentials abridged. The reader is invited to try to judge from this text, how and why Gutenberg may have diverted some of the money loaned to him.

Be it known to all those who examine, read or listen to this public document, that in the year 1455, in the third indiction, on Thursday the sixth of November, in the first year of the reign of Pope Calixtus III, between the hours of eleven and twelve at noon in the large refectory of the convent of the barefoot friars at Mainz in the presence of myself, a public notary, and of the witnesses hereinafter named, that honourable and prudent man Jakob Fust, citizen of Mainz, was present and on behalf of his brother also there present, Johann Fust, declared that, in the proceedings between his brother Johann Fust on one side and Johann Gutenberg on the other, a term was set for this day, hour and place for the said Johann Gutenberg to see and to hear Johann Fust take an oath pursuant to the wording and content of the judgment between the parties. In order that the friars of the said convent, who were still assembled in the hall, should not be disturbed, Jakob Fust did ask through his messenger whether Johann Gutenberg or anyone representing him were present in the convent ready to take cognizance of the matter. On this enquiry, the honourable Heinrich Günther, sometime minister of St Christoph's, Heinrich Keffer and Bechtolff von Hanau, servants of Johann Gutenberg, entered the refectory. And when they had been asked by Johann Fust about what they were doing there, and why they were come and whether they had been authorized by Johann Gutenberg, they answered jointly and severally they had been sent by their master Johann Gutenberg, to hear and to see what should happen in this matter. Thereupon Johann Fust declared that he wanted to abide by the day appointed, and that since he had been waiting until twelve o'clock, and was still waiting, for his opponent Johann Gutenberg who, however, had not appeared in person, he announced himself ready to proceed according to the judgment passed upon the first article of his claim. He thereupon caused the verdict together with his plaint and [Gutenberg's] answer to be read out word for word as follows:

And then Johann Fust affirmed to the above-named Johann Gutenberg: firstly, that he, in accordance with their written agreement, had in good faith advanced to Johann Gutenberg 800 gold gulden with which he was to finish the work – and whether it would cost more or less was of no concern to him [Fust] – and that Johann Gutenberg was to pay six per cent interest for this money. Now he [Fust] borrowed the 800 gulden for him against interest and gave it to him, but he was not satisfied, and complained that he did not yet have [all of] the 800 gulden, or enough therewith. So [Fust], wishing to oblige him anyway, borrowed for him over and above the said 800 gulden, secondly, 800 gulden more than he was obliged to under the above-mentioned contract; and he therefore had needed to pay out a further 140 gulden in interest on this additional 800 gulden he had borrowed. And although the said Gutenberg was contractually obliged to pay him interest at six per cent on the first 800 gulden, yet he did not pay it in any year, and he [Fust] had to pay it himself to the amount of at least 250 gulden.

And since Johann Gutenberg has never settled for or paid to him such interest, namely the six per cent for the first 800 gulden and then also the interest for the other 800 gulden, which interest he [Fust] had to raise among Christians and Jews, and to pay about 36 gulden for in compound interest conservatively estimated, which, together with the principal and interest on the main debts, amounts to not less than 2020 gulden, and he calls upon Gutenberg to make good and reimburse him this sum without deduction, etc.

Whereupon Johann Gutenberg answered, that Johann Fust was to have advanced him 800 gulden so that with this money he [Gutenberg] should fashion and make his equipment, and with such money he was to be satisfied and to use it for his own gain, and that this equipment was to be the said Johann's security, and that this Johann [Fust] was to give him each year 300 gulden for expenses and also supply workmen's wages, rent, vellum, paper and [printing] ink, etc.

Should they no longer be in agreement, he [Gutenberg] was to repay him his 800 gulden and the lien on his equipment was to be released. It being well understood that he should finish this work [i.e. making equipment] with his [Fust's] money which he had lent him against security, and hopes that he was under no obligation to him to apply the said [first] 800 gulden to the work of the books. And although according to the written contract he was to pay six per cent interest, Johann Fust had told him that he would not insist on this interest. Moreover he had not received the [first] 800 gulden immediately and in full according to agreement, as he [Fust] had announced and declared in the first article of his claim; and with regard to the remaining 800 gulden he [Gutenberg] was desirous to render an account to him. And therefore he concedes to Fust [on the second 800 gulden] no interest or compound interest, and trusts that he is not obliged thereto by law, etc.

Since then this plaint, rejoinder, claim and counterclaim have been set forth in these and many other words, we now pronounce judgment as follows:

When Johann Gutenberg has submitted an account of all receipts and expenditures which he has incurred on the work to their common profit, any money which he has received and taken in over and above this shall go to the account of the [first] 800 gulden. But should it appear from the figures that he [Fust] had given him more than 800 gulden not devoted to their common profit, he [Gutenberg] shall return to him [this surplus] also. And if Johann Fust proves by oath or reputable witness, that he raised the above-mentioned sum on interest and did not advance it from his own money, then shall Johann Gutenberg make good and pay him this interest as well according to the wording of the contract.

When this judgment as reported here had been read out in the presence of the above-named gentlemen, Heinrich etc., Heinrich and Bechtolff, servants of the said Johann Gutenberg, the said Johann Fust swore, confirmed and vowed personally, with his fingers laid on the saints' [relics] in my, the public notary's, hand, that everything contained in a document required by the court, which he then handed to me, was entirely true and concordant, so help him God and the saints. The said document reads word for word as follows:

I, Johann Fust, have borrowed 1550 gulden, which were partly given to Johann Gutenberg and partly devoted to our common work, for which sum I have paid yearly interest and compound interest and still owe a part. For each 100 gulden which I so borrowed, as written above, I reckon 6 gulden interest annually. For what he has received of the said borrowed money that has not been expended on our common work, as revealed by the account, I demand of him the interest according to the terms of the judgment. And that all this is true, I am willing to affirm, as is legal, according to the terms of the decision on the first article of my claim which I have made against the said Johann Gutenberg.

Another memorandum by the notary Helmasperger is annexed to this text:

Of all the above-mentioned matters Johann Fust has required of me, the public scribe [notary], one or more copies, as many as he may need. And all the matters written down took place on the said date in the presence of the honourable men Peter Granss, Johann Kist, Johann Kumoff, Johann Yseneck, Jakob Fust, citizens of Mainz, Peter Gernsheim and Johann Bonne, clerics of the city and diocese of Mainz, as witnesses especially requested and summoned (Schorbach, 1900: 195ff, doc. XIX and Geldner, 1972a: 92ff).

What was the 'work of the books'?

IN THE MIDDLE AGES it was considered dishonourable to loan money at interest. But if the lender was able to show that he had needed to borrow the money in question himself at an equivalent rate of interest, then he had nothing to be ashamed of. This is exactly what Fust declared on oath in the dining hall of the Franciscan convent in Mainz, where the secular court had convened. Everything which he chose to put forward concerned his money. He even went so far as to distance himself from shared responsibility: 'whether it would cost more or less (to produce the tools and equipment and set up the printing works) was of no concern to him'. He was only the money-broker; perhaps we may be able to exonerate him from any active participation in the invention. A small defect in Fust's methods is revealed by his stating in complaint that Gutenberg had received 800 gulden from him on each occasion, while under oath he casually changes this to admit that he loaned only 1550 gulden. He also does his best to ignore the different character of these sums advanced to Gutenberg. The initial 800 gulden constituted a loan to Gutenberg, who pledged for it the equipment (*geczuge*) it enabled him to make. The second 800 gulden represented an operating investment for their 'common work'. But the central point at issue in the plaint, that some of this business outlay for the 'common work' or 'work of the books' was used for quite a different purpose by Gutenberg, is something which the inventor does not attempt to refute (Blum, 1954, and Kapr, 1981: 126ff).

Gutenberg explicitly protests in his rejoinder that he was not obliged to use the first 800 gulden for the 'work of the books'. It is generally assumed that the 'work of the books' refers to the Bible only, although Gutenberg was just as interested as Fust in completing the B42. It is however my view that, according to the clearly distinguishable phraseology of the Helmasperger Instrument, the 'work of the books', 'work to their common profit' and the 'common work' should all be taken to mean the same thing. Can one just take it for granted of devout men, that they would describe the Bible as a work for their common profit? Even if applied not to the Bible itself, but to its production, it still strikes me as an unwarranted profanity, as an improper expression for printing the Holy Scriptures. Still less would the word 'work' have been understood at that time to mean book; by substituting 'the book of books' for 'the work of the books' it is true that the expected sense emerges, but a similar exchange of synonyms from 'work to their common profit' back into 'book to their common profit' makes a nonsense of this interpretation. I accept though, that the description 'book of books' for the Bible, leads by analogy to the conclusion: that the 'work of the books' could have referred to the *42-line Bible*, if in fact it was being printed at that time.

Changes of meaning can be read into many words, which were understood quite differently during the Middle Ages from today. Some words have had an assortment of meanings. In medieval usage, '*Werk*' or 'works' (frequently used as a plural in English, and in contrast to mere labour or toil) could be used in any of the following senses:

(a) A planned undertaking, usually used for a grand-scale conception.

(b) Making and doing; for example, the labour on a large planned enterprise.
(c) That which was produced; that is, the results of creative activity.
(d) The establishment where an activity took place, for example workshops or manufacturing sites.
(e) Gradually *Werk* came to stand also for book or *opus*, but this meaning probably only became widespread later on (Grimm, 1852– : 14, I, ii: 196ff).

To resolve the question of what the 'work of the books' may actually have been, it is necessary to test out all five of these possible meanings to find in which sense the word 'work' is being used wherever it appears. Gutenberg said in his rejoinder that it was '... well understood that he should finish this work [i.e. making the tools or equipment] with his [Fust's] money which he had lent him against security, and hopes that he was under no obligation to him to apply the said [first] 800 gulden to the work of the books'. The first use of the word 'work' here quite clearly refers to making and doing something as part of a large planned enterprise in concrete terms, such as the production of punches, matrices, types and other equipment to be used for printing. All this equipment will naturally be needed when it comes to that which is to be produced, that is to say for the planned book or for printing books in general. It would therefore be impossible for Gutenberg to have meant '... that he hopes that he was under no obligation to him to apply the said [first] 800 gulden' for producing printed books. But a new sense altogether is revealed if we allow the word 'work' in 'work of the books' to mean the workshop or manufacturing site or printing works. And surely this is precisely what the 'common work' or 'work to their common profit' was: a workshop for the production of books, a printing works. Since the name of 'printing works' had not yet been given to a manufacturing workshop of this particular kind, and since this works also housed a composing room and typefoundry as well as the printing room, so for the inventor, who was at last ready to put his revolutionary ideas into practice on a large scale in great books – through the Bible, and with a psalter or possibly a missal to follow – the description 'work of the books' would have seemed perfectly fitting. Gutenberg must have thought it sensible that the little *Donatuses*, indulgences and calendars should be produced alongside other small-scale printing, that is to say in the works at the Gutenberghof, so as not to interrupt the working schedule for the Bible at the Humbrechthof. For Fust, on the other hand, all that mattered was the shared property, and for him the 'work of the books' meant the 'works for their joint profit', their 'common works'. The two parties to the contract differed about the works at the Humbrechthof and the works in the Gutenberghof, in that Gutenberg still directed the latter, in which Fust had no say at all.

Fust was presumably basically opposed to the continued existence of the original printing house. It probably ran counter to his direct interests for Gutenberg to be working on both the psalter-types, and maybe even printing the *Mainz Psalter*, before he had received back his loan or his business share. Naturally Fust must have been angry that part of his capital – in other words part of the second 800 gulden – was not being used for their joint enterprise, but that Gutenberg had diverted this capital for another purpose, for new work which he had begun at the first printing works in the Gutenberghof. These days this would be called embezzlement. In reality Fust's accusation – that the second 800 gulden clearly represented a share in the business – had not been refuted by Gutenberg, who merely observed that he was not obliged to use the first 800 gulden in its entirety for the 'work of the books', or their common enterprise (Geldner, 1972a: 117, and Blum, 1954: 69ff). He went out of his way to avoid giving a straight answer to this second part of the plaint. Therefore the court required him to render a written account of all his receipts and expenditures in connection with the work to their common profit. If this statement proved that any of the money received had not been used for the common profit, then it should be returned. Unfortunately this important balance-sheet has not survived.

Most historians have accepted that Fust swindled the inventor and then brought Gutenberg's work to a fruitful conclusion. A great deal of thought has been expended over what made Fust decide to bring his action at that particular time. We know that, having made his decision, he sued for the following items:

1.	First capital advance	=	800 gulden
2.	Six per cent interest on same	=	250 gulden
3.	Second capital advance	=	800 gulden
4.	Interest on the foregoing	=	140 gulden
5.	Compound interest	=	36 gulden
	Grand total of the debt		2026 gulden (Schorbach, 1900: 203).

But all control calculations based on this data, including those that narrow down the dates between which the loans were made – while highlighting a few discrepancies – take us not a single step forward with the central question. It has hitherto been assumed that Fust waited before bringing his action until the printing of the Bible had been completed, but it had not yet been sold. This would have been just the moment when Gutenberg had all his capital tied up in the venture, and consequently could not satisfy the demands of his creditors. Certainly such behaviour on Fust's part was incompatible with Christian moral teaching; but then he was a typical representative of the new generation of early capitalist entrepreneurs then growing up in the lap of the established feudal order, and would have taken his cue from other successful merchants and financiers of the aspiring middle classes. An all too obvious villainy would not have been upheld by the court. Neither could the judges be expected to recognize the historical import of the invention. They judged in accordance with the legal norms of their age. It is also likely that in a relatively small town, word got about that Gutenberg was running two printing works, and that he was involved in other matters besides printing bibles, and that he needed to withdraw capital or materials for these purposes from the works at the Humbrechthof. Thus the inventor's reputation was not exactly spotless. Some part at least of Fust's plaint had substance behind it. But since the recent discovery of Piccolomini's letter to Cardinal Carvajal, it has become necessary for these problems to be thoroughly re-examined.

It seems indisputable that Gutenberg lost the action Fust brought against him. According to the contract for the first loan of 800 gulden, Fust would have received the pledged equipment, the workshop, the presses, the B42-types in addition to the large and small psalter-types, and equally any printing that may well have already begun on the *Mainz Psalter*, of which we have still to speak (Thiel, 1939: 62ff, and Geldner, 1972a: 120). Within the meaning of the other contract for the second 800 gulden, provided as a business investment for their common advantage, the court ought to have decided that both partners should receive an equal share from printing the Bible, whether as income from copies already sold or as printed sheets in quinternions ready for binding. Gutenberg's calculations of expenditure and income were presumably decisive in determining how many unsold copies went to Fust to satisfy his claims and as his share in the profits, and how many Gutenberg should receive for contributing his inventive genius to the success of the venture. I am absolutely convinced that Gutenberg did not come out of this dispute empty-handed.

A hypothetical balance-sheet for the 42-line Bible

BEFORE EMBARKING ON THIS THEME, it is worth mentioning relative monetary values in the Rhineland at about 1450. At the same time, comparative rates are given for other coinages sometimes referred to in the text, although it should be noted in passing, that the ratio between gold and silver coins was constantly shifting.

1 Rhenish gold gulden	= 24 schillings, or
1 Rhenish gold gulden	= 1 silver pound + 4 schillings, or
1 Rhenish gold gulden	= 26 albi = 12 old turnosgroschen
1 silver pound	= 20 schillings = 240 heller, or
1 silver pound	= 1 pound heller = 1 denar (Strasbourg)
1 schilling	= 12 heller = 6 pfennigs, or
1 schilling	= 1 halfturnose

Four old hellers were usually exchanged for three newly minted ones. A Bohemian groschen was worth three times as much as an ordinary one because of its high silver content. To convey the purchasing power of the gulden the relevant literature has constant recourse to shopping basket comparisons: an ox ready for slaughter would fetch 6 to 8 gulden in Mainz, a stone-built mansion 80 to 100 gulden. A master craftsman earned between 20 and 30 gulden a year. A hen or ten eggs cost a pfennig, and beef 2 pfennigs a pound.

In nearly all descriptions, Gutenberg is portrayed as the inventor who brought ideas, resolve and organizational talent to the common undertaking, while Fust is merely cited as the provider of capital (Ruppel, 1967: 145). Peter Schöffer's comment – as reported by Abbot Johann Trithemius in his *Annales Hirsaugienses* of 1515 – that the printing of the Bible had already cost 4000 gulden by the time the first three quinternions had been completed (Corsten, 1979: 57) induced me to attempt a fresh costing. It is of course possible that Peter Schöffer, when talking to Trithemius some 30 years before the latter's book went to press, thus in about 1485, concerning events still further distant in time, may have been trying to calculate the total cost of developing the invention since its beginnings at Strasbourg in about 1436. Or was he simply exaggerating in order to show Fust's financial help in the best light?

Although Otto Hupp, Paul Schwenke, Gottfried Zedler, Aloys Ruppel and most recently Severin Corsten, have all pondered the expenditure entailed, a great deal remains unclear (Corsten, 1979: 66). While Paul Schwenke unquestionably overestimates the cost of paper, Severin Corsten probably errs on the low side. I also have to part company with him when he concludes that four usable double-page sheets could be obtained from a single calfskin, since he bases this on modern experience, whereas the animals of that period were considerably smaller. Furthermore, no provision is made in any of the above-mentioned estimates for new presses, for new typefounder's hand-moulds, or for the handwritten Bible that would unquestionably have been required, not to serve as manuscript alone but as printing exemplar as well: that it is to say, a volume to be disbound into individual sheets which could then be followed page for page, line for line, practically letter for letter, so that different compositors could set simultaneously while maintaining extent and continuity (Todd, 1982).

Though Corsten has argued that there were only four presses (Corsten, 1979), I remain in favour of six presses – as has been generally held hitherto – on the strength of the clear stylistic evidence that six compositors were at work. I would like to base the use of the more expensive but efficient iron screw on the document of 4 July 1444 relating to the appearance of Procopius Waldvogel in Avignon, which speaks of a steel screw that could probably only have come from the first Strasbourg press from whence it had vanished shortly after Andreas Dritzehn's death. Accordingly, the first press which Saspach built in 1438 may already have had a steel (iron) screw.

A note about pricing the paper: it is not acceptable to draw direct comparisons between the prices for the B42 paper and that for the *Catholicon*. The entire paper stock for the *42-line Bible* had to be imported from Italy, most likely from Turin, whereas paper of German manufacture was available for use in the *Catholicon* and the *36-line Bible*. Transporting the paper over the Alps alone must have added very significantly to its cost. So I am unable to agree with Severin Corsten that the price of paper for the Bible would have been as low as 300 gulden.

Leonhard Hoffmann, who has researched the calculation of wages, concludes that, when set against customary rates for comparable work, not more than 13 to 16 persons could have been engaged on the Bible (Hoffmann, 1983: 529). In view of the detection of the hands of six different compositors, it follows that twice that number of pressmen would need to be paired with them, not counting the typefounders and other assistants required. Maybe a solution to this discrepancy was found in some kind of agreement for an employee to work for a reduced wage in return for a copy of the printed Bible.

1.	Production of 6 hand-presses, probably with iron screws, at 40 gulden each	=	240 gulden
2.	Costs for typecases and frames, workshop furniture and fittings	=	60 gulden
3.	Rent for the Humbrechthof for 3 years	=	30 gulden
4.	Heating for living quarters, workshop and stoves for metal casting for 3 years	=	20 gulden

5.	Production of 3 typefounder's hand-moulds at 20 gulden each	=	60 gulden
6.	Cost of steel, copper, lead and antimony	=	100 gulden
7.	Cost of manufacturing ink	=	30 gulden
8.	Paper for 150 copies	=	400 gulden
9.	Vellum for 30 copies	=	300 gulden
10.	Wages for between 12 and 20 employees over 30 months including bed and board	=	800 gulden
11.	A handwritten Bible of high quality as manuscript and exemplar	=	80 gulden
	Total of probable expenditure		2120 gulden

But we know from the Helmasperger Instrument that the most Fust can have invested was 1600 gulden. So where did the other 500 gulden come from? Is it conceivable that Gutenberg had this sort of money at his disposal? Could it have been that, as in Strasbourg, the inventor produced and sold holy mirrors for the Aachen pilgrimage, which took place in 1447, in order to raise such a large sum? Or possibly Heinrich Eggestein or others, perhaps even Heinrich Keffer and Bechtolff von Hanau, may by then have had certain savings to invest in the new printing office?

A hypothetical estimate of income is quite as difficult as calculating the expenditure. A handwritten and illuminated Bible on vellum is supposed to have cost 60 gulden in Strasbourg. In another case, 100 gulden was paid for a manuscript Bible. Paul Schwenke imagined that a paper copy of B42 in loose sheets would cost 34 gulden and a copy on vellum 42 gulden. The first of these valuations is probably too generous, and the second too low (Ruppel, 1967: 146). Throughout the entire incunabula period there was a steady price ratio of 1:3 between copies on paper and on vellum. In any event, prices would naturally have been open to negotiation. The paper copy of a *Catholicon* preserved at Gotha contains an entry recording that 27 gulden was paid for it. However, a rubricated and bound paper copy of the selfsame *Catholicon* was purchased by the cathedral of Bamberg for 47 gulden and a pound. The abbey of St Nikola near Passau had to pay 48 gulden for a copy on vellum, but the Carmelite monastery in Bamberg acquired its paper copy of the *Catholicon* for a mere 16 gulden (Geldner, 1978: 170ff). The cost of having such a volume rubricated may be reckoned at between 6 and 10 gulden according to its elaborateness, with a full binding in leather costing about the same or perhaps slightly more. On the assumption that the offer of a relatively large number of copies of the

Bible within the Mainz catchment area, and Gutenberg's pressing need to recover his capital, may have driven prices downwards, I would propose the following minimum prices for the B42 in printed sheets:

30 vellum copies @ 50 gulden	=	1500 gulden
150 paper copies @ 20 gulden	=	3000 gulden
yielding a total of	=	4500 gulden

From this common income it should have been possible to repay Johann Fust's demand without more ado, for Gutenberg to have kept control of the works at the Humbrechthof and still have had an appreciable working capital at his disposal. Where is the hidden error in this hypothetical calculation of returns?

First, it is possible that each time Gutenberg ran short of cash he pledged his employees a printed copy of the Bible on paper. The acceptance of payment in this form brought with it an obligation to maintain secrecy, particularly where specialized skills were involved. This practice could easily account for a shortfall of 20 paper copies for sale and a consequent reduction of income by about 400 gulden. Maybe there were other creditors as well – Heinrich Eggestein, Heinrich Keffer and Bechtolff von Hanau have been mentioned as potential ones – who took an agreed number of bibles as their share in the profits.

Second, hypothetical estimates of income rest on the basis of what Piccolomini's letter has to say about the number of copies and their sale. But if one takes instead of his last-mentioned edition of 180 copies, the earlier report he had heard of only 158 copies, then once again the proceeds shrink by some 500 gulden (see Piccolomini's text on p. 170). Yet even with his receipts down to 3500 or 3000 gulden the inventor should still have been able to pay off his debts without undue difficulty.

Third, the passage in the letter of Enea Silvio Piccolomini reports that the entire edition of the Bible had been sold immediately on completion. Perhaps his sources had not informed him with total accuracy that these folded sheets were only being delivered or bound to the orders of subscribers, who had not yet paid for their purchase. The morality of settling bills in the fifteenth century was terribly lax, and creditors were made to wait for payment for years on end. Moreover, the reform monasteries of the Benedictines, Franciscans, and Augustinians had been exhorted by their hierarchies to possess and to study a well-edited Bible, without settling how this was to be funded. Only if it is accepted that by the date the lawsuit was heard, on 6 November 1455, most copies of B42 had still to be paid for, does it become apparent why Gutenberg was unable to pay his debts. It is quite clear that for lack of capital Gutenberg was unable to meet his liabilities and therefore had to surrender the joint printing works at the Humbrechthof to Fust.

Ambitious but abandoned plans

A BOOK IS ONLY COMPLETE after binding, and in the Middle Ages a fine book would also have called for rubrication and illumination. Evidently it would have been part of the inventor's eventual planning that all those operations which fell within the compass of the 'works of the books' should be carried through according to commission, as was normal practice in monastic scriptoria. He sought to apply the advantages of a manufacturing business, with its higher rate of output and economically favourable series production, to these finishing stages of the book, but was prevented from putting such plans into practice through the lawsuit brought by Fust and the end of their partnership.

There are three distinct aspects of this work to discuss: first, rubrication (inserting non-illustrative initials, paragraph marks, and upright red strokes to capitals which mark sentence openings, as well as writing in chapter titles and running headlines); second, illumination (decorative and figurative marginal illustration and initials); and third, sewing the sections and binding them into leather-covered and decorated wooden boards. These three successive operations would have occupied about six to nine months. The final job at the printing office was to gather the single-folded printed sheets into sections (quinternions) and collate or check them. So that the work of the rubricator should be free from mistakes, Gutenberg took the trouble to print the eight-page guide mentioned earlier, a *tabula rubricarum*, which was issued with each set of the folded sheets, and of which two copies have been preserved (Schmidt, 1979).

There is a most interesting hypothesis which concerns the illumination of the *Gutenberg Bible*. Hellmut Lehmann-Haupt has drawn attention to a series of correspondences between border illustrations in one copy of B42 and those in a manuscript known as the *Giant Bible of Mainz*, which was produced in Mainz at roughly the same time as B42 was being printed there. The coloured illustrations in both these books exhibit a further distinct resemblance to drawings by a Middle Rhenish artist, the so-called 'Master of the Playing Cards'. A collaboration between the 'Master of the Giant Bible of Mainz' and Gutenberg is conceivable, and from here Lehmann-Haupt ventures to develop the thesis that Gutenberg may have been occupied with some mechanical means for the multiplication of border illustrations (Lehmann-Haupt, 1962: 360ff, and König, 1979: 71ff, 95ff). The outlines of these drawings might have been printed in an early copper engraving technique, and while the print was still moist it could have been transferred face down to the margins of the printed Bible page by rubbing from the back. Working to these pre-printed outlines, the miniaturist could then have made his painting in egg tempera. The earliest dated copper engraving only goes back to the year 1446, and this accordingly makes it feasible for Gutenberg to have been involved with the invention of intaglio printing as well. Goldsmiths had been familiar with the techniques of engraving on metal from a far earlier date, but only when practised as a means of permanently incising drawn decoration onto weapons and suchlike (Mayer, 1983: 104). Disagreement is possible over the precise technique adopted by Gutenberg, but its guiding principle was close to that of typography. Hand-burnished proofing would enable him to combine and recombine on the page an assortment of stock pictorial motifs: tendril scrollwork, roses, blossoms, bears, lions, birds, wildmen and so forth. Lehmann-Haupt suggests that a kind of model book with patterns of this sort was being drawn up to Gutenberg's commission, and that after the loss of the court action, the master draughtsman who had been engaged on this work converted it on his own initiative into a motif book for playing cards, and completed it as a volume of 60 leaves.

It so happens that in these Bible illuminations – unlike handwritten

Comparison of a subject from the Master of the Playing Cards with miniatures from B42.
Left: the climbing bear in the engraved playing cards.
Centre: the corresponding miniature in the Giant Bible of Mainz.
Right: the same motif as a miniature in the B42 in the Scheide Collection.

Comparison of a subject from the Master of the Playing Cards with miniatures from B42.
Left: bird and snake in the engraved playing cards.
Right: the same motif as a miniature in the B42 in the Scheide Collection.

bibles of that time or earlier – no use is made of religious motifs. These deer, bears, birds and lions are much closer to playing-card subjects, and the wildman can even be mistaken for the heathen Wotan. One explanation may be that these motifs reflect courtly fashion, where hunting subjects were all the rage; another argument may be that only thematic material that was distanced from the biblical text could be put through endless variations in this way. Similarly, Gutenberg may also have planned to sell his Bibles, or some of them at least, as bound books. The copy that was rubricated, illuminated and bound by Heinrich Cremer may provide one piece of evidence for this. But even more remarkable is the fact that the master bookbinder Johann Fogel – famous as the 'Binder with the Lute-player and the Knots' because of his use of these two motifs on his blind-stamped bindings – was enrolled at Erfurt University from 1455 as 'Johannes Voghel de Francfordia'. He was no student, but rather attached to the university as its bookbinder, and as such he bound a number of *Gutenberg Bibles*. In the case of the Eton College B42, this attribution is cast iron, for it carries his name, stamped in blind, on the covers. The vellum copy bound in four volumes at Leipzig University, the copy in the Hessische Landesbibliothek Fulda, and the one belonging to the Scheide Collection, now housed at Princeton University, all use those stamps of the lute-player and the knots characteristic of Fogel. The Scheide Bible is of course the copy containing the illustrations which have just been identified with the Master of the Playing Cards (Mazal, 1979: 157; Corsten, 1979: 56; Knaus, 1956: 315). This brings to four those bindings which may be firmly or strongly attributed to Fogel, and in the nature of things there may have been more that have since been destroyed. How can Fogel have come by these commissions? Could it be that he was a bookseller as well as a bookbinder, who had acquired the unbound copies in Mainz and then bound them in Erfurt for resale? It is a striking coincidence that he should have appeared in Erfurt so soon after the printing of B42 had been completed, and Gutenberg had severed his connection with the former partnership printing works following his legal dispute with Fust. At the very least Fogel appears to have been well-informed about developments in Mainz, and may even have been a close collaborator of Gutenberg; or perhaps he should be counted as one of the still unidentified investors whose existence the hypothetical calculation of production costs leads us to surmise.

There are about ten *Gutenberg Bibles* left in the world in their original bindings, of which four are by Fogel; three or four were bound in Mainz itself, one in Lübeck, and the Huntington Library example was bound by Johann Wetherhan, a bookbinder active at Leipzig University from 1446 onwards. All these surviving original bindings have wooden boards covered in blind-stamped leather. In the mid-fifteenth century it was the practice to bind in cowhide, calf or pigskin, and front and back boards were decorated in relief or stamped with brass dies, rolls and panel stamps. The flexible leather spine was attached direct to the back of the book, and divided into compartments by bands covering the raised cords onto which the sections were sewn. Brass fittings protected the corners, and clasps at the fore-edge kept out dust and moisture.

Gutenberg definitely had far-reaching plans. It may have been his own intention – for the illumination and binding of the printed sheets to be executed by means of series manufacture – that resulted in a wait-and-see policy towards selling, which in turn brought about the cash-flow crisis of 1455. His foremost objective until that time was probably still the production of the standard missal which Nicholas of Cues had advocated as an essential part of his ecclesiastical reforms. Now, however, the typographic resources previously lacking for this work had been assembled, the technology perfected, and a team of craftsmen well rehearsed. The larger sizes of type were ready to be tested out on a psalter. But as a result of legal action everything lay in ruins.

CHAPTER EIGHT

Unequal competition

Justice or injustice

ON THE PROCEEDINGS as set forth in the Helmasperger Instrument the point at issue is: who was in the right? The fifteenth century, which witnessed the gradual emergence of the middle classes in Germany as elsewhere, was a time of uncertainty for the legal system, particularly in the area of credit transactions. Scholasticism upheld the view that money was infertile and that accordingly no interest could be imposed on a loan. There were a number of ways around this difficulty, including life annuities or pension contracts, whereby privileged citizens could secure an income for life by means of a capital deposit. We know that Gutenberg was able to count on standing annuities from the city of Mainz up to 1448 and from Strasbourg until 1453. Another exception was sanctioned under canon law, provided a creditor could furnish proof that he himself had to pay interest on money that he had loaned out. This is exactly what Fust was obliged to state on oath before the court in the convent of the barefoot friars, since any such legal transaction had to be put to the test to establish whether it was usurious in character.

As social change gathered momentum, above all in the Italian cities, economic conditions called for access to greater capital sums with growing frequency. Although the Church maintained its stand against usury on principle, it increasingly tolerated the circumvention of its own rules. Since the beginning of the fifteenth century, the Franciscans in Italy had set up pawnbroker's shops for granting loans to the needy. It came about in Germany, too, that religious institutions swelled the funds flowing into their prebends and sinecures by credit operations and interest payments. It will be remembered in this connection that Gutenberg personally took out a loan of 80 denars on 17 November 1442 from the St Thomas Chapter in Strasbourg. As early as 1425, Pope Martin IV had pronounced the purchase of annuities not to be usurious if they were issued by rulers, cities, or monasteries, or guaranteed on landed property. Legal conceptions framed in Rome had become generally accepted in Germany by the mid-century, and we heard earlier how Mainz's clerical creditors were able to go so far as to procure the excommunication of that insolvent city in 1448. This measure, taken by the Church in a legal matter that did not exactly involve Christian issues, was incomprehensible to ordinary people; it fuelled antagonisms and lent support to the unrest which prefigured the Reformation.

It is idle to conclude with hindsight that Gutenberg was totally in the right, and that Johann Fust, as a self-seeking financier, was somehow historically offside – although it was not for want of trying that the descendants of Johann Fust and Peter Schöffer failed to wangle the inventor's laurels for their forefathers. Gutenberg lived at a time of change, and his sense of right and wrong was based to some extent on the German or old canonical law, while on the other hand he accepted the advantages of the new Roman law. The disparity between them determined Gutenberg's conduct. His aims and ideals may, however, have shocked current social standards as being egocentric and only explicable by the desire for gain.

The Cyprus Indulgences

IN THE EFFORT TO SEE GUTENBERG above all as the Bible-printer of genius, only passing reference is usually made to his also having printed papal indulgences in 1454 and 1455, with printed years of issuance, the first of which represents the earliest piece of western typography with an exact date. Moreover, these indulgences provide the key to understanding various problems concerning early Mainz typography and the proof that two printing works were operating there concurrently (Kapr, 1968).

The Turks captured the city of Constantinople on 29 May 1453. A diet was convened in Regensburg at the end of April 1454 to discuss a campaign against the Turks. Because of its inconclusive outcome, a second assembly on the same theme was held that autumn in Frankfurt, and Enea Silvio Piccolomini, in the service of pope and emperor, energetically drummed up support for the war. At the same time the zealot Giovanni di Capistrano preached in the Römerberg or town hall square and in the cathedral churchyard to recruit troops for this crusade against the Turks. Capistrano is known to have been present from 1 October to 2 November 1454, which prompts the conclusion that the first *Indulgences for the aid of the kingdom of Cyprus* – of which the earliest copy to have survived is hand-dated 21 October – may have been on sale during the wandering preacher's mass oratory. And it is equally probable that when Enea Silvio visited Frankfurt he saw not only the Bible-printing of that 'astonishing man', but copies of printed indulgences as well.

What were the circumstances surrounding such letters of indulgence? Since the earliest Middle Ages it has been normal to make temporal atonement for certain ecclesiastically imposed penalties through good works, almsgiving, fasting, prayer, pilgrimage or the payment of sums of money. Later the legislation of the Church was extended to allow its representatives to remit divine punishment for specified sins against appropriate penance. During the time of the crusades it become customary for all participants in a crusade to receive plenary indulgence (full remission of their sins). From the thirteenth century onwards, receipts were written out for donations purchasing entitlement to the remission of sins, which included a charge for the document itself. The holder of such a certificate could go on to a confessor, present it and make a confession, whereupon remission would be officially pronounced. These letters of indulgence (*litterae indulgentiales*) gave the source or occasion for the issue of an indulgence and its standard wording; with spaces for the purchaser's name, date of transaction, and sometimes the signature of the 'pardoner' or seller of indulgences, to be entered. This last signature did not need to appear if the seal of the issuing authority was affixed to signify prior payment had been made for the document.

It would be unhistorical to try to impose our modern moral verdict on the sale of indulgences on the people of the fifteenth century. The fierce attacks by Wyclif, Hus, Luther and other reformers on indulgences held it against the Catholic Church that it conferred on itself the power of the keys, and thereby the judgment over sins and with it the remission of sins. In its claims to take these decisions, the Church was appropriating the role of purgatory, whose cleansing fires existed to afford penance for temporal sin.

In reality, of course, indulgences constituted a special tax for the Church to apply in particular contingencies. In the present case, the kingdom of Cyprus had sent an appeal in 1450 for papal aid in defending the island against a threatened Turkish invasion. On 12 August 1451, Pope Nicholas V granted the king of Cyprus, John II of Lusignan, a plenary indulgence for three years, to run from 1 May 1452 to 30 April 1455. The king of Cyprus commissioned the Cypriot councillor Paulinus Zappe or Chappe with the implementation of the indulgence, with two deputies, Giovanni de Castro Coronato and Alberto de Albe Lapide, to assist him (Beyer, 1937: 43ff). These in turn delegated the work to a large number of agents, of whom at least eight are known by name. A less well-known fact is that fully half of the money collected flowed into the archbishop's coffers and that one of the two deputies, de

Castro, embezzled 14,000 gulden (which would have been the proceeds from the sale of about 3000 indulgences) and consequently ended up in Erfurt gaol. It seems likely that only a tiny proportion of this income ever reached the hands of the Cypriot king, where the money should have paid for mercenaries to protect against the Turks (Zedler, 1913: 13).

As early as 2 May 1452 the papal legate Nicholas of Cues had authorized the prior of St Jakob's in Mainz to have 2000 hand-written(?) indulgences ready for sale to the citizens of Frankfurt by the end of the month (Mori, 1928: 6). (There have even been conjectures that these 2000 letters of indulgence may have been printed by Gutenberg using the DK-type. But unfortunately no single copy of any kind has survived; Kapr, 1982: 161.) For the printed *Indulgences of 1454 and 1455*, there are sound reasons for believing that the editions were very much higher than this. For a start the distribution area was not restricted to a designated town, but covered both extensive archdioceses of Mainz and Cologne at least. Another difference was in the period over which they could be sold, which at seven months was seven times longer than those from St Jakob. Finally, the popular enthusiasm to contribute to a war against the Turks would have increased considerably since the loss of Constantinople.

What is striking about the *Indulgences for Cyprus* is that they have the same text, but exist in two variant settings which are produced in totally independent typefaces. Some interpreters would explain this as a consequence of the extremely high edition. But the essence of Gutenberg's typography is that multiple matrices can be struck from the same punch, and then huge quantities of types cast from each matrix. For both these variants it is not simply a question of the texts having been set up separately, but of having to cast supplies of the two distinct text types. And both these typeface designs were specially cut for these indulgences (Ruppel, 1967: 154).

One differentiates between the *30-line* and the *31-line Indulgence* on the usual ground of the number of lines of type made by each setting of the standard text. But there is a whole series of further characteristic differences. Although both offer the same text, the *31-line Indulgence* opens with the initial 'V', and the other one with the initial 'U', because in the Middle Ages it was permissible to write or set interchangeably the same Latin word, either as *Vniversis* or as *Universis*. The other pairs of initials, with which the other two paragraphs begin, also have different forms of decorative uncial types then current. The DK-type is used for the displayed lines of the *31-line Indulgence*, it was also used at roughly the same time in the Gutenberghof for setting and printing the *Türkenkalender*, and in addition the *Türkenbulle*, or Latin and German texts of

Vniuersis Cristifidelibꝫ p̄ntes litteras inspecturis **Paulinus** Chappe Consiliari⁹ Ambasiator ⁊ pcurator generalis Serenissimi Regis Cypri ī hac pte Salutē in dn̄o Cū Sāctissim⁹ ī xp̄o pr̄ ⁊ dn̄s nr̄. dn̄s Nicola⁹ diuīa puidētia. papa v⁹. Afflictiōi Regni Cypri misericorditer ꝯpatiēs. contra pfidissiōs crucis xp̄i hostes. Theucros ⁊ Saracenos gratis ꝯcessit omībꝫ xp̄ifidelibꝫ vbilibet ꝯstitutis ipōs p aspsionem sāguīs dn̄i nr̄i ihū xp̄i pie exhortādo qui infra triēniū a prima die Maii Anni dn̄i Mcccclii incipiendum p defensiōe catholice fidei ⁊ Regni p̄dicti de facultatibꝫ suis magis vel min⁹ prout ipōꝝ videbit̄ ꝯscientiis. procurībꝫ vel nūciis Substitutis pie erogauerint vt Confessores ydonei seculares vel Regulares per ipsos eligendi ꝯfessionibꝫ eoꝝ auditis. p ꝯmissis etiā Sedi aplīce reseruatis excessibꝫ crimībꝫ atqꝫ delictis quātūcūqꝫ grauibꝫ p vna vice tātū debitā absolutionē impēdere ⁊ penitētiā salutarē iniūgere Necnō si id huīliter petierīt ipōs a quibuscūqꝫ excōicationū suspensionū ⁊ Interdicti Aliisqꝫ sentētiis cēsuris ⁊ penis ecclesiasticis a Iure vel ab hoīe pmulgatis quib⁹ forsan innodati existūt absoluere. Iniūcta p modo culpe penitētia salutari vel aliis que de Iure fuerint iniūgenda Ac eis vere penitētibꝫ ⁊ confessis. vel si forsan propter amissionem loquele ꝯfiteri non poterint signa ꝯtritionis ostendendo plenissimā oīm pctōꝝ suorū de quibꝫ ore ꝯfessi ⁊ corde ꝯtriti fuerīt Indulgētiā ac plenariā remissionē semel in vita et sel in mortis articulo ipīs aūcte aplīca ꝯcedere valeāt. Satisfactōe p eos fcā si supuixerint aut p eoꝝ heredes si tunc trāsierint Sic tn̄. q̄ post indultū ꝯcessum p vnū ānū singulis sextis feriis vel quadā alia die ieiunēt. legitiō impedimēto ecclesie pcepto Regulari obseruātia. pnīa iniūcta voto uel alias non obstan̄. Et ipīs impeditis in dicto āno uel eius parte Anno sequenti uel alias quamprimū poterint ieiunabunt. Et si ī aliquo ānoꝝ vel eoꝝ parte dictū ieiuniū cōmode adimplere nequiuerint Confessor ad id electus in alia ꝯmutare poterit caritatis opera que ipī facere etiā teneāt̄ Dūmodo tn̄ ex ꝯfidentia remissionis hmōi quod absit peccare non presumant Alioquī dicta concessio quo ad plenariā remissionē in mortis articulo et remissio quo ad pctā ex ꝯfidentia vt pmittit̄ ꝯmissa nulli⁹ sint roboris uel momēti Et quia deuoti [illegible] Otto [illegible] filii Anna [illegible] filie —
Iuxta dictū indultum de facultatibus suis pie erogauerunt merito huiusmodi indulgentiis gaudere debet In veritatis testimonium Sigillum ad hoc ordinatum presentibꝫ litteris testimonialibꝫ est appensum Datum [illegible] Anno dn̄i Mcccclv [illegible]
die uero [illegible] Mensis Ianuarii

Forma plenissime absolutionis et remissionis in vita

Misereatur tui ⁊c̄ Dn̄s nr̄ ihesus xp̄s p suā scīssimā et piissimā mīaꝫ te absoluat Et aūcte ipi⁹ beatoꝝqꝫ. petri et pauli aploꝝ ei⁹ ac aūcte aplīca michi ꝯmissa et tibi ꝯcessa Ego te absoluo ab omībꝫ pctīs tuis ꝯtritis ꝯfessis ⁊ oblitis Etiā ab omībꝫ casib⁹ excessibꝫ crimībꝫ atqꝫ delictis quātūcūqꝫ grauibꝫ Sedi aplīce reseruatis Necnon a quibuscūqꝫ excōicationū suspensionū et interdicti Aliisqꝫ sniīs cēsuris ⁊ penis ecctiasticis a Iure vel ab hoīe pmulgatis si quas incurristi dando tibi plenissimā oīm pctōꝝ tuoꝝ indulgentiā ⁊ remissionē Inquātū claues sancte matris ecctie in hac pte se extendūt. In nomine patris ⁊ filii et spiritus sancti Amen.

Forma plenarie remissionis in mortis articulo

Misereatur tui ⁊c̄ Dn̄s noster ut supra Ego te absoluo ab omībꝫ pctīs tuis ꝯtritis ꝯfessis ⁊ oblitis restituendo te vnitati fideliū ⁊ sacramentis ecctie Remittendo tibi penas purgatorii quas propter culpas et offensas incurristi dando tibi plenariam oīm pctōꝝ tuoꝝ remissionē. Inquātū claues scē mrīs ecctie in hac parte se extendūt. In noīe pr̄is et filii et spūs sancti Amen.

[illegible]
Theoder[illegible] Nycolai [illegible]

the papal bull of Calixtus III. To serve this same display purpose in the *30-line Indulgence*, the B42-type itself was employed, with which the Latin Bible in two volumes was of course at this same time either still being printed or had recently been completed at the partnership works in the Humbrechthof.

The type used for the text of the *31-line Indulgence* is a Gothic bastarda face, closely modelled on the normal hand of the day in Germany for written documents. It derives a few characteristics from the Schwabacher letter, but also inclines towards a rotunda or round Gothic. Compared to the textura types that we have looked at so far, it is a very much smaller typeface, set on a body of about 14 typographic points or 5 mm. There are 60 characters in all, only one of which is a joined character or ligature.

The type of the *30-line Indulgence* – about one point smaller – fits a body of about 4.5 mm. Among its 67 characters, eight are ligatures. Once again the typeface closely imitates the bastarda hand. (This suggests that both punchcutters may have had handwritten letters of indulgence in front of them to follow – very similar products but from two different scribes.) The lower-case letters with straight descenders are tapered and slightly oblique, unmistakably reflecting the French style of written bastarda. This leads me to suspect that this text face, as well as the somewhat more elegant initials of the *30-line Indulgence*, may have been cut by Peter Schöffer – an experienced calligrapher who would have grown familiar with the French *lettre bâtarde* during his stay in Paris. Text area and vellum format – all surviving indulgences are printed on vellum – are similar for both productions. But there are significant minor differences in the typography, which have not received much attention hitherto. The *31-line Indulgence* has uneven line lengths and accordingly follows closely the look of a written document. In contrast, the *30-line Indulgence* has text lines of equal length, with a straight edge to the right margin, but the hyphens used in word division are allowed to overhang the text as an optical refinement, just as they do in the B42.

From the surviving 41 copies of the *31-line Indulgence*, it is possible to establish seven edition variants. Whoever placed the printing contract would not have been able to judge the market demand at the outset of the sales campaign, and this must have exceeded expectations. In the meantime, further impressions would have been put in hand. The earliest surviving of these indulgences bears the date of 22 October 1454 and the final one that of 30 April 1455, which also happens to be the

31-line Indulgence for Cyprus.
Variant year-dates for 1454 and 1455 within the same edition.
Reduced.

Universis Cristifidelib; p̄ntes lr̄as inspecturis **Paulinus** Chappe Cōsiliari⁹ Ambasiator ⁊ pcurator generalis Serenissimi Regis Cypri in hac parte Salt̄m ī dn̄o Cū Sāctissim⁹ ī xp̄o pr̄ ⁊ dn̄s nr̄ dn̄s Nicolaus diuīa puidēcia pp̄ quint⁹ afflictiōi Regni Cypri misericorditer cōpatiēs cōtra pfidissīos crucis xp̄i hostes Theucros ⁊ Saracenos gratis cōcessit omib; xp̄ifidelib; vbilibet ɔstitutis ipos p aspsionē sanguīs dn̄i nr̄i ihū xp̄i pie exhortādo qui infra trienīū a prima die Maij Anni dn̄i Mcccclij īcipiēdū p defēsiōe catholice fidei ⁊ regni p̄dicti de facultatib; suis magis uel min⁹ put ipoꝝ videbitur ɔsciētijs pcūtorib; uel nūcijs substitutis pie erogauerint ut ɔfessores ydonei seculares uel regulares p ipos eligēdi ɔfessionib; eoꝝ auditis · p cōmissis etiā sedi aplice reseruatis excessib; criminib; atq; delictis quātūcūq; grauib; p vna vice tātū debitā absolutionē impēdere ⁊ penitētiā salutarem iniūgere Necnō si id hūiliter petierīt ipos a quibuscūq; excōicationum suspensionū ⁊ interdicti alijsq; sentencijs cēsuris ⁊ penis ecclesiasticis a iure uel ab hoīe pmulgatis quib; forsan innodati existūt absoluere · Iniūcta p modo culpe penitētia salutari uel alijs q̄ de iure fuerit iniūgēda ac eis vere penitētib; ⁊ ɔfessis · uel si forsan propter amissionē loq̄le ɔfiteri nō poterit signa ɔtricōnis ostēdēdo plenissimā oīm pccōꝝ suoꝝ de quib; ore ɔfessi ⁊ corde ɔtriti fuerint Indulgentiā ac plenariā remissionē semel in vita ⁊ semel in mortis articulo ipis aūcte aplica ɔcedere valeāt · Satisfactione p eos facta si supuixerint aut p eoꝝ heredes si tūc trāsierīt Sic tamē q̄ post indultū ɔcessum p vnū annū singulis sextis ferijs uel quadā alia die ieiunēt · legittimo impedimēto ecclesie p̄cepto regulari obseruātia pnīa iniūcta voto uel alias nō obstan̄ · Et ipis impeditis in dicto āno uel eius parte · anno sequēti uel alias quam primū poterint ieiunabūt Et si in aliquo annoꝝ uel eoꝝ parte dictū ieiuniū cōmode adimplere nequiuerīt Confessor ad id electus in alia ɔmutare poterit caritatis opa q̄ ipi facere etiā teneātur Dūmodo tū ex ɔfidentia remissionis hmōi quod absit pccare nō p̄sumāt Alioquī dicta ɔcessio quo ad plenariā remissionē in mortis articulo et remissio quo ad pccā ex ɔfidentia ut p̄mittitur ɔmissa nullius sint roboris uel momenti Et quia deuoti in cristo Cord quander Et hampe bron eius sue conthoralis legitima et Tilche munder iuxta dictum indultū de facultatibus suis pie erogarunt merito huiusmodi indulgentijs gaudere debēt · In veritatis testimoniū sigillū ad hoc ordinatū p̄ntib; lr̄is testimonialib; est appensum Datū in Grimsink Anno dn̄i Mccccl quinto die vero vicesima quarta mensis Aprilis

Forma plenissime absolutionis et remissionis in vita

Misereatur tui ⁊c̄ Dn̄s noster ihesus xp̄s p suā sanctissimā et pijssimā miāq; te absoluat Et aūcte ipi⁹ beatoꝝq; petri ⁊ pauli aploꝝ ei⁹ ac aūcte aplica michi ɔmissa ⁊ tibi ɔcessa Ego te absoluo ab omib; pccīs tuis ɔtritis ɔfessis ⁊ oblitis Etiā ab omib; casib; excessib; criminib; atq; delictis quātūcūq; grauib; sedi aplice reseruatis Necnō a quibuscūq; excōicationū suspensionū ⁊ interdicti Alijsq; sentencijs censuris ⁊ penis ecclasticis a iure uel ab hoīe pmulgatis si quas incurristi dando tibi plenissimā oīm pccōꝝ tuoꝝ indulgentiā ⁊ remissionē Inquātū claues sancte matris eccl̄ie in hac parte se extendūt · In noīe patris ⁊ filij ⁊ spiritus sancti Amen ·

Forma plenarie remissionis in mortis articulo

Misereatur tui ⁊c̄ Dn̄s noster ut supra Ego te absoluo ab omib; pccīs tuis cōtritis ɔfessis et oblitis restituendo te vnitati fideliū ⁊ sacramentis ecclesie Remittendo tibi penas purgatorij quas propter culpas ⁊ offensas incurristi dando tibi plenariā oīm pccōꝝ tuoꝝ remissionē · Inquantū claues sancte matris eccl̄ie in hac parte se extendūt · In noīe patris ⁊ filij ⁊ spiritus sancti Amen ·

last day of the validity of the issue (Geldner, 1972b: 175). It is noteworthy that nearly all these surviving indulgences with the requisite handwritten entries were sold within the bounds of the archdiocese of Mainz itself.

The *30-line Indulgence* is only known from eight extant copies which represent six edition variants. The earliest is dated 27 February 1455, and once again the last dated one was sold on 30 April 1455, the final day of issue. Apparently the sales territory for the *30-line Indulgence* lay mainly in the archdiocese of Cologne. When isolated examples come to light spread through the same district, then it is always possible that they got there through one person who bought them by request, or brought them home as travel gifts for family and friends. In any case it looks as though substantially fewer of the *30-line Indulgences* may have been printed. It is probably the more recent edition, and the *31-line* version could have been taken as its exemplar.

What is still being debated in Gutenberg circles is the conclusion that the *31-line Indulgence* must have been set and printed at the Gutenberghof, while the *30-line Indulgence* was produced at the Humbrechthof (Ruppel, 1967: 153n.). But how could it have been otherwise, when the B42-type used for the displayed headings in the latter indulgence was only to be found at the Humbrechthof, where it was in use for setting the Bible (Geldner, 1972b: 177)? Correspondingly, the DK-type used for the headings in the *31-line Indulgence* points to the first printing works at the Gutenberghof, which used it exclusively.

It appears that Gutenberg, who at the time still controlled both printing works, would have linked the contract for printing the indulgences to the Gutenberghof. This served as the workshop for small projects, or for what later came to be known as 'jobbing printing'. It may well be that he undertook this commission out of support for the war against the Turks; stemming from his own patriotic and religious convictions, and his desire to perform a service for friends in clerical high places in Mainz, and likewise to Cardinal Nicholas of Cues. But his acceptance of such a contract must have been activated primarily by the need to earn money towards repayment of his debt to Fust.

I suspect, in any case, that the printing of these indulgences provided the real cause of the dispute between Gutenberg and Fust. Perhaps Gutenberg diverted some of the money which Fust had made available 'for the work to their common advantage', to the manufacture of types for the *31-line Indulgence*, which was certainly intended to be printed at

30-line Indulgence for Cyprus.
Variant year-dates for 1454 and 1455 within the same edition.
Reduced.

the Gutenberghof and so not to be set against their joint profit and loss account. This then would have constituted a misappropriation of Fust's business investment. It would seem that Fust was angered because Gutenberg had placed this lucrative contract within his own original workshop. Only through negotiations with indulgence-dealers could Fust retaliate, by ensuring that at least the contract for printing indulgences for issue by the Cologne archdiocese came to the Humbrechthof.

But could these letters of indulgence have been sufficiently important, when set against the magnificent Bible, for the two partners to have fallen out over them; and what made them so attractive financially to both Mainz printing houses? What would such a certificate of indulgence – slightly smaller than an A4 letterheading – have been worth altogether? It may be assumed that the cost of having such a letter written by hand, inclusive of the parchment, would have been three albi, or three silver pfennigs. A scribe or calligrapher, working at the rate of two documents a day, would consequently earn four albi, after allowing for the cost of his materials (principally the parchment and seal). The same would be charged for a printed letter of indulgence. As 26 albi make one gold gulden, then nine indulgences would fetch roughly a gulden, or 9000 indulgences represent 1000 gulden. It appears likely that indulgences were printed in far greater numbers than this at the Gutenberghof alone. Naturally, when considering these figures, the costs of developing a typeface, the typesetting, vellum and operating expenses need to be taken into account. But even after these costs were deducted, a sufficiently impressive profit must have remained to give ample cause for dissension between the partners.

Furthermore, in the course of preparing vellum for Bible printing, a huge quantity of offcuts must have been left which were eminently suitable for indulgence slips. An almost irresistible opportunity had arisen to put these parchment remnants to good use at the Gutenberghof. This or any similar misappropriation of expensive printing materials purchased for the Bible can only have exacerbated the conflict.

For the first copies of the *31-line Indulgence* to be on sale in Frankfurt on 1 October 1454, Gutenberg would have needed an order perhaps three months earlier; for he and his craftsmen would have required that sort of time in which to engrave the punches, strike and justify the matrices, and to cast supplies of type in readiness. It is unlikely that the quarrel between the two partners developed until after the first issue had sold out, for only then would Fust have woken up to the full financial import of indulgence printing. Out of this clash between the partners must have come Fust's plan to secure a share of this potentially massive trade for himself at the printing works at the Humbrechthof – in fact precisely that share which was at the disposal of the indulgence traders for the see of Cologne. This may have been the financier's first active intervention in the inner workings of a printing house. As cash ran short, then Gutenberg would soon find himself in difficulties over paying the workmen, and Fust could have taken advantage of the situation to strengthen his grip over the workshop. By then he may have placed his adopted son, the cleric and calligrapher Peter Schöffer, in a position of trust within the works, and put him in charge of devising a typeface for the *30-line Indulgence*. This could have taken place in about November 1454. The commission seems to have been despatched with great rapidity and remarkable skill, for at the very beginning of the new year, Fust and Schöffer's *30-line Indulgence* left the printing works at the Humbrechthof.

These dates broadly coincide with the timing of Fust's lawsuit. The dispute between the two proprietors had repercussions for their co-workers. The talented Peter Schöffer and the cleric Johann Bonne, who would have worked alongside Heinrich Günther as proofreader for the Bible, were firmly in Fust's camp. Financial resources had triumphed over inventive genius. Although an eventual breach between Gutenberg and Fust may have been inevitable, it was the *Cyprus Indulgences* which brought matters to a head. Strange to reflect that what took place in 'far-off Turkey' should have had so direct a bearing on events in Mainz!

Peter Schöffer of Gernsheim

AT THE CLOSE OF PROCEEDINGS before the secular court held in the refectory of the barefoot friars, there were two printing workshops operating in Mainz, which confronted one another as more than straightforward business rivals because of what had taken place. Until a few decades ago, eminent Gutenberg scholars shared the view that Gutenberg would have abandoned his first printing works in the Gutenberghof on terminating his partnership with Fust, and that in the period from 1455 to 1462 only a single printing workshop existed in Mainz, namely that of Fust and Schöffer. But there are compelling grounds for assuming that two workshops were active concurrently. To sidestep this controversy and avoid even greater problems, the *Gesamtkatalog der Wiegendrucke* (1925 – in progress) decided to refer to an 'unknown printer' who was active in Mainz from 1455 onwards, but independently from Fust and Schöffer; but this seems to me a position which is no longer tenable today (Ruppel, 1967: 154).

One thing is certain: the invention was brought to its fruition as Gutenberg's personal achievement. Of course he was open to suggestions of a technical and aesthetic kind; but it would be quite wrong to wish to place Gutenberg and Fust on the same level in consideration of their respective contributions to the invention. It is true that Fust should not be dismissed as a mere money-lender and exploiter; his father had been a goldsmith and his younger brother Jakob also worked as one, and this would have given him some familiarity with engraving and metal-casting. Undoubtedly the profit motive remained uppermost in his mind, but, since he was uniquely placed to see the new art of printing reach maturity, he must have devoted all his efforts towards its success.

The invention of printing, as emphasized earlier, was no sudden brainwave, but a creative process which lasted from about 1437 to 1445, a process which had its setbacks, periods of stagnation and a succession of fresh problems to solve. Even when the *42-line Bible* could finally be presented as conclusive evidence for the superiority of this new way of producing books, this did not mean that there were not many technological and aesthetic questions still to settle.

The period of competitiveness between the two Mainz printers opened with the workshop at the Humbrechthof well in the lead. All the conditions and facilities for mass-producing books were in place there. Paper and parchment as well as inks were stored there, and four to six sturdy presses were in good working order. Above all, this was where the experienced team of compositors, printers, typefounders and other specialists was based. What is more, Gutenberg had just prepared or finished for them two new typefaces, the large and small psalter-types. In all probability some of the *Mainz Psalter* had already been printed.

But what was lacking was a master printer. The embittered inventor had retreated to the Gutenberghof. Who now possessed sufficient authority and expertise to carry forward such a complicated enterprise? The most experienced printers would have been Berthold Ruppel and Heinrich Keffer, yet both were close friends and associates of Gutenberg and worked at the Gutenberghof. Fust, at this stage sole proprietor, needed a capable man on whom he could depend, and he chose the cleric Peter Schöffer as his new works manager.

Who was this Peter Schöffer? Little enough is known about his early years. He was born between 1420 and 1430 in the small town of Gernsheim on the Rhine, which lies between Mainz and Worms, and where the Gernsheimers erected a monument in 1836 to their most famous son. His father must have died while he was young, for Abbot Trithemius, writing in his *Annales Hirsaugienses* as printed in 1515, describes Peter Schöffer as the fostered and adopted son of Johann Fust

(Geldner, 1974: 418ff). It is unfortunate that this passage has been overlooked by scholars until quite recently, for it allows us to conclude that, since Peter Schöffer grew up in the goldsmithing Fust household, he must have gained some knowledge of metalworking as well as a natural allegiance to his adoptive father. Fust apparently sent him to Erfurt University in 1444, as there is an entry for one 'Petrus Ginsheym' in the register for the summer semester of that year. A later entry for the winter semester of 1448/9 shows a 'Petrus Opilionis' studying there. Schöffer may well have Latinized his name by then, so that *Schäffer* (or shepherd) became *Opilionis* (Weissenborn, 1881: I, 199, 218).

Portrait of Peter Schöffer.
Aquatint plate after an earlier painting (from Linde, 1886).
Reduced.

We next encounter him in 1449 as a cleric at the University of Paris. He would have needed Latin not only to become a cleric, but to have been admitted into minor orders. He appears to have worked at the Sorbonne as a scribe or calligrapher. A splendid example of his writing was kept in Strasbourg University Library until it was destroyed by Prussian troops in 1870. Even from an engraved facsimile one can recognize the work of a skilful calligrapher.

It is likely that Fust recalled his adoptive son from Paris to Mainz in about 1452 in order to make use of his expertise within the partnership works; for one thing he knew Latin, for another he was a good scribe, and moreover he may have been well versed in the goldsmith's crafts. Fust could not have found a better man. By all appearances he became Gutenberg's eager master-class student, and soon penetrated the secrets of the new art. One assumes his collaboration on the large and small psalter-types. The type of the *30-line Indulgence* also seems to reveal his own hand. It is fitting that Schöffer's name should appear with those of other witnesses for Fust in the Helmasperger Instrument, where he is described as a cleric of the diocese of Mainz.

Calligraphy by Peter Schöffer.
(from Schöpflin, 1760). Reduced.

There is an alternative romanticized version, according to which Fust fetched the young cleric back from Paris as tutor to his daughter Christine, and Schöffer fell in love with the schoolgirl and abandoned his religious vocation in order to win her hand. His adoptive father (and future father-in-law) encouraged the young cleric's attentions, so that this gifted man would have been obliged to transfer his loyalty from his then employer, Gutenberg, and act in accordance with Fust's personal interests. In other words, Peter Schöffer ceased to support the master who had taught him all he knew of the craft, out of familial solidarity with the new proprietor. However, all that can be proven about this tale is that Peter Schöffer did in fact wed Fust's daughter Christine in the end.

Evidence of this is given in the colophon of Abbot Trithemius's *Annales*, where Peter Schöffer's son relates these circumstances:

> This present work of the chronicles was printed and completed in the year of the Lord 1515, on St Margaret's Eve, in the noble and celebrated city of Mainz, the first inventress of this art of printing, by Johann Schöffer, grandson of Johann Fust, citizen of Mainz, first author of the said art, who began to conceive and fathom the art of printing through his own talents in the year 1450. In the year 1452 only, he perfected it, with the help of God, and made it serviceable to the printing of books, but with the help and many necessary additional inventions of his assistant and adopted son, Peter Schöffer of Gernsheim, to whom he gave his daughter Christine as wife, in just reward for all his labour and numerous inventions. Both Johann Fust and Peter Schöffer kept this art secret, and bound all their workmen and members of their house by an oath not to make it known in any way. From 1462 onwards, this art was spread, however, by these same workmen in diverse countries of the world, by which means it took further wing (Ruppel, 1937: 53).

The Latin wording of this colophon has for a long time only been looked at for the light it sheds on Johann Schöffer's attempts to mislead posterity, by concealing Gutenberg's achievement and exaggerating that of Fust. In fact Johann Schöffer's purpose is blatantly transparent, and can be shown to have been set in motion in the later colophons of his father, Peter Schöffer – although it should be said that similar historical obfuscations are not uncommon throughout the Middle Ages; the legends formed about saints and rulers show a comparable disregard for the truth.

Despite these minor flaws in his character, Peter Schöffer remains an outstanding figure, whose contributions to the further development of the invention deserve to be rated very highly indeed. He carried forward the 'work of the books' in the spirit of the inventor. His earlier calling as a calligrapher offered him the finest grounding for the cultivation of printing – above all in its aesthetic aspects.

ON 14 AUGUST 1457, a magnificent work of 340 folio pages appeared from the Humbrechthof workshop, every copy of which was printed on vellum. This was a *Psalterium Moguntinum*, or the *Mainz Psalter*. For the first time a printer's imprint is given, showing the producers to be a Mainz citizen, Johann Fust, and Peter Schöffer from Gernsheim. In one of the surviving copies a printer's mark is to be found for the first time as well – the celebrated mark of Fust and Schöffer – printed in red. The colophon makes this the earliest printed work to state when, where, and by whom it was produced. Attention is drawn to the fact that this entire book was printed, right down to its coloured initials.

Pñs psalmoꝝ codex · venustate capitaliū decoratꝰ
Rubricationibusq̃ʒ sufficienter distinctus,
Adinuētione artificiosa imprimendi ac caracterizandi ·
absq̃ʒ calami ulla exaracōne sic effigiatus, Et ad euse-
biam dei industrie est ɔsummatus, Per Johem fust
Ciuē maguntinū · Et Petrū Schoffer de Gernszheim,
Anno dñi Millesiō · cccc · lvij · In vigilia Assūpcōis,

Colophon of the Mainz Psalter *with the printer's mark of Fust and Schöffer. Reduced.*

Even today the *Mainz Psalter* has to be considered as one of the world's loveliest books. As an artistic achievement it stands shoulder to shoulder with the *Gutenberg Bible*. Naturally, the large and small psalter-types make their début, but what is really special about these pages are the magnificent printed initials in two colours and the printed rubrication in Lombardic or uncial letters. The large psalter-type is furnished with no fewer than 228 different characters, and the small psalter-type with 215 sorts. In addition, there are 24 uncial initials related to the large psalter-type, and 29 to the smaller size. Altogether this gives a range of 496 types, which is 200 more than were available for setting the *42-line Bible*. But the resources for embellishing the *Mainz Psalter* are then further extended by a total of 288 fitted initials in three different sizes (Ruppel, 1967: 162). There can be no other book for which comparable pains were taken in the preparation of its typographic repertoire as well as in the actual printing. The faultless colour register of the great initials – for which red and blue are alternated for each successive initial and its close-fitting lily of the valley decoration – leads to the conclusion that this could only have been achieved by withdrawing the two parts of these initials from the inked forme, cleaning and re-inking them separately in colours and replacing them within the black text, so that all three colours could be printed in a single impression. Although there are slightly differing hypotheses about the possible construction of these two-colour initials, their technical precision leads almost everyone to agree that this must have been achieved through the metalworking ingenuity of Gutenberg himself (Rosenfeld, 1972: 202–3).

The cutting and proofing of both psalter-types, and of the uncial letters and colour-combined initials, must all have been well advanced before proceedings were instigated between Fust and Gutenberg. The actual printing would have begun by 1456 and may even have continued while the lawsuit was being heard, so that one still has to regard the *Mainz Psalter*, or at least some part of it, as the work of Gutenberg. At the same time it confirms how Fust and Schöffer were able to carry the inventor's work forward with mastery. It must have been their intention to demonstrate to the employees of their printing office and to all observers of the scene in Mainz that the new managers were in no way inferior to their predecessor. They sought rather to surpass him and obliterate him from memory. In this, one can guess that Fust would have been primarily motivated by commercial interests, whereas Schöffer was driven by ambition.

A psalter is a book of psalms, but the *Mainz Psalter* is not simply a collection containing these songs of praise and thanksgiving, popular psalms and those for use in the Temple, psalms concerning the coming of the Messiah, songs of kings and lamentation, as well as penitential psalms. Rather it is a breviary, because it disposes the liturgical psalter according to the canonical hours, with seven songs of praise, prayers and poems from the Old Testament and three from the New Testament. Then follow the 150 psalms as described above, with their respective antiphons. After that came the collects, the litany of all saints, the vigils

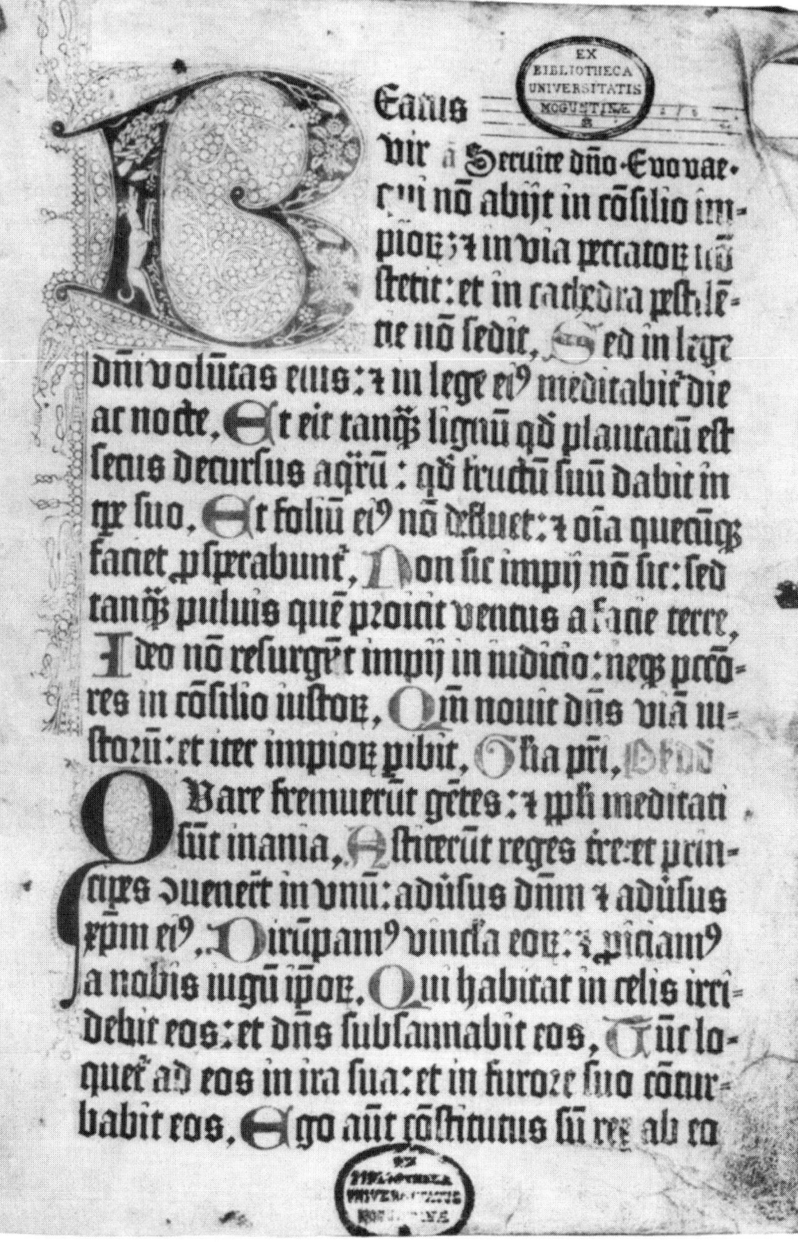
EX BIBLIOTHECA UNIVERSITATIS MOGUNTINAE

Beatus
vir Seruite dño. Euouae.
q̃ nõ abijt in cõsilio impioꝝ: ⁊ in via peccatoꝝ nõ
stetit: et in cathedra pestile-
ne nõ sedit. Sed in lege
dñi volũtas eius: ⁊ in lege eiꝰ meditabit̃ die
ac nocte. Et erit tanq̃ lignũ qd̃ plantatũ est
secus decursus aq̃rũ: qd̃ fructũ suũ dabit in
tp̃e suo. Et foliũ eiꝰ nõ defluet: ⁊ oĩa quecũq̃
faciet psp̃erabunt̃. Non sic impij nõ sic: sed
tanq̃ puluis quẽ proicit ventus a facie terre.
Ideo nõ resurgẽt impij in iudicio: neq̃ pccõ-
res in cõsilio iustoꝝ. Qm̃ nouit dñs viã iu-
storũ: et iter impioꝝ pibit. Gl̃ia patri. Euouae
Quare fremuerũt gẽtes: ⁊ ppl̃i meditati
sũt inania. Astiterũt reges t̃re: et prin-
cipes conuenerũt in vnũ: adũsus dñm ⁊ adũsus
xp̃m eiꝰ. Dirũpamꝰ vincla eoꝝ: ⁊ piciamꝰ
a nobis iugũ ipoꝝ. Qui habitat in celis irri-
debit eos: et dñs subsannabit eos. Tũc lo-
quet̃ ad eos in ira sua: et in furore suo cõtur-
babit eos. Ego aũt cõstitutus sũ rex ab eo

EX BIBLIOTHECA UNIVERSITATIS MOGUNTINAE

A page from the Mainz (Benedictine) Psalter *of 1459.*
Reduced.

of the dead, and finally the *hymnis* or hymnal – a collection of short poems for religious festivals.

Any book of this kind needs to be printed in large types so that the precentor and if possible the members of the choir can all read it

Two-colour initial from the Mainz Psalter *of 1457.*
Actual size.

E igit' clemētissime pr̄
per ihesū xp̄m filiū tuū
dn̄m nostrū supplices
rogamus ac petimus.
uti accepta habeas et
bn̄dicas. hec do ✠ na.
hec mu ✠ nera. hec sancta ✠ sacrificia il=
libata, In p̄mis que tibi offerimꝰ pro
eccl'ia tua sancta katholica. quā pacificāe.
custodire. adunare. ⁊ regē digneis. toto
orbe terraꝝ. una cū famulo tuo Papa no=
stro. N. et rege nr̄o. N. ⁊ antistite nostro
N. ⁊ oībꝫ orthodoxis. atqꝫ katholice et
apostolice fidei cultoribꝫ.
Memento dn̄e famuloꝝ famulaꝝqꝫ
tuarū. N. Hic fit memoria vivoꝝ.
et oīm circūastātiū quoꝝ tibi fides cogni=
ta est et nota devocō pro quibꝫ tibi offeri=
mus. uel qui tibi offerūt hoc sacrificium

A page from the Canon Missae. *Mainz, 1458. Reduced.*

ad celestis regni libitatē gaudiu. ac claritatē et ad
supim regis thalamu trãsducunt. vn in cantic. veni
electa mea et ponã in te thronu meu. Nudis capitibz
obuiã veniut et pontifex cãtando dicit illis. venite
Et ipe similr cantãdo respõdent. Et nuc sequitur. ad
reputandu q in cantic legit. Surge amica mea spõsa mea onde michi faciē tuã z sonet vox tua i auribz
meis. Rursus denudacõ capitu. depositõem z abre-
nũciacõez mũdanoz cõgrue desigt. nudato eniã capite ecclia ingrediut. ad nõndu q velut formose
et spõso placide in ipi9 sponsi tabnaclm introducunt.
Iux illd cãtic. Nigra su sed formosa. Et introduxit
me rex in tabnaclm suu Ter aut dicit eis venire
ad nõndu q ad h triplicit debet venire. s. p abdica-
tionē pctatis. p votu castitatis z p sponsionē obe-
dientie. Debet qdã venire. rimo p abdicacõez
pctatis de duersacõe mũdana. de sruitute egiptia-
ca. de carcē. de laqueis z de retibz vn ps. Cadet in re-
tiaclo ei9 peccores. Et sapiētie. xiiij. b. creature dei facte sut in tēptacõez aie hoim z in muscipulã pedibz
insipientiũ. Scdo debet venire p votu castitatis.
de declaracõe carnali. z de immũdicia. z de loco toxi-
cato. de quo si qd aia sumit z pniētiã nõ tetit. mori-
tur morte etiã. ercio p spõsionē obediētie. de
ppria volũtate. sic. De corrupcõe z dibano accenso
et de babilonica fornace. z ideo cu pueris qui erat in
fornace illa dicunt. et nuc sequim in toto corde et
time9 te z qrim9 faciē tuã. daniel iij. par an ps bn-
dicite. De quolibz aut istoz excũdu ēhrmo cordis
pposito soiemoni voto z toci9 vite pseueratia z hec
sut qsi tres diete. exo. iij. g. Viã triũ dierũ ibimus
in solitudinē. qs tres dietas pmisse tres vocacões
triplicit facte designt. Quia vēo post susceptu tam
laudabile ppositu restat insidie z tēptacões demo-
nu. atq acrima cõtra mũdu carnē z demones cer-
tamia. et insup regulais obsuãtie difficultas. q mlie-
bris infirmitas sufficient per se sustinē nõ possi Ido
diuinu auxiliu z scõz suffragia p letaniã que sbicit
implorant. Cõsequent deponut vestes vetes et
induut nouas bndicãs. ad nõndu q in hoc pposito
vetus homo exuit et nouus induit q sicut legit
ephi. iiij. f. Creat9 est in iusticia z sanctitate veritatis. et debet esse vestes mũde z cãdide ad designdu
q q3 dei filio despõsant. debet de cetero se scãs z mũ-
das absq macla pbuare vel cõsuac Iux illud apli.
Despõdi eni vos vni viro ugmē castam exhibere
xpo hec eni candor seu mudicia vestis ondit vnde
ecclīastes. ix. c. Omi tpe vestimēta tua sint cãdida
et hoc sũptũ est a btã cecilia. q exterius veste fulge-
bat. intus castitate nitebat. z ab angelis. qui in xpi
resurrectõne visi sut in vestibz albis. vel si sit niger
habit9 sigficat carnis mortificacõem. qz eni xpus
spõsus suus mortuus ē p ipis. debet z ipe cõmori p
illo vn gal. v. Qui xpi sut carnē sua crucifixert cu
vicijs z cõcupiscētijs. Et ro. vj. Si cõplãtati facti
sum9 silitudinē mortis xpi siml et resurrectõis eim9
Rursus ingredo habit9 est contemptus virilis am-
plexus. Sbsequent indute vestibz bndcis ũsus
epm veniut. qsi ipo actu dicãt. Regnu mũdi z oēz
ornatu secli cõtemsim9 ppt amorē dni nri ihu xpi zc.
Vela q sup scapulas z pectora dependētia ex insti-
tucõne sotheis ppe. cum signo crucis earũ capitibz
imponunt pmo ad sighcand q p xpo debet mũdũ
humilit corde z ope cõtemnē et sensus velae ac memoria passiois xpi munire. ne ad mũdana lasciuiedo
exeãt vel illa ad illaz sensus intrēt Iux illud gal. v.
Michi mũdus crucifixus ē z ego mudo. Secudo
velant quia nõ sut imago dei. Tercio ut ondat sb-
iecte. Quto ut illicite cuctis viris appareãt. Quito
ne spes eaz occasio inspectoribz sit peccandi quia ps
ait. Dne delectasti me in factura tua. z creature dei
facte sut in tēptacõez ut pmissum ē. Velu ergo est
signu pudois z futuri honoris. Deinde q xpo despon-
sat qui ē alpha et o. i. pncipiu z finis. Ideo dat eis
ãnulus q rotũdus ē. pncipio z fine cares et ponit in
qrto digito. ex quo vena quedã sanguis ad cor ptē-
dit. ut sciat se sponsu suu xpm toto corde debē dili-
gere. et ei insepabilr adherē. ostremo vēo co-
rone capitibz eaz imponut. Iux illd in cãtic. veni
spõsa xpi accipe coronã zc. Ad nõndu q qn virgo p
cõsecrationē sũmo regi despõsat regina efficit id ē
se et alios in ũtutibz regens vn. pu. j. vt addat gra
capiti tuo z torques collo tuo in q coronacõe põtifex
cãtat illud canticu leticie veni electa mea zc tanq
celestis spõsi paraniphus. et hinc est q illaz amici z
cõsangnei in hac cõsecrõe letant. Leo pp pm9 insti-
tuit in cõcilio calcedon q ipe celebrauit solas ũgies
debē velari Quia vero in pmissis de velo mencõ
facta ē Ideo nõndu est q velu aliud est cõuersionis
aliud cõsecracõis aliud pfessiois aliud ordinacõis
aliud placõnis. Velu cõuersiois aliq de seclari vita
ad religionē trãsiens assumit z tuc si p annu int ve-
latas steterit vlterius exire nõ poterit. Velu cõsecracõ-
nis a solis epis solis ũginibz z solu in festiuis et dnī-
cis diebz dat. urgētē tn necitate sicut et baptism9
omi die dari possz nõ dat etiã nisi in vicesimoquito
ãno illud recipiētis nisi forte despēsacie elu aut
professiois suscipit a ũgine. qn cõtinentiã pfitetur
nõ tamē an duodecimu ãnu qm nec ante illud tpus
bndicit. Dat velu huiusmoi cu bndictõne solēni.
et cu letania hoc velu null9 epus dat viduis vel cor-
ruptis h ipamet de altai ut dicut qdã assumunt Sane ũgo et nõ vidua ideo ab epo velat. quia ũgo in
hac despõsacõne typu gerit ecclie. q pura et ũgo vni
nupsit viro. i. xpo. Et in signu hui9 rei velat ab epo
qa a xpo recipit in cõiugiu In cui9 psona dictu est
ãnulo suo sbarrauit me dns h vidua nõ gerit in tali
facto typu ecclie sicut ũgo cu non sit integra mente
et corpe sicut illa vn nõ sic cõiugit xpo ut rñtet eccle
cõiũctiõi qre nõ velat. Pretea sacdos phibet secũ-
dis nuptijs interesse z sup scdo nubētes bndictionē
infundē put dcm est in pma pte sb ti. de sacramētis
sed hec vidua quasi scdo nubit pmo homi postea in
pfessione xpo Ideoq ei qsi celebrãti scdas nuptias
nõ porrigit velu cõsecracõis. nec etiã pfessiois. sed
ipa illud suscipit de altai. Aiut tn quidã q licet nõ
ab epo. potest tn a sacdote velo pfessiois ul cõuersionis velari. a quo seu a cui9 mistro. habitu seu ve-
stem religiosam assumit. In libro tn põtificali scdm
ordinē romanu habet bndictio vidue cõtinentiã
pfitentis z veli eius. Nã et dns sareptenã viduã per
helia ppham cõsolat9 ē. Et vidim9 in vrbe episcopu
hostien. mt virgines bndicē duas viduas moiales
Velu ordinacõis olim diaconisse in quadragesimo
ãno dabat ut possz legē euãgeliu in nocturnis in cõcilio laudicen. statutu ē. ut mlieres q apud grecos

A page from Rationale divinorum officiorum *by Durandus.*
Fust and Schöffer, Mainz, 1459. Reduced.

together. Mainz cathedral treasury still houses choirbooks which could have served as models for this aspect of the design. As in these handwritten volumes, the *Mainz Psalter* of 1457 has plainchant neumes or musical notation entered by a rubricator or choirmaster. Since a psalter was indispensable to conducting services, a constant demand on the part of monasteries and churches may be taken for granted. The *Mainz Psalter* probably not only brought ecclesiastical favour to both its master printers but also contributed to their future business success.

Furthermore, the *Mainz Psalter* of 1457 was also issued in a second issue with only 246 pages, since a considerable number of psalms were never called upon in the usual services. Five copies are known to survive of each of these two versions, which would make it today no less valuable a book than a *42-line Bible*.

It has repeatedly been said that the most important book in the Middle Ages was the missal. Originally, Gutenberg had the aim of working towards the standardized missal which would become necessary as a result of the efforts of the reform party. But any such unification of the missal had since become quite out of the question. On the contrary, all notions of reform which had been expressed at the Council of Basle had been rigorously suppressed by the Holy See. As things now stood, Fust and Schöffer could not have contemplated this plan. Each diocese required a mass-book of its own, as had always been the case, and every edition must conform to the number of copies currently called for by a particular see. However, there was one part of any missal that had to remain identical for all Roman Catholics throughout the world, and that was the *Canon missae*, or canon of the mass, which ran from the sanctus to the communion. This section was printed, it is thought in 1458, in the large and small psalter-types and to the same superlative quality standards as the *Mainz Psalter*, but occupying a mere 24 folio pages. One of the most beautiful of all the two-colour initials was cut especially for this *Canon missae*.

As early as 1459 a modified reprinting of the *Mainz Psalter* appeared from Fust and Schöffer, which is known as the *Benedictine Psalter*. The sequence of the psalms and other matter was changed in accordance with the reformed monastic breviary of the Bursfeld Congregation. The page size was increased and now harmonizes even better with the huge sizes of type. For beauty of typography and quality of printing this impression almost outdoes the original edition of 1457. It is quite possible that this commission for printing the *Psalterium Benedictinum* was placed directly by the Benedictine order. Incidentally, this and other printing contracts point to ties between Schöffer and the Benedictines, whereas Gutenberg seems to have favoured the Franciscans. Later monastic

iudeoꝝ septingẽtas quadragintaquinq;.
Omnes ergo anime: quatuor milia sexcẽte. Et
factum est in tricesimoseptimo āno trāsmi-
grationis ioachin regis iuda duodecimo
mense vicesima quīta mensis eleuauit euil-
merodach rex babilonis ipso āno regni sui
caput ioachin regis iude: et eduxit eum de
domo carceris: et locutus est cum eo bona.
Et posuit thronū eius sup thronos regū q̃
erāt post se in babilone: et mutauit vestimēta carceris ei9: et comedebat panē corā eo
semp cūctis diebus vite sue. Et cibaria ei9
cibaria ꝑpetua dabant͛ ei a rege babilonis
statuta per singulos dies: vsq; ad diem
mortis sue cunctis diebus vite eius.
Explicit ihēremias ꝑpheta. Incipiūt lamēta-
cōes eius que cynoth hebraice inscribūt͛
Et factū est postq̃ in
captiuitatē redactus
est israhel et iherusalē
deserta est: sedit ihere-
mias ꝑpheta flens et
planxit lamētatione
hac in ihrlm: et amaro
animo suspirās et eiulās dixit. Aleph Quō
sedet sola ciuitas plena pplō. Facta est q̄i
vidua domina gentiū: princeps ꝓuinciaꝝ
facta est sub tributo. Beth. Plorans plo-
rauit in nocte: et lacrime eius in maxillis
eius. Non est qui consoletur eam: ex omī-
bus caris eius. Omēs amici eius spreuerūt
eā: et facti sunt ei inimici. Gimel Migrauit
iudas ꝑpter afflictōem et multitudinē serui-
tutis. Habitauit inter gētes: nec inuenit re-
quiē. Omēs psecutorēs eius apphenderūt
eā inter angustias. Deleth Vie syō lugēt:
eo q non sint q̄ veniant ad solemnitatē. O-
mnes porte eius destructe: sacerdotes eius
gemētes. Virgines eius squalide: et ipsa
oppressa amaritudine. He. Facti sūt hostes
eius in capite: et inimici ei9 locupletati sūt:
q dominus locutus est sup eā ꝑpter multitudinē iniquitatū ei9. Paruuli eius ducti
sunt in captiuitatem: ante faciē tribulātis.
Vau. Et egressus ē a filia syon omīs decor
ei9. Facti sūt pncipes eius velut arietes nō
inueniētes pascua: et abierūt absq; fortitu-
dine āte faciē subsequētis. Zay. Recordata

ē ihrlm dieꝝ afflictōnis sue. et puaricacōis
oīm desiderabiliū suoꝝ. q̄ habuerat a dieb9
antiquis: cū caderet ppl's eius in manū hosti-
li: et nō esset auxiliator. Viderūt eā hostes: et
deriserūt sabbata ei9. Heth Peccatū pecca-
uit ihrlm: ꝑpterea instabilis facta ē. Omes
qui glorificabant eā spreuerūt illā: q viderūt
ignominiā eius. Ipsa aūt gemēs: et cōuersa
retrorsū. Teth Sordes eius in pedib9 eius:
nec recordata ē finis sui. Deposita ē vehemē-
ter: nō habēs cōsolatorē. Vide domine affli-
ctionē meā: qm̄ erectus est inimicus. Ioth
Manū suā misit hostis ad omīa desiderabilia
eius: q vidit gētes ingressas scūarium suū:
de quib9 pceperas ne intrarent in ecciam tuā.
Caph. Omīs ppl's eius gemēs: et querens
panē. Dederūt pciosa q̄q; ꝑ cibo: ad refocil-
landā aīam. Vide dn̄e et cōsidera: qm̄ facta
sū vilis. Lamech O vos omēs q̄ transitis ꝑ
viam attendite et videte: si est dolor sicut dolor meus. Quoniā vindemiauit me ut locutus ē dominus: in die ire furoris sui. Mem.
De excelso misit ignē in ossib9 meis: et erudi-
uit me. Expandit rethe pedib9 meis: cōuertit
me retrorsū. Posuit me desolatam: tota die
merore cōfectā. Nun Vigilauit iugū iniq̄-
tatū meaꝝ in manū ei9: cōuolute sūt et imposite
collo meo. Infirmata ē v͛tus mea: dedit me
dominus in manū de q̄ non potero surgere.
Samech. Abstulit omēs magnificos meos dominus de medio mei: vocauit aduer-
sū me tps: ut cōtereret electos meos. Torcu-
lar calcauit dn̄s v͛gini filie iuda. Ayn. Idcir-
co ego plorās et oclus meus deducēs aq̄s:
q longe fcūs ē a me cōsolator: cōuertēs ani-
mā meā. Facti sūt filij mei pditi: qm̄ inualuit
inimicus. Phe. Expādit syon manus suas:
non ē qui cōsolet͛ eā. Mandauit dn̄s aduēsū
iacob: in circuitu eius hostes ei9. Facta est
ihrlm quasi polluta menstruis inter eas.
Sade Iustus est dominus: q os eius ad
iracundiam ꝓuocaui. Audite obsecro vniu͛-
si ppli: et videte dolorē meū. Virgines mee
et iuuenes mei abiert̄ i captiuitatē. Coph
Vocaui amicos meos: et ipsi deceperūt me.
Sacerdotes mei et senes mei in vrbe cōsūpti
sūt: q quesierūt cibū sibi ut refocillarēt ani-
mas suas. Res. Vide domine qm̄ tribulor:

A page from the 48-line Bible *by Fust and Schöffer.*
Mainz, 1462. Reduced.

dissension would bring renewed significance to these alliances.

The fourth distinguished product of the Fust and Schöffer workshop, the *Rationale divinorum officiorum* of Guillelmus Durandus, was finished on 6 October 1459. Schöffer designed a new and extremely small type-face for this work, which is a very readable Gothic roman *(fere-humanistica)*, cut in imitation of one of the humanist hands then in use. Double-column setting is used on its folio pages, and the lines – with very few exceptions – are justified, or brought out to equal breadth. As the book begins, coloured initials are printed in with the text, but for the remainder of a total of 161 leaves they are subsequently added by hand. This is another title for which a commission may have been offered, since Durandus was valued and promoted as the main authority for the origin of ritual and its symbolic relation to buildings, furnishings and vestments.

A number of books of canon law appeared in this same typeface, which met a real need, particularly on the part of students of ecclesiastical jurisprudence. The printing of the *Constitutiones* of Pope Clement V dates from 1460, and 1465 saw the appearance of the *Liber sextus Decretalium* of Boniface VIII. Schöffer was developing into a printer who supplied the literature the Church required.

Altogether, it is fair to judge that the house of Fust and Schöffer always preferred such texts as promised an assured sale. At the same time, Gutenberg's successors aspired to the same aesthetic standards and objectives. Peter Schöffer in particular deserves credit for the high artistic quality of these books. On 14 August 1462 – that is to say, shortly before the fall and pillage of Mainz – the *48-line Bible* was issued in a large new size of Gothic-roman type from the Fust and Schöffer works once again, and here for the first time a printer's mark is fitted next to the colophon for the whole edition. There will be more to say about printing the *Indulgences for Neuhausen* (nowadays a part of Worms), and also printing *Broadsides* for both warring Mainz archbishops, at the Humbrechthof works.

Small publications and calendars in the DK-type

ON RETURNING TO THE ORIGINAL PRINTING HOUSE in the Gutenberghof, it has to be remembered that it was here that *27-line Donatuses* had been printed since 1448. There is every likelihood that the very first of the 12 editions so far identified were produced in Strasbourg, where the *Sibyllenweissagung* has been dated to between 1440 and 1444. In the years from 1450 to 1455, while Gutenberg's energies

Eyn manūg d' cristēheit widd' die durkē

O Almechtig' kōnig in himels tron
Der vff ertrich ein dorne crone Vñ
sin strijt baner vō blude roit Das heilge
crutze in sterbend' not Selb hat getragē
zu d' mart' grois Vñ dē bittri dot nackt
vñ blois Dar an vmb mentschlich heil
gelittē Vñ vns do mit erloist vñ erstrittē
Vñ den bosē fyant vb wūden Hilff vns
vorbas in allē stūden widd' vnser fynde
durcken vñ heiden Mache en yren bosen
gewalt leidē Den sie zu cōstantinopel in
kriechē lant An manchē cristē mentschē
begangē hant Mit fahen martin vñ dot
slagē vñ vsmehē Als den aposteln vor
zijtē ist geschen Vmb die xij stucke des
heilgen glaubē gut Halt xij die gulden
zale in hut Auch werden dis iar xij nu-
wer schin Disiceren die xij zeichē des him
mels din Als mā zelet noch diñ geburt
offenbar M · cccc · lv · iar Siebē wochē

The opening page of the Türkenkalender *for the year 1455. Original size.*

were devoted to establishing the partnership works at the Humbrechthof and to printing the *42-line Bible*, Heinrich Keffer and Bechtolff von Hanau appear to have continued the work of the Gutenberghof largely on their own initiative. Although the Helmasperger Instrument refers to them as Gutenberg's 'servants', this term should not be taken in its modern literal sense. Heinrich Keffer and Berthold Ruppel – as the latter became better known – are sooner to be regarded as junior associates of Gutenberg, especially after the master suffered his financial setback, and in view of their own later distinguished careers. Perhaps, just like the partners in the Strasbourg undertaking, they may have had a fixed financial share in the Gutenberghof venture and were accordingly concerned for its profitability. Considerable income must have flowed into the Gutenberghof as a result of printing the *31-line Cyprus Indulgences*. Seven editions of the *30-line Donatus* were fitted into the interval between 1454 and 1456.

This ongoing printing of *Donatuses* could always be interrupted, though, for the production of other small items in the DK-type. Calendars were very popular at that time. Their fairly assured sale and calculable economic return must have helped decide the print run.

However, an exception to this has to be made for the so-called *Türkenkalender* for the year 1455. This was in effect a piece of political polemic, in which the monthly divisions and calendar characteristics are used as a vehicle to summon up the might of Christendom against the peril of invasion by the Turks, who had captured Constantinople on 29 May 1453 and now menaced south-eastern and central Europe. The *Türkenkalender* consists of six quarto leaves, opening with the heading or title *Eyn Manung der christenheit widder die durken*, and then one after another the spiritual and secular heads of the Christian world are exhorted into battle: in January the pope; in February the emperor; in March the rulers of the Balkans; assorted European monarchs in April; the archbishops in May; the dauphin of France in June; the dukes of Burgundy, Savoy, Lorraine and elsewhere in July; Venice and other Italian cities and princes in August; in September '*Germania die edle deutsche Nation*', in October the German princes, in November the free imperial cities, and for December news is mentioned of a repulse of the infidels at the Hungarian border, which reached Frankfurt on 6 December 1454. On these grounds we may safely assign the printing of the calendar to a slightly later date, but presumably not after 1 January 1455, since the text ends with the first New Year's greeting to be set in movable types: *Eyn gut selig nuwe Jar* (Mori, 1928; and Geldner, 1972b: 162–3).

The observation that some of the calendar information follows Strasbourg custom – i.e. the mention of St Margaret's Day and a report of the ravages caused by the Armagnacs – leads one to speculate that the author may have been Alsatian. Ferdinand Geldner invites us to consider Heinrich Eggestein, who had served alongside Gutenberg as a constable in Strasbourg, relinquished his Strasbourg seal of office and his citizenship for a time between 1455 and 1457, and later became

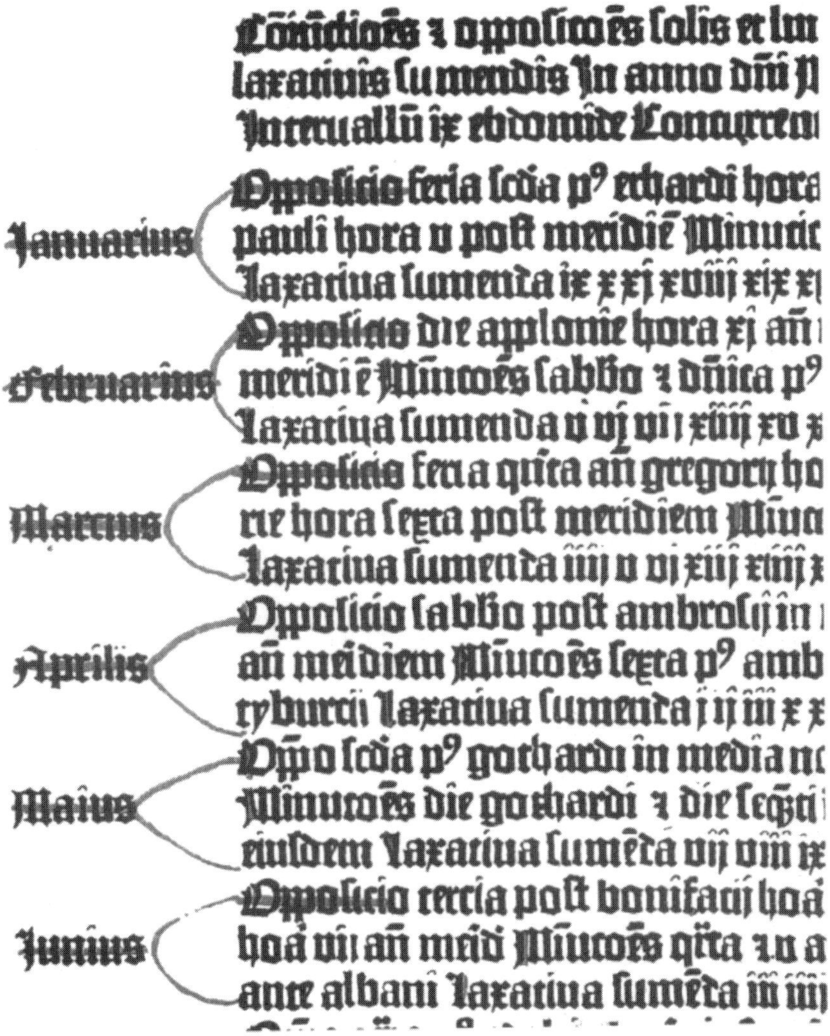

The Aderlass- und Laxierkalender *for the year 1457.*
Detail from the surviving fragment. Reduced.

Strasbourg's first printer (if one leaves Gutenberg himself out of contention). Eggestein would probably have been present during the printing of the B42, and have continued to work with Gutenberg after the lawsuit was over. But it must remain an open question whether Heinrich Eggestein could have secured the order for printing the *Türkenkalender*.

It is possible to be quite sure about when the *Aderlass- und Laxierkalender* was printed too, although only a single fragment of this broadside has come to light. This calendar must have gone to press in 1456, since it was intended for use in the following year. It specifies the most propitious days for bloodletting and administering laxatives during the year 1457 according to astrological indications.

The *Cisianus zu deutsch* is likewise a broadside. It functions as an aid to learning the calendar dates as applicable to every year. It is generally accepted that the *Cisianus*, a translation into German of a Latin calendar which opens with the words *Cisio Janus*, must have been printed after the *Aderlass- und Laxierkalender*, since the types of the *Cisianus* show greater signs of wear. The unique surviving leaf is printed on a paper size of $17\frac{3}{4} \times 12\frac{1}{4}$ inches; a paper which has the Bull's-head-X watermark, similar to that occurring in the *42-line Bible*.

Also by 1456, even perhaps by late in 1455, the *Türkenbulle* of Calixtus III, who had become pope on the demise of Nicholas V, would have been printed. On 29 June 1455, the new pope had appealed for a crusade against the Turks, which was due to commence on 1 May 1456, and it is certain that his text, published in both Latin and German versions, would need to be disseminated some months ahead of this deadline. The Church's propaganda in Germany had been delegated to the Koblenz-born bishop of Trondheim, Heinrich Kalteisen, who had translated the bull into German himself. He or one of his staff may have seen the advantages offered by placing an order to have this publication printed.

The German language version of the *Türkenbulle* is headed: 'Dis ist die bulla und der ablas zu dutsche ... widder die bosen und virfluchten tyrannen die turcken Anno MCCCCLVI ... '. It consists of 14 leaves of paper, $8\frac{1}{4}$ inches $\times$ $5\frac{1}{2}$ inches, only 25 pages of which are printed (Ruppel, 1967: 127).

It seems reasonable also to assign to 1456, judging from the state of the DK-type and the style of setting, an edition of the *Provinciale romanum*, or list of all archbishoprics throughout the world. Of the entire copy, which was discovered in Kiev in 1941, only the first and last leaves are missing, while pages 3 to 18 are well preserved. The name '*Alemania*' at the head of the roll-call of German bishoprics is distinguished by a rubricated initial, from which it could be assumed that whoever ordered this piece of Latin printing entertained a particular interest in the German provinces of the Church. There may have been some possible connection between the printing of the *Provinciale romanum* and the fact that Calixtus III had sought to delegate his cardinal, Nicholas of Cues, to visit the Rhenish electors. But Nicholas had withdrawn from this commission, and so one has to look for the prime mover behind this piece of printing among those close to the archbishop of Mainz, or to the Mainz patrician, Johann Guldenschaph, with whom Nicholas of Cues had stayed on previous visits, and who was later to establish a printing office of his own (Lübke, 1968: 184).

A broadside, the Latin prayer *Respice domine sancte pater*, written by Ekbert von Schönau, ought again to date from this slightly earlier phase, since it displays irregular line endings besides some dancing about in the fitting and alignment of characters and a lack of crispness to the edges of types. The leaf size is 11½ inches × 8 inches. Damage to the head margin, which appears to be caused by hanging the sheet from a peg, brings us back to Nicholas of Cues, who had expressed his eagerness

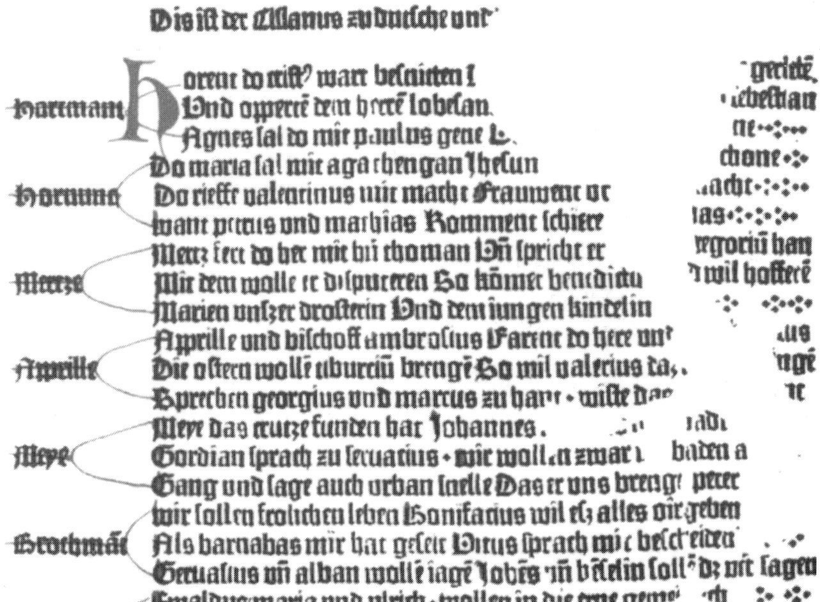
Dis ist der Cisianus zu dutsche unt

Hartman — Horent do mit? wart besnitten
Und opperte dem herrē lobesan.
Agnes sal do mit paulus gene
Do maria sal mit aga brengan Jhesun
Hornung — Do riefte valentinus wir machē Frauwent ce
want petrus und mathias Kommendt schiere
Mertze — Mertz secz do her mit bii thoman Un spricht er
Mit dem wolle er dispuciren So kömmet benedictus
Marien unszer drostern Und dem iungen kindelin
Apprille — Apprille und bischoff ambrosius Farent do here un
Die ostern wollē tiburciū brengē So wil valerius da
Sprechen georgius und marcus zu hant wiste das
Meye — Meye das crutze funden hat Johannes.
Gordian sprach zu servacius wir wollen zwar
Gang und sage auch urban snelle Das er uns brengē
Brachmāt — wir sollen frolichen leben Bonifacius wil es alles dir geben
Als barnabas mir hat geseit Vitus sprach mit beschriben
Gervasius un̄ alban wollē iagē Johēs un̄ bēlein soll
Ewaldus maria und ulrich wollen in die erne geen

Cisianus. *Probably 1456. German translation of a Latin calendar. Detail from the only known copy: Cambridge University Library. Reduced.*

Dis ist die bulla und der ablas zu
dutsche die uns unser aller heil-
gister vatter und herre babst calist9
gesant und geben hat wider die
bosen un verfluchten tyrannen die
turcken Anno M cccc lvi 1 cetera

Calistus ein diener der diener
gottes Den wirdigen userz-
welten brudern Patriarchen Ertz-
bischoffen bischoffen und yren lie
ben kindern yn geistlichen sachen
vicarien ebren und allen geistlichē
personē die durch die gantz cristēheit gesessen sint selikeit uns unser
bebstlichen gesegenūg · wante yn
den ṽgangen iaren der ungnedigē
und unmilder ṽfolger des cristlichē
namens der tyranne der turcke ·:·
Noch der zijt als er ṽtrucket hat

The Türkenbulle *of Pope Calixtus III. German version.*
Printed 1455/56. Enlargement of opening page.

on previous inspections of the German dioceses for the texts of important prayers to be hung up in churches so that worshippers could learn them properly.

The last of these calendars and small items printed in the DK-type to be discussed is that still generally referred to as the *Astronomische Kalender für 1448*. This achieved central importance for Gutenberg

Provinciale romanum.
An index of archbishoprics and bishoprics within the Catholic Church. The only known copy. Kiev: Vernadsky Central Scientific Library of the Ukrainian Academy of Sciences. Detail.

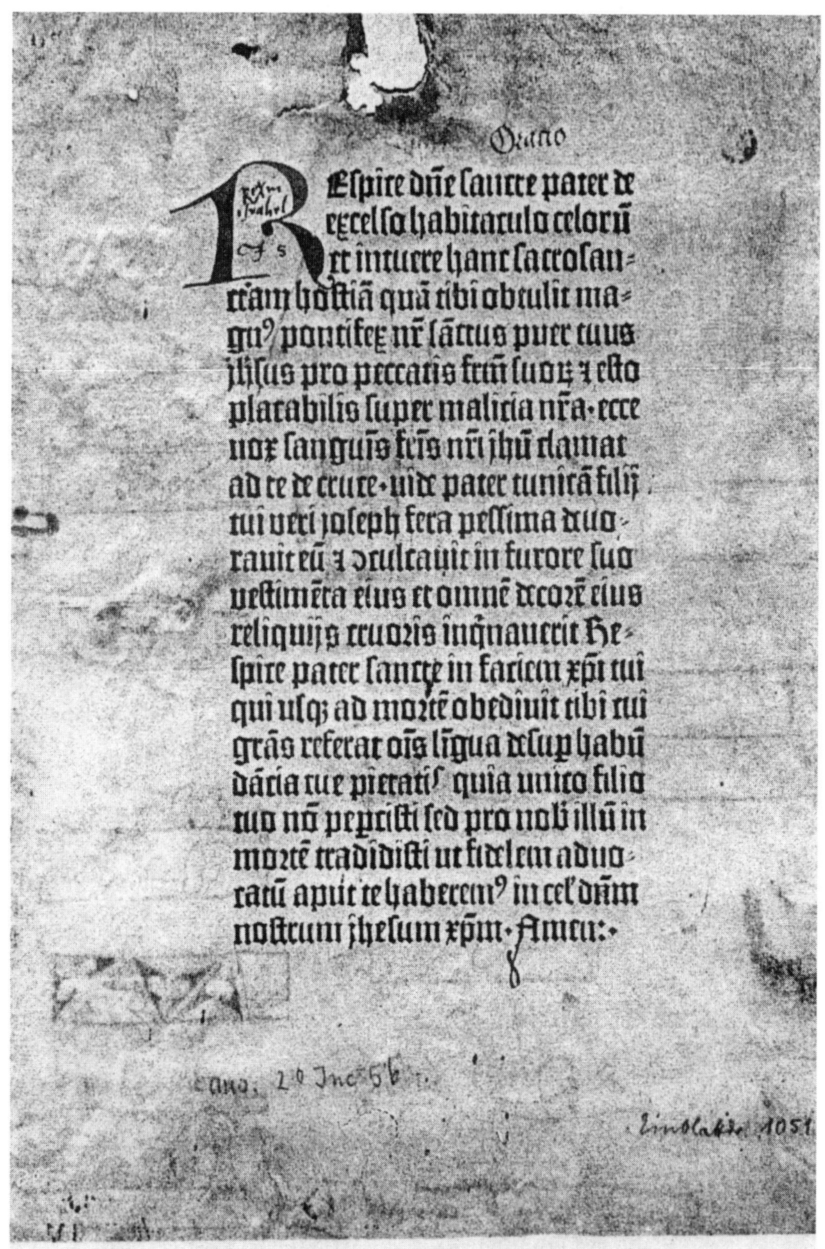

Oracio

Respice dn̄e sancte pater de
excelso habitaculo celorū
et intuere hanc sacrosan-
ctam hostiā quā tibi obtulit magnus pontifex nr̄ sanctus puer tuus
ihesus pro peccatis fratrū suorū et esto
placabilis super malicia nr̄a. ecce
vox sanguinis fr̄is nr̄i ihū clamat
ad te de cruce. vide pater tunicā filii
tui veri ioseph fera pessima devo-
ravit eū et conculcavit in furore suo
vestimēta eius et omnē decorē eius
reliquiis cruoris inquinavit Respice pater sancte in faciem xp̄i tui
qui usque ad mortē obedivit tibi tui
grās referat oīs lingua desuper habū
dācia tue pietatis quia unico filio
tuo nō pepercisti sed pro nobis illū in
mortē tradidisti ut fidelem advo-
catū apud te haberemus in cel' dn̄m
nostrum ihesum xp̄m. Amen.

Latin prayer: Respice domine sancte pater,
Broadside. The only known copy. Munich University Library. Reduced.

research as a whole, for while its date could be firmly assigned to 1448, it provided a foundation stone for dating the entire edifice of early printing. This broadside, with its imposing size of about 28¼ inches × 26½ inches, must have consisted of six pieces pasted together, each having a printed area of 10½ inches × 7 inches, and of which only those parts from January to April have been preserved. The make-up of these single leaves lets us conclude that the presses in question could not have coped with an effective printing area greater than about 12 inches x 8 inches. The *Astronomische Kalender* does record a whole number of calculations which refer specifically to 1448. But this 'calendar' was really intended as a table for the use of lay astrologers, showing the position of the planets in the zodiac at the new and full moons for the purpose of casting horoscopes, knowing that this data would remain basically valid for a period of some 20 to 30 years after the year of 1448 for which it had been compiled. (Widmann, 1972b: 17). It has been known for a long time that the later celebrated astronomer, Regiomontanus, had undertaken as an early student assignment in Leipzig to recalculate the astronomical information for that very year of 1448. Georg von Purbach and Regiomontanus became the first in modern times to plot a lunar eclipse precisely, on 9 September 1457 at Melk (Zinner, 1938: 128ff). Yet again we stumble across another enthusiasm of Nicholas of Cues, who had foreseen the necessity of calendar reform and a revision of the Alfonsine Tables at the time of the Basle Council; and had set to work on the project in collaboration with his friend the Greek cardinal, Bessarion, and with Purbach and Regiomontanus (Lübke, 1968: 216, 237). I would not go so far as to suggest that Gutenberg may have received the manuscript of the *Astronomische Kalender* from Nicholas himself, but his general interest in the field may have been awakened by the cardinal.

In 1948 Carl Wehmer established conclusively – on evidence supplied by newly discovered proofs set in the type of the *Astronomische Kalender*, and supported by an investigation by Viktor Stegemann into its astronomical relevance – that the *Kalender* could not have been printed until some ten years later, that is to say in 1457/58 (Wehmer, 1948). It is clear that any calendar which is intended, as this one was, to serve as a basis for casting horoscopes, must also supply the constellations for those born earlier, and consequently the calendar's year and planetary positions must be considerably older than the date of printing. This early dating had previously been called into question in any case, since the state of the type suggested that it could only have been printed after the *Türkenbulle*. Moreover, individual characters crop up in the *Astronomische Kalender* which otherwise make their first appearance after the DK-type had been refashioned for printing the *36-line Bible*. This provides absolutely no justification, though, for advancing the early dating of the *27-line Donatuses* or the *Sibyllenweissagung*. It is quite right to place the items printed in the DK-type in a sequence determined by the state of the type material, but at the same time external factors, such as political or social considerations, need to be taken into account in dating any piece of printing.

Taken together, it should be noted that of all the small jobs printed

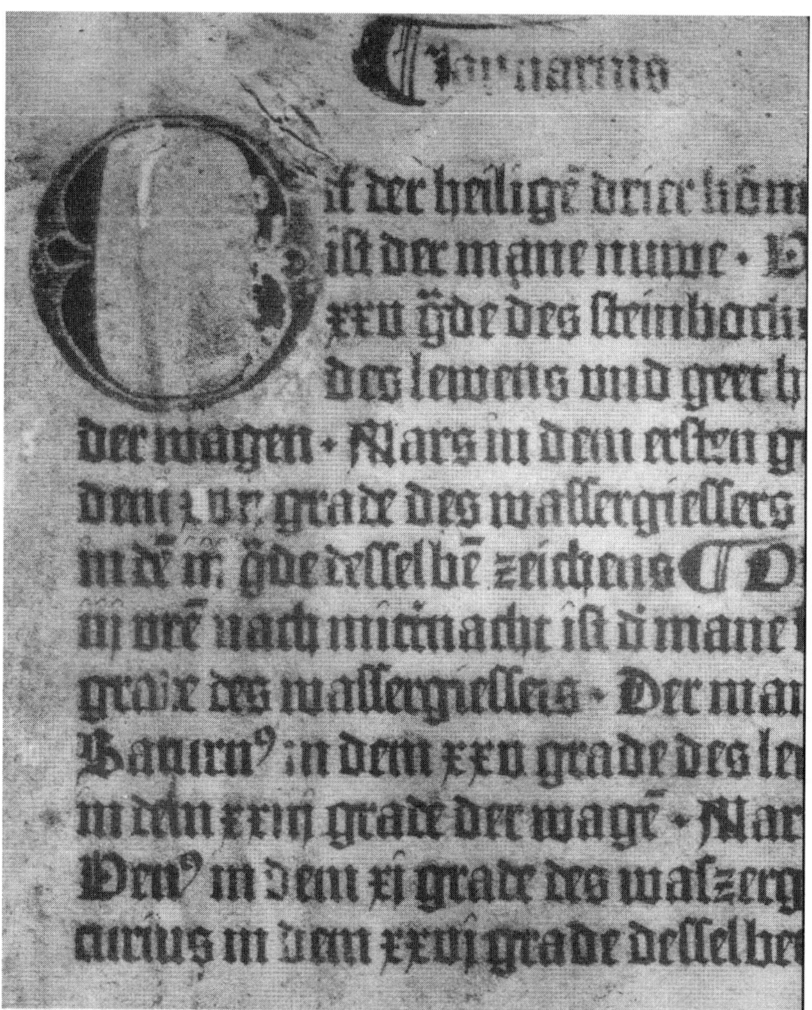

The so-called Astronomical Calendar for the year 1448.
Detail.

in DK-types, about half have survived either in a single copy or as an incomplete fragment. This prompts the conclusion that still other similar items may have disappeared without trace or are yet waiting to be discovered. The main business at the Gutenberghof works seems to have consisted in printing *Donatuses*. The seven editions of the *30-line Donatus* were apparently followed by two more *26-line* settings, in which the state of the DK-type comes to resemble more closely that of the *Astronomische Kalender*; from which it follows that these were probably produced in 1457/58 as well.

To what degree would Gutenberg have been personally involved with these small publications? It is understandable that he should have regarded the lost lawsuit, the forfeiture of the Humbrechthof printing house, and the shattering of his far-reaching plans as personal setbacks, although he probably emerged from these entanglements far from penniless. Certainly he must have found it hard to be forced back upon the limited printing capabilities of the Gutenberghof. But it may be possible to detect his not inconsiderable influence, merely from the choice of subject matter behind such titles as the *Türkenbulle* and *Türkenkalender*, not to mention the *Astronomische Kalender*.

On 21 June 1457, Gutenberg's name appears as a witness in a Mainz legal document (Schorbach, 1900: 211–2, doc. XXI). Its content is scarcely of any importance. It deals with the sale of a property that was encumbered with a perpetual interest obligation in favour of the church of St Viktor in Mainz, to which the new purchaser was obliged to assent. This treaty of sale was witnessed at the residence of Leonhard Mengoss, a canon of St Viktor's. At least this document shows Gutenberg as a respectable and probably a property-owning citizen at the time. It further admits the conclusion that he may have been a member of the St Viktor Brotherhood by then. Entries in the account books of the St Thomas Chapter of Strasbourg make less pleasant reading, showing that since 1458 Gutenberg had defaulted on the four pounds in annual interest due on the loan of 80 pounds or denars which he had taken out in 1442. As early as 1457/58 an outlay of two schillings is recorded for attempting to arrest Johann Gutenberg and his guarantor Martin Brechter (Schorbach, 1900: 213, doc. XXII). It has to be assumed that the interest for this particular year was eventually paid. Thereafter St Thomas's account books continue to enter interest for each successive year as remaining unpaid. Even writs sent to Mainz met with no success. Gutenberg was clearly in financial difficulties.

The 36-line Bible

GUTENBERG SCHOLARS in the first half of the twentieth century had a hard nut indeed to crack, and one which is hardly remembered nowadays. A key problem for much of this period was whether it was the *36-line Bible* or the *42-line Bible* which had come first. Thirteen copies altogether of a Latin Bible in two volumes, although sometimes bound as three volumes instead, were to be found in libraries, set in Gutenberg's original typeface: the DK-type. And from this fact alone, it seemed to follow that the *36-line Bible* must be the earlier. That the *36-line Bible* was not so well printed as the *42-line* version added weight to this argument. True, every character in the DK-type had been newly cast and accurately dressed for printing this Bible, but nonetheless it lacked the ultimate splendour. A certain confusion had persisted, because leaves one to four of the first volume and both opening leaves of the second volume had been set from an unfamiliar manuscript source. But as soon as it was established that for the entire remaining text the B42 must have served as manuscript and exemplar, the question of priority had naturally been resolved.

Gutenberg, who has to be recognized as the owner of the DK-type, would not, however, while presumably printing the *Catholicon* at the Gutenberghof between 1458 and 1460, have been able to produce the massive *36-line Bible* at the same time. In the Bibliothéque Nationale, Paris, there is a single leaf of B36 to be found with a rubricator's note stating that his work had been finished in 1461 (Geldner, 1964: 48). Accordingly, the B36 must have been printed between 1458 and about the beginning of 1460. Since then it has been ascertained that the Bamberg printer Albrecht Pfister was already working with the B36-types in 1460/61, by which time the *Ackermann aus Böhmen* had appeared; but this book is full of typographic defects of a kind which could never have arisen had Albrecht Pfister been involved in printing the B36 immediately beforehand.

There are various other arguments in favour of Bamberg as the place of printing. No fewer than ten different kinds of paper are used in B36, and nearly all of them come from paper mills in the vicinity of Bamberg. Among these papers, not a single one is to be found that was used for printing in Mainz at that time. Paper evidence proves an important scientific aid to incunabula research, since on the basis of watermark designs – formed of thin wire sewn onto the moulds used by the papermaker – it is often possible to tell the place and date of origin of the paper in question (Geldner, 1970: I, 47). The original provenance of nearly all surviving copies and fragments of B36 centre

bro· Et quosdā quidē posuit deus in ecclīa· primū aplos· secūdo ꝓphetas· tercio doctores: deinde uirtutes· exinde gratias cu-
racionū: opitulationes guber-
nationes· genera linguarꝫ: int-
pretationes sermonū· Nunqd
oēs apli? Nunqd omnes ꝓphe-
te? Nūquid oēs doctores? Nūqd oēs uirtutes? Nūqd oēs
gratiā habēt curationū? Nūqd
oēs linguis loquūtur? Nun-
quid oēs interp̄tant? Emula-
mini autē carismata meliora·
Et adhuc excellētiorē uiā uobis
demonstro· XIII

Si linguis hoīm loquar et
angelorꝫ: caritatē aūt nō
habeā: factus sum velut es so-
nās aut cimbalū tinniēs· Et si
habuero ꝓphetiam· ⁊ nouerim
misteria oīa ⁊ omnē scientiā
⁊ habuero omnē fidē ita ut mō-
tes trāsferam· caritatē aūt non
habuero: nichil sum· Et si distri-
buero in cibos pauperū oēs
facultates meas· et si tradidero
corp9 meū ita ut ardeā: carita-
tem aūt nō habuero: nichil michi ꝓdest· Caritas patiēs est: be-
nigna est· Caritas nō emulatr·
nō agit perperā: nō inflatr· nō
est ambiciosa: nō querit q̄ sua
sūt· Nō irritatr: nō cogitat ma-
lū: nō gaudet sup iniq̄tate: con-
gaudet aūt ueritati· oīa suffert·
oīa credit· oīa sperat: oīa
a sustinet· Caritas nūq̄ excidit·
Siue ꝓphetie euacuabūt: siue
lingue cessabūt: siue sciētia de-
struetr· Ex parte eñi cognoscim9:
⁊ ex parte ꝓphetam9· Cū aūt ue-
nerit qd p̄fectū ē: euacuabitr qd
ex parte est· Cum essem paruulus loquebar ut paruulus: sa-
piebā ut paruul9: cogitabā ut
paruulus· Quando aūt factus
sum uir: euacuaui q̄ erant par-
uuli· Videm9 nūc p speculū in
enigmate: tunc aūt facie ad fa-
ciem· Nunc cognosco ex parte:
tunc aūt cognoscā: sicut ⁊ cog-
nitus sum· Nūc autē manēt fides spes caritas tria hec· Maior
aūt horꝫ est caritas· XIIII

Sectamini caritatē: emula-
mini spūalia: magis aūt
ut ꝓphetis· Qui eñi loquitr lig-
ua: non hoībus loquitr· sed
deo· Nemo eñi audit· Spiritus
aūt loquitr misteria· Nā qui ꝓ-
phetat: hoībus loquitr ad edifi-
cationē et exhortationem et cō-
solationem· Qui loquitr ligua·
semetipm edificat: q̄ autē ꝓphe-
tat ecclesiā dei edificat· Volo aūt
oēs uos loqui liguis: magis
aūt ꝓphetare· Nam maior ē q̄
prophetat q̄ qui loquitr liguis
nisi forte interpretetr: ut ecclesia e-
dificationem accipiat· Nūc autem frēs· si uenero ad uos ling-

A page of the 36-line Bible. *Probably printed in Bamberg between 1457 and 1458 by Albrecht Pfister and Heinrich Keffer. From the copy in Leipzig University Library. Reduced.*

on monasteries and collections in Bamberg or its sphere of influence. Finally it is on record that the prince-bishop of Bamberg, Georg I von Schaumberg, presented the Franciscan monastery in Coburg in 1463 with a Bible printed on vellum. Three vellum leaves of the B36 were discovered at Coburg in 1940 (Geldner, 1970: I, 48).

Perchance the notary, Ulrich Helmasperger, who described himself in his well-known legal instrument as a cleric of the bishopric of Bamberg, may have informed his prince-bishop of the new art of printing, and Georg I von Schaumberg, as a connoisseur and patron of several arts, may have initiated the project in consequence. It is likely that the B36 would have been a straightforward commission, with the bishop meeting the costs of paper and printing and taking delivery of the entire edition – which, by the way, must have been increased a number of times, as emerges from the variant issues of the first sections. Perhaps the B36 was originally conceived in Mainz, for a trial proof, albeit in 40 lines, has been discovered overprinted on a waste page from a manuscript account book kept by a Mainz cloth-cutter. Another possibility is that the entire type supply may have been cast at the Gutenberghof and then transported to Bamberg.

It has been assumed that Heinrich Keffer and a few other colleagues, whose names are not known to us, accompanied this transfer of equipment. Gutenberg himself must eventually have stayed in Bamberg from time to time, as a new workshop was furnished and printing commenced, in order to support the work that was taking place there from his wealth of experience. Another name to be mentioned in this connection is that of Johann Sensenschmidt from Eger, for later on, between 1469 and 1470, Keffer and Sensenschmidt opened the first printing office in Nuremberg. Sensenschmidt may well have worked with Gutenberg and Keffer in Mainz, as probably did the Mainzer, Konrad Zeninger, and Ulrich Han from Ingolstadt, who went on to become Rome's first printer; whereas Johann Nicolai of Bamberg, who printed in Perugia from 1471 onwards, and Georg Herolt, also from Bamberg, who worked in Rome after 1481, probably learned the 'black art' in their home town either while the B36 was being printed there or later in Albrecht Pfister's workshop. It is interesting enough in itself that Bamberg should have developed into a centre from which printing was to spread to other countries and cities in the future.

In setting out to print the new Bible a page depth of 41 lines in the improved DK-type was envisaged, but aesthetic arguments for finer proportions led to an eventual reduction to 36 lines, although the work's extent was vastly increased thereby. While the *42-line Bible* had made 1286 pages in all, the same text set in the larger typeface would have occupied 1768 pages. So the *36-line Bible* was 462 pages longer, and this increased bulk accounts for why some copies were bound in three volumes. Despite the bigger task, it is probable that only two presses were available for printing these volumes; which in turn would call for four compositors to handle the typesetting. As a result of the larger typesize, and a more restricted fount of 186 characters, line-endings could not be justified with quite the finesse of its exemplar, the *42-line Bible*. Notwithstanding this, the B36 is indisputably a masterpiece, and its creation between about 1458 and 1460 is now generally accepted (Ruppel, 1967: 131; Wehmer, 1948: 20-21; Rosarivo, 1955: 70ff). Whether it can also be considered as the work of Gutenberg remains to be seen. The decisive elements, the typeface and its typographic arrangement, may have been Gutenberg's contribution, but Heinrich Keffer is likely to have taken the entire project through to completion. From being Gutenberg's servant and assistant, as he is described in the Helmasperger Instrument, he had become a master printer in his own right.

An edition size for the B36 is hard to estimate. Thirteen copies have been preserved, with a few additional fragments and individual leaves on vellum. An average of the estimates which have been made would indicate 20 copies on vellum and 60 paper copies. Such numbers would have met the current need of the Bamberg diocese.

The entire type material for B36, as well as a printing workshop and both presses installed for this purpose, were sold to Albrecht Pfister not long after the Bible printing was finished. Pfister had served until then as secretary to the dean and (after 1459) prince-bishop of Bamberg, Georg I von Schaumberg. Pfister recognized further uses for the printer's craft, and he specialized – after first issuing a *Donatus* – in a series of little popular works, mostly in German. In 1461, *Der Ackermann aus Böhmen* was published, and a second edition was called for by 1463 which contained five full-page woodcuts. A collection of fables by the Swiss writer Ulrich Boner, *Der Edelstein* (1461), was to become equally well known; it was decorated with 200 woodcuts, even if some of the same blocks are repeated from time to time. This makes Pfister the earliest printer to unite typography with printed illustrations, and, although his typesetting and presswork could never be compared to the quality achieved by Gutenberg or Fust and Schöffer, his products were quickly sold for their texts and illustrations (Geldner, 1970: I, 49).

With this Bamberg printing office, later to become the Pfister works, the *nova forma scribendi* had spread beyond the walls of Mainz. It should not be overlooked that active patronage must have linked the two cities, and that Bamberg's distinctive contribution was the woodcut illustration, which from now on accompanies the further spread of the printed book.

Heinrich Keffer is most likely to have returned to the Gutenberghof. Had he remained in Bamberg, then it is fair to expect that the quality of Pfister's early printing would have been far higher.

Who was the printer of the Catholicon?

GUTENBERG MUST INEVITABLY HAVE FELT CONSTRICTED by the limited printing resources of the Gutenberghof. The routine production of *Donatus* and *Kalender* editions can have afforded him scant creative satisfaction. He had some new and different kind of venture in mind, which called for the enlargement of his printing establishment at the Gutenberghof, and he staked his remaining financial resources to this end. This may explain why he was no longer able to meet interest payments on the Strasbourg loan. Presumably normal productivity and supplying types for the prince-bishop of Bamberg, Georg I von Schaumberg, also yielded certain revenues. But the necessary outlay involved a much vaster sum; almost on a par with that estimated for printing the *42-line Bible*. The inventor needed a new financial backer. He found him in Dr Konrad Humery, town clerk of Mainz. Once again he was able to offer as security those instruments and types that were to be manufactured using the capital borrowed.

And so he re-embarked on that course which had ended so disastrously over the *42-line Bible*. This time, the master probably had even less chance of profit or business success. The triumphant vindication of his invention through the completion of the *42-line Bible* signified a boost to his ego after decades of wrestling. Since then it must have dawned on him what tremendous implications his discoveries held for the spread of knowledge and culture. Whereas Fust and Schöffer continued to attach great importance to maintaining the secrecy that had always enveloped the new art, the inventor himself had apparently changed his mind. Printing could not have taken place in Bamberg without his active approval. By 1457 or thereabouts, Heinrich Eggestein must have left Mainz to return to Strasbourg, because from as early as 1458 the first books start to appear from the Strasbourg workshop of Heinrich Eggestein and Johann Mentelin. These chronological links between the beginning of printing in Bamberg and Strasbourg and Gutenberg's failure to make payment to St Thomas's Chapter in Strasbourg, as well as his presumed borrowing from Konrad Humery and starting work on printing the *Catholicon*, may all be connected with each other, and still await a thorough reconsideration. It looks as though

The type of the Catholicon.
Original size.
Reconstructed by Gottfried Zedler.

Gutenberg did not wish to see the undeserved superiority of Fust and Schöffer's office become a monopoly for his unloved rivals, and took steps to ensure that the new art could spread in free and open competition.

The *Catholicon* of Johann Balbus de Janua which appeared in 1460 in Mainz is a work best described as a great Latin dictionary with a Latin grammar, which also served the educated person of that age as a sort of encyclopaedia (Zedler, 1905, and 1942: 461ff). Since its first compilation in 1246, it must have been copied out many hundreds of times. An assured sale for such a famous and important book could plainly be anticipated.

To commence a work like that, extending to 744 pages in folio, and in a relatively high printing which has been estimated to be in the region of 300 copies, represented a massive undertaking for the time. And yet there are 64 paper and 10 vellum copies surviving today (although there are recent conjectures, which will need to be gone into later, according to which these numbers have to be divided between either two or three editions). This vast quantity of text called for a smaller typeface; in fact for the smallest size that had ever yet been used for typesetting. It is a Gothic roman of the kind written by contem-porary humanist scribes. In contrast to liturgical texts – such as the *Gutenberg Bible* or the *Mainz Psalter* – for which textura was seen as the most suitable typeface, or the *30-line Indulgence* where a Gothic bastarda appeared more appropriate, for the 'data bank of learning', if the *Catholicon* may be so described, an early form of roman with consider-able vestiges of Gothic influence was used.

The setting is in double columns as with the *Gutenberg Bible*. However, lines are not of equal length as we find them in the Bible, but instead the right column edges are irregular as happens with fixed-space typewriting. This style of typesetting, known as 'ragged' composition, is still used nowadays and is appropriate for text matter that is not

The four small typefaces in use by 1460. Actual size.

ut ipoꝝ videbit̃ ꝯſcientiis.ꝓuociinbꝫ vel nūcius Sub-
ꝯeligendi ꝯfeſſionibꝫ eoꝝ audits.ꝓ ꝯmiſſis etiā Sedi
ū debitā abſolutionē impēdere ꝛ penitētiā ſalutarē
ū ꝛ Interdicti aliiſqꝫ ſentētiis cēſuris ꝛ penis eccleſia-
iūcta ꝑ modo culpe penitētia ſalutari vel aliis que
r amiſſionem loquele ꝯfiteri non poterint ſigna ꝯtri.

Type of the 31-line Indulgence for Cyprus.

is attemptaui cū quasi nulle sint. s; consummacō
nis fiduciam laboris q; mercedem totaliter in sa
maritano pulso timore figens. qui prolatis in pro
curatione seminiui duobus denarijs superoganti
cūcta reddere e est professus. delectat nos sane ueri
tas pollicentis s; terret immensitas laboris. desideriū

The Catholicon *type.*

iariꝰ Ambasiator ⁊ ꝓcurator generalis Serenissimi
olaus diuīa ꝓuidētia pp quītꝰ afflictis Regni Cypri
s gratis cōcessit omībꝫ xpifidelibꝫ ubilibet ɔstitutis
die Maij Anni dñi Mcccclij icipiēdū ꝓ defēsiōe catho
ɔsciētijs ꝓcūtoribꝫ uel nūcijs substitutis pie erogaue
ditis. ꝓ cōmissis etiā sedi aplice reseruatis excessibꝫ

Type of the 30-line Indulgence for Cyprus.

eū omia ɔdidit siue iussit. imago dicit᷑ ꝓpter parē
similitudinē pris. Siquidē apud xpianos seculares
psone laici dicunt᷑. laos eni grece dicit᷑ ppls latine
Cleicales sūt. q̄ in ecclia deseruiūt vel ipm regūt. a de
ros qꝫ ē sors ꝓut iā dicet᷑. Hee aūt subdiuidunt᷑ in
monachos. i. insingłarit' degētes. Nā monos grece

The Durandus *type.*

intended for sustained reading; whereas in texts meant for continuous reading – represented at that time by the Bible and in our own day by novels and academic texts – lines of even length are more readable and are always to be preferred on functional grounds. It has been maintained that on no account could the printer of the *42-line Bible* be identical with the printer of the *Catholicon*, because the Bible is so much finer and more harmonious in its typesetting (Ruppel, 1938b: 83ff). This seems to me a hasty judgment; I believe that then, just as now, great pains were taken to find a visual solution which corresponded to the content and literary genre of the text in question.

In the hunt for the printer of the *Catholicon* one immediately encounters the Latin colophon, which runs as follows in English:

> By the help of the most high, at whose bidding the tongues of children become eloquent, and who often reveals to the lowly what he conceals from the wise; this noble book, *Catholicon*, in the year of our Lord's incarnation, 1460, in the

Gummi.a gutta dr hoc gummi indeclinabile lac
ma arbor q est quasi gutta et pmo gutta exit a
ligno.et inde durescit et fit gummi.et hinc gūmo
Gurdus.a guttur dr gurdus a ū. Jus sa sum
ineptus.stultus.inutil.importunus.et pcipue in
Gurges itis mas. Comesacōnibus recipiendis
ge ppriie locus altus in flumine p tapinosim.tn
sepe ponit pro mari ul p loco pfundo in mari.
quā tapinosim solent etiā autores eleuare p ad
iuccōnem eppteti istius scz magnus ul altus uel
uastus ul consimiliū.et dr gurges a guttur.quia
e quasi guttur fluminis.A gurges deriuat gurgi
to as.uorare ul implere.Et componit ingurgito
as implere ul deuorare.Et e gurgito actiū cū di
bus suis compositis.Et cor pnl sicut et gurgites
in obliquis.Vnde ouidius de arte.Quo minime
credis gurgite piscis erit.Gurgito as in gurges e
Gurgulio.a guttur dr hic gurgulio onis quedā
ps in ore cui pximū est rumen.cuius meatus ad
os et nares ptendit.habens uiam qua uox ad
linguam transmittit.ut possit uba collidere.Item
gurgulio inuenit pro quodam uime que comedit
legumina.Sed in hac significacōne debet potius
scribi per c.vnde in c dixi de curculio.
Gurgustiū.a guttur ul gurgulio quod e potius
curculio dr hoc gurgustiū tij cella modica uel do
mus paupeu angusta secreta et tenebrosa uel lo
cus tabernau tenebrosus ubi turpia cōuiuia fiūt.
ul ubi pisces mittūtur ul rete piscatou.quia in
aquis curculiones dephendē solent.Vnde in iob
qdragesimoprimo.Nūqd implebis sagenas pelle eius
Gurgustiuus a ū et gurgustium capite illius
ad gurgitē ptinens.et dr a gurges itis.et prod ti
Gustito as pnl cor ūbū fre.i.freqūter gustare
Gusto tas in gustus uide.
Gustus.a guttur dr hic gustus tus tui.vnus de
qnqz sensibus corpis.et inī gusto as aui are.i.liba
re quod uulgo dr assazare.Et componit aggusto
as.i.ualde ul iuxta gustare.Item congusto as.i.
simul gustare.Itez degusto as.i.ualde ul deorsuz
ul de aliquo gustare.Item pgusto as plibare.aū
gustare.Item regusto stas.id est iterum gustare
Gusto et eius composita neutra sunt.
Gutta te e aqua que stat et pau fluit.stilla uo
que cadit.hinc stillicidiū stilla cadens.Stiria eniz
grecū est.i.gutta.et inde diminutiue dr stilla.dū
autē stat aut pendet de tectis ul arboribus.quasi
glutinosa gutta est.vnde gutta quasi gluta.Inde
glutinosa a glutine dū ceciderit stilla.Gutta etiaz
dr quedā infirmitas.Et scribit p duo t fm pris.
Et a gutta dr gutto as.i.guttatim cadere ul gut
tatim fundere.ul guttis perfundere.vnde hec gutta
men inis.Gutto componit congutto tas.Degut
to as.Ingutto as.Pergutto as.Regutto as.Sug
gutto as.i.sub ul pau guttare.Gutto as pro gut
tatim cadē neutu est.Alias cū suis compositis e
actiuum.Item a gutta guttosus sa osum plenus
guttis.uide in grando et in uentus.
Gutto as in gutta exponitur.
Guttim.i.guttatim aduerbium.a gutta dicitur
Guttula le diminutiuuz parua gutta.
Guttulus li quid minutus piscis.et dr a gutta
Guttur neu ge dr a garrio ris et dr guttur qua
si garrur.quia inde garritus pcedit.Et producit
pmā pōne.Vn in auro.Quod guttur transit nō
Gutturna.a guttur dr guttur compitur ibi
na ne infirmitas gutturis que solet cū inflatione
gutturis euenire.vnde gutturnosus a um illam
Gutturniū nij quoddam habens infirmitatē
uas aquatile in inferiori pte pforatum quod in
ferius deguttat aquam.Et dicitur a gutta.
Guttus ti mas ge.genus uasis vnguentarij p
breuitate a gutta dcūs.vnde hoc guttū ti vngentū
in eodem repositū.Vn iuuenalis.Nec ex opposito
pauidus tegit inguina gutto.
Guua ul guuia uas uitreū ul cucurbita qd uero
sa dicit.et uidet dici a gula quasi gulosa in sang
uine accipiendo.ul a cucurbita pter similitudi
nem.ul qr de ea fit fm hug.Pap uo dicit.Guua
uas uitreum que a latinis a similitudine cucurbi
te uentosa uocatur.que animata spiritu per igni
culum in superficiem trahit sanguinem.
HAbel interptatur iustus ul
luctus.quo nomine pfigu
rabat occidendus.Id et ua
nitas.quia cito solutus est
et subtractus.
Habena.Ab habeo dr hec
habena ne.i.lorum.retina
culū freni.qr ea habemus
.i.retinemus equos.Vnde
habenatus ta tū.i.habenam habens.ul habena
ornatus.et habeno as.i.habenā regere ul habe
nam preparare et ornare.Et producit be.
Habenula le dimi.parua habena.Et cor penl.
Habeo es ui itū componit cū ad et dr adhibeo
es.Item cū con et dr cohibeo es.Item cū ex et dr
exhibeo es.Item cū in et dr inhibeo es.Item cū
p et dicit phibeo es.Item cū pre et dicit pbibeo
es.Item cū per et dicit phibeo es.Item cuz re et
dr rehabeo es.habeo et eius composita sunt ac
tiua pter cohibeo quod e neutu.Item omnia fa
ciunt pteritū in bui et sup in bitū.et omnia cor
Habilis.ab habeo bes dr hic et hec ha ba ul bi
bilis et hoc bile.ad habendū commodus aptus et
oportunus.congruus.Et compatur.vnde habili
ter lius me.et hec habilitas tatis.et componit in
habilis.i.non habil.vnde hec inhabilitas et cor bi
Habitabil.ab habeo es.uel habito tas.dr hic et
hec habitabil et hoc le.qd habitari pt.Et componit
inhabitabilis.i.non habitabil.et hoc habitaculū li
Habito.ab habeo bes bui bitū bitu.u in o.fit
habito tas Et componitur cū con.et dr cohabito
tas.i.simul habitare Itez cū in.et dr inhabito tas
.i.incolē.intus habitare habito et eius compo
sita omnia.sunt neutra.Licet enim habito sit fre
quentatiū.tamen qr significacionem mutauit sui
simplicis.mutauit et genus cū significacōne.quā
tamen non omnino mutauit qr qui habitat locū
aliquem frequenter illum hz.vnde cuz homo est
in expedicōne non dr habere loca in quibus ma
net ad tempus.quia non frequenter illa habet.
Habitudo habitudinis In habitus est.
Habitus.ab habeo es dr hic habitus us.i.quali
tas corpis p applicacōnez adueniens.difficile mo
bil.habitus iste nichil aliud e qz habilitas ad ac
tū.Itez habitus.i.uestimentū.ut iste monachus
habitū gerit monachalem.Item habitus.i.status
ul uolūtas.ul appetitus.ul actus siue passio hū
di.Item ab habeo habitus ta tū pticipiū.Itē ha
bitus ta tum ponit pro pingui.Et compatur et
or simus.et ab habitus deriuat hec habitudo di

A page from the Catholicon *of Johann Balbus de Janua.*
Published in 1460 in Mainz.
Reduced.

mother city of Mainz of the renowned German nation (which the clemency of God has deigned with so lofty a light of genius and free gift to prefer and render illustrious above all other nations of the earth), without help of reed, stylus or quill, but by a wonderful concord, proportion and measure of punches [*patronae*] and formes [*formae*] has been printed and finished. Hence to thee, holy Father, thyself, the Son together with the Holy Spirit, praise and glory be rendered, the triune Lord and one; and thou, devout believer in the universe, who never ceasest to praise the blessed Mary; join your approval with tribute to the Church for this book. Thanks be to God.

Altissimi presidio cuius nutu infantium lingue fi
unt diserte. Qui q̃ nũo sepe puulis reuelat quod
sap entibus celat. Hic liber egregius. catholicon.
dñice incarnacionis annis M cccc lx Alma in ur
be maguntina nacionis inclite germanice. Quam
dei clemencia tam alto ingenii lumine. dono q̃ g̃
tuito. ceteris terrarum nacionibus preferre. illustrare
q̃ dignatus est Non calami. stili. aut penne suffra
gio. s; mira patronarum formarum q̃ concordia pro por
cione et modulo. impressus atq̃ confectus est.
Hinc tibi sancte pater nato cũ flamine sacro. Laus
et honor dño trino tribuatur et uno Ecclesie lau
de libro hoc catholice plaude Qui laudare piam
semper non linque mariam DEO. GRACIAS

Printer's imprint to the Catholicon.
Natural size.

What have the Latin verses of this colophon to tell us? They make known in terms of glowing civic and national pride that the book, *Catholicon*, was accomplished in Mainz. Next, a number of hints are dropped about the new technology, in an attempt to convey the wonderful harmony and modular nature of type and its setting into pages, similar to the way in which this is referred to in the scientific writings of Nicholas of Cues (Schmidt-Künsemüller, 1951: 61). Lastly, there is praise of God, who makes the tongues of children eloquent. Even this conspicuously parallels the spiritual ethos of Nicholas, who concludes his *De conjecturis libri duo* with the words:

Praise be to God, that he avails himself of my own lack of erudition in order to open thine eyes to the spirit ... Just as uprightness itself is the ideal and fidelity, truth, proportion or justice, the regard for or perfection of all existence and the exact, unclouded reality of all realities and possibilities; so thou too will find this fundamental and flawless truth (Lübke, 1968: 322, 326, and see also Kapr, 1972: 32ff).

The text of the *Catholicon*'s colophon could only have been compiled by a devout and theologically sophisticated mind, familiar with the Biblical sources (Wisd. 20, 21, Matt. 11, 15, and Luke 19, 21) and able to conflate them.

As with everything Gutenberg may have printed, the printer's name is not given. It is still contested up to this day whether Gutenberg himself was in fact the printer (Ruppel, 1967: 169ff). As it happens, the evidence for this can only be furnished in connection with the later deployment of the Catholicon-type. It is unlikely that the colophon text would have been drafted by Gutenberg personally, but rather – under his supervision of course – by the parish cleric, Heinrich Günther, who presumably also read the *Catholicon* proofs.

Another explanation to account for why Gutenberg's name never appears is that he was not the proprietor, but only a works manager or partner, and this may well be so; and yet a more persuasive motive for the master's anonymity may be sought in his basic religious outlook – one in which the individual ego was subordinated to the community and the service of God.

The contrasting texts of the printer's imprint to the *Catholicon* and those to the *Psalter's* reveal different, almost conflicting views of the world, which typify the late Gothic age and the period of transition leading to the Renaissance and early capitalism. The printer of the *Catholicon* is still firmly part of the community of the Church and the faithful, to whom the invention is a divine gift, which he thankfully receives. The printers at the Humbrechthof refer proudly to their personal achievement in what is practically a commercial advertisement; their thinking has freed itself from the notion of a medieval hierarchy of values and now pursues a course of individual business development.

The *Catholicon* group is still full of problems. It was recognized quite early on that the *Catholicon* existed in three distinct variants, one on vellum and on paper watermarked with Bull's Heads and a red-printed *incipit*, one on paper incorporating the D-formed watermark of the Galliziani papermill near Basle without the printed *incipit*, and a third with an admixture of papers with a Tower and a Crown as watermarks. The paper researcher Theo Gerardy then established that the papers with Tower and Crown watermarks could not have existed in 1460 and recommended that 1468 should be accepted as the probable date of printing (Gerardy, 1973: 105). But by 1465 the Marienkloster in Altenburg had purchased a *Catholicon* for 41 *Schock* (threescore) of groschen (about 27 gulden), as a contemporary ownership entry proves. There are a variety of other factors which argue decisively in favour of the *Catholicon* having been printed by about 1460, including the fact that

Mainz itself fell in October 1462 and was sacked by the troops of the archbishop, Adolf von Nassau. The Gutenberghof was made over to a loyal supporter of the new archbishop and Gutenberg exiled from the city. It is inconceivable that sufficient typesetting of the *Catholicon* could have been set up, and left undisturbed by this armed conflict, to be useful for subsequent editions.

I find it quite possible, though, that the printing of the *Catholicon* was divided between various working partnerships. It is to be assumed that Gutenberg was the initiator and Dr Konrad Humery the principal financier for the project. Heinrich Keffer, who in 1459 had completed the printing of the *36-line Bible* in Bamberg, may have engaged with the Bamberg notary, Helmasperger, to produce a co-edition from the same typesetting. A third team made up of Heinrich Günther and Berthold Ruppel, or possibly others, may likewise have shown interest in a division of costs and labour. It seems natural that different printing papers with different watermarks should have been employed to identify the assorted editions. The technical difficulty of this kind of co-production would arise in transferring the pages from one press to another. This could only be overcome if all three presses were housed in the same room, as would have been possible at the Gutenberghof.

The results of paper research have led the American scholar Paul Needham to the ingenious hypothesis that the *Catholicon* was not printed from movable types at all, but from some form of castings – invariably taken from pairs of lines (Needham, 1982: 395–456). He had observed that in both page columns here and there either two or four lines (i.e. never one or three) are alternately set slightly out or slightly back from the left edge, and he concluded from this that these pages were composed of indissoluble two-line slugs. It would follow from this that Gutenberg was also the inventor of stereotyping. One can in fact think out several ways in which either moulds or thin stereo plates could be stored with a view to producing later impressions as needed. But to affix all these two-line metal plates to a wooden printing surface – that is to say to stick or nail them to a smoothly planed plank – would have been extremely impractical and time-consuming, if not beyond the technology of the fifteenth century, and would have negated the advantages of Gutenberg's invention. The occasional displacement of pairs of lines has its origin in a not yet fully explained way of lifting the lines out of the composing stick and placing them on a galley, and in a sometimes inexact method of locking up the page on the bed of the press. In any case, the *Catholicon* and the other works set in the same type are printed from movable types.

The *Dialogus rationis et conscientiae*, a tract by Matthias de Cracovia, bishop of Worms, also appeared in the Catholicon-type. This may have preceded the *Catholicon* as a piece of trial printing, as there is quite a lot of space between the lines. In the *Catholicon* the lines are much nearer together, indicating that the hand-mould had been more closely adjusted for a fresh casting. The tract is set in single column and consists of just a few quarto leaves. In the Paris copy of the *Dialogus rationis* there is a note to show that the owner of this volume, Heynricus Keppfer (Heinrich Keffer), had lent it and no longer demanded its return. It can be assumed that Keffer had taken some part in the production of this little book, even though he had moved away to Bamberg in order to supervise the printing of the *36-line Bible* there (Geldner, 1950: 109). This lends further support to my suggestion that apparently it was customary in the Gutenberghof printing works for associates to receive one or more copies of titles they had worked on, to sell for their own benefit.

In addition a little work of St Thomas Aquinas, *Summa de articulis fidei*, comprising no more than 14 quarto leaves, appears to predate the commencement of setting for the *Catholicon*. A later impression was issued, for which each page depth was increased from 34 lines to 36. The *Dialogus rationis* was likewise followed by a further impression. Needham supposes that both these booklets as well as their reissues were printed from two-line slugs.

But not until we reach further items printed in the Catholicon-type will the question of who actually printed the *Catholicon* be resolved.

CHAPTER NINE

The Mainz archbishops' war

Considerations of church politics

GUTENBERG WAS REPEATEDLY AFFECTED by the tumultuous events of his age. As a child, he was forced to flee Mainz with his family, and may have been brought up for part of his childhood outside the parental home. As a young man, he emigrated from Mainz because of the political conflicts between patricians and guilds, and had to establish himself afresh in Strasbourg. Just as the cooperative venture there – the 'adventure and art' – showed signs of success, his associate Andreas Dritzehn fell sudden victim to the Black Death, and the venture received a serious setback. As soon as Gutenberg had succeeded in rebuilding his enterprise, and in all probability the first printed items had been issued, the advance of the Armagnac horde caused him to abandon Strasbourg. Back in Mainz, where he sought to crown his work as an inventor with the *42-line Bible*, it was of course the civil suit brought by Fust which forced him to relinquish the Humbrechthof works and his ongoing plans for the future. Once the *Catholicon* had been completed at the Gutenberghof and the *36-line Bible* produced in Bamberg using the improved DK-type, new storm clouds gathered. Only an exceptionally single-minded character could have found new energies in these circumstances when others would have given up the struggle long ago; and only an incessantly creative personality could have completed such a tremendous accomplishment, which was to have undreamed-of significance for learning and culture in the centuries to come.

Bit by bit the edifice of the old social order was crumbling away. The outlines of a new middle-class structure were gradually sketched out in the course of the fifteenth century. Conflicts were building up behind the façade of the ecclesiastical hierarchy, within a historical context of which people at that time were still unaware. They glimpsed the world around them as shadowy shapes caught by summer lightning, whose meaning and activities remained obscure and inaccessible to them. And no one suspected that one of their contemporaries had already forged the key that would open the doors of knowledge to all mankind, and with it an understanding of social and scientific processes and interrelationships.

This chapter once again has to begin by looking at some contemporary international issues, since the events of the next few years, as enacted on stage at Mainz, represent a scene in the world theatre of that century. Again we meet in changed circumstances three characters who had encountered each other long before in Basle, when all were prominent representatives of the conciliar or reform party. First, Enea Silvio Piccolomini, now Pope Pius II, the most powerful man in the western world; it is true he remains in the background, but he is puppet-master all the same. However, as Holy Father he does not exercise convincing stage direction. Even his former allies have ceased to trust him. Many Mainzers refuse to approve all his decisions. One of his best friends, Nicholas of Cues, who genuinely wished to bring about a long overdue reform of the Church, has yielded to the force of the Austrian archduke, Sigismund, and withdrawn himself as prince-bishop of Brixen back to Rome, where he, once more in vain, is seeking to bring about improvements within the *curia*.

Pope Pius II recorded in his *Commentaries* what Nicholas of Cues had said to him:

> You wish to use me as a tool to further your own ambition. I can and will not concur in this; flattery is hateful to me. If you can bear to hear the truth, I like nothing which goes on in these curial circles; everything is corrupt, and no one does his job honourably. Neither you nor the cardinals take the interests of the Church truly to heart. Who has any regard for canon law? Where should we seek proper reverence in divine service? All are out for their own advancement and greed. If ever I speak in a consistory about reform, I am simply laughed at. I am quite superfluous in all this. Allow me to withdraw. Such a situation has become unbearable for me ...

Nicholas requested the pope to let him retreat into seclusion. The pope refused, and Cues gave way. As a solution Pius persuaded his friend to take a break in the immediate surroundings of Rome. In July 1459, Nicholas betook himself to Subiaco near Rome (Lübke, 1968: 186–7). Can it be pure coincidence that brought the German printers, Sweynheym and Pannartz, to open Italy's first printing house at Subiaco in 1465?

Archduke Sigismund, who had driven Cues from his bishopric of Brixen, now had strong support from Gregor von Heimburg – a nationwide campaigner against papal encroachment – who, on completing his studies at Bologna, had first encountered Cues as opposing counsel in a Mainz lawsuit. When the Council of Basle began, Piccolomini, Cues and von Heimburg had presented a united front for the reform of the Roman *curia* (Brockhaus, 1969: 212 and 35). And now von Heimburg was about to make another appearance in Mainz.

Germany was still split into those two parties which had emerged from the politics of the Council of Basle, the papal adherents and the conciliar reformists. The party which supported the pope had gained ground through adroit and stubborn policies. Ever more clearly, German politics were being directed from Rome. In Enea Silvio Piccolomini and Nicholas of Cues two of the most influential personalities of the age had changed camps: from being conciliar supporters they had embraced Roman centralism. One had been rewarded with a cardinal's red biretta and the other with the papal tiara itself. The third, the only one to remain true to his former principles, Gregor von Heimburg, had entered into renewed dispute with his former friend and present pope in 1459 in Mantua, and had been excommunicated for his pains. The conciliar party of reform was weakened above all by the equivocation among the German princes, who put their dynastic interests above those of the realm (Hiksch, 1978: 11ff).

The stirrings of national consciousness recalled one of the ideas of the Council of Basle, according to which at certain intervals there should be a general council on the problems of the Church and all Christian nations, at which even infringements by the pope himself could be criticized. Attention focused increasingly on Mainz, because only its archbishop, who ranked first among the imperial electors, was empowered to convoke the imperial assemblies (*Reichstag* and *Fürstentag*), and through him alone was the gathering of a new council to be expected.

As characteristic of the basic attitude of many Mainz burghers, which Johann Gutenberg in all probability would have shared, I should like to quote from a letter that Martin Mayer, chancellor of Archbishop Dietrich von Erbach, wrote in 1457 to Enea Silvio Piccolomini, who was still a cardinal at that time:

> Thousands of means have been devised, whereby the Roman see can take our money away from us in its own fashion, as though we were barbarians. So it has come about, that our nation, once so renowned, which through its courage and blood established the Holy Roman Empire and made her mistress and queen of the world, is now reduced to poverty, servitude and paying tribute. However, our princes have now awakened from their slumbers and begun to consider how they can best combat this disaster, indeed, they are resolved to shake off this yoke once and for all and to restore the old freedoms. (Piccolomini, 1962: 34).

Incidentally, Mayer's letter gave Enea the occasion to make an impressive case to the *curia*, thus improving his own image as a candidate in the following papal election.

The Neuhausen Indulgences *of 1461 and 1462*

DIETHER VON ISENBURG-BÜDINGEN secured election as the new archbishop of Mainz on 18 June 1459 by the majority of a single vote, in a restricted committee drawn from the full cathedral chapter. The election had straightforward political implications, and the chapter was well aware of Diether's aversion to the democratic process. Diether had to pledge to wage war against Frederick I, elector palatine of the Rhine, as an additional condition for the ratification of his election (Menzel, 1868). It is not difficult to recognize the interests of the papal party behind this last demand, since to bring about a war between two electors would prevent any future assembly of the German princes for a few years at least, and the prospect of their meeting in council was a constant headache for the pope.

What reason induced Diether to redeem his election commitment so promptly is not immediately obvious, but by 14 July 1460 he had been defeated by Elector Frederick on the battlefield near Pfeddersheim (*Mainz*, 1968: II, 171). It must have caused some embarrassment at the time that the church and monastery of St Cyriacus at Neuhausen near Worms should have fallen prey to destruction in the course of a war that had been started by the archbishop, and apparently Archbishop Diether was every bit as interested as his opponent in its rapid reconstruction. Both adversaries concluded peace, while simultaneously entering into a friendly alliance for 20 years, on 4 August 1460 at Hemsbach on the Bergstrasse. The pope must have viewed this treaty with Frederick – a character who had already incurred much displeasure in Rome – as one more ground for that distrust of Diether which came into the open as the archbishops' war ran its course. Pope Pius II, himself a former cathedral provost of Worms, would not have been surprised to be approached through Rudolf von Rüdesheim, dean of Worms and later bishop of Maribor and Wroclaw, for his support in rebuilding the monastery. The pope granted an indulgence and entrusted its administration to Rudolf von Rüdesheim, who belonged to his close circle of acquaintances, and to Reinhard von Sickingen, bishop of Worms (*Mainz*, 1968: II, 16, and Schmidt, 1911: 65).

And now we come to a replay of a situation which is familiar from the printing of the *Cyprus Indulgences*. The *Indulgence for the Benefit of the Cyriacus Church at Neuhausen near Worms* is found to be printed in an almost identical text, but in two different typefaces. The Catholicon-type is used for one setting, and the Durandus-type for the other. Both settings have two variants, namely for male and female indulgence purchasers, and each of these four versions has survived in a further reprinting for 1462. Once again it is only possible to explain these settings of the *Neuhausen Indulgences* in two distinct typefaces through the coexistence of two printing offices. The Durandus-type was to be found at the Fust and Schöffer works. This has been proved beyond doubt, and with it the printer for the letters of indulgence set in the Durandus-type is established. It is true that there are still various schools of thought on who may have been the printer of the *Catholicon*. But if no alternative and more valid reason can be offered for setting the same text in different types than that there were still two separate printers at work, then this second printing house can only have been the one at the Gutenberghof. And if the Catholicon-type was located at the Gutenberghof, then the *Catholicon* too must have been printed there (Kapr, 1976: 101–2).

Notū sit: vniūsis pñtes lrās inspecturis. Q̄d q̄ [illegible] vir Albertus [illegible] dioc. p repacōe eccīe
sci Ciriaci Nuhusen̄ z ad opus fabce ipius mtm̄ ɔtribuit q̄ laborās apd̄ eādē p duodeci dieb; dispo-
m posſit. Jdeoq̄ p.ceps indulgētiaꝝ in fauorē dcē eccīe p scīssimū dnm nr̄m Piū ppā; scd̄; ɔceſſaꝝ ēē
debebit. vic; q̄ elig̃e posſit ɔfessorē idoneū q̄ eū ab omib; snis excomūicacōis z alijs cēsuris in q̄s nondū me-
diſſe declaratus z denūciatus ē. necnō z ab omib; crimib; pcc̄is z delictis suis in q̄buscū; casib; etiā sedi aplice
resuatis semel in vita absoluē ac ei salutarē pniā; iniūgē. necnō plenariā remiſſionē oim pccōꝝ suoꝝ semel
in mortis articlo aūcte aplica impriri z ɔcedē ac vota oia. exceptis votis ad limina aplōꝝ Petri z Pauli Terre scē ac sancti Jacobi in alia pietatis opera maxime p fabrica p̄dicta ɔmutaē posſit et valeat. sic tn̄ q̄ satisfaciat. si alicui p eū satisfactō impēdenda sit. z ɔcēptor sedis aplice z libertatis status ecciastici nō fueit neq̄ sit.
Et singlis sextis ferijs p annū vel loco sexte ferie qn̄ aliūde in illa ieiunare tenet alio die in septiana ieiunet
Et si in p̄dicto āno vel aliq̄ eius pte esset legitie impeditus. āno sequen̄ti vel alias q̄ primū potueit mō simili huiusmodi ieiumū supplē teneat. Et si in toto vel in pte adimplē ɔmode nequerit eo casu ɔfessor ipm ieiumū in
alia pietatis opa ɔmutet. iux q̄ in bulla dci dni ppe Pij plenius ɔtinetur. In cuius testimonū sigillū p reue-
rēdos pres dnos Reynhardū Epm et Rudolphū decanū wormcien p hac indulgētia ordinatū put sup hiis
a dco dno Pio summo pontifice ē data facultas pñtib; ē appēnsū. Datū Anno dni. M. cccc. lx. secūdo die [illegible]
[illegible] datū ut supra in Newhusen

The Neuhausen Indulgence *in the Durandus-type.*
1461/62. Reduced.

An interesting aspect is raised by considering the possible commissioners. One was the bishop of Worms, Reinhard von Sickingen, the other Rudolf von Rüdesheim. From the Stuttgart copy of the *Neuhausen Indulgence* in the Catholicon-type, which was made out on 10 April 1462 for Frau Anna Vogtin from Ellwangen, hangs a seal impressed with arms of Rudolf von Rüdesheim. These arms show three figures, one of which depicts St Viktor with the banner of the cross. Rudolf von Rüdesheim also acted as provost of St Viktor, and in this capacity he had succeeded Diether von Isenburg, who was provost from 1442 to 1459 (Schmidt, 1911: 131ff). And Gutenberg was a member of the St Viktor Brotherhood. The members of this brotherhood were bound to hear four masses each year and at times to make an appropriate gift at the altar. On the death of a member the burial ceremonies would be attended to by the brotherhood. Gutenberg's ties with the foundation of St Viktor have in any case been well established (Ruppel, 1967: 70–1). So it does not seem unreasonable to assume that the inventor should have undertaken to print the *Neuhausen Indulgences* at the request of the provost of his foundation. As the competition between both printers was no secret in Mainz, it would follow for the other buyer, Reinhard von Sickingen, to seek the services of Fust and Schöffer.

Notum sit vniu̾sis p̄ntes l̃as inspecturis Q quia dicta [illegible] augusten̄
dioc̄ pro repacōne ecclie scti Cyriaci Nuhusen̄ et ad op9 fabrice ip̄i9 intantū contribuit q laborās
apud eādē pro duodecim dieb9 disponi possit. Ideoq3 particeps Indulgenciaꝝ in fauorē dicte ecclie
per sctissim̄ dn̄m nrm̄ pium papā scdm̄ concessaꝝ esse debebit videlicet q eligē possit confessorem
ydoneu3 q eam ab oib9 Sentencijs excōicacōis et alijs cēsuris in q̄s nōdum incidisse declarata
et denūciata est Necnon ab om̄ib9 crim̄ib9 pctis et delictis inqbuscūq3 casibus etiam sedi aplice
resuatis semel in vita absoluē ac ei salutarē peñiam iniungē necnō plenariā remissionē oīm
pctoꝝ suoꝝ semel in mortis articulo aucte aplica impartiri et concedē ac vota oīa exceptis votis
ad limīa aploꝝ pet̾ et pauli: tre sctē. ac scti Jacobi in alia pietatis opera maxīe pro fabca p̄dicta
ɔmutaē possit et valeat: Sic tn̄ q satisfaciat si alicui p eā satisfactio impendēda sit Et contemptrix
sedis aplice et l̾ibtatis stat9 ecctiastici nō fueit neq3 sit Et singul̾ sextis feijs per annū l̾ loco sexte
feie qn̄ aliunde in illa ieiunaē tenet̄ alio die in septiana ieiunet Et si inp̄dicto anno vl̾ aliq̄ ei9
parte esset legittime impedita āno seqnti vl̾ alias quāp̄mu potuerit mō simili huiusmodi Ieiuniu3
supplere teneat̄ Et si in toto ul̾ in parte adimplere cōmode nequeit eo casu confessor ip̄m Ieiu=
nium in alia pietatis opera ɔmutet. Juxta q in bulla dicti dn̄i pape pij pleni9 continetur In cui9
testimonium Sigillum p Reuēndos prēs dn̄os Reynhardū Ep̄m et Rudolphu3 decanū wōmacien̄
pro hac Indulgēcia ordiatū put sup B eis a dicto dn̄o pio sūmo pōtifice ē data facultas p̄ntib9 ē
appensum Datum [illegible] die [illegible] Mensis [illegible] Anno dn̄i. M. cccc. sexagesimo secūdo .

The Neuhausen Indulgence *in the Catholicon-type. 1462. Reduced.*

There is yet another argument which speaks in favour of Gutenberg having printed the *Neuhausen Indulgences* in the Catholicon-type. Their setting reuses two abbreviation signs from the typeface created for the *31-line Indulgence for Cyprus*. The printer who set in the Catholicon-type must accordingly have had access to the punches, matrices, or types of the *31-line Indulgence*; in just the same way that when printing the *31-line Indulgences* he was able to make use of Gutenberg's original typeface, the DK-type, for the headings. And there remains yet one more argument which will come into play later. Not only the Catholicon-type but also the 31-line Cyprus Indulgence-type are encountered again at the Bechtermünze printing office in Eltville, a place with which only Gutenberg maintained close connections (Hensel, 1952).

Both versions of the *Neuhausen Indulgences* are printed on vellum, plainly, and with less aesthetic interest than the *Cyprus Indulgences*. They have the look of simple receipts, their form adding nothing to the display of the message or content, possibly reflecting the designers' detachment from affairs in Neuhausen.

The *Neuhausen Indulgences* mark simply a preliminary skirmish in the archbishops' war, at which stage Mainz book printing was still only participating from the sidelines. But political events were to unfold rapidly.

Diplomacy, pamphleteering, war

SHORTLY AFTER THE ELECTION OF DIETHER as archbishop, the chapter of Mainz cathedral appointed a legation headed by its canon, Münch von Rosenberg, to travel to Rome to apply for confirmation of the election and for the pallium, or vestment. Pope Pius II, who at this time was in congress in Mantua to prepare a crusade against the Turks, and who properly expected Diether to attend in person, received these ambassadors curtly. He made the conferring of the archbishop's pallium conditional on his fulfilling three conditions: the archbishop elect should pledge that he would never summon a general council; that he should never convene a *Fürstentag* unless the pope had previously granted express permission; and finally, that he should assure one tenth of the entire income of the archdiocese to the pope for the war against the Turks. These ignominious demands made of Diether as the first elector of the empire were rejected by his legation (Zedler, 1905:57).

Diether sent a fresh delegation to Mantua in December 1459, led by the cathedral's theologian, Volbrecht von Ders, and in which the margrave of Brandenburg and the eloquent Gregor von Heimburg could now be brought into action on his behalf. This time the pope gave his assent to Diether's election and pallium; stipulating that the archbishop must pay his customary fees within a year. This condition was accepted by the delegates, who were afraid that otherwise the pope might install an archbishop of his own choosing. But they were unaware of the intention to raise the pallium and benefice taxes to 20,500 gulden in the meantime. They paid a tiny proportion of these dues from the means at their disposal, and took out a loan for the balance from a Roman banking consortium that was effectively subordinate to the papal treasury. In so doing, the Mainz delegation had signed a promissory note containing a clause that, in the event of nonpayment of the loan, the debtor would be subject to excommunication (Erler, 1964: 1).

The large amounts due for conferment of the pallium, consecration in office or award of benefice, were constant bones of contention between the papal party who defended such payments, and the party of reform who held them to be unreasonable. Pallium fees, which had been abolished at the Basle council, had been recognized again for Germany under the later Vienna concordat. But hitherto the pallium fees for the archbishop of Mainz had amounted to 10,000 gulden, and now the pope had arbitrarily and without agreement doubled this sum. Diether informed the Vatican that he was indeed prepared to contribute pallium fees, but only at the level which had been customary until then. Back from the Vatican came the reply that the sum had in fact already been paid in full, as reference to his own bankers would confirm. In effect the bankers were working in collusion with the *curia*, which had promised to honour the sum advanced by the banks, in the event that Diether failed to pay. Diether let the time limit elapse, and was promptly excommunicated or suspended from communion with the Church. In accordance with the rules of canon law he was required to relinquish his office as archbishop forthwith.

He acted to the contrary, summoning an assembly of the imperial electors at Nuremberg for February 1461, and appointing Gregor von Heimburg, the most determined spokesman for the reform party, as his adviser. However, Gregor von Heimburg and his archduke, Sigismund of Austria – who had ventured to take prisoner the prince-bishop of the Tyrol, Cardinal Nicholas of Cues, on Easter Day 1460 – had also been placed under the papal ban (Erler, 1964: 2). The excommunicated archbishop had accordingly chosen a fellow excommunicate as his advocate. This was a blatant affront to the pope, and it was in this atmosphere that the *Fürstentag* met in Nuremberg. A few significant passages from the surviving minutes of its proceedings merit quotation for the light they shed on the political background:

> When the archbishop of Mainz, the count palatine of the Rhine and Frederick, margrave of Brandenburg, in their own persons, and emissaries from the archbishop of Trier and sundry other princes and nobles had gathered for the conference on the Sunday called *reminiscere*, and had deliberated together about such evident impositions and issues whereby they, their lands and peoples and the whole German nation had for so long been and were daily burdened and would continue to be thus oppressed by the papal court in Rome, and to be precise: 1. through imposing the tenth, twentieth and thirtieth penny, 2. through annulment of the constitutional right to call for a general council, 3. through raising and multiplying the payment for livings or benefices above the levels customary earlier, 4. through violating the decrees enacted and adopted at the holy Councils of Constance and Basle, and which had been ratified by the pope himself, 5. through breaking off and infringement of the concordat between the German nation and the Roman see, and 6. through all kinds of other encumbrances imposed by the Roman see at present and which it would be able to inflict in the future: and so, with the aim of bringing about a full general council of the Christian Church, the electors, princes and emissaries previously named have unanimously agreed upon the following closing resolutions:
>
> 1. That the said electors and other princes and nobles of the German nation should send their councillors to Frankfurt for the Friday after Sunday *exaudi* [22 May] to discuss the matter and agree the best and quickest means to put a stop to these abuses for all time and to bring about a general council.
>
> 2. These same councillors were to remain in Frankfurt until Sunday *trinitatis* [31 May] to debate and resolve these issues further with the princes and nobles themselves, who would arrive there on that day. This assembly should not be

dissolved until it had devised effective ways and means for the German nation to rid itself of these burdens for evermore.

3. Those electors, princes and nobles, who had attended at Nuremberg in person or had sent representatives, must not enter into any understanding, neither with the pope nor any other person, which might hinder their plan and endanger the removal of oppression from the German nation, but rather they must all, until things were brought to a successful conclusion, keep their own counsel and remain united.

4. The archbishop of Mainz shall advise the electors, princes and nobles of the German nation, who have not appeared in Nuremberg at the present time, of the conferences which are to be held in Frankfurt on the Friday after *exaudi* and on Sunday *trinitatis*, and of the agendas and shall urge their participation.

5. Margrave Frederick of Brandenburg shall send these final resolutions to Frederick, duke of Saxony, and persuade him to support these decisions; what he achieves in this quarter he shall make known to the archbishop of Mainz.

6. The concerted agreement to counter oppression through this levying of tithes, and double or triple dues to Rome, which had been resolved in Nuremberg and underwritten by the attendant princes and ambassadors, was to be signed and sealed in Frankfurt on Sunday *trinitatis*, and the princes or their ambassadors should be sure to bring along their seals so that the appropriate documents could be drawn up and sealed on the spot (Menzel, 1868: 103ff).

This resolution received the signatures and seals of Archbishop Diether, Elector Frederick and the envoy of the archbishop of Trier. Frederick, margrave of Brandenburg declared the support of Peter Knorr, archbishop of Salzburg, the bishops of Bamberg, Würzburg, Constance and Hildesheim and also that of Louis, duke of Bavaria-Landshut.

At this, Archbishop Diether provoked a counter-attack. With the call for a general council the pope sensed that his Achilles' heel was endangered. Diether had not appealed to the *curia* as defined by canon law with a plea for his excommunication to be lifted, but instead he used the opportunity to convene a council. He met with the ready approval of many German princes and bishops who, like the Mainz archbishop, felt led by the nose from Rome.

The pope's countermeasures took their hidden course, flexibly and extremely adroitly. Although he was entitled under canon law to install a new archbishop without more ado, he began by isolating Diether from his allies. He appointed two legates, Rudolf von Rüdesheim, already mentioned as dean of Worms, and the scholarly canon, Francis of Toledo. These went to see Diether's individual supporters, made concessions over the anti-Turkish contributions, gave rise to expectations, and clarified the legal standpoint of the papacy. In parallel to this, Johann Werner von Flassland, dean of Basle, was charged with a papal commission to pave the way for electing a new archbishop of Mainz. In the meanwhile, Diether called a new *Fürstentag* to Frankfurt, inviting the emperor and all the princes, adding that, in the event of their absence, decisions would be taken without them. But the emperor and German king opposed this meeting. At his behest, the city of Frankfurt closed its gates to the diet.

Diether then summoned the *Fürstentag* to Mainz for 4 June. Although all his princely colleagues and naturally enough the king himself stayed away, Diether remained optimistic at the outset, but must soon have realized that he and his secretary Heimburg were on their own. The papal legates had gained the upper hand through their powers of persuasion, and finally wrested from him the retraction of the Nuremberg appeal on the question of fees payable on assuming office in the Church. In return they held out the prospect that the pope would take a lenient view over his own pallium fees.

At the same time, however, Flassland had been negotiating with the candidate who had been defeated in the 1459 election for the archbishopric, Adolf von Nassau, and they had reached agreement. The emperor also favoured the planned removal of Diether and the election of Adolf von Nassau. Accordingly, Flassland hurried back to the pope, who pronounced the deposition of Diether von Isenburg and the appointment of Adolf von Nassau as new archbishop. Flassland carried the corresponding papal bull of 21 August 1461 to Mainz and handed it over to Adolf von Nassau. Meanwhile a papal brief was issued to all princes, in which the pope promised that the ecclesiastical tithe might only be raised with their consent. This concession won the pope the neutrality of the German princes in what amounted to the outrageous removal from office of the first elector of the German nation (Menzel, 1868: 125ff).

The next scene between the immediate participants followed in accordance with a secret stage direction on 26 September 1461. Diether was with his capitularies, to whom Adolf von Nassau also belonged, in the cathedral chapter at Mainz. Then Adolf stepped forward with both legates and read out the papal bull concerning Diether's deposition and his own appointment. The cathedral canons were completely taken by surprise and withdrew for debate. Their decision eventually swung in favour of Adolf von Nassau. In this the canons submitted to the directions of the pope. The cathedral theologian, Volbrecht von Ders, ascended the choir-screen, and the same man who had brought back the pallium for Diether now proclaimed to the public the name of their new archbishop, just as two years earlier he had announced that of his predecessor.

Gregor von Heimburg was no longer staying in Mainz by this time. Under the pressure of papal threats he had cut himself off from Diether, for the excommunicated Heimburg had left himself wide open to attack by his enemies. It must also have become apparent to Heimburg after the abortive Mainz *Fürstentag* that there was nothing further to be expected from Diether in support of those reform politics which he himself pursued. As his new adviser, Diether had turned to Dr Konrad Humery, who has already been mentioned because of his connections with Gutenberg. Through Humery, the presumed financier and possibly even the owner of the printing works in the Gutenberghof, the conflict between both archbishops now directly touches upon the inventor, and during its course I think there is every reason to assume that Gutenberg remained thoroughly in sympathy with the political aims of Archbishop Diether.

Diether alone was prepared to conclude an agreement with Adolf von Nassau as the pope envisaged, but Frederick, elector palatine of the Rhine, stepped in and offered Diether the support of his entire fighting force. An alliance was formed between Diether, Elector Frederick and Philipp, count of Katzenelnbogen. Thereafter the Mainz citizenry moved away from Adolf and declared their support for the Isenburger, now that his power had been strengthened, and especially since he had promised the city council that the so-called 'priests' revenge' of 1435 granting oppressive privileges to the clergy would be abolished. A number of wavering cathedral canons – the custodian Ruprecht von Solms, Raban von Liebenstein, and Damo von Fraunheim – returned to the ranks of the old archbishop. Diether could claim a clear endorsement in any appeal. The city council under Humery's leadership followed this example and accordingly demanded of every cleric an oath that he would protect the city from harm. On this account, some of the clergy and those members of the cathedral chapter who stood on Adolf's side had to withdraw to Bingen under protest.

On 1 February 1462, the pope ordered all archbishops, bishops and prelates to proclaim each day in their churches the anathema upon Diether and his supporters. However, no attention was paid to this papal command in the city of Mainz (Erler, 1964: 6).

Broadsides appeared in quick succession, all of them produced in the Fust and Schöffer printing works and some taking Diether's part and others that of Adolf. The precise dates of printing are mostly indeterminable; they can only be placed in sequence according to the flow of events. First, after 8 August 1461, came Frederick III's *Confirmation of the deposition of Diether von Isenburg*, which is set in a new typeface for the Fust and Schöffer office: that to be used for the *48-line Bible*. Afterwards, there followed a notice sheet containing the *Papal Bull of Pius II concerning the deposition of Archbishop Diether* of 21 August 1461. The next printed item comprises a *Brief to Adolf von Nassau sanctioning his election to the archbishopric* of the same date, which is also known in a surviving variant issue. There is a further printed notice containing the *Brief to the Cathedral Chapter of Mainz concerning the election of Adolf von Nassau*. All these broadsides or notices are set in Fust and Schöffer's Durandus-type (Erler, 1964: 9).

On 30 March 1462, Diether also allowed a manifesto, probably written by Dr Humery, to be printed and sent out to principalities and cities, as well as to guilds in various towns. In it he volunteered to let the conflict that had arisen come before an arbitration tribunal, to consist of the king of Bohemia, the electors of the Palatinate, Cologne and Saxony, the bishop of Augsburg and a number of other judges. This proposal was politically unrealistic; it was only intended to serve as propaganda in a war that was now clearly to be anticipated. It is reported in an early chronicle of 1612 (Lehmann's *Chronica von Speier*), that Mainz's first printer, Johann Gutenberg, had printed a circular letter for Diether von Isenburg (*Mainz*, 1968: II, 45). But there is no evidence for this, in that all surviving broadsides, including this one of Diether's, are produced in the types of Fust and Schöffer.

At an unascertainable date during the spring of 1462, a manifesto appeared from Adolf in response to Diether's accusations, with the opening words: *Wir haben vernommen, dass Diether von Isenburg ...* . Both this, and a printed appeal from Diether to Pope Pius II: *Beatissime pater* ... , were not addressed to their recipients so much as thought of as propaganda for general publication. All these pamphlets were aimed at gaining public support for the respective protagonists and defaming their opponents. To the *matériel* of warfare – halberds, rapiers, swords, harquebuses and cannon – psychological weapons had been added, which could be delivered by means of the printing press.

Elector Frederick won a decisive victory over the allied forces of Adolf von Nassau at Seckenheim near Schwetzingen on 30 June 1462. He was able to take the counts of Württemberg and Baden as well as the bishop of Metz as prisoners back to his castle at Heidelberg. Popular regard for Diether rose to new heights in consequence.

The fall of Mainz

Doing away with the 'priest's revenge' – which conferred privileges and tax-exemption on the clergy – had won for Diether von Isenburg the hearts and minds of a great many more Mainz citizens. The triumph of Elector Frederick prevailed on the councillors to strengthen their support, but this meant that they needed to give greater consideration to the security of the city. The elector and the count of

Katzenelnbogen had offered the city 200 to 300 mounted mercenaries for its protection. The burgomasters declined, presumably in order to save money, or possibly even because the city treasury had run out of funds. For all that, some 200 inhabitants of the city were open supporters of the Nassau cause, in part in order to comply with the pope's directives, but in other cases out of selfish expediency, hoping to receive some eventual reward from Adolf von Nassau for their loyalty.

The Nassau faction, which was based in Eltville, exploited these weak points to contrive a plot down to the last detail. A number of macabre documents have survived, which show how the spoils were to be divided. Wine, grain and crops, and similarly artillery and weapons, were to be equally shared between Adolf von Nassau and his allies: Ludwig von Veldenz (known as the 'Black Duke'), Eberhard von Eppenstein and Wirich von Falkenstein. All jewellery, cash and household valuables – excepting the cathedral chapter reserves and the treasures and utensils of churches – should go half to Adolf von Nassau and Ludwig von Veldenz and the other half to be shared among their remaining confederates. The two princes together should have exclusive jurisdiction over the prisoners. Albig von Sulz, as chief war-lord, was to receive one-tenth of the booty, and the other high commanders had been promised 5000 gulden apiece. Whichever soldier was first over the wall would be rewarded with a town house and 1000 gulden (Erler, 1964: 274ff). An earlier commentator labelled this agreement a thieves' contract, which ill became an archbishop whom the pope himself had installed.

The confederates had found out about a meeting which had been planned for 27 October in Mainz between Diether and the elector and count of Katzenelnbogen. They intended to attack the city by surprise at that time and take all three of their foes prisoner. But this conference was postponed by a day. It was said that the elector, Frederick, having reached Oppenheim on his route there, was warned by his chaplain, Matthias von Kemnat, who was able to read the stars, and so turned back.

The attack came just before dawn on St Simon's day, on Thursday 28 October 1462, at a point near the Gautor where the wall enclosed vineyards and orchards which separated it from houses. Bold fighters used ladders to scale the wall. They opened the Gau and Abtmünster gates to admit some 500 armed soldiers. From the Rhine signals of fire extended along the Rheingau or left bank. Altogether about 3000 men took part in the assault, 1000 horse-soldiers and 2000 on foot, among whom were 400 Swiss mercenaries.

At five in the morning the alarm bell was sounded from St Quintin's tower. Some of the inhabitants ran for the walls, others to the guild-halls. Those who gathered in front of the Rathaus were the Isenburg forces, under the civil command of Reinhard von Baldesheim and Kunz Echte. They succeeded in forcing back the insurgents towards the Gautor. Burgomaster Diemerstein met his death. The count of Königstein spurred on his troops: 'Strike dead the heretics, take no prisoners!' One group of defenders especially distinguished itself – that led by Burgomaster Jakob Fust, younger brother of Johann Fust.

Archbishop Diether and the count of Katzenelnbogen, who had spent that night within the city, now made good their escape over the city wall and across the Rhine. Before that the archbishop had told the citizens to do their utmost to defend themselves, and that he would return from Hochheim with reinforcements. All the time, renewed enemy forces were pressing forward and overcame resistance in the city centre. When troops eventually came to aid the Isenburgers, it was too late. Some were immediately taken prisoner. Of those Mainzers who had taken part in battle, 400 citizens had fallen. As evening approached the war was over. Patrician houses, and equally those of the clergy and the Jews, fell prey to plundering.

On the following day the victor, Archbishop Adolf von Nassau, entered the city on horseback. The city was obliged to hand all its letters of privilege to him. On the Saturday, all citizens were summoned to the Dietmarkt, and some 800 appeared in the expectation that they would be required to swear loyalty to Nassau. But they found themselves encircled by armed Rheingau and Swiss mercenaries – like sheep in a pen, as an early account puts it. The archbishop railed at them, declaring that through their disobedience to pope and emperor their lives were forfeit, but that he would temper justice with leniency and only banish them from the city. The Mainzers implored mercy, but in vain. All were driven out through the Gaupforte. Their route to the city walls was lined by troops; on one side were the Swiss with taut crossbrows, and on the other armed Rheingau forces, who reviled the Mainzers as perjurers and heretics. Those exiled lost all they owned; their homes were expropriated and handed over to the new archbishop's followers. All money in the city treasury, cloth in store and vast treasures fell into the hands of the conquerors. The lords and commanders took the lion's share, but each horseman received 15 gulden and every foot soldier half that sum.

When those who had been driven out were readmitted to Mainz at Shrovetide 1463, 15 of them were arrested and imprisoned, about 300 who had not participated in the battle were allowed to remain in the city, and the remaining 400 or more were bound on oath for life never to approach within a mile's distance of the city and to stay clear of the Rheingau and the area ruled from Königstein. As they left two by two by the Gaupforte, scribes listed their names in a book. Despite having been plundered, all had to pay an extra fine of half a gulden. In exactly the same way all creditors of the city and all recipients of annuities had their entitlements annulled, or in other words, the archbishop assumed responsibility for none of the city's debts. Total losses through the war have been roughly calculated at two million gulden. First and foremost this money flowed to Rome. All papal rights were re-established. The peace talks dragged on for roughly another year (*Mainz*, 1968: II, 176, 178 and 109). Diether von Isenburg renounced his title as archbishop and received substantial compensation in return. At a glittering assembly held in Frankfurt on 24 October 1463 he relinquished the electoral sword and in bowed attitude received absolution through a papal legate (*Mainz*, 1968: II, 32ff). In this way, at least to outward appearances, papal supremacy in worldly matters as well was reasserted.

How may Gutenberg and both the Mainz printing houses have fared in all this? The inventor has for the most part been viewed by researchers as a supporter of Diether's party, while Johann Fust's brother, Jakob Fust, is to be found among the nine traitors known by name. There is some unexplained discrepancy in the latter case, since the burgomaster and goldsmith Jakob Fust is known to have been severely wounded in defence of the city on 28 October and to have died in consequence. Fust and Schöffer's printing works, which undertook printing commissions not only for the Nassauers but equally for the Isenburgers, in all probability remained closed from 28 October 1462 until Shrovetide 1463. It is likely that owner and printer were driven from the city as well. Yet after that the *Türkenbulle* promulgated by Pius II on 22 October 1463 was published in both German and Latin editions – a publication remarkable for having a caption printed on a preliminary leaf as forerunner of the title page: 'Dis' ist die bul zu dutsch die vnser allerheiligster vatter der babst Pius herusz gesant hait widder die snoden vngleubigen turcken'. [This is the bull in German which our holiest father Pope Pius has sent us against the despicable infidel Turks.]

It is certain that Gutenberg had been dispossessed, as the Gutenberghof was leased for life to a supporter of Adolf von Nassau, Conrad Wilvung. The inventor and his associates must have been driven out of the city on 30 October 1462. He was in no position to assemble a new group of colleagues to continue to print further editions of the *Catholicon*. Singly or in groups most of the compositors and pressmen from both printing works set out for other cities and lands. Perhaps some took with them on the way a few tools of the trade or samples of printing; the most vital item they were able to take with them was their working experience of printing with metal types. The destinies of some of these dispersed printers will be examined later.

Ironically, the victor of the day, Adolf von Nassau, has been forgotten and his name is familiar now only to historians. The loser, Diether von Isenburg, was later – after Adolf's death some years later and once more to the pope's intense annoyance – again elected as archbishop of Mainz, and is still remembered today as the founder of its university. But one man, who paid scant attention to the warring between both factions, emerged with imperishable fame. And in fact it was his weapons which could have prevailed over crossbows and cannon, and the ravages and exactions of war.

However, there are still a few aspects of that capitular feud to be elucidated. Whoever enquires into Gutenberg's political stance in this dispute cannot afford to ignore a controversy that raged, at least intermittently, between the Benedictine and Franciscan orders. When Adolf's troops occupied Mainz, all Franciscans were excommunicated and chased out of the city, and the Franciscan church turned into stabling for horses. A majority of German Franciscans had striven for the figurehead system, according to which the pope in effect still remained the supreme leader of the Catholic Church, but the regional churches retained a degree of autonomy. Diether could depend on the Mainz Franciscans for support in his disputes. And we know of Gutenberg that his bones, together with those of his parents and many ancestors, were interred in the Franziskanerkirche. Gutenberg's attitude in the dominant ecclesiastical conflict may also have been influenced through his personal collaboration with Dr Humery, secretary to the Isenburg archbishop.

The Benedictines manifestly occupied another position. Their best known representative, Gabriel Biel, who had also been active as cathedral preacher at Mainz cathedral since 1460, found himself expelled from the city with the other brethren of his order as supporters of Adolf von Nassau. On 18 September 1462, he wrote in bitter language about Diether's partisans, who:

> ... in committing grave sins against the rule of God and his holy Church, for what is this other than that which the accursed Jews and heathens did, who defiled the blood of our dear Lord ... and therefore I exhort you all through the love of our Lord Jesus, that you yourselves ... for God's sake refrain from all communion with the aforenamed.

In this sense which Biel intimates, the Benedictines sapped the power of Diether von Isenburg. It may be assumed that Peter Schöffer maintained certain connections with the Benedictines. As mentioned earlier, he probably printed the second *Mainz Psalter* to the commission of the Bursfeld Congregation of Benedictines. Furthermore, it is known that in 1473 Schöffer established a foundation for a mass at the Benedictine abbey of Mainz.

How then can it be explained that all this polemical printing, not only that for the Nassauers (which comprised the apostolic letters of 21 August 1461 deposing Diether, the emperor's confirmation, and the papal letters sanctioning Adolf's election as archbishop), but also Diether's publications, and especially his manifesto of 30 March 1462, came out from the same Fust and Schöffer printing works? In the case of the broadsides for Adolf, Schöffer's sympathies towards the Benedictines may have been motive enough. Conversely, the Isenburg broadsides could have been introduced to the order book through Johann Fust, whose brother Jakob was later to give up his life in Diether's cause while a burgomaster, especially since the guilds as a whole stood up for the claims the Isenburgers made against the papacy. It may equally have seemed an advisable policy to Fust, that his printing works should be seen to be impartial.

A few final words about these military and political events: in several publications about the Mainz archbishops' conflict, I have come across the view that the regime of the guilds in Mainz was to blame for neglecting the defences of the city. In other cities, such as Strasbourg, by contrast, the guilds' administration had earlier reinforced their defensive measures. According to some reports, various Mainzers were in league with the Nassau party, and traitors were involved: Hermann Sternberg, a gardener and treasurer at the time, Dudo Fischer and Henn Ortwein, both master builders, Ortwin the rope-maker and Dude the fisherman. An itinerant labourer, Heinz von Hechtsheim, had opened the parleying with the Nassau camp and he and Dude had bribed the watchmen to leave the Gautor gate open that night (Menzel, 1868: 309). It has to be assumed that the seeds of betrayal were implanted among the populace above all through the clergy, and Benedictine influence in particular, and that the traitors acted under moral pressure from the Church, in order to carry out the pope's instructions.

On All Saint's Eve in 1463, the new archbishop issued a remarkable document, which no longer permitted any assembly of electors or other princes without the emperor's approval. That was to put an end to thoughts of reform and conciliar objectives for a long time. But with the resolution of the Mainz archbishops' war, neither the problems of the Church nor the political issue of the dependence of Germany upon Rome had been settled. These tensions heightened and became identified with the social concerns of an oppressed peasantry and flowed ultimately into the religious, political and social movement of Martin Luther and Thomas Müntzer.

CHAPTER TEN

Memento mori

The last exile – Eltville

ON 30 OCTOBER 1462, Gutenberg probably had to stand with 800 of his fellow citizens in the Dietmarkt and then pass with his printers through the cordon of Swiss and Rheingau troops. It is possible that his colleagues gathered outside the city walls with the elderly inventor and talked about their intended routes and working destinations. Some went to Strasbourg and Bamberg, where printing was already established, others to Basle or Cologne, and several set out to try their luck in the Italian cities. Circumstances had freed them all from their agreement to maintain secrecy about the art. However, the closing pages of this book will be devoted to the incunabula printers and their successors.

Where could Gutenberg have turned to? One possibility that has to be taken into account is that the inventor may have moved to Frankfurt to stay with the daughter of his late sister, also called Else, and now the widow of Henne Humbrecht, who is described as Gutenberg's heiress by Aloys Ruppel (Ruppel, 1967: 28). But this overlooks the fact that a territorial ban had been imposed on the inventor in the meantime.

It will be recalled that during 1442 Gutenberg raised a loan from the St Thomas Chapter in Strasbourg of 80 denars, equivalent to about 67 gulden, and that he had last paid the 4 denars annual interest on this sum in 1457. The foundation sued Gutenberg and his guarantor, Martin Brechter, in the imperial high court at Rottweil after letters of reminder for the interest due in 1459 and 1460 proved of no avail. Since then the court had sent three official summonses by messenger to Gutenberg in Mainz. After the defendant failed to appear, he was outlawed, that is, deprived of his rights and legal competence. Furthermore, he could be arrested at any time. He had been protected from this by virtue of being a Mainz citizen, since the archbishop of Mainz recognized only the jurisdiction of the Mainz courts; but following his expulsion from his home city, he now had to guard against entering Frankfurt territory (Schorbach, 1900: 215ff, docs XXIII, XXIV).

There remained only one place for him to retreat to: Eltville. Although Gutenberg's brother Friele was no longer alive, his daughter Odilgen and her husband, Johann Sorgenloch, also known as Gensfleisch, seem to have kept up good relations with Gutenberg. Moreover, Gutenberg knew Gretgen Swalbach, whose property was close to that of Odilgen and who had since married Heinrich Bechtermünze. It is even possible that it was in the company of Heinrich or Nicolaus Bechtermünze, both Mainz patricians he had known since childhood, that he left Mainz for Eltville.

The son-in-law of Heinrich Bechtermünze, Jakob Sorgenloch, is known to have been a partisan of the new archbishop. At some time in May 1462 he had gone from Eltville to Mainz to agitate on behalf of the Nassauers. As his boat pulled into Eltville on the return journey, he was set upon and wounded by Isenburg supporters (Schweinsberg, 1900: 77, 88, 253 n.349). Gutenberg was not without intercessors in his new exile.

Nicholas Jenson and Eltville

WHO MAY HAVE ACCOMPANIED THE INVENTOR to Eltville? Was he attended as ever by his servant Beildeck and his wife, or were they no longer in the land of the living? Did Wiegand Spiess – who was later to take part in the Bechtermünze printing venture – join him? There are indications regarding the subsequent activities of the Frenchman, Nicholas Jenson, at the monastery of Marienthal in the Rheingau, which was being built at that time, and which give rise to the possibility of his spending some time beforehand with Gutenberg in neighbouring Eltville (Muzika, 1965: II, 102ff).

Jenson emerges as one of the most fascinating figures of the incunabula period. His artistic talent and his technological skills place him in the front rank of early printers. He was despatched to Mainz by a decree dated 4 October 1458 by Charles VII of France – who had come to hear of the new Mainz discovery – in order to learn the art of printing from 'Jehan Guthemberg, Chevalier' and bring it back to France; he was accordingly engaged in a kind of official industrial espionage. He had originally been a painter, and then worked as an engraver in the *Monnaie de France* or royal mint in Paris, ending up as master of the mint at Tours. He is sure at least to have begun to work for Gutenberg in accordance with his commission, probably eventually letting the master into his mission and gaining his trust. At all events he was never to return to France, presumably since, after Louis XI's accession, he could no longer expect a friendly reception in his own country (Świerk, 1972a: 80; but note that Lowry, 1991: 49ff calls this traditional account into question).

Through the fall of Mainz, Jenson was caught up in the whirl of political and military events. His veneration for the inventor could have led him to accompany Gutenberg on his departure from Mainz. Of course it remains uncertain whether Jenson passed the years 1464 and perhaps 1465 working with the Brethren of the Common Life at Marienthal, where he may perhaps even have cut a typeface that was later used there. The building of their monastery at Marienthal had begun in 1463, and it appears that Gutenberg kept up good contacts with the Brethren, for these 'brothers of the pen' proved quick enough to exchange the pen for the composing stick in various of their establishments, in order to be able to produce more books.* Jenson was later to cut a typeface in Venice for the first printers of that city, Johann and Wendelin of Speyer. Thereafter he continued to work in Venice, and from his hand came the finest and most mature roman of the fifteenth century. But before that, back in 1463, he may well have helped the inventor with the establishment of a small printing works in Eltville.

Gutenberg and the Bechtermünze printing office

IN THE LATE 1970S, a previously unknown indulgence which had been printed in the Catholicon-type in 1464 came to the attention of the editors of the *Gesamtkatalog der Wiegendrucke*. Pope Pius II had granted this *Indulgence to Frater Radulphus*, general of the order of Trinitarian friars – popularly known as the 'donkey's brethren' on account of their

*Frank Falk, using Bodmann and the '*Hauschronik*' as his sources, quotes:

> In the year 1463, the steadfast nobles Ulrich, Diether and Reynfried von Rüdesheim as brothers and as feudal lords of Marienthal, with the consent and approbation of Adolf, archbishop of Mainz, have given over the *jus patronatus* thereof with the office of the bells, along with all annuities, revenues and income, to the brethren *sive canonicis de communi vita*, so that from amongst the society of brethren at Weidenbach near Cologne some may be sent thence to incorporate a common table (Falk, 1882: 4).

Since Falk wrote, this foundation charter by Adolf von Nassau has been exposed as a Jesuit forgery of the mid-seventeenth century. It has been shown that the monastery at Marienthal was established by Adolf in 1464–5 at the instigation of Gabriel Biel. The printing activity of the brethren is thought to have begun with an *Indulgence for Adolf II* of 30 August 1468 (Struck, 1979: 167). I suggest that Gutenberg may have been encouraged to help set up this printing press by Gabriel Biel, who was known to him, and that Jenson had gone to Marienthal to supervise its establishment.

preferred mode of travel – in 1458, to enable their mission, which was to liberate Christian prisoners and slaves. Hitherto this indulgence was only known in one edition, also printed in 1464, but at the Fust and Schöffer works, and set in the Durandus-type with the B48-type used for display (Hoffman, 1979: 202).

This provides the third instance – after the *Cyprus Indulgences* for 1454 and 1455 and the *Neuhausen Indulgences* of 1461 and 1462 – in which the same text is found printed from two distinct type settings. And again we must conclude that two separate printers were involved. Concerning Fust and Schöffer's office, the only place where the Durandus-type (used for the text) and the B48-type (used for emphasis) were to be found, this only confirms what we knew all long: that they continued to reuse the old types. But since printing had ceased at the Gutenberghof by then, this indicates that in the meantime the Catholicon-type had become available for use at another printing workshop. We know that the *Catholicon* printing was likely to have been either commissioned or largely financed by Dr Konrad Humery, and that consequently he has to be regarded as the owner of the Catholicon-type. We learn that later a new printing works had emerged in Eltville, in all probability with direct assistance from Gutenberg, and that it was most likely to have been on the instructions of Archbishop Adolf himself or one of his closest associates that part of the contract for the Trinitarians was granted to this new printing enterprise. For the installation of such a new printing house, it must have been important (equally with the approval of the supposed owner, Dr Konrad Humery) to transport a typefounder's hand-mould, matrices and supplies of the Catholicon-types, and whatever other printing equipment could be conveniently conveyed from the Gutenberghof to Eltville.

The *Indulgence to Frater Radulphus* in the Durandus-type recalls, through the initial 'U' used for the abbreviated word *Uniuersis*, a similarity to the *30-line Indulgence for Cyprus*. This initial is certainly not identical with that of the *30-line Indulgence*, but is cut in very close imitation. For the *Indulgence for Frater Radulphus* in the Catholicon-type, as in the *31-line Indulgence for Cyprus*, an initial 'V' is once again used for *Vniuersis*, but here the variations which indicate that it is in fact a recutting are even more minor and subtle (Hoffman, 1979: 204–5). One can, nevertheless, as various researchers have found in the case of the *Cyprus Indulgences*, easily distinguish a 'U' Indulgence from a 'V' Indulgence. These differences and points in common stress the conclusion that there must have been close connections between the printer of the *31-line Indulgence for Cyprus* and the printer of the *Indulgence for Frater Radulphus* in the Catholicon-type. It is not all that surprising, if the

Uniuersis p̄ntes lr̄as inspecturis. Frater radulphus maior minister totius ordis scē trinitatis ⁊ re-
demptōis captiuoꝝ. Salm̄ in dn̄o. Cū felicis recordacōis dn̄s Allexnder pp̄ qr̄tus. Et dn̄s clemēs pp̄ sextus. et
ipoꝝ quilibꝫ. omibꝫ xp̄ifidelibꝫ q̄ ad sustentacōꝫ ordinis p̄dicti manus porrexerint adiutrices. tres ān̄os ⁊ xl.
dies de iniūctis eis penitēcijs piter in dn̄o relaxauerint. Volentes insup ac statuētes ꝙ ɔfratribꝫ ⁊ ɔsororibꝫ
fraternitatis ordinis eiusdēꝫ. si eccie ad quas spectauerint forēt interdicte. ipos[que] mori ɔtigerit. nisi excōicati
aut noiatim interdicti fuerint. sepultura nō negeꝰ ecciastica. Preterea vero dn̄s Clemēs p̄fatus licētiaꝫ ɔcessit ɔfratribꝫ ⁊ sororibꝫ eisdē. ut ipi annuatī p̄sbiterū idoneū in ɔfessorē eligē possīnt. q̄ eos ⁊ quēlibꝫ eorūdeꝫ absoluat ab omibꝫ pccis. exceptis casibꝫ sedi aplice refuatis. Nouissime aūt dn̄s nr̄ Pius pp̄ scd̄us per suas lr̄as
aplicas datas Rome Anno dn̄ice incarnacōis. M. cccc. lviij. x vj. kl. februarij. Pontificatus sui anno p̄mo.
Confirmādo p̄dcās ⁊ alias quaslibꝫ indulgētias ⁊ grās ordis p̄dci. Eosdē[que] p̄decessoꝝ suoꝝ ān̄os. et totidē
quadragenas. singulis bn̄factoribꝫ de iniū ctis eis penitēcijs misericorditer in dn̄o relaxauit. Necnō ɔfratribꝫ
et sororibꝫ p̄fatis licentiā ɔcessit. ut ipi hmōi ɔfessoreꝫ eligē possīnt. qui eos ⁊ quemlibꝫ eorūdeꝫ. etiā a casibꝫ sedi aplice quolibꝫ refuatis. Et de quibꝫ sedes ip̄a ē merito ɔsulenda. semel in vita aūcte aplica absoluē. et p
ɔmissis pniaꝫ salutarē ipis iniūgē valeat. Nos siquidē attestamꝰ ꝙ Bertoldus kolentzen et margareta eius filia
hodie suis exigentibꝫ meritis. p nos eidem fraternitati p̄dce ⁊ illius ɔsorcio aggregati. has in testimōniū sibi
ɔcedētes lr̄as. Datū sub sigillo quo vtimꝰ in talibꝫ. Anno dn̄i. M. cccc. lxiiij. die vero quarta mensis aprilis

Forma absolucōnis quā ɔfessor dicat semel in vita put iacet. Alijs
vero annis cōfessor p̄cauebit ne dicat de casibꝫ sedi aplice refuatis.

Misereatur tui deus ⁊c. Dn̄s nr̄ ihūs xp̄s qui est pius ⁊ misericors. p suā pijssimā miscdiaꝫ te absoluat.
Et ego aūcte aplica michi ɔmissa ⁊ tibi concessa te absoluo ab omibꝫ pccis tuis ore confessis ⁊ corde ɔtritis.
Etiā a casibꝫ sedi aplice quolibꝫ refuatis ⁊ de quibꝫ sedes ip̄a ē merito ɔsulenda. Necnō oblitis ⁊ de quibꝫ
nō recolis In noie p̄ris ⁊ filij ⁊ sp̄ūs s[ancti]. Amen

Indulgence to Frater Radulphus for the Benefit of the Trinitarian Order
in the Durandus-type.
Mainz, Fust and Schöffer. 1464. Reduced.

Indulgence in the Durandus-type, which preceded the other, is more handsomely set, the more so as a typeface was available for display use. For the *Indulgence* set in the Catholicon-type, it was clearly necessary to engrave those words requiring emphasis in typemetal and to fit them as small blocks into the text. This task presented no technical challenge, it simply discloses the paucity of types available at the new Eltville printing works. (There is technical confirmation of such engraved lettering appearing in combination with the type later used by the Brethren of the Common Life at Marienthal, but there is insufficient basis for attributing this to the same authorship.)

It is historically certain that the new printing house belonged to the brothers Heinrich and Nicolaus Bechtermünze, and was located in the Bechtermünzer Hof on the west side of the Kirchgasse. It was here that the *Vocabularius ex quo* was printed between 1465 and 1467, a Latin vocabulary that early studies had rather vaguely labelled as an abridgement of the *Catholicon*, which had seen the light of day at the Gutenberghof seven years previously, and had now been greatly altered and expanded with numerous German terms. Its 166 single-column quarto leaves made only about one-seventh of the extent of the *Catholicon*, but naturally it was correspondingly cheaper, and quickly went through four successive editions. A smaller format allowed it to be printed in sheets, which means in this case

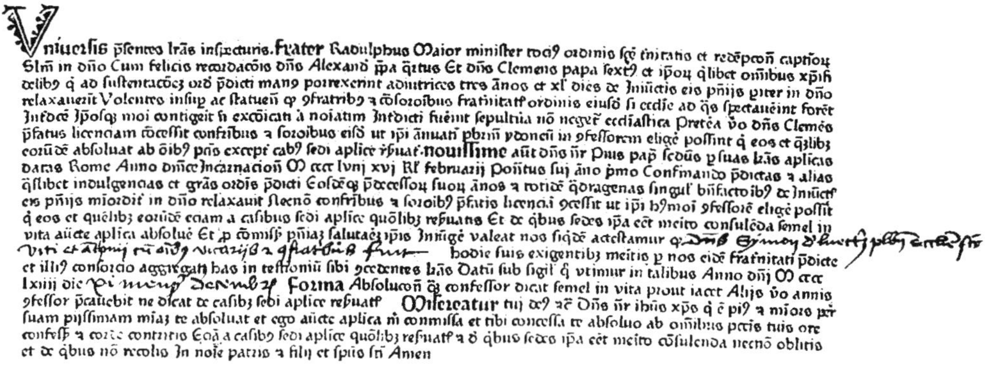

Vniuersis p̄sentes lr̄as inspecturis. **Frater** Radulphus Maior minister tocius ordinis scē trinitatis et redēpcōn̄ captiuo͛
Slm̄ in dn̄o Cum felicis recordacōis dn̄s *Alexand* pp̄a q̄rtus Et dn̄s *Clemens* papa sextus et ipo͛ q̄libet om̄ibus xp̄ifi
delibus q̄ ad sustentacōe͛ ord̄ p̄dicti manus porrexerint adiutrices tres ān̄os et xl dies de Iniūctis eis pn̄ijs p͛ter in dn̄o
relaxauerit Volentes insup ac statuen̄ q̄ confratribus ⁊ cōsororibus fratnitatis ordinis eiusd̄ si eccl̄ie ad q̄s spectauerint forēt
Interdcē Iposq̄ moi contigerit si excōicati à noiatim Interdicti fuerint sepultura nō negeẽ ecclastica Pretēa vo dn̄s Clemēs
p̄fatus licenciam concessit confratribus ⁊ sororibus eisd̄ ut ipi ānuati p̄bīm ydoneū in confessorem eligē possint q̄ eos et q̄libs
corūdē absoluat ab oībus p̄ns except casibus sedi aplice r̄suat. **nouissime** aūt dn̄s nr̄ Pius pap̄ secūs p suas lr̄as aplicas
datas Rome *Anno* dn̄ice Incarnacioñ M cccc lvuj xvj Kl februarij Pōtus suj ān̄o p̄mo Confirmando p̄dictas ⁊ alias
q̄slibet indulgencias et grās ordis p̄dicti Eosdē q̄ p̄decesso͛ suo͛ ān̄os ⁊ totidē q̄dragenas singul bn̄factoribus de Iniūcti͛
eis pn̄ijs miordit in dn̄o relaxauit Necnō confratribus ⁊ sororibus p̄fatis licenciā concessit ut ipi hmoi confessorē eligē possit
q̄ eos et quelibz eorūdē eciam a casibus sedi aplice quolibz reseruans Et de q̄bus sedes ipa eēt merito consulēda semel in
vita aūcte aplica absoluē Et p cōmissis pn̄iaz salutarē ipis Iniūgē valeat nos siqdē actestamur q̄ [illegible]
[illegible] hodie suis exigentibz meritis p nos eidē fratnitati p̄dicte
et illius consorcio aggregati has in testioniū sibi concedentes lr̄as Datū sub sigil q̄ vtimur in talibus Anno dn̄j M cccc
lxiiij die [illegible] **Forma** *Absolucōn̄* q̄s confessor dicat semel in vita prout iacet Alijs vo annis
confessor p̄caue͛bit ne dicat de casibz sedi aplice reseruatis **Misereatur** tui deus ⁊c Dn̄s nr̄ ihūs xp̄s q̄ ē pius ⁊ miors p͛
suam pijssimam miaz te absoluat et ego aūcte aplica m̄ commissa et tibi concessa te absoluo ab om̄ibus pctis tuis ore
confessis ⁊ corde contritis Eciā a casibus sedi aplice quolibz reseruatis ⁊ d̄ q̄bus sedes ipa eēt merito cōsulenda necnō oblitis
et de q̄bus nō recolis In noīe patris ⁊ filij et spūs scī *Amen*

Indulgence to Frater Radulphus for the Benefit of the Trinitarian Order
in the Catholicon-type.
Eltville, Heinrich and Nicolaus Bechtermünze. 1464. Reduced.
(The handwritten entries show that this example was made out for a clergyman on 11 December 1464.)

that there would have been two pages side by side on the press at a time, to be printed together. The *Vocabularius ex quo* takes its title from the two opening words 'Ex quo'. It has a printer's colophon which follows a similar formula to that of the *Catholicon*, except that the brothers Heinrich and Nicolaus Bechtermünze are named as printing masters (Ruppel, 1967: 175–6; Hoffman, 1979: 203; Widmann, 1975: 39). (In his paper, Widmann describes the *Vocabularius ex quo* as a compilation designed to serve as a schoolbook for basic Latin teaching.)

Once again there is an abundance of theories concerning the printer of the *Vocabularius*. The fact that not only was a (revised!) abridgement of the *Catholicon* made available, but its typeface also – and newly cast and sharp-edged types were used – clearly indicates that the printer of the *Vocabularius* must have been closely associated with the printer of the *Catholicon*. In agreement with his financial backer, Humery, Gutenberg must have placed a quantity of the Catholicon matrices at the disposal of the Bechtermünze brothers, so that new letters could be cast from them in Eltville. After Heinrich Bechtermünze's death, his brother Nicolaus combined with Wiegand Spiess of Ortenberg for a second edition of the *Vocabularius*, which appeared in 1469 (Geldner, 1970: I, 108). Now it is scarcely to be credited that Nicolaus, or his brother Heinrich before him, would have done any actual printing for themselves. They were very much more the printing masters, the owners of Eltville's printing works, which had been set up by Gutenberg and was run by his journeymen. It may well have been that Wiegand Spiess himself was one of these printers, and had formerly learned his craft at

Exquo vocabularij varij autētici videlʒ
hugwicō katholicō breuilogꝰ pappas
alij que codices sūt i opacōne p̄ciosi in
collectōe ,plixi et itellcōe obscuri et in
mimico multi im paupes scholacs cosēe de facili ꝛ
ꝓ p̄cio cōpetēti ratōe eoꝝ paupꝛtatꝭ habere ac sibi
procurae nō valeant Vt tn̄ eo facilius sacrā scrip
turā litteralit intellige pn̄t qlibet pmmo scriptū
latinicale pro vtilitate et necessitate collectus ē
p̄ns vocabularius ꝑm ordinē alphabeti ita q lati
nū p̄cedat ꝛ teutonicū subiūgit et an̄ h' cuiꝰ gnis
et cꝰ ordinacōis seu cꝰ ptis oroīs qlibʒ dcō fuelt
et ānexū quē qlibʒ fidelis q potest melioare te
nē ut vitā eternā possiꝺʒ q ꝓmitti elucidātibꝰ
sapiāʒ sicut scriptū ē de sapia i lib sapie octauo ca
pitulo. Qui lucidāt me vitā etnā habeāt Amē:

p̄o A.i. sine
Alma interptat' ugo absconditā
h m Aron interptat' mōs fortis l' mōs
fortitudinis ꝛ ē ꝓpium nomē vin
p̄o Ab t. von ul' est nomen indeclinabile mens
augustus scd̄m ebreos
m s Abactus ta tū.i. fugatus sepatus t gedcplt
a p Abalieno nas nare cōponit' ex ab et alieno
ps.j. Abalienati sunt retrorsū.i. alieni facti
adu Abante t zuvor
Abarim mōs i quo obijt moyses ut habet'
deutronomij xxxij.
m s Abauus est pater proaui
h m Abba est nomē ebraicū Et dr pater latine
f p Abbacia ab abbas dr h' abbacia ep̄n eptij
f p· Abamita ē soror aui ex ab ꝛ amita cōponit'
f p. Abbatissa est monachaꝝ mat' t epn eptyn
m t Abbas tis est monachoꝝ p̄r t epn apt
a p Abbreuio as are t vorkurtzigen

Vocabularius ex quo. *1467.*
Eltville, Office of the Bechtermünze Brothers. Original size.

the Gutenberghof before moving with the inventor to Eltville. The inferior typographic quality of the *Vocabularius* in comparison with the *Catholicon* has to be viewed in relation to Gutenberg's age and to his deteriorating eyesight. The Eltville printing works probably also provided for his social support, since it appears that his entire property and all his annuities had been confiscated.

A third edition of the *Vocabularius ex quo* appeared in 1472, printed from a fresh casting of the types of the *31-line Indulgence for Cyprus*. Only Gutenberg himself or his former financier Dr Humery were in a position to make the corresponding matrices available to the Bechtermünze works. This again shows that the *31-line Indulgence for Cyprus* can only have been produced at the Gutenberghof.

It is remarkable in itself that a tiny town like Eltville on the Rhine should be one of the first places in the world where printing took place, and thus find itself in the same league as large and important cities such as Mainz, Bamberg, Strasbourg, Basle and Rome. The only explanation for this can be that Johann Gutenberg was personally involved in the establishment of the printing house at Eltville.

Gutenberg as court pensioner

THE FOLLOWING LETTER bearing the seal of his new master, Archbishop Adolf II von Nassau, and dated 17 January 1465, was delivered to Johann Gutenberg, and is headed in a contemporary copy book which survives: 'How my gracious lord of Mainz appointed Johann Gutenberg as his Excellency's servant and courtier':

> We, Adolf, etc., declare and manifest publicly by this document that we have recognized the agreeable and willing service which our dear, faithful Johann Gutenberg has rendered, and may and shall render in future time to us and our diocese; therefore, and by special dispensation, have we admitted and received him as our servant and courtier, and receive and admit him presently by virtue of this document. Moreover, we will not and shall not deprive him of such service as long as he lives, and, in order that he may benefit all the more by such service, we shall, each and every year when we clothe our ordinary courtiers, clothe him at the same time like one of our noblemen, and have our court clothing given to him and, each and every year, twenty *Malter* of grain and two *Fuder* of wine for the use of his household, yet so that he shall neither sell it nor give it away, and let it enter free of tax, duty and toll, into our city of Mainz; and also exempt him graciously, as long as he lives, and will be and remains our servant, from watch duty, military service, taxation, and sundries, which we have already imposed, or shall hereafter impose upon our citizens and residents of our said city of Mainz. And about this the aforesaid Johann Gutenberg has faithfully promised us and personally sworn an oath upon the Saints to be faithful and loyal to us, to avert harm from us and foster our interest and do everything a faithful servant is in duty bound and obliged to do on behalf of his rightful master. All the above-written items, points and articles we agree and promise in good, true faith, by virtue of this document, to observe truly, steadfastly, firmly and inviolably, not to act contrary thereto, nor cause such action to be taken in any form, all deceit and falsehood excluded; in wit-

> ness whereof we have attached our seal to this document, which was issued at Eltville, on Thursday the day of St Anthony, *Anno domini millesimo quadringentesimo sexagesimo quinto. Dedit literam reuersalem etc.* (Schorbach, 1900: 220, doc. XXV, and Ruppel, 1967: 56).

After the peace that was concluded on 5 October 1463 between Adolf II and Diether von Isenburg, the new archbishop sought to subdue political protest within his diocese and, at least to some extent, to settle ongoing injustices. One of his bitterest opponents, Dr Konrad Humery, even received monetary compensation for losses he had suffered. It may easily have been on a suggestion direct from Rome itself, through the influence of Cardinal Nicholas of Cues, or from the prince-bishop of Bamberg, or possibly even from the University of Paris, that Adolf was prevailed upon to bestow attention and recognition on the new art of book printing and its inventor. But ultimately the archbishop had experienced for himself during the recent war what a powerful weapon the printing press could become, and that it was important to keep such weapons available close at hand.

What does this document reveal in detail? Its substance is the public honouring of the inventor, who is admitted as a nobleman to a milieu which had been unkindly disposed towards him. In addition, it provided for the social protection of a man who was still being pursued by the imperial court at Rottweil for an unsettled loan and was liable at any time to be cast into debtor's prison. He received the clothing of the court each year, and a supply of about 2180 kilos of grain and 2000 litres of wine – duty-free and for his own personal use. At least he could ask his friends round for a convivial evening and was free from the fear of hardship.

The document makes it plain that wine and grain could be delivered to Gutenberg within the city of Mainz. It follows that he was no longer accounted among those who had been banished, and were never again to set foot in the city. Probably he lived for part of the year in Mainz, spending the summer and autumn in Eltville, as had long been the custom for many patricians. This brought to an end his exile dating from 30 October 1462 and the temporary need to reside exclusively in Eltville.

The 'agreeable and willing service' that Gutenberg had rendered, and might continue to render, to the archbishop, may have consisted in organizing a printing establishment at Eltville. In thus elevating Gutenberg, Archbishop Adolf may also have been hoping to enhance his own standing with the papal *curia*, where several influential figures were following the introduction of book printing with interest. The question of who was doing whom the greater honour in this context is one which need never be asked. Archbishop Adolf has to be considered as the destroyer of the formerly proud city of Mainz, as the man who abolished the freedom of the city, humiliated its citizens, and handed over to Rome many of the traditional rights of the first elector of the German nation. It was Gutenberg who paid tribute to this prince in accepting the honour from his hands. For Gutenberg, this distinction was to be viewed as a disposition of God, with the archbishop acting as his instrument.

Document of 17 January 1465 confirming Gutenberg's appointment as an electoral courtier. Reduced.

IN THE MIDDLE AGES, death constituted the greatest adventure for the individual. Where the lines of pointed Gothic windows and door arches converged, there at the apex one imagined death, but not as a finality, rather as judgment and as verdict. The life of the faithful was aligned towards a blessed death, to the assurance of life after death. Diffuse and muddled notions existed about this afterlife. Most people anticipated their resurrection in full physical perfection, decently clothed in their final apparel. In France, for example, it was thought gruesomely appropriate that a robber or murderer should be hauled out fully naked by his or her victim, so that the criminal would have to appear before the redeemer at the Last Judgment without the means to cover his or her nakedness. The unjustness of oppression and exploitation was only made bearable through this faith in the justice of the hereafter – as in his *Divina Commedia*, the poet Dante is conducted through hell and purgatory, and depicts the justice of God, whose mercy can only be attained through good acts and intercession.

Gutenberg had certainly long prepared himself for death, and especially through his membership of the St Viktor Brotherhood. This brotherhood ensured for all its members a devout burial and a mass for the souls of the departed (Schorbach, 1900: 222, doc. XXVI). He could await his final day with composure.

His appointment as a courtier is the last record of the master during his lifetime. There are, to be sure, traditional and questionable reports that he became blind during his final years (Ruppel, 1967: 66). With advancing age it would have been natural enough for his eyesight to have deteriorated to the point that he could no longer engrave punches or discern letters clearly, and knowledge of making spectacles was only just reaching Germany from Italy.

Gutenberg lived on until the year 1468. There is a marginal note in the manuscript known as the *Zimmersche Chronik*: 'Hansz Gutenberger wohnet in der Algescheimer Bursch' (Ruppel, 1967: 64). This refers to the Algesheimer Hof next to the church of St Christoph and near the Gutenberghof, and it later became a student hostel for the university. Similarly to the Gutenberghof, this large house had been sequestrated by Archbishop Adolf during the sack of Mainz, and occupied by one of his adherents. As early as 1463, this particular house had been leased by Adolf to Ludwig zu Lichtenberg. It is quite possible that later on Johann Gutenberg held domestic authority here and that the archbishop awarded him this Mainz residence when he was made a courtier. In his last years he can hardly have failed to receive more and more news from other cities concerning the spread of his 'adventure and art', and in the summer months, while staying in Eltville, he would have visited Nicolaus Bechtermünze's workshop.

A message must have reached him from abroad that his earlier partner and adversary Johann Fust died of the plague in 1466 in Paris (Geldner, 1970: I, 37). This news is confirmed, as Fust is named as a printer in the endowment of a requiem mass for him at St-Victor in Paris.

On 26 February 1468, Doctor Konrad Humery certified the receipt of printing equipment from the estate of Gutenberg, who must have died shortly prior to that date. His letter takes on this obligation in the following terms:

> I, Conradt Humery, doctor, make known by this letter: Whereas the most reverent prince, my gracious and beloved lord, Lord Adolf, archbishop of Mainz, had graciously permitted sundry forms, letters [characters], instruments, tools and other things pertaining to the work of printing, which Johann Gutenberg has left after his death, and which have belonged and still belong to me, to come into my possession, therefore, I, to honour and please his Grace, did bind, and do bind myself by this document, to wit: That should I now or hereafter make use of the said forms and tools for printing, I will do so within the city of Mainz and nowhere else; that, likewise, in case I should desire to sell them and a citizen should be willing to give me as much for them as a

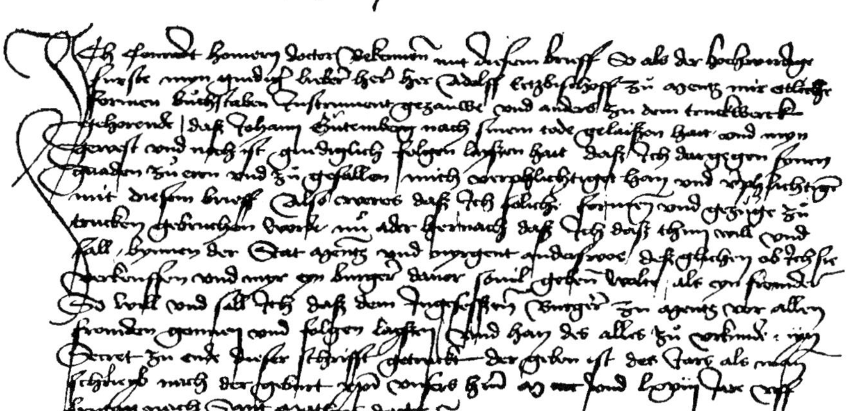

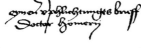

Letter of undertaking by Dr Konrad Humery regarding the equipment left by Gutenberg. Mainz, 26 February 1468. Reduced.

> stranger, then will and shall I give and deliver them to the resident citizen of Mainz in preference to all strangers; in witness of which I have impressed my privy seal at the foot of this document, which was done on Friday following St Matthew's Day, in the year of our Lord Jesus Christ, 1468 (Schorbach, 1900: 227, doc. XXVII).

In order to comprehend this document better, there is an entry which ought to be considered first, which was written in a book printed soon after Gutenberg's death – probably by the priest at Eltville and canon of the St Viktor Foundation, Leonhard Mengoss. It states in a fifteenth-century Gothic hand: 'Anno Domini M°cccc°lxviij uff sant blasius tag starp der ersam meinster Henne Ginsfleiss dem got gnade' [AD 1468 on St Blasius's Day died the honoured master Henne Ginsfleiss on whom God have mercy] (Ruppel, 1967: 70). Mengoss had known Gutenberg

A note of Gutenberg's death made by Leonhard Mengoss.

reasonably well. Both had appeared together in 1457 as special witnesses to the purchase of a property in Bodenheim by Gutenberg's niece Odilgen and her husband Johann Gensfleisch von Sorgenloch, which was encumbered with a perpetual interest obligation to the St Viktor Foundation. Gutenberg had further contacts with Mengoss, who came from an ancient Eltville knightly family, through their membership of the St Viktor Brotherhood and his own frequent stays in Eltville. He would often have attended the priest's services there. After Mengoss had later acquired this printed book from the Schöffer workshop, he must have remembered his acquaintance with the inventor himself and have noted his date of death beneath the printer's mark.

According to this entry by Mengoss, Gutenberg died on 3 February 1468, which is consonant with the dating of Konrad Humery's undertaking, on 18 February of the same year, not to allow the printing tools left by Gutenberg to be resold outside Mainz. From this latter document it follows indisputably that Gutenberg continued to operate a printing works after the breach with Fust in 1455, and that this had been financed by Humery. Presumably, among the printing projects supported by Humery, the *Catholicon* has to be included – the costs of which must have been fairly considerable. For all that, Humery was a wealthy man and open to the spread of learning. Similarly, he would doubtless have agreed to make the Catholicon-types available to equip the Bechtermünze printing works at Eltville. The political head of the guild party, and guiding light within the secretive fraternity of hearty *bon-viveurs* described earlier, now proved himself a patron of the inventor of far higher moral stature than the profit-seeking Fust. Humery's promissory letter was plainly written at the instigation or request of the archbishop, whose interest lay in not exporting the established art of printing outside his own sphere of influence. It would have been in the interests of the master printers Schöffer and Bechtermünze to have backed such a demand.

Gutenberg's mortal remains were interred, as is amply testified, in the church of St Francis (Ruppel, 1967: 71). A distant relative of his, Adam Gelthus, published this inscription – resembling a funerary tablet – in a book printed 31 years afterwards in Mainz:

In foelicem artis impressorie inuentorem.
D[eo] O[ptimo] M[aximo] S[acrum].
Joanni Genssfleisch
artis impressorie repertori
de omni natione et lingua optime merito
in nominis sui memoriam immortalem
Adam Gelthus posuit.
Ossa eius in ecclesia diui Francisci Maguntina
foeliciter cubant (Ruppel, 1967: 72).

[To Johann Gensfleisch, the inventor of the art of printing and deserver of the highest honours from every nation and tongue, Adam Gelthus places {this memorial} to the immortal memory of his name. His remains rest peacefully in the church of St Francis at Mainz.]

This Adam Gelthus was the son of Adam Gelthus von den jungen Aben and of Margarete von Fürstenberg. Both families counted as relatives of Gutenberg's grandparents. Arnold Gelthus zum Echtzeler had helped Gutenberg obtain the first loan he took out on his return from Strasbourg. As the parents of Adam Gelthus had married in 1457, it is still possible that the writer of the epitaph could have recalled the inventor. Adam Gelthus was a licentiate of law, altarist of the St Nicholas altar at St Quintin's in Mainz and chaplain of a similar altar endowed to that saint in the parish church at Eltville (Ruppel, 1967: 73–4).

As we do not know the inventor's year of birth nearly as accurately as the year of his death, but assume him to have been born in about 1400 or a few years later, he could have reached the age of about 68. For men of the fifteenth century – who were more prone to death through battle, pestilence and sickness than those living today – a life of 68 or perhaps 65 years was a considerable span for one who had led a chequered career and had always put his unremitting energy into his work. Since his work represented for him a development of the creative process, the relentless pursuit of his goal always brought renewed powers, which we can believe kept him young and enthusiastic.

CHAPTER ELEVEN

Eternal fame

The spread of printing before 1500

AFTER THE FALL OF MAINZ in 1462, as a result of which most printers were driven from the city, the new art spread with astonishing speed across the whole of Europe. Especially in the great mercantile and university cities, an immense need for books arose which could only be met with help from the new technology. Following the pattern set by the Mainz printing offices, the new workshops in many places began by cutting punches, striking matrices and casting characters; and new presses and fittings were constructed to the Mainz model. With such preliminary work to be accomplished, and allowing for typesetting and printing, one to two years would have elapsed before the first books were ready for sale. For this reason many new establishments were dependent on the search for a financier, whose name would become the one to appear on the printer's mark or colophon. Another feature of early printing was that a printer usually had to become his own publisher at the same time, and to market and distribute the books which he produced. Only later did specialization within the trade begin to emerge. Printers sold their characters to others. And so the first type-foundries were established. A few travelling book salesmen and book-sellers with fixed locations ordered complete editions. Independent publishing houses initially began in this way. This differentiation between publishing, printing and typefounding can be observed earlier in Italy and France than in Germany.

In Mainz, the house of Peter Schöffer developed along prosperous lines. The publication of theological texts continued to predominate. One after another, Schöffer printed missals for Breslau, Cracow and Meissen, then a further one for Cracow, one for Gnesen, for Cracow yet again and finally one for Mainz. All these editions were revised for the usage of the appropriate episcopal authority, and undertaken for each diocese, which in turn supplied them to its monasteries and priests. This involved scarcely any financial risk at all. Schöffer paid attention to good quality at high prices. He reaped where Gutenberg had sown. He died a respected citizen and civil judge of the city of Mainz in 1503 (Geldner, 1970: I, 37–8).

IOſeph quid agis, Rē profecto oparis
q̄ me profundiſſima admiratōe ſuſpē
dit, herodem timens ne puerum perdat,
in egiptuȝ cum puero ⁊ matre eius fugis
O res ſtupenda nonne puer iſte eſt paruu
lus ille qui paucos ante dies natus eſt no
bis, cuius imperiuȝ ut propheta ſanctus
ait ſuper humerū eius, deus fortis pater
futuri ſeculi, princeps pacis, Nimis profe=
cto arbitratus es herodis potētiā, ut me=
tueres ne paruulū pderet, cui eſt poteſtas
immēſa, maieſtas infinita, et inſupabilis

The Meditationes *of Johann de Turrecremata.*
Printed by Johann Numeister, with metalcuts copied from the woodcut illustrations to an earlier edition by Ulrich Han in Rome.
Mainz, 1479.

Bernhard von Breydenbach's Pilgerreise ins Heilige Land.
Woodcuts by Erhard Reuwich. Printed by Peter Schöffer. Mainz, 1486. Reduced.

Dem hochwirdigsten vatter yn cristo·vnd herren hern Bertholdō: deß heyligen stůles zů Mentz Ertzbischoff·des Römschen riches Ertzkantzler durch tütsche lande vnd kurfursten ꝛc·mynem gnedigsten herren Jch Bernhard vō Breydenbach deß selben hohen stifftes yn mentz dechan vnd Camerer ꝛc Myn schuldigen willigen dienst vnd vndertenige gehorsame·allezyt dienstlich zů vor·

HOchwirdigster vatter yn cristo vnd gnedigster furst vnd herr·Daz ich mich wyder myn gewonlich gebruch vermessen hab an vwer hochwirdikeyt vnd furstlich gnad nit alleyn kunlich vnd fruntlich schriben· sunder auch ettwas bewysen· anzeugen·ja opferen daz vwrer furstlichen gnaden tapfferheit vnd ernsthafftikeit nit werdt ist geantwort oder furbracht zů werden·ist die vrsach·kommend vß dißem grund alleyn·daz ich mich yn gegenwirtikeit uwrer furstlichen gnaden angeborner tugend vnd gutte größlichen gebruch·begerend vnd bittend in sollicher zůuersicht|zů erst·daz uwer furstlich gnad diß myn vermessenheit (dasß eyn gůtt zuversicht genāt als auch ym grund ist) nit wol in vbel verstan· besunder so ich gar by schympflichen hādelen mit uwer furstlichen gnaden möchte geurteylet werden·derren wißheyt doch mir vnd menglich wöl bekant ist·vor ab angesehen vnd gemerckt· daz ich diß alles in gemüt vn̄ in maß eyner fruntlichen erzeugūg mynes gutten willens vn̄ eyner besunder reuerentz oder eerbewisung thun·vngezwifelt· Jch werde auch glichmutiglichen lyden vnd dulden· ob uwer furstlich gnade oder yeman ander kluger man·mich wurde versehen in dissem handel· nit gnůg tapferlichen thůn·mynem stat oder ampt nach·Ob mich dan eyn menschliche bekorung hyryn begrifft oder eyn furwitzikeit villicht vermeynet mir nit wol anstende· wöl mir uwrer furstlichen gnaden· Auch ander wysen menner (fur die diß wurdt kommen) bescheydenheit vnd menschlikeit in keynem argen vff nemen· Diß wol gehoffnet·kom ich also vff myn meynūg·daz mancherley vbūg vn̄ gebruch sy menschlicher vernunfft vnd synn· vnd keyn end nuwer bucher zu machen (ob joch etwas diser zyt möchte nuwe genant werden· solichs meyn ich daz alleyn vßwendig eyn ander kleydūg enpfahet· oder mit eyner anderen farbe vberstrichen wurdt dan eß vorhyn hette· doch die substantz von ynnen vnveranderet verlyben·vnder anderem vnd anderem vßwendigem vn̄ zukōmendem zuvall) wer das nit enweiß oder mercket vor ab ytz der zyt so nuw fundikeit seer vber handt nymmet· vnd eyn yeder in synem synn rich ist·meyn ich nyman mogen werden gefundē· der syner vernunfft mechtig ist·erkennet daz eß vor lang dar zu kommen ist· daz nach gemeynem spruch· wer alleyn den stilum oder die sunderlich wiß

The other Mainz printers did not display the same brilliance as Peter Schöffer. Johann Numeister can fairly be described as a typical journeyman printer, who probably learned his craft in the Gutenberg and Fust partnership works, had gone on to print in Foligno and Perugia, returning to Mainz, where he brought out the *Meditationes* of Johann de Turrecremata in 1479, before continuing his later work in Albi and Lyon. His Mainz printing is noteworthy for its fine metalcuts, which are modelled on an edition issued in Rome by Ulrich Han in 1467 (Geldner 1970: I, 39).

A remarkably handsome book was published in Mainz by the Utrecht-born painter Erhard Reuwich, about a pilgrimage made to the Holy Land in 1483 by the dean of Mainz cathedral, Bernhard von Breydenbach, whose travel account is provided with many full-page woodcuts. Although Reuwich is named as printer in the colophon, it appears that the book, which went through repeated editions, was printed by Schöffer to Reuwich's commission. Another Mainz printer, Peter von Friedberg, printed a series of shorter texts which are interesting for their range of content.

The printing of the *36-line Bible* in Bamberg on behalf of the prince-bishop, Georg von Schaumburg, has already been mentioned, as has the fact that the B36-type ended up in the printing works of Albrecht Pfister, where it was used for popular books issued with hand-coloured woodcuts. Those most likely to have shared in producing the B36 include Heinrich Keffer, Johann Sensenschmidt and probably Johann Numeister as well. After *Der Ackermann aus Böhmen* and Ulrich Boner's *Der Edelstein*, Pfister brought out the *Vier Historien* as well as German and Latin versions of the *Biblia pauperum*.

Later Johann Sensenschmidt and Magister Heinrich Petzensteiner from Leipzig were invited to set up a press in the Michelsberg monastery near Bamberg, and produced as their first book in 1481 a splendid *Missale Benedictinum*. Sensenschmidt's liturgical printing was highly acclaimed, and he received commissions from Peter Drach, one of the first wholesale booksellers and publishers, for a *Missale Olomucense* and a *Missale Pragense*: works which would then be sold by Drach's representative Johann Schmidhöfer in Bohemia and Moravia. Sensenschmidt could also be described as a travelling printer. To meet the wishes of several bishops who themselves wanted to become acquainted with and supervise the printing, he produced the first editions of the *Missale Ratisbonense* (1485) in Regensburg; *Missale Frisingense* (1487) in Freising; and *Missale Augustense* (1489) at Dillingen, residence of the

Biblia pauperum. *Printed in the B36-type (DK-type). Bamberg, Albrecht Pfister. About 1462.*

David. Herre rich das plut deiner heiligen.

Salomō. Ein prūmender leo und ein zorniger pere ein pos furst.

Jeremias. Die stym ist gehort wordē des schreiens und des heulens.

David. Sie haben geherscht aber nicht aus mit.

Saul. Die prister

Die schar. dy schwester des kunigs

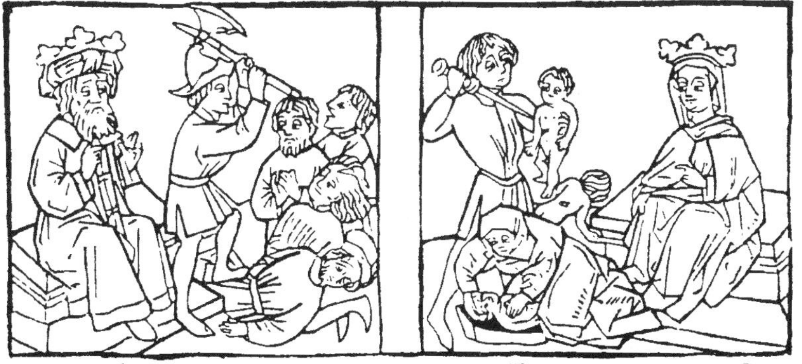

wir lesē in dem puch dʼ kunig in dē .xxij. ca. Das saul liesz totē all prister des herrē darumb das sie dauid dʼ do fluchtig was ein namē vñ ym das heilig prot gabē zu einer speisz. Saul bedeut herodē dauid xpm die prister die kinder die herodes liesz toten durch xpm. wir lesē ym puch dʼ kunig ym .xxj. ca. Do athalia die kunigyñ sach das ir sun tot was do liesz sie totē all kinder des kunigs das sie icht besessē das reich nach irem vater vñ die schwester des kunigs v̄parg heimlich dē jungsten sun und wart zu kunig. Die vnlustige kunigin bedeut herodē der durch xpm willē liesz totē die kindʼ. Aber das kint das v̄porgē wart bedeut xpm

Augsburg archbishop. A *Missale Bambergense* did not appear from him until 1490.

After Johann Sensenschmidt's death, Johannes Pfeyl continued to print liturgical books as well as the usual official ephemera. Another Bamberg printer, Hans Sporer, produced popular booklets which to some extent heralded the approaching Peasants' War: with titles such as Konz Has's *Geschichte von der Welt Lauf*, the *Bauernlob* and the *Pfennigmünzer*. For printing a verse satire on the failure of Duke Albrecht the Courageous of Saxony to be elected bishop, Sporer was banned from Bamberg and moved on to Erfurt (Geldner, 1970: I, 49ff).

Strasbourg constitutes one of the most important fifteenth-century printing cities, in fact the third in chronological sequence (Geldner, 1970: I, 55ff). So states the literature on the German incunabula printers; though my interpretation of the printing of the *Sibyllenweissagung* – that earliest European example of printing from movable type – which according to its links with the election of Frederick III as German king and the Armagnac campaign may be assigned to between the years 1441 and 1444, would demonstrate that printing took place in Strasbourg earlier than anywhere else. However, the art was perfected in Mainz, and it was from that city that it spread throughout the world.

Leaving aside Gutenberg's earliest experiments, Heinrich Eggestein and Johann Mentelin are to be accounted Strasbourg's first printers. Both may be presumed to have worked together with Gutenberg during his Strasbourg period. Eggestein, who was an official of Bishop Ruppert of Strasbourg, went to Mainz, most probably in 1454, in order to become familiar with the subsequent development of the 'adventure and art', returning to Strasbourg in 1457 to establish a printing office with Mentelin, who can be shown to have practised as goldsmith and notary in Strasbourg since 1447. The *49-line Bible* appeared in two volumes in the course of 1460 and 1461. After 1465 both of them ran a workshop of their own. Mentelin completed the *First German Bible* on 21 June 1466, which Eggestein followed with an almost word-for-word reprint in 1470. The translator is said to have been a Waldensian and the manuscript exemplar to have dated back to the fourteenth century. The bad German of this first Bible to appear in any vernacular language has been repeatedly criticized. But when Archbishop Berthold of Mainz on 22 March 1485 forbade the printing and sale of bibles in the German language, it is more likely that he feared that laymen would be able to read into the Holy Scripture an interpretation that was rebellious and out of line with that of the Church. Mentelin published mainly theological and philosophical texts. Printing had made him a very wealthy and respected citizen by the time of his death in 1478.

gen peide vogel unde thier · Ein groszer krieg wart
gar schir · yder wenne er het recht · Do komen rit=
ter unde knecht · Der streit wart grosz und hert · Sy
hertē gerne erwert · Dē vogeln do ein wāg gescha=
ach · An eim do das ersach · Die fledermausz liesz ir
schar · Und flog zu den thierē dar · Sie sazten sich
wider die dier · Als ir verzagtes herz rier · Sie flog
do man ir bedorffte wol · Des was sie lasters vol ·
Der adeler gestosē kam · Vil sere schrei er die vogel
an · Er gab in herz unde mut · Als noch vil der rec
ken thut · Und machtē blosz die fledermausz · Vñ
stissen sie vil schnelle ausz · Do wart ir das zu pusz
gegeben · Das sie des nachts ir leben · Speisen und
auch fliegē sol · Der do zweiē auch diner wol · Das

Ulrich Boner's Der Edelstein.
Printed by Albrecht Pfister in the B36-type. Bamberg, 1462.
Reduced.

Eggestein concentrated more on medieval literature and the Latin classics in German translation. He printed for his travelling salesmen what is probably the earliest leaflet to advertise books, and Mentelin and Schöffer were quick to follow this example.

Mentelin's son-in-law, Adolf Rusch, carried on his office. He printed primarily humanistic and classical literature. Of the remaining Strasbourg printers, the most important were Heinrich Knoblochtzer, printer of the *Entekrist*, a book famous for its powerful and expressive woodcuts, and Johann Grüninger. At least 50 different printing establishments were active in Strasbourg by the close of the century.

In Cologne by that time there may have been perhaps 30 printing concerns. Its first printer, Ulrich Zell, had matriculated at Erfurt in 1453, and then learned the crafts of printing with Fust and Schöffer before having himself registered in the university faculty of arts at Cologne in 1464. At the same time he must have started his own printing office, for his first edition was ready in 1465. He issued mostly theological and classical texts in Latin. From among the rest of Cologne's printers, Bartholomäus von Unkel and Heinrich Quentell are best known for their North German and Saxon dialect bibles containing a wealth of woodcut illustrations. Heinrich Quentell managed to issue no fewer than 400 bibliographical items in the 21 years from 1479 to 1500, making him one of the most prolific printers of his age (Geldner, 1970: I, 86ff).

Berthold Ruppel, a former apprentice of Gutenberg, began printing in Basle. By 1468 a large Latin Bible had issued from his presses. This brought him early prosperity, although growing competition was to force him into the background. Another enterprising printer, Michael Wenssler, came from Strasbourg and founded a business which again began well. He printed missals for Cologne, Mainz, Basle, Trier and Salisbury and had made available more than two dozen texts of various kinds. But then economic decay set in, his office went bankrupt and he was forced to flee. Johann Amerbach and Johann Froben are regarded as the most celebrated Basle printers. They enjoyed fame as scholar-printers and cultivated the friendship of the foremost intellectuals in Europe. Amerbach in particular placed himself at the service of humanism. His printing was extolled for its meticulous editing; it would cause a sensation to find a printer's error slip through. Johann Bergmann von Olpe has to be mentioned among the Basle printers as the publisher of Sebastian Brant's *Narrenschiff*, which contained woodcuts by the young Albrecht Dürer (Geldner, 1970: I, 111).

It is not practical to consider here all the more than 60 German-speaking cities and locations in which printing took place during the fifteenth century. But in conclusion there has yet to be mentioned the

Deuteronomi

ſprach zů moyſes. Rede zů den ſūnē iſrl: vñ ſprich
zů in. So ir vberget den iordan in das land chanaan
ſchaut welche ſtett do ſüllen ſein zů der hilff ð flůch:
tigen · die do vnwillent vergieſſent das plůt: ſo der
flůchtig fleůcht in ſy: der freůnd des derſchlagen ð
mage in nitt derſchlagen: vntz das er ſtee in der be
ſcheůde der menig · vnd ſein ſach die werd geurteilt
Wann von den ſtetten die do werden geſcheiden zů
der hilff der flůchtigen der werdent · iij · anderthalbe
des iordans vnd · iij · in dem land chanaan · als wol
den ſůnen iſrl als den frembden vnd den ellenden: dz
der flich zů in · der do hat vergoſſen das plůt vnwil
lent. Der do ein ſchlecht mitt eim eyſen vnd ſtirbt ·
der in hat derſchlagen · der wirt ſchuldig der mann
ſchlacht: vnd er ſelb ſterbe. Ob er wirfft den ſtain ·
vnd er ſtirbt von dē wurff: er werde gepeiniget ze:
geleicher weys. Ob er ſchlecht mit dem holtz vnd er
ſtirbt: er werd gerochen mit dē plůt des ſchlachers.
Zehant ſo in begreift der neſt des derſchlagen : er:
ſchlach in vnd derſchlach den manſchlechten . Ob
etlicher quelt den menſchen durch haſz oder yemant
wirfft an in durch die lagen: oder in ſchlecht mit ð
hant ſo er iſt ſeī feind vñ er ſtirbt : ð ſchlacher wirt
ſchuldig der manſchlachte. Zehant ſo in vindet der
freůnd dez derſchlagē er wurg in. Vñ er tůt keins
dirr ding on vngluck vñ on haſz vñ on veindſchaft
vnd ditz wirt gehort vnd bewert von dē volck · vnd
die frag wirt vnderſcheiden zwiſchē dē neſten vnd
dem ſchlacher des plůtz: der vnſchuldig wert erlöſt
von der hant dez rechers · vnd wider gefůrt durch dz
vrteil in die ſtat zů der er wz geflochē: vnd er belaibe
do vntz das ð michel pfaff geſtirbet der do iſt geſalbt
mit dem heiligen ol. Ob der derſchlaher wirt fundē
auſwendig der ſtett die do ſeint geacht dem ellenden
vnd wirt er geſchlagen von dem der do iſt ein recher
des blůtz: ð in hat erſchlagen der wirt vnſchuldig.
Wann der flůchtig der ſolt ſein beliben in der ſtatt
vntz an den todt des biſchofs . Wann dornoch ſo er
abget der manſchefftig kert wið zů ſeim land. Vnd
ditz werdent ewig geſetzt · in all eur entwelungen .
Der manſchlecht der werd gepeiniget vnder dē ge:
zeůgen. Keiner werd verdampt zů dem gezeůg eins.
Nit enphacht dē werd von dem der do iſt ſchuldig
des blůtz: vnd zehant ſterb er . Die ellenden vnd die
flůchtigen die mügen in keiner weys wið keren in
ir ſtett vor dem tode des biſchoffs das ir icht entzeů:
bert das lande ewer entwelung dz do wirt entzeůbert
in dem plůt ð vnſchedlichen: noch mag anders wer:
den geheiligt neur durch das plůtt des · der do ver:
geůſt das plůtt eins andern: vnd alſuſt wirt gerei:
niget ewer beſitzung die weil ich entwele mit eůch
Wann ich bins der herre : ich do entwele in mitzt
der ſůn iſrahel.

xxxvi

Wann auch die fürſten der ingeſinde galaad
die ſůne machir die ſůn manaſſe von dem
ſtamme ð ſůn ioſephs : die genachentē ſich
vñ redten zů moyſes vor den fürſten iſrl vñ ſprach
en. Der herr hat dir gebotten vnſerm herren das du
teilſt das lande mitt dē loſz den ſůnen iſrl: vnd dz du
den tőchtern ſalphaad vnſers brůders gebeſt die ge:
ordenten beſitzung des vatters: ob die weiber nemēt
mann eins andern geſchlechtz · ir beſitzung die vol
ge vnd werde vbertragen zů eim andern geſchlecht
gemynnert von vnſerm erbe : vnd es werde gethan
alſo ſo das vmbgende iar der derlöſung zůkumpt ·
das iſt zewiſſen das · l · die teilung des loſz werde ver
wůſt vnd die beſitzung ð andern vbergeen zů dē an
dern. Moyſes ð antwurt den ſůnen iſrl: do es ð herr
gebott vnd ſprach. Das geſlecht der ſůn ioſephs hat
recht geredt: vnd ditz iſt die ee vber die tőchter ſal:
phaad vnd iſt deroffent vom herren. Sy gemecheln
mit wem ſy wellen allein das es ſey mit den leůtten
irs geſchlechtz: das die beſitzung der ſůn iſrahel icht
werd vermiſcht von geſchlecht in geſchlecht. Wañ
alle die mann fůrent weiber von ir geburt wañ vō
dem geſchlecht · vnd alle die weiber die nement die
mann von dem ſelben geſchlecht: das das erbe beleib
vnder den ingeſinden noch die geſchlechte werdent
in vermiſchet: wann das ſy beleiben alſo als ſy ſint
geſcheiden von dem herren. Vnd die tőchter ſalpha:
ad die detten als in was gebotten · vnd maala vnd
therſa vñ egla vnd melcha vnd noa die gemecheltē
mit den ſůnen irs vettern von dem geſchlecht ma :
naſſe der do was der ſun ioſephs: vnd die beſitzung
die in was zů dem zinſz die beleibt vnder der geburt
vnd vnder dem ingeſinde irs vettern. Ditz ſint die
gebott vñ die vrteil die ð herr gebott durch die hand
moyſes zů den ſůnen iſrl in den velden moab vber
den iordan gegen iercho . Hie endet das buch
Numeri vnd hebt an das buch deutro
nomij Das erſt Capitel

Ditz ſint die wort die moyſes
redt zů allem iſrahel andert:
halbe des iordans in der einð:
de des veldes bey dem rotē me:
re zwiſche pharan vnd top:
hel vñ laban vñ aſeroth. Xi ·
tag durch den weg der berge
ſeir vō oreb: do do iſt vil gol
des vntz zů cadeſbarne an dē · xl · iar an dem · xi · mo
ned an dem erſten tage des monedz moyſes der redt
zů den ſůnen iſrl alle ding die im der herr hett gebot
ten · das ers in ſagt: dornach do er ſchlůg ſeon dē ků
nig der amoreer · der do entwelte in eſebon: vnd og
den künig baſan der do beleib in aſeroth vñ in edrai
anderthalb des iordans in dē lande moab. Vñ moy
ſes der begunde zeroffen die ee vnd zeſagen. Der her
re euwer gott der rede zů eůch in oreb ſagent. Eůch
begnůgt das ir beleibt an diſē berge. Kert wider vñ
kumpt zů dem berg der amoreer vnd zů den andern
veldē die im ſint nachē vnd die berg vñ die kranck:
en ſtett gegen mittemtag vmb den iordan vnd bey
dem geſtatt des meres in daz land der chananeer vñ
libani biſz zů dem groſſen fluſz effraten. Er ſprach .
Secht ich habs eůch geantwurt. Geet ein vnd beſitzt
es: vber daz der herr ſchwůr ewern vettern abraham
yſaac vnd iacob : das er es in gebe vnd irem ſamen
nach in. Vnd ich ſprach zů dem ſelben zeit zů eůch .
Jch enmag eůch nit allein enthaben wann der herr
ewer gott der hat eůch gemanigualtigt: vnd ir ſeit
heůt manige als die ſtern des himels. Der herr gott
ewer vetter der hat zůgelegt vil tauſent zů der zal:

Page from the First German Bible.
Printed by Johann Mentelin. Strasbourg, 1466. Reduced.

largest printing enterprise of them all. Anton Koberger in Nuremberg, who had the necessary means at his disposal, ran printing and the allied book trades as a capitalist undertaking. He is said to have employed over 100 craftsmen and to have owned 24 presses. His travellers visited all the big trade fairs. He had branches in Venice, Milan, Paris, Breslau, Vienna, Passau, Cracow and Buda. Since at times his own vast work-shops lacked sufficient capacity, he farmed work out to printers in other cities; even those in Basle and Strasbourg worked for him. Predominantly he published theological, philosophical, legal and liturgical works. Hartmann Schedel's *Nuremberg Chronicle*, with its 1809 woodcuts after 645 drawings by the Nuremberg artists Michael Wolgemut and Wilhelm Pleydenwurff, became his best-known publication. But the most signifi-cant artistic achievement of Koberger's workshop was of course Albrecht Dürer's woodcuts to *The Apocalypse* in its Latin and German editions, for which the artist retained the publishing rights and himself supervised the printing. Koberger had some 30 different type designs at his disposal to select from, according to the style his market was accustomed to reading, or the requirements of a particular literary genre. For example, for the German edition of Schedel's *Weltchronik* he used a Schwabacher, while for the Latin edition he used the rotunda that was popular in Italy. Within his business organization Koberger realized what Gutenberg had striven to achieve, namely a liberal division of labour, with input from important artists and the coordination of the production processes and selling all under one person's control (Geldner, 1970: I, 162).

There were about 300 hundred printing offices at work in 60 German centres by the year 1500. But long before that printing had crossed the frontiers of the German empire. Printers from Germany travelled to Italy, France and Spain. In many cases they proved unable to cope with the difficulties of a foreign environment. It is true that they brought with them the knowledge of printing, and sometimes met with success, but as competition from local printers grew they were frequently driven out again.

To illustrate this situation, a letter may be cited which Giovanni Andrea Bussi, bishop of Aleria, who had been secretary to Cardinal Nicholas of Cues for several years and thereafter chief librarian of the Vatican Library, sent to Pope Sixtus IV. This takes the form of a plea to the pope for financial help from the German printers, Sweynheym and Pannartz. It lists all 28 titles which they had issued from 1465 to March 1472, at first from Subiaco and then at Rome in a total output 'unless we are mistaken' of 12,475 copies. The petition ends with the following lines:

Sebastian Brant's Narrenschiff.
Printed by Johann Bergmann von Olpe. Basle, 1494.

Den vordantz hat man mir gelan
Dañ jch on nutz vil buͤcher han
Die jch nit lyß / vnd nyt verstan

Von vnnutzē buchern

Das jch sytz vornan jn dem schyff
Das hat worlich eyn sundren gryff
On vrsach ist das nit gethan
Vff myn libry ich mych verlan

> Due to the expenses just in printing the Nicolaus de Lyra *Postilla super Bibliam* volumes, our house is full of unsold quires, but empty of the means to live. If we were able to sell our work, not only would we not implore your charity, but, mindful of pressing demands on your time, do ask only that you scan the list of our books in the hope that the mere sound of such illustrious names may move you to provide assistance. Broken in strength we implore your gracious help, in return for which we will gladly give you as many copies of our handiwork as you may choose to have. May you benefit from health and contentment, Holy Father. Rome, 20 March 1472, in the first year of your pontificate (Geldner, 1970: II, 25ff).

Evidently this letter to the pope brought no financial help, for Italy's first printers were unable to renew their type and their printing deteriorated. Pannartz was dead by 1476, and Sweynheym had devoted himself to map-engraving. But both had encountered competition long before that. Ulrich Han from Ingolstadt, who had studied at Leipzig in 1443 and may have worked in Bamberg under Albrecht Pfister, achieved great success. He used the rotunda letter that was favoured in Italy and in some cases decorated his books with woodcuts, which were later coloured by hand. Recent research has revealed that for the 34 woodcut illustrations to Johann de Turrecremata's *Meditationes* he copied a fresco-cycle in a Roman monastery attributed to Fra Angelico. He later printed papal bulls, orations and ordinances, and became first to print musical notation together with text in 1476 (Geldner, 1970: II, 30ff). The colophon specially claims this missal to be: 'printed with the notes to be sung, which has never happened until now' (Geldner, 1970: II, 35).

German printers – most of whom were clergymen or scholars – were able to maintain their ascendancy in Rome until the turn of the century. In Venice, however, where humanism had its cultural capital and which was to become the most important centre of early printing as well, the German master printers were to encounter the stiffest competition from their Italian colleagues. Venice's first printer was Johann von Speyer, probably identical with that Hans von Spyre who is encountered as a witness to certain Mainz documents of 1460 and 1461 and who may have learned printing from Gutenberg. His first book was printed as early as 1469. He worked together with his brother, Wendelin von Speyer, who continued the printing works after Johann's early death (Geldner, 1970: II, 62ff). It seems remarkable to me that Wendelin should have been able to issue the first Bible in the Italian language by 1471.

One of the most important Venetian printers, and certainly the best

Diomedes, De Arte Grammatica.
Printed by Nicholas Jenson in a particularly fine and readable roman. Venice, 1480. Reduced.

cætera. Hio hias ex quo iteratiuum figuratur hiato: hiatas. Inchoatiuum uero figuratur hisco hiscis cum dicimus.

Sed quanq̃ ita se habeant tamen plus esse uidetur ĩ eoquod ẽ hiscer̃ q̃ hiare. Hiat eĩm qui ore patet uel tacitus tm̃ quod in rebus fictis animaduerti põt. hiscere uero incipere loqui. Illud præterea nõnullis libuit animaduertere ꝙ actiuis acti ua nõnulla figurata ĩchoatiua r̃periũtur etiã passiua: quale ẽ gelo gelas: cuius inchoatiuum facit gelasco quod ẽ ĩcipio gelare.

Item cum ẽ lento lentas: Vnde Virgilius: Lentandus remus ĩ unda. Ex hoc inchoatiuum lentesco facit ut idem Virgilius Et picis in morem ad digitos lentescit habendo. Eiusmodi figuratio parum admisit ex se perfectum: nec conuenit ad mittere ut aut possit: aut debeat cum cæteris temporibus ꝑ totam declinationem uim incipiendi significare. Absurdũ ẽ ergo ea quæ sunt inchoatiua perfecto tempore definire: & mox futurum declinando inchoatiua esse demõstrare. Nec enim potest cum tota uerbi species inchoatiua dicatur alia parte finitiua uideri ut perfectum admittat. Nec enim pale sciui: horresciui dicimus. per aliam tamen transfigurationẽ hæc uerba quidam declinare consueuerunt. ut palesco: pale factus sum: liquesco liquefactus sum. quãuis quidam ad ꝑ fectum inchoatiuum uenerint modo primitiui ut horresco horrui ex eo quod ẽ horreo. Nec tamen omnia inchoatiua habent primam positionem. Albesco enim nõ habet albeo licet figuranter Virgilius: Campiq; ĩgentes ossibus albent. Item putresco: grãdesco: siluesco: uilesco: brutesco: iuuene sco nõ habet iuueneo. Nam senesco & seneo apud ãtiquos dicebatur. Vnde & Catullus nunc recondita senet.

Deducuntur item inchoatiua a neutris uerbis & appellationi bus. ex uerbis: ut caleo calesco: deliteo delitesco: frõdeo frõ desco: floreo floresco. Et sunt hæc quæ a perfecta forma ue niũt. Sũt itẽ quæ originẽ sui nõ habẽt: ut cõsuesco: cõquie sco. Sunt quoq; alia inchoatiuis similia quæ inchoatiua nõ esse temporum consideratione pernoscimus. ut compesco

type designer, was Nicholas Jenson. It has already been mentioned that he was sent to Mainz from Paris in 1458, and may have spent a few years with the Brothers of the Common Life at Marienthal. From there he went on to Italy and may initially have served a little time with Johann and Wendelin von Speyer. By 1470 he had his own workshop, which he later expanded into a company with other German printers and under the financial control of the wealthy Frankfurt merchant Ugelheimer. A book was published in 1470 in Jenson's splendid roman typeface, which foreshadows all the roman types which have followed (Geldner, 1970: II, 65-6). The early printing types were in most cases interpreted with a sensitive artistic understanding from prevalent styles of handwriting, and it fell to Jenson to realize the clear readability of the humanist lower-case directly into type. He died in 1480 in prosperous circumstances.

Erhard Ratdolt from Augsburg, working with his countrymen Peter Löslein and Bernhard Maler, also won renown in Venice through the 60 or so mainly scholarly books which they printed there. Many of his pages were framed with scrollwork borders in white line cut by Bernhard Maler. Some of these woodcuts were overprinted from several blocks in different colours. He was elderly by the time he transferred his printing business to Augsburg, but the fashion for his Venetian ornamental initials and borders spread to other German cities as well, and he became a popular printer for liturgical books (Geldner, 1970: II, 72ff).

The most celebrated Italian printer and publisher of the incunabula period, which is to say up to the arbitrary year 1500, was the humanist Aldus Manutius, who printed editions of the Greek and Latin classics in Venice. His punch-cutter, Francesco Griffo of Bologna, created for him an entire range of Greek and roman typefaces. He introduced a narrow italic, based on the current handwriting of the humanists, which was used for inexpensive books set in pocket format and produced in relatively large editions. The *Hypnerotomachia Poliphili* of Francesco Colonna is considered to be the loveliest book which Aldus printed; it appeared in 1499 with 170 fine woodcuts in black outline to balance the weight of the text. Without hesitation this can be nominated as the highpoint in the book arts of the Renaissance, and the only work that may be placed on the same aesthetic plane as the *42-line Bible* published some 44 years earlier.

In Venice alone by 1500, more than 4500 titles had issued from 150 printing houses in typical editions of between 200 and 500 copies. Besides Rome and Venice, there were 51 other Italian centres of printing by then. Italy's economic development was so far advanced that by the turn of the century it was poised to overtake the land where printing

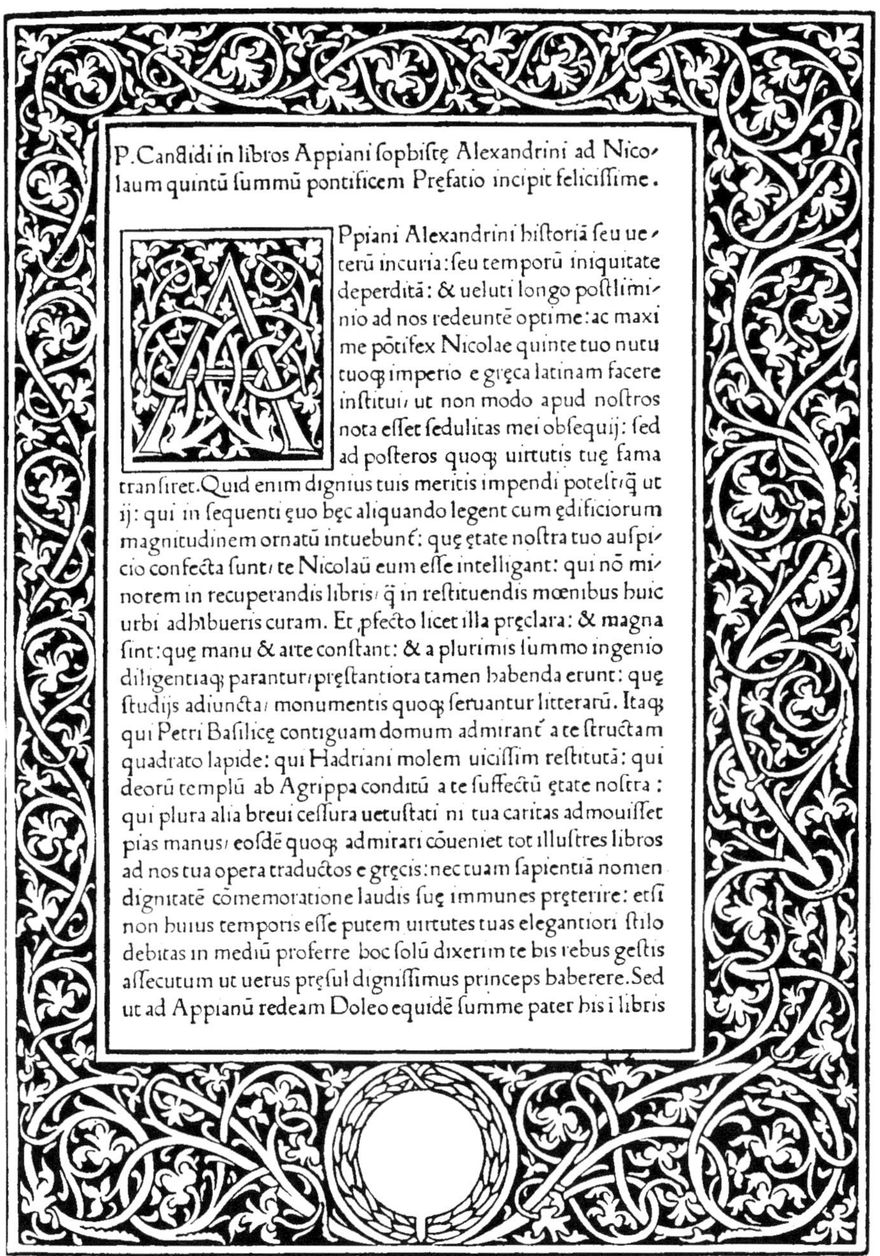

P.Candidi in libros Appiani sophistę Alexandrini ad Nico-
laum quintū summū pontificem Prefatio incipit felicissime.

A Ppiani Alexandrini historiā seu ue-
terū incuria: seu temporū iniquitate
deperditā: & ueluti longo postlimi-
nio ad nos redeuntē optime: ac maxi
me pōtifex Nicolae quinte tuo nutu
tuoq; imperio e gręca latinam facere
institui, ut non modo apud nostros
nota esset sedulitas mei obsequij: sed
ad posteros quoq; uirtutis tuę fama
transiret. Quid enim dignius tuis meritis impendi potest, q̄ ut
ij: qui in sequenti ęuo hęc aliquando legent cum ędificiorum
magnitudinem ornatū intuebunt': quę ętate nostra tuo auspi-
cio confecta sunt, te Nicolaū eum esse intelligant: qui nō mi-
norem in recuperandis libris, q̄ in restituendis mœnibus huic
urbi adhibueris curam. Et ꝑfecto licet illa pręclara: & magna
sint: quę manu & arte constant: & a plurimis summo ingenio
diligentiaq; parantur, pręstantiora tamen habenda erunt: quę
studijs adiuncta, monumentis quoq; seruantur litterarū. Itaq;
qui Petri Basilicę contiguam domum admirant' a te structam
quadrato lapide: qui Hadriani molem uicissim restitutā: qui
deorū templū ab Agrippa conditū a te suffectū ętate nostra:
qui plura alia breui cessura uetustati ni tua caritas admouisset
pias manus, eosdē quoq; admirari cōueniet tot illustres libros
ad nos tua opera traductos e gręcis: nec tuam sapientiā nomen
dignitatē cōmemoratione laudis suę immunes pręterire: etsi
non huius temporis esse putem uirtutes tuas elegantiori stilo
debitas in mediū proferre hoc solū dixerim te his rebus gestis
assecutum ut uerus pręsul dignissimus princeps haberere. Sed
ut ad Appianū redeam Doleo equidē summe pater his i libris

Appianus, Historia Romana.
Printed by Erhard Ratdolt. Venice, 1477. Reduced.

was invented, in terms of the quantity as well as the quality of its books (Muzika, 1965: II, 121ff, and Barge, 1940: 100).

Second only in importance to Venice as a focus of early printing was the French capital, which had a population of 200,000 at that time. Two academic dignatories at the Sorbonne, Guillaume Fichet and Johann Heynlin, invited three German printers to Paris: Ulrich Gering from Constance, Michael Friburger from Colmar and Martin Crantz from Strasbourg. Their printing works was accommodated as part of the university library under Heynlin's scholarly, and Fichet's financial, supervision. Their first book ends with a colophon in four Latin distichs:

> As the sun its light, so you shed learning through the globe,
> Royal nourisher of the Muses in Paris.
> Therefore accept that almost divine art.
> Which Germany invented, of artificial writing.
> Behold, the first books, created by these means,
> In France's land, and within your walls.
> Michael, Ulrich, and Martin, the masters,
> Have printed these, and will produce yet more.

The patronage of the university proved relatively short-lived, and the printers moved to the Rue Saint-Jacques, although a series of entrants to printing continued to be drawn directly from the Sorbonne. Graduates of German origin had probably first to serve as correctors of the press before setting up their own establishments or going into partnership with trained printers. This appears to have been so for Berthold Remboldt, Peter Wagner (Petrus Caesaris), Simon Doliatoris, Georg Wolf and others. Thielman Kerver became an important Parisian printer, who received so many orders for his popular Books of Hours that he had other printers working for him. As a publisher, Jean Petit similarly gave out contracts to various printers (Geldner, 1970: II, 189ff). The progressive strengthening of central authority caused the book trade to flourish in France, so that by the second half of the sixteenth century it had become the leading country in the book arts.

Lyon developed as a further metropolis for Gutenberg's invention. Many German printers struck up good working relations with French booktraders there. Johann Trechsel, for example, brags about this in one of his colophons: 'The Frenchman and the German find my books surround him. All of France praises, admires and buys my books. Here [my work] is clasped to the bosom, there held in the hand. See, there

Francesco Colonna's Hypnerotomachia Poliphili.
Printed by Aldus Manutius. Venice, 1499. Reduced.

EL SEQVENTE triúpho nõ meno mirauegliofo dl primo. Impo che egli hauea le q̃tro uolubile rote tutte, & gli radii, & il meditullo defu fco achate, di cádide uéule uagaméte uaricato. Ne tale certam͞te geftoe re Pyrrho cú le noue Mufe & Apolline í medio pulfáte dalla natura íp͞ffo.

Laxide & la forma del dicto q̃le el primo, ma le tabelle erão di cyaneo Saphyro orientale, atomato de fcintillule doro, alla magica gratiffimo, & longo acceptiffimo a cupidine nella finiftra mano.

Nella tabella dextra mirai exfcalpto una infigne Matrõa che dui oui hauea parturito, in uno cubile regio colloca ta, di uno mirabile pallacio, Cum obftetrice ftu pefacte, & multe altre matrone & aftante Nymphe Degli quali ufciua de uno una flammula, & delal tro ouo due fpectatiffi me ftelle.

* *
*

GEOR.

Phillyrides Chiron, Amythaoniusq; Melampus.
Sæuit et in lucem stygiis emissa tenebris
Pallida Tisiphone, morbos agit ante, metumq;,
Inq; dies auidum surgens caput altius effert,
Balatu pecorum, et crebris mugitibus amnes,
Arentesq; sonant ripæ, collesq; supini.
Iamq; cateruatim dat stragem, atq; aggerat ipsis
In stabulis, turpi dilapsa cadauera tabo,
Donec humo tegere, ac foueis abscondere discunt.
Nam neq; erat coriis usus, nec uiscera quisquam,
Aut undis abolere potest, aut uincere flamma.
Nec tondere quidem morbo, illuuieq; peresa
Vellera, nec telas possunt attingere putres,
Verum etiam inuisos si quis tentarat amictus,
Ardentes papulæ, atq; immundus olentia sudor
Membra sequebatur, nec longo deinde moranti
Tempore, contactos artus sacer ignis edebat.

P.O.N. *in quartum Georgicorum, argumentum.*

Protinus aerii mellis redolentia regna,
Hyblæas et apes, aluorum et cærea tecta,
Quiq; albi flores, examina quæq; legenda
Indicat, humentesq; fauos, cœlestia dona,

P.V.M. GEORGICORVM, LIBER QVARTVS.

Protinus aerii mellis, cœlestia dona
Exequar, hanc etiam Mæcenas aspice partem.
Admiranda tibi leuiū spectacula rerū,
Magnanimosq; duces, totiusq; ex ordine gentis
Mores, et studia, et populos, et prælia dicam.
In tenui labor, at tenuis non gloria, si quem
Numina leua sinunt, auditq; uocatus Apollo.
Principio, sedes apibus, statioq; petenda,
Quo neq; sit uentis aditus (nam pabula uenti
Ferre domum prohibent) neq; oues, hædiq; petulci
Floribus insultent, aut errans bucula campo
Decutiat rorem, et surgentes atterat herbas.
Absint et picti squalentia terga lacerti
Pinguibus à stabulis, meropesq;, aliæq; uolucres,
Et manibus progne pectus signata cruentis.
Omnia nam late uastant, ipsasq; uolantes,
Ore ferunt, dulcem nidis immitibus escam.
At liquidi fontes, et stagna uirentia musco
Adsint, et tenuis fugiens per gramina riuus,
Palmaq; uestibulum, aut ingens oleaster obumbret,
Vt cum prima noui ducent examina reges
Vere suo, ludetq; fauis emissa iuuentus,
Vicina inuitet decedere ripa calori,
Obuiaq; hospitiis teneat frondentibus arbos.
In medium, seu stabit iners, seu profluet humor
Transuersas salices, et grandia coniice saxa

The Aldine Virgil edition, set in the first italic type, that designed by Francesco Griffo of Bologna. Venice, 1501. Reduced.

is one who becomes pallid, astonished, disbelieving; that Johann Trechsel has engraved such types' (Geldner, 1970: II, 233ff).

Printing spread to Spain and Portugal, and to the Netherlands, Belgium, England, Switzerland, Poland and – still within the fifteenth century – to Bohemia, Moravia, Hungary, Yugoslavia, Denmark and Sweden as well, and thereafter progressed by stages to cover the whole world. Roughly one half of all incunabula were theological works. Second came editions of the classics, except in Italy where they always held pride of place. Popular books, calendars and other literature in the vernacular took third place. It is interesting to enquire from which professions the early printers were recruited. Most of them were clergymen, others goldsmiths, and a number came from occupations already associated with books or printing; such as woodblock cutters, secular copyists, printers of devotional woodcuts, scribes and rubricators.

Guillaume Fichet, professor and rector of the Sorbonne in Paris, who has already been mentioned, wrote in 1471 in a foreword:

> Johann Gutenberg, who first of all men thought out the art of printing by which books are made, not written with a reed as former books were made, nor with a pen as we make them – but by metal letters, and that indeed with speed, elegance and beauty. He was a man surely worthy of having all the muses, all the arts, and all the voices of those who delight in books honour him with divine praise (Geldner, 1970: II, 191ff).

A little before that, the following Latin epigram appeared in a book published in 1470 in Paris: 'Germany has created much that is immortal, but the greatest is the art of printing' (Ruppel, 1967: 186). The following lines were printed in Siena in 1487: 'What formerly took a swift scribe a year to complete, this gift from Germany now yields us in a day' (Ruppel, 1967: 186). And Werner Rolevinck wrote in his *Fasciculus temporum*: 'The art of printing discovered in Mainz is the art of arts and the science of sciences; through its rapid dissemination the world is enriched and illuminated with a priceless and hitherto buried treasure of knowledge and wisdom' (Ruppel, 1967: 206).

Up to 1500, at some 255 printing locations, at least 30,000 printed items must have been published, in a total edition of 20 million copies. Gutenberg's work had not been in vain.

The history of Gutenberg studies

EVEN THE LABYRINTH OF GUTENBERG RESEARCH allows only an incomplete assessment of Gutenberg's personality and achievement (see also Ing, 1988). One remains optimistic that new discoveries will lead to fresh insights and that these outlines will continue to be corrected and sharpened.

It only remains to cast a backward glance, and one forward to the future. Naturally it is not possible to speak of Gutenberg research in the sixteenth century; but it is nevertheless rather dismaying to find how quickly recollection of the inventor vanishes at that time. With dishonest intent, Johann Schöffer, son of Peter Schöffer, phased out Gutenberg's name from his successive colophons and credited only Johann Fust and his own father as the inventors. Apparently neither Ulrich von Hutten nor Erasmus of Rotterdam any longer knew of the real master. Then came a retrospective disclosure from the Strasbourg printer, Johann Schott, naming Johann Mentelin, one of Strasbourg's first printers, as the inventor of the process – a legend which attracted credulous supporters. Schoolbooks in the Low Countries related how Laurens Janszoon Coster discovered printing. And in the northern Italian town of Feltre stands a monument to the physician and poet, Pamfilo Castaldi, to whom the invention was also attributed. On St John's Day in 1640, a bicentenary commemoration of the invention was organized in Leipzig by the co-rector of St Nikolai, Sebastian Gottfried Starck, at which Fust and Schöffer were hailed as the inventors and Gutenberg described as their assistant (Debes, 1968: 41). When the tercentenary was celebrated, and sermons on the beneficial invention were delivered in all Leipzig's churches, then once again at the university only Fust and Schöffer were mentioned in the address by Johann Christoph Gottsched (Debes, 1968: 57).

Gutenberg research in the modern sense dates from the publication in 1741 of Johann David Köhler's *Hochverdiente und aus bewährten Urkunden wohlbeglaubte Ehren-Rettung Johann Guttenbergs*, which may be translated as 'The Vindication of Johann Gutenberg'. Ever more documents and sources then came to light, theories and counter-arguments were presented, scholarly disputes conducted that sometimes dragged on for decades, experts recruited from other disciplines; and in general, despite confusion and hair-splitting, much fruitful work was carried out. Certainly, some long-running debates – such as that involving the so-called *Missale speciale* – led up a blind alley (Corsten, 1972: 185ff). Scholars of such fame and merit as Otto Hupp, Adolf Schmidt, Gottfried Zedler, Konrad Haebler and Paul Schwenke almost came to blows over it. This work, which was at first considered to be the 'oldest printed book in the world', had finally to be recognized – on the basis of scientific watermark and paper evidence – as a relatively late Basle impression of 1473. In the present book, I have deliberately not stirred up again this and similar dead side-issues. Perhaps such fruitless controversies lead to a certain resignation. They stress again how little we really know of Gutenberg and warn us against speculation.

The standard book on Gutenberg has long been that by Aloys Ruppel, for many years director of the Gutenberg-Museum in Mainz, and this still has to be regarded (despite a few *a priori* and pro-Mainz assumptions) as a landmark. Besides a number of interesting studies on individual aspects, recent decades have brought notable works of synthesis, from which I would single out those of Ferdinand Geldner and Hans Lülfing, as well as Hans Widmann's important work on the present state of Gutenberg research, and the commentary volume which accompanies the B42 facsimile published by Idion-Verlag. New findings are published in an exemplary manner in the *Gutenberg-Jahrbuch* of the Gutenberg Society.

While sensational discoveries are scarcely to be hoped for, Gutenberg research in the near future might focus more on the environment and

Hochverdiente
und aus bewährten Urkunden wohlbeglaubte
Ehren-Rettung
Johann Guttenbergs,
eingebohrnen Bürgers in Mayntz,
aus dem alten Rheinländischen Adelichen Geschlechte
derer
von Sorgenloch, genannt Gänsefleisch,
wegen der ersten Erfindung
der nie gnug gepriesenen Buchdrucker-Kunst
in der Stadt Mayntz,
Zu unvergänglichen Ehren der Teutschen Nation,
und insonderheit
der löblichen uralten Stadt Mayntz,
mit gäntzlicher und unwiedersprechlicher Entscheidung
des darüber entstandenen dreyhundertjährigen
Streits,
getreulich und mit allem Fleiß ausgefertiget
von
Johann David Köhler,
Hist. P. P. O. zu Göttingen.

Leipzig,
Bey Caspar Fritschen, 1741.

Johann David Köhler's Hochverdiente und aus bewährten Urkunden wohlbeglaubte Ehren-Rettung Johann Guttenbergs.
Leipzig, 1741.

contacts of the inventor. Many of the leading figures of the time, not only Nicholas of Cues and Enea Silvio Piccolomini, but also Gregor von Heimburg, Peter Knorr and others, were aware of the invention and may have had something to say about it in still undiscovered places. Perhaps there were other associates and guarantors of Gutenberg in Strasbourg and Mainz who await investigation. There are also high expectations that recent electronic techniques for printing ink and paper analysis may yield new conclusions about production methods (Schwab *et al.*, 1983). More precise and large-scale photographic comparison of different copies of the same piece of printing are needed to generate more data, nowhere perhaps more significantly than in the current debate about the *Catholicon*. But even the greatest possible expenditure of time and effort will hardly suffice to illuminate all the dark areas that shroud much of Gutenberg's life and achievement.

Gutenberg today

WHAT HAS GUTENBERG'S INVENTION ACHIEVED? An answer is difficult and could never be comprehensive. It would also need to consider the proposition that the discovery of typesetting and printing was a response to a social need, and that in any case within a generation or so someone else would have come up with similar ideas. But here we are not going to be drawn into a discussion of the significance of the individual within the historical process. Recent approaches to the theme of the printing revolution have opened up different historical perspectives and a new field of studies (see Febvre and Martin, 1958; Eisenstein, 1979).

Education spread at differential rates, as Gutenberg's invention brought books and knowledge within the reach of ever-widening sectors of society. Books promoted economic progress through the diffusion of practical skills and scientific discovery. It was through printed books, for example, that Columbus came to know that the world was round and that India could be approached from a westerly direction as well. Books accelerated the development of learning. All progressive ideas took advantage of printing. Martin Luther praised the printing press as a mighty helper in carrying through the Reformation. Without tens of thousands of broadsheets, the peasants' demands could not have been so effectively circulated in 1525. And Friedrich Schiller wrote in 1788 in his *History of the Secession of the United Netherlands*: 'It is remarkable, what a vital role printing and pamphleteering played in the Netherlands uprising. Through this organ a few turbulent heads addressed millions.' It was for this reason that reactionary and established powers everywhere were quick to shackle the press through censorship and other means imposed by the state. Karl Marx wrote: 'It is plain what makes the press the mightiest lever for the cultural and intellectual education of the masses, it turns a material battle into one of ideals, a battle of flesh and blood into a spiritual one, a battle of needs, appetites and empiricism into one of theory, reason and form.' Heinrich Mann put the same thing a different way: 'The books of today are the deeds of tomorrow.'

In this sense the importance of the book still continues to grow. The emerging nation-states of the world have to confront the illiteracy of hundreds of millions. Each country has to create a literature and strive for a book culture of its own. Experience has shown that printing supports education in the vernacular and encourages the growth of its literature. At the same time it facilitates and promotes cultural and literary exchange between peoples.

A vital consequence of printing has always been and remains the opportunity it offers for gifted children from disadvantaged backgrounds of all kinds to discover for themselves the sources of education and culture. This in turn leads to a relative democratization – at least the ruling élite are constrained to take public opinion into account in reaching their decisions.

Last but not least, printing and the book have influenced the whole world of the appreciation of the arts. The multiplication of works of literature, visual art and music has provided access to cultural life and standards to countless people who would otherwise have remained isolated. Offset, gravure and other processes have supplanted letterpress in providing improved pictorial reproduction.

And now a glance to the future. What does Gutenberg signify for us in an age where metal typesetting has been superseded, first by incorporeal photocomposition, and latterly by digitization? The Canadian communications guru Marshall McLuhan spoke of an end to the 'Gutenberg galaxy' and predicted a denouement between alphabetical and electronic formats. In his view, the future belonged to the 'global village' brought into being through radio, television and the new electronic media (McLuhan, 1962: 65ff). Whoever sees and wills the end of the book, plays into the hands of those who wish to have a manipulable society and a retreat into a modern form of illiteracy.

The technology of typesetting and printing has been transformed, and the form of the book is also adaptable to change. Gutenberg was not in any case the inventor of the codex form of the book. His name is synonymous with the concept of joining together single preformed characters into words and texts. And this basic principle of typography remains intact, whether these letters are cast from a lead-tin-antimony alloy, or set by cathode-ray stroboscopically at an electronic speed of 400,000 characters an hour (when this book was first written in Leipzig in 1986), or whatever the state of the art may become.

Gutenberg's name has, moreover, become synonymous with a balance which has to be sought between technological innovation and aesthetic quality. Our present situation is directly comparable in many respects to Gutenberg's age. It is possible to speak in the same breath of the transition from the written book to the printed one, and of the transition from typesetting to incorporeal data storage and transmission through a new information technology. Gutenberg's striving towards a form of book adapted to the eyes and hands presents an unchangeable challenge as a new, electronically conditioned era begins. The book does not have to be converted into some technological reading apparatus or other; it must continue to be designed with the same imagination and energy as hitherto because it is still one of the prime vehicles of our culture. It is for this reason that Gutenberg remains a living figure today and sets an ideal for the future.

Chronology

Economic, political and cultural events from near and far are set beside some important dates from Gutenberg's life and the history of early printing.

1386	Marriage of Gutenberg's parents.
c. 1388	Chaucer wrote his *Canterbury Tales.*
1390	Germany's first papermill established near Nuremberg by Ulman Stromer.
1399–1413	Henry IV king of England.
1400–1403	Johann Gensfleisch, later known as Gutenberg, born in Mainz.
22 October 1401	Nicholas of Cues (Cusanus) born.
1403	King Tadchong set up a large new printing house in Korea with hundreds of thousands of bronze types.
1410–1437	Sigismund German king and Holy Roman Emperor.
1413–1422	Henry V king of England.
1414–1418	Council of Constance.
1415	Jan Hus burned at the stake in Constance as a heretic.
1417–1431	Pope Martin V.
1418	First dated woodcut in Europe.
1418–1419	One Johannes de Alta villa (=Eltville) studies at Erfurt University.
1419	Death of Gutenberg's father, Friele Gensfleisch zur Laden.
1422	Accession of infant Henry VI as king of England, Bedford as regent.
c. 1422	Probable date of birth of William Caxton, England's first printer and publisher.
1427–8	Gutenberg is first named as 'Hengin zu Gudenberg' in a Mainz document.
1428	The guilds took over the leadership of Mainz city council after a fierce struggle.
1428	Gutenberg left Mainz for an unknown destination.
30 May 1431	Joan of Arc burned at Rouen on charge of witchcraft.
1431–1447	Pope Eugenius IV.
1431–1448	Council of Basle (Nicholas of Cues, Enea Silvio Piccolomini and Gregor von Heimburg first met as representatives there).
1439–1449	Amadeus VIII, duke of Savoy, elected pope by Council of Basle; becomes Felix V, antipope to Eugenius IV.
Summer 1433	Gutenberg's mother dies.
14 March 1434	Gutenberg first known to be in Strasbourg.
1436	The goldsmith Hans Dünne receives from Gutenberg over 100 gulden 'solely for that which pertains to the use of a press'.
1437	Gutenberg taught the wealthy Strasbourg citizen, Andreas Dritzehn, 'stone polishing'.

1437	Nicholas of Cues travelled to Constantinople to collect a delegation of the Greek Orthodox Church on behalf of Eugenius IV.
Start of 1438	Andreas Dritzehn, Andreas Heilmann, Hans Riffe and Johann Gutenberg form a partnership to produce devotional mirrors.
1438–1439	Albert II German king.
26 December 1438	Andreas Dritzehn dies of the Black Death.
1438–1443	Cooperative partnership formed for the 'adventure and art'.
12 December 1439	Judgment given in the Strasbourg action brought against Gutenberg by Jörg and Claus Dritzehn.
1440–1493	Frederick III German king.
1440–1444	It is suggested that one of Gutenberg's earliest pieces of printing, the *Fragment vom Weltgericht*, is assigned to between these years.
1443	Death of Gutenberg's sister, Else.
12 March 1444	Final reference to Gutenberg in Strasbourg.
1444–1446	Procopius Waldvogel teaches an 'art of writing artificially' in Avignon.
30 November 1444	New council elected in Mainz under the secretarial leadership of Dr Konrad Humery, from which the patricians were debarred.
1447–1455	Pope Nicholas V.
17 October 1448	Gutenberg takes out a loan of 150 gulden in Mainz with the help of his relative Arnold Gelthus.
1448	The so-called original Mainz printing shop was established in the Gutenberghof, and here the *Donatuses* and jobbing work were the main products.
1449	Beginning of collaboration with Johann Fust, from whom Gutenberg received at first a loan of 800 gulden, and later a business investment, again of 800 gulden.
1450	Establishment of the Gutenberg-Fust joint printing office, the 'Work of the Books', in the Humbrechthof.
May 1451	In Mainz, 70 Benedictine abbots take an oath before the papal legate Nicholas of Cues to reform their monasteries.
1452–1455	Printing of the *42-line Bible* in 2 volumes.
29 May 1453	The Turks capture Constantinople.
October 1454	Enea Silvio Piccolomini reported that at this time he was able to see some sections of B42 in Frankfurt.
1454–1455	Printing of the *31-line Indulgence for Cyprus*.
End of 1454	Printing of the *Türkenkalender* for the year 1455.
1455–1458	Pope Calixtus III.
c. 1455–1485	Wars of the Roses: civil wars during reigns of Henry VI, Edward IV and Richard III of England.
6 November 1455	The notary Helmasperger records the lawsuit Fust vs Gutenberg in a legal instrument.
1455	Johann Fogel, the master bookbinder later to bind several *Gutenberg Bibles*, is found on the rolls of Erfurt University as 'Johannes Voghel de Francfordia'.

Chronology

August 1456	Heinrich Cremer noted in the Paris copy of B42 that at this time he had just completed its rubrication, illumination, and binding.
1456	Gutenberg's older brother Friele died in Eltville.
1456	The *Türkenbulle* of Calixtus III printed in Latin and German versions.
14 August 1457	The *Mainz Psalter* is issued by the Fust and Schöffer printing house.
1458–1460	Printing of the *36-line Bible* in Bamberg.
1458–1460	Printing of the *Catholicon* at the Gutenberghof works.
1458–1461	Printing of the *49-line Bible* in Strasbourg.
1458–1464	Papacy of Pius II.
18 June 1459	Diether von Isenburg chosen as archbishop of Mainz.
1461	Albrecht Pfister printed in Bamberg.
1461–1462	Both the *Indulgences for Neuhausen* printed.
1461	The imperial court at Rottweil brought legal pressure to bear against Gutenberg for non-payment, since 1458, of annual interest due on a Strasbourg loan.
26 September 1461	Adolf von Nassau designated archbishop of Mainz by Pius II.
28 October 1462	Fall of Mainz.
1464	Printing of both *Indulgences for the Order of the Holy Trinity* (Frater Radulphus) in Mainz and Eltville.
1464–1471	Pope Paul II.
1465–1467	The *Vocabularius ex quo* is printed in Eltville.
1465	Sweynheym and Pannartz print in Subiaco near Rome.
14 January 1465	Gutenberg is appointed a court pensioner.
1466	Ulrich Zell prints in Cologne.
1467	Ulrich Han prints in Rome.
1467	Berthold Ruppel prints in Basle.
3 February 1468	Gutenberg dies.
26 February 1468	Dr Humery acknowledges the return of printing equipment from Gutenberg's estate.
1473–1476	William Caxton prints the first book in English, *The Recuyell of the Historyes of Troye* in Bruges (late 1473/early 1474), and the *Canterbury Tales* may have left his Westminster press in 1476 (for significant revisions to Caxton's chronology, see Hellinga, 1982).

Bibliography

BARGE, H. (1940), *Geschichte der Buchdruckerkunst*, Leipzig.

BARTHOLD, F.W. (1842), 'Der Armegeckenkrieg im Jahre 1444 und 1445', *Historisches Jahrbuch*, Leipzig.

BENARY, F. (1919), 'Via antiqua und via moderna auf den deutschen Hochschulen mit besonderer Berücksichtigung der Universität Erfurt', *Zur Geschichte der Stadt und Universität Erfurt*, Gotha.

BEYER, F. (1937), 'Gedruckte Ablassbriefe und sonstige mit Ablässen in Zusammenhang stehende Druckwerke des Mittelalters', *Gutenberg-Jahrbuch.*

BIBLE, GUTENBERG: see *Faksimile-Ausgabe*, 1979.

BIEREYE, J. (1940), 'Erfurts besonders berühmte alte Bürgerhäuser', *Mitteilungen des Vereins für die Geschichte und Altertumskunde*, 53.

BIGMORE, F.C. AND WYMAN, C.W.H. (1978), *A Bibliography of Printing*, reprint of the 1888 edn, London and Newcastle.

BLUM, R. (1954), *Der Prozess Gutenberg gegen Fust: Eine Interpretation des Helmaspergerschen Notariatsinstruments in Rahmen der Frühgeschichte des Mainzer Buchdrucks*, Wiesbaden.

BOGENG, G.A.E. (1930–41), *Geschichte der Buchdruckerkunst*, 2 vols, Hellerau.

BROCKHAUS, C. (1969), *Gregor von Heimburg*, reprint of the 1881 edn, Wiesbaden.

CARTER, H. (1969), *A View of Early Typography up to about 1600*, Oxford.

CARTER, T.F. (1925) , *The Invention of Printing in China and its Spread Westward*, New York.

CORSTEN, S. (1966), 'Wann wurde Gutenberg geboren?', *Gutenberg-Jahrbuch.*

— (1972), 'Das Missale speciale', in Widmann (1972a).

— (1979), 'Die Drucklegung der zweiundvierzigzeiligen Bibel: Technische und chronologische Probleme', *Kommentarband zur Faksimile-Ausgabe*, Munich.

COSACCHI, S. (1965), *Makabertanz: Der Totentanz in Kunst, Poesie und Brauchtum des Mittelalters*, Meisenhein am Glan.

CROUS, E. AND KIRCHNER, J. (1928), *Die gotischen Schriftarten*, Leipzig.

DAVIS, H. AND CARTER, H. (1958), *Mechanick Exercises on the Whole Art of Printing by Joseph Moxon (1683–4)*, London.

DEBES, D. (ed.) (1968), *Gepriesenes Andenken von Erfindung der Buchdruckerei: Leipziger Stimmen zur Erfindung Gutenbergs*, Leipzig.

DECKERT, H. (1961), 'Von Gutenberg oder nicht? Zum 500. Geburtstag des "Catholicon", *Marginalien*, 12.

DE VINNE, T.L. (1876), *The Invention of Printing*, New York.

EICHLER, F. (1950), 'Kleine Randbemerkungen zur Gutenbergischen Drucktechnik', *Gutenberg-Jahrbuch.*

EISENSTEIN. E. (1979), *The Printing Press as an Agent of Change*, 2 vols, Cambridge.

ERLER, A. (1964), *Mittelalterliche Rechtsgutachten zur Mainzer Stiftsfehde 1459–1463*, Wiesbaden.

Faksimile-Ausgabe der 42-zeiligen Bibel nach dem Exemplar der Staatsbibliothek Preussischer Kulturbesitz Berlin (1979), 2 vols, with *Kommentarband zur Faksimile-Ausgabe*, ed. Schmidt and Schmidt-Künsemüller, Munich.

FALK, F. (1882), *Die Presse zu Marienthal im Rheingau und ihre Erzeugnisse*, Mainz.

FEBVRE, L. AND MARTIN, H.-J. (1976), *The Coming of the Book*, London (from the French: *L'Apparition du livre*, Paris, 1958).

FISCHER, J. (1958), *Frankfurt und die Bürgerunruhen in Mainz (1332–1462) (Beiträge zur Geschichte der Stadt Mainz*, 15), Mainz.

FORMAN, W. AND BURLAND, C.A. (1970), *Die Reisen des Marco Polo*, Vienna and Munich.

FÖRSTEMANN, E.G. (1828), *Die christlichen Geisslergesellschaften*, Halle.

FRANZ, A. (1902), *Die Messe im deutschen Mittelalter*, Freiburg i. Br.

FRIEDERICHS, H.F. (1968), 'Der Erfinder Johannes Gutenberg', *Genealogisches Jahrbuch*, 8.

— (1972), 'Gutenbergs Herkunft: Eine genealogisch-soziologische Studie', in Widmann (1972a).

FUHRMANN, O.W. (1940), *Gutenberg and the Strasbourg Documents of 1439*, New York.

— (1950), 'A note on Gutenberg's typemetal', *Gutenberg-Jahrbuch*.

FUNKE, F. (1963), 'Vorformen des Buchdrucks in China', *Buchkunst*, 4, Leipzig.

GABAIN, A. VON (1967), 'Die Drucke der Turfan-Sammlung', *Sitzungsberichte der Deutschen Akademie der Wissenschaften zu Berlin*, 1/1967.

GECK, E. (1968), *Johannes Gutenberg: From Lead Letter to the Computer*, Bad Godesberg.

— (1972), 'Bibliographie der seit 1940 erschienenen Literatur zu Gutenbergs Leben und Werk', in Widmann (1972a).

GELDNER, F. (1940), 'Ein unbeachteter Einblattdruck in der Type der 36zeiligen Bibel in der Universitäts-Bibliothek zu München', *Zentralblatt für Bibliothekswesen*, 57.

— (1950), 'Hat Heinrich Keffer aus Mainz die 36zeilige Bibel gedruckt?', *Gutenberg-Jahrbuch*.

— (1961), 'Das "Catholicon" des Johannes Balbus im ältesten Buchdruck', *Festschrift für F. Juchhoff*, Cologne.

— (1964), 'Ein neuer Hinweis auf Bamberg als Druckort der 36zeiligen Bibel: Das Wappen Peter Knorr im Exemplar der Bibliothèque Nationale', *Gutenberg-Jahrbuch*.

— (1968), 'Johannes Gutenberg, Johannes Fust und Dr Konrad Humery', *Börsenblatt*, 24.

— (1970), *Die deutschen Inkunabeldrucker*, 2 vols, Stuttgart.

— (1972a), 'Das Helmaspergersche Notariatsinstrument in seiner Bedeutung für die Geschichte des ältesten Mainzer Buchdrucks', in Widmann (1972a).

— (1972b), 'Die ersten typographischen Drucke', in Widmann (1972a).

— (1974), 'Peter Schöffers Frühzeit', *Archiv zur Geschichte des Buchwesens*, 14.

— (1976), 'Der junge Gutenberg', *Gutenberg-Jahrbuch*.

— (1978), *Inkunabelkunde*, Wiesbaden.

GERARDY, T. (1973), 'Wann wurde das Catholicon mit der Schlussschrift von 1460 (GW 3182) wirklich gedruckt?', *Gutenberg-Jahrbuch.*

GERHARDT C.W. (1970), 'Was erfand Gutenberg in Strassburg', *Gutenberg-Jahrbuch.*

— (1971), 'Warum wurde die Gutenberg-Presse erst nach über 350 Jahren durch ein besseres System abgelöst?', *Gutenberg-Jahrbuch.*

— (1975), *Die Geschichte der Druckverfahren. Teil II: Der Buchdruck*, Stuttgart.

— (1976), *Beiträge zur Technikgeschichte des Buchwesens*, Frankfurt.

GERMAN HISTORY (1983) = *Deutsche Geschichte. Bd. II: Die entfaltete Feudalgesellschaft*, ed. by an authors' collective, Berlin.

GESSNER, J.F. (1740), *Die so nöthig als nützliche Buchdruckerkunst und Schriftgiesserey* ..., Leipzig.

GOFF, F.R. (1970), *The Permanence of Johann Gutenberg*, Austin.

GOODRICH, L.C. (1972), 'Two New Discoveries of Early Block Prints', in Widmann (1972a).

GRABES, H. (1973), *Speculum, Mirror und Looking Glass: Kontinuität und Originalität der Spiegelmacher in den Buchtiteln des Mittelalters* ..., Tübingen.

GRIMM, J. AND W. (1852–), *Deutsches Wörterbuch*, Leipzig.

GUIGNARD, J. (1960), *Gutenberg et son oeuvre*, Paris.

HAEMMERLE, A. (1971), 'Das Rätsel um das Wappen des Johannes Gutenberg', *Gutenberg-Jahrbuch.*

HAUPT, H. (1890), 'Konrad Schmid', *Allgemeine deutsche Biographie*, 31, Leipzig.

HÄUSER, H. (1968), 'Zur Berechnung von Gutenbergs frühestmöglichem Geburtstag', *Gutenberg-Jahrbuch.*

HELLINGA, L. (1982), *Caxton in Focus: The Beginning of Printing in England*, London.

— (1989), 'Analytical Bibliography and the study of early printed books with a case-study of the Mainz Catholicon', *Gutenberg-Jahrbuch.*

— (1992), 'Slipped Lines and Fallen Type in the Mainz Catholicon', *Gutenberg-Jahrbuch.*

— (1993), 'The Codex in the fifteenth century: Manuscript and Print', in *A Potencie of Life* ..., ed. Barker, London.

HENSEL, K. (1952), 'Das Stift St Viktor vor Mainz', diss., Mainz: Gernsheim/Rhein.

HIKSCH, J. (1978), 'Gregor von Heimburg (um 1400 bis 1472): Politiker zwischen Mittelalter und Neuzeit', diss., Potsdam.

HIRSCH, R. (1974), *Printing, Selling, Reading 1450–1550*, 2nd edn, Wiesbaden.

HOFFMANN, L. (1979), 'Ist Gutenberg der Drucker des Catholicon?', *Zentralblatt für Bibliothekswesen*, 93.

— (1983), 'Gutenberg, Fust und der erste Bibeldruck: Eine Untersuchung auf der Grundlage neuer Quellen', *Zentralblatt für Bibliothekswesen*, 97, continued in 98 (1984), 100 (1986), 101 (1987).

— (1993), 'Die Gutenbergbibel: Eine Kosten- und Gewinnrechnung auf der Grundlage zeitgenössischer Quellen', *Archiv für Geschichte des Buchwesens.*

HONG, HI-JU (1963), 'Der Druck mit Metall-Lettern in Korea', *Buchkunst*, 4, Leipzig.

HUIZINGA, J. (1965), *The Waning of the Middle Ages*, Harmondsworth.

ING, J. (1988), *Johann Gutenberg and His Bible: A Historical Study*, New York and London.

JENSEN, H. (1958), *Die Schrift*, 2nd edn, Berlin.
JUCHHOFF, R. (1950), 'Was bleibt von den holländischen Ansprüchen auf die Erfindung der Typographie?', *Gutenberg-Jahrbuch.*

KAPR, A. (1968), *Johannes Gutenberg und die Cyprischen Ablassbriefe 1454/5*, Leipzig.
— (1972), 'Gab es Beziehungen zwischen Johannes Gutenberg und Nikolaus von Kues?', *Gutenberg-Jahrbuch.*
— (1976), 'Die Ablassbriefe für Neuhausen bei Worms 1461 und 1462', *Gutenberg-Jahrbuch.*
— (1977), *Johannes Gutenberg: Tatsachen und Thesen*, Leipzig.
— (1980), 'Hat Johannes Gutenberg an der Erfurter Universität studiert?, *Gutenberg-Jahrbuch.*
— (1981), 'Was war das "Werk der Bücher"?', *Gutenberg-Jahrbuch.*
— (1982), 'Der Erfurter Ablassbrief von 1473', *Albert Kapr: Schrift- und Buchkunst*, Leipzig.
— (1983), *The Art of Lettering*, Munich, New York, London, Paris.
— (1994), 'Andreas Venzke: Johannes Gutenberg', *Marginalien*, 134.
KAZMEIER, A.W. (1952), 'Wasserzeichen und Papier der 42zeiligen Bibel', *Gutenberg-Jahrbuch.*
KIRNBERGER, A. (1952), *Neues über Gutenberg und die Gutenberghäuser in Mainz*, Mainz.
KLEINEIDAM, E. (1964), *Universitas Studii Erffordensis, Teil I: 1392 bis 1460*, Leipzig.
KNAUS, H. (1956), 'Einbände von Johannes Fogel in Düsseldorf und Bielefeld', *Gutenberg-Jahrbuch.*
KÖNIG, E. (1979), 'Die Illuminierung der Gutenbergbibel', *Kommentarband zur Faksimile-Ausgabe*, Munich.
— (1984), 'Möglichkeiten kunstgeschichtlicher Beiträge zur Gutenberg-Forschung: Die 42zeilige Bibel in Cologny, Heinrich Molitor und der Einfluss der Klosterreform um 1450', *Gutenberg-Jahrbuch.*
— (1987), 'The history of art and the history of the book at the time of transition from manuscript to print', *Bibliography and the Study of 15th-Century Civilisation*, London.
KOPPITZ, H-J. (1994), 'Zwei neue Bücher über Gutenberg und die Erfindung der Druckkunst', *Gutenberg-Jahrbuch.*
KOSCHORRECK, W. (1955), 'Zum Prozess Fust gegen Gutenberg', *Gutenberg-Jahrbuch.*
KÖSTER, K. (1972), 'Mittelalterliche Pilgerzeichen und Wallfahrtsdevotionalien', *Rhein und Maas: Kunst und Kultur 800–1400*, exhibition catalogue, Cologne.
— (1973), *Gutenberg in Strassburg*, Kleine Drucke of the Gutenberg-Gesellschaft, 23, Mainz.
— (1983), 'Gutenbergs Strassburger Aachenspiegel-Unternehmen von 1438–40', *Gutenberg-Jahrbuch.*
KRATZ, W. (1962), *Eltville: Baudenkmäler und Geschichte*, 2 vols, Eltville.
KRISTELLER, P. (1921), *Kupferstich und Holzschnitt*, Berlin.
KYRISS, E. (1943/4), 'Schriftdruck vor Gutenberg', *Gutenberg-Jahrbuch.*

LEHMANN, P. (1921), 'Konstanz und Basel als Büchermärkte während der grossen Kirchenversammlungen', *Zeitschrift für Buchwesen und Schrifttum*, 4.
LEHMANN-HAUPT, H. (1950), *Peter Schoeffer of Gernsheim and Mainz*, Rochester.
— (1962), 'Gutenberg und der Meister der Spielkarten', *Gutenberg-Jahrbuch.*
— (1966), *Gutenberg and the Master of the Playing Cards*, New Haven.
LINDE, A. VAN DER (1886), *Geschichte der Erfindung der Buchdruckkunst*, 3 vols, Berlin.
LOWRY, M. (1991), *Nicholas Jenson and the Rise of Venetian Publishing in Renaissance Europe*, Oxford.
LÜBKE, A. (1968), *Nikolaus von Kues*, Munich.
LÜLFING, H. (1969), *Johannes Gutenberg und das Buchwesen des 14. und 15. Jahrhunderts*, Leipzig.
— (1972), 'Schreibkultur vor Gutenberg', in Widmann (1972a).

MCLUHAN M. (1962), *The Gutenberg Galaxy*, Toronto and London.
MCMURTRIE, D.C. (1941), *The Gutenberg Documents, with translations of the texts into English, based with authority on the compilation by Dr Karl Schorbach*, New York.
— (1942), *The Invention of Printing: A Bibliography*, Chicago.
— (1943), *The Book: The Story of Printing and Bookmaking*, New York
MAINZ (1968) = *Die Chroniken der mittelrheinischen Städte: Mainz I und II*, unrevised reprint of the 1881 edn, Göttingen.
MASSON, I. (1954), *The Mainz Psalters and Canon Missae 1457–1459*, London.
MAYER, R. (1983), *Gedruckte Kunst*, Dresden.
MAZAL, O. (1979), 'Die Bucheinbände der erhaltenen Exemplare der zweiundvierzigzeiligen Bibel', *Kommentarband zur Faksimile-Ausgabe*, Munich.
MENZEL, K. (1868), *Diether von Isenburg, Erzbischof von Mainz 1459–1463*, Erlangen.
MEUTHEN, E. (1982), 'Ein neues frühes Quellenzeugnis für den ältesten Bibeldruck', *Gutenberg-Jahrbuch.*
MORAN, J. (1973), *Printing Presses: History and Development from the Fifteenth Century to Modern Times*, London.
MORI, G. (1928), *Der Türkenkalendar für das Jahr 1455: Eine druckhistorische Studie*, Mainz.
MUSPER, H.T. (1961), *Die Urausgaben der holländischen Apokalypse und Biblia pauperum*, Munich.
MUZIKA, F. (1965), *Die schöne Schrift*, 2 vols, Prague.

NEEDHAM, P. (1982), 'Johann Gutenberg and the Catholicon Press', *Papers of the Bibliographical Society of America*, 76.
— (1986), 'The Type-Setting of the Mainz Catholicon: A Reply to W.J. Partridge', *The Book Collector*, 35.
— (1993), 'Slipped Lines in the Mainz Catholicon: A Second Opinion', *Gutenberg-Jahrbuch.*

PAINTER, G.D. (1970), 'Gutenberg and the B36 Group: A Re-Consideration', *Essays in Honour of Victor Scholderer*, Mainz.
PARTRIDGE, W.J. (1986), 'The Type-Setting and Printing of the Mainz Catholicon', *The Book Collector*, 35.
PICCOLOMINI, E.S. (1962), *Deutschland, ein Brieftraktat an Martin Mayer*, Graz.

PRESSER, H. (1966), *Gutenberg, Eltville und die Schwarze Kunst*, Wiesbaden.
— (1967), *Johannes Gutenberg in Zeugnissen und Bilddokumenten*, Hamburg.

RACHEWILTZ, I. DE (1971), *Papal Envoys to the Great Khans*, London.
RICHTER, P. (1902), *Die Geschichte des Rheingaues*, Coblenz.
RÖLL, J. (1994), 'A Crayfish in Subiaco: A Hint of Nicholas of Cusa's Involvement in Early Printing?', *The Library*, 16/2.
ROSARIVO, R.M. (1955), 'Der goldene Modul der 36zeiligen Bibel: Die Entdeckung eines Werkstattgeheimnisses Johannes Gutenbergs, *Gutenberg-Jahrbuch*, and in an extended version (1961) as *Divina proportio typographica,* Krefeld.
ROSENFELD, H. (1972), 'Buchschmuck als typographisches Problem bei Gutenberg', in Widmann (1972a).
— (1974), 'Gutenbergs Wappen, seine Entstehung und die angeblich jüdischen Ahnen Gutenbergs – zugleich ein Beitrag zur Namens- und Kulturgeschichte des ausgehenden Mittelalters', *Gutenberg-Jahrbuch.*
— (1975), 'Zur Datierbarkeit früher Spielkarten in Europa und im Nahen Orient', *Gutenberg-Jahrbuch.*
RUPPEL, A. (1937), *Peter Schöffer aus Gernsheim*, Mainz.
— (1938a), *Eltville als Frühdruckstadt*, Mainz.
— (1938b), 'Probleme um das Mainzer Catholicon', *Gutenberg-Jahrbuch.*
— (1940), *Die Technik Gutenbergs und ihre Vorstufen*, Berlin.
— (1943), 'Ein bisher unbekannter Gutenberg-Druck aufgefunden: Das Provinciale Romanum', *Archiv für Buchgewerbe*, 3/4.
— (1948), 'Heinrich und Nikolaus Bechtermünze', *Nassauische Lebensbilder*, 3.
— (1964), *Die Stadt Mainz und ihr grosser Sohn Gutenberg*, 2nd edn, Mainz.
— (1967), *Johannes Gutenberg: Sein Leben und sein Werk*, 3rd edn, unrevised reprint, Nieuwkoop.
— (1968), *Gutenbergs Tod und Begräbnis*, Mainz.
— (1969), 'Gutenberg in Strassburg und die Uranfänge der Buchdruckerkunst', *Refugium animae bibliotheca: Festschrift für A. Kolb*, Wiesbaden.

SCHAAB, K.A. (1969), *Diplomatische Geschichte der Juden zu Mainz*, unrevised reprint of the 1855 edn, Wiesbaden.
SCHADE, O. (1854), *Geistliche Gedichte des XIV. und XV. Jahrhunderts vom Niederrhein*, Hanover.
SCHEIDE, W.H. (1973), 'A Speculation Concerning Gutenberg's Early Plans for his Bible', *Gutenberg-Jahrbuch.*
SCHMIDT, A. (1911), 'Die Ablassbriefe für Neuhausen bei Worms: 1461 und 1462', *Zeitschrift für Bücherfreunde*, Leipzig.
SCHMIDT, W. (1955), 'Das Berliner Exemplar der Gutenberg-Bibel', *Edwin Redslob zum 70. Geburtstag*, Berlin.
— (1979), 'Zur Tabula Rubricarum', with facsimile, *Kommentarband zur Faksimile-Ausgabe*, Munich.
SCHMIDT-KÜNSEMÜLLER, F.A. (1949), 'Das Schriftmetall der ältesten deutschen Druckerzeugnisse', *Zentralblatt für Bibliothekswesen*, 69.
— (1951), *Die Erfindung des Buchdrucks als technisches Phänomen*, Mainz.
SCHOLDERER, V. (1970), *Johann Gutenberg: The Inventor of Printing*, 2nd edn, London.

SCHÖPFLIN, J.D. (1938), *Vindiciae Typographicae*, translated from the Latin edition (Strasbourg, 1760) by C.A. Nelson, New York.

SCHORBACH, K. (1900), 'Die urkundlichen Nachrichten über Johann Gutenberg', *Mainzer Gutenberg-Festschrift 1900 (see* McMurtrie, 1941).

— (1932), *Der Strassburger Frühdrucker Johann Mentelin*, Mainz.

SCHRÖDER, E., ZEDLER, G. AND WALLAU, H. (1904), *Das Mainzer Fragment vom Weltgericht*, Mainz.

SCHWAB, R.N. *et al.* (1983), 'Cyclotron Analysis of the Ink in the 42-line Bible', *Papers of the Bibliographical Society of America*, 77.

— (1985), 'New Evidence on the Printing of the Gutenberg Bible: The Inks in the Doheny Copy', *PBSA*, 79.

— (1986), 'Ink Patterns in the Gutenberg New Testament: The Proton Milliprobe Analysis of the Lilly Library Copy', *PBSA*, 80.

— (1988), 'New Clues about Gutenberg in the Huntington 42-line Bible: What the Margins Reveal', *Huntington Library Quarterly*, 51.

SCHWEINSBERG, FRH. SCHENK ZU (1900), 'Genealogie des Mainzer Geschlechtes Gänsfleisch', *Mainzer Gutenberg-Festschrift 1900*.

SCHWENKE, P. (1903), *Die Donat- und Kalendertype*, Mainz.

SEYBOTH, A. (1890), *Das alte Strassburg: Vom 13. Jahrhundert bis zum Jahr 1870*, Strasbourg.

SOHN, POW-KEY (1971), *Early Korean Typography*, Seoul.

— (1972), 'Early Korean Printing', in Widmann (1972a).

— (1983), *Frühe koreanische Druckkunst / Early Korean Printing*, exhibition catalogue, Mainz.

SPULER, B. (1965), *Die Mongolen in Russland*, 2nd edn, Wiesbaden.

— (1968), *Die Mongolen in Iran*, 3rd edn, Berlin.

STAMM, K. (1960/61), 'Gutenberg und seine Zugehörigkeit zum Mainzer St Viktor-Stift – eine Fälschung Bodmanns?: Eine Stellungnahme zur Behauptung Zedlers in der Mainzer Zeitschrift', *Mainzer Zeitschrift*, 56/57.

STEIGER, G. AND FLASCHENDRÄGER. W. (eds) (1981), *Magister und Scholaren: Professoren und Studenten*, Leipzig.

STENZEL, K. (1915), *Die Politik der Stadt Strassburg am Ausgang des Mittelalters in ihren Hauptzügen dargestellt*, Strasbourg.

STEVENSON, A. (1967), *The Problem of the Missale Speciale*, London.

STILLWELL, M.B. (1972), *The Beginning of the World of Books 1450 to 1470*, New York.

STÖWESAND, R. (1956), 'Heinrich Günther und Gutenberg', *Gutenberg-Jahrbuch*.

STRASBOURG (1870–71) = *Die Chroniken der oberrheinischen Städte, vols 8/9: Strassburg*, Leipzig.

STRUCK, W.H. (1979), 'Marienthal', '*Monasticon Fratrum Vitae Communis*', *Archives et Bibliothèques de Belgique*, special issue 19.

SWIERK, A. (1972a), 'Johannes Gutenberg als Erfinder in Zeugnissen seiner Zeit', in Widmann (1972a).

— (1972b), 'Was bedeutet "ars artificialiter scribendi"?', in Widmann (1972a).

THIEL, R. (1939), 'Kritische Gutenberg-Studien', *Gutenberg-Jahrbuch*.

TODD, W.B. (1982), *The Gutenberg-Bible: New Evidence of the Original Printing*, Chapel Hill.

TÖPFER, B. (1964), *Das Kommende Reich des Friedens: Zur Entwicklung chiliastischer Zukunftshoffnungen*, Berlin.

TSIEN, TSUEN-HSUIN (1985), *Paper and Printing*, being vol V:1 of Needham, J., *Science and Civilisation in China*, Cambridge.

ULLMANN, C. (1841), *Reformation vor der Reformation, vornehmlich in Deutschland und den Niederlanden*, Hamburg.

VARBANEC, N.V. (1980), *Johannes Gutenberg and the Beginning of Printing in Europe* (in Russian), Moscow.

WEHMER, C. (1948), *Mainzer Probedrucke in der Type des sogenannten Astronomischen Kalenders für 1448. Mit einer Untersuchung von Viktor Stegemann: Der Astronomische Kalender, eine Planetentafel für Laienastrologen*, Munich.

WEISSENBORN, J.C.H. (ed.) (1881), 'Akten der Erfurter Universität', *Geschichtsquellen der Provinz Sachsen*, 8, I–III.

WIDMANN, H. (1969), 'Der Mainzer Psalter von 1457', *Antiquariat*, 19.

— (ed.) (1972a), *Der gegenwärtige Stand der Gutenberg-Forschung*, Stuttgart.

— (1972b), 'Gutenbergs Wirken: Versuch eines Umblicks' *Der gegenwärtige Stand der Gutenberg-Forschung*, Stuttgart.

— (1972c), 'Zur Überlieferung über den Zeitpunkt von Gutenbergs Erfindung', *Mainzer Festschrift für Fritz Arens*, Mainz.

— (1973), *Vom Nutzen und Nachteil des Buchdrucks – aus der Sicht der Zeitgenossen des Erfinders*, Mainz.

— (1975), 'Mainzer Catholicon (GW 3182) und Eltviller Vocabularii', *Gutenberg-Jahrbuch*.

WINTERSTEIN, C. (1977), *Goldgulden von Basel*, Basel.

WITTE, H. (1890), 'Die Armagnaken im Elsass', *Beiträge zur Landes- und Volkskunde von Elsass-Lothringen*, 11.

WOLF, H.J. (1974), *Geschichte der Druckpressen*, Frankfurt.

ZEDLER, G. (1902), *Die älteste Gutenberg-Type*, Mainz.

— (1904), *Das Mainzer Fragment vom Weltgericht*, (with E. Schröder and H. Wallau), Mainz.

— (1905), *Das Mainzer Catholicon*, Mainz.

— (1913), *Die Mainzer Ablassbriefe der Jahre 1454 und 1455*, Mainz.

— (1921), *Von Coster zu Gutenberg*, Leipzig.

— (1934), *Gutenbergs älteste Type und die mit ihr hergestellten Drucke*, Mainz.

— (1942), 'Das Mainzer Catholicon von 1460', *Zentralblatt für Bibliothekswesen*, 59.

ZINNER, E. (1938), 'Der astronomische Kalender von 1448, *Beiträge zur Inkunabelkunde*, new series, 2.

Glossary

ABBREVIATION – shortened word form, usually indicated in MSS and early printing by a modified character or special sign; i.e. *dn̄s* = *dominus*; see also *contraction*.

ABECEDARIUM – single-sheet or primer giving letters of the alphabet and elementary Latin instruction.

ALBUS/ALBI – medieval unit of currency in use at Strasbourg, also known as white (i.e. silver) pfennig (1 Rhenish gulden = 26 albi).

ANOPISTHOGRAPHIC – manner of printing early block books by burnishing on one side of the leaf only (thus disfiguring the reverse side, the pages of which are concealed by being folded or pasted together).

ANTIMONY – metal added to type alloy to render types tough and sharp enough for the ordeal of the press.

ANTIPHON – brief Latin liturgical chant, sung to introduce psalm or in procession. Antiphonal or antiphonary is choral book, whereas words to be spoken by priest appear in *breviary*.

ASCENDER – stroke of lower-case letter which projects above the x-height; as b, d, h, etc.

BASE LINE – common alignment of all characters at foot, excluding descenders; as g, j, p, etc.

BENEDICTINES – monks, living according to the rule of St Benedict of Nursia.

BIBLIA PAUPERUM (poor man's Bible) – popular devotional book of late Middle Ages pairing Old and New Testament scenes, with text and pictures printed from woodblocks.

BINDERY – workshop for forwarding and finishing books, i.e. binding written or printed sheets of a single copy or batch to order.

BLACK ART – the proper medieval term for magic; which was later also used as a synonym for Gutenberg's invention.

BLOCKBOOK – popular book in which woodcuts, frequently hand-coloured, are usually accompanied by brief woodcut or, occasionally, typeset texts.

BODY – cast metal cube carrying the face of a type: the body determines the size of a type, which (in its other dimensions) is standard in height-to-paper, and adjustable in width to the character it carries.

BREVIARY – book containing the offices for the canonical hours for priests and members of religious orders.

BRIEF – papal encyclical bearing the pope's seal but not his signature.

BROADSIDE – sheet of paper printed on one side only, often for public display.

BULL – important written pronouncement of the pope, bearing his signature.

BURSFELD CONGREGATION – union of Benedictine monastic houses committed to reform in the spirit of the Council of Basle.

CASE – tray (or an upper and lower pair) divided into compartments to hold type and spaces.

CAST-TYPE – supplies of characters produced from a typefounder's hand-mould or later by casting machine.

CATHARS – sect persecuted for heresy in the Middle Ages.

CATHOLICON – Latin dictionary with grammar.

CHAP-BOOK – a pamphlet or popular romance or ballad of the kind hawked by chapmen or pedlars.

CHASE – metal frame into which type and blocks are locked by means of quoins or wedges.

CHORAL TYPE – smallest typesize required in a missal; to print the words beneath the plainchant.

CLERIC OR CLERK – one of the body of men set apart by ordination for religious service in the Catholic Church.

CODEX – handwritten book.

COLOPHON – note, usually appearing at the end of a book, giving details of its title, printer, date and place of printing. The 1457 *Psalter* of Fust and Schöffer contains the first printed colophon and printer's mark.

COMPOSING STICK – hand-held gauge into which lines of type are set.

COMPOSITOR – craftsman who sets type.

CONCILIAR MOVEMENT – effort at reform, which placed the authority of an oecumenical council above that of the pope.

CONCORDAT – agreement between the Roman See and a secular government relative to matters which concern both.

CONTRACTION – abbreviation which includes the first and last letter of the full form of the singular.

COUNCIL OR CONSILIUM – general assembly of the Church.

CURIA – the whole body of administrative and judicial institutions through which the pope governs the Church and, by extension, the persons who form part of it and the Roman See as such.

DENAR – medieval unit of currency in use at Strasbourg. (1 denar = 1 silver pound = 240 heller).

DESCENDER – stroke of lower-case letter which projects below the x-height; as g, j, p, etc.

DOMINICANS – friars of an order of preachers, charged with the conversion of heretics.

DONATUS – shorter form of the Latin grammar of Aelius Donatus.

DONATUS AND KALENDAR (DK) TYPE – Gutenberg's first typeface, which went through several phases of development before becoming the type of B36, and ending its days in Pfister's Bamberg workshop.

DURANDUS-TYPE – small typeface devised by Fust and Schöffer and first used in their 1459 edition of the *Rationale divinorum officiorum* by Durandus.

EM – the square of any type size. The 12pts em (pica) is still a standard unit for measuring print.

ENGRAVING – copperplate and wood engraving generally flourished later than the incunabula period, during which prints and book illustration were primarily made by woodcut, although soft metal (or type alloy) was often substituted for wood.

EPISTOLAR OR EPISTOLARY – liturgical book containing those parts of the letters of the apostles used in the mass.

EVANGELIUM OR EVANGELY – liturgical book containing all four gospels in unabbreviated form.

EVANGELISTARIUM OR EVANGELISTARY – liturgical book containing those parts of the gospels used in the mass.

EXCOMMUNICATION – action of excluding an offender from the sacraments (in its lesser form), or from all communication with the Church and its members.

EXEMPLAR – edited copy of a text which serves as model both for composition and layout.

FOLIO – book size resulting from folding a sheet with one fold; thus giving pages half the size of the full sheet. Kapr suggests that most incunabula were printed one page at a time; thus each side of a sheet required two impressions because of the limited power of the press. It is important to remember that each folio (or leaf of paper or parchment) in a MS or incunabulum is numbered on – or counted from – the front or recto only, whereas modern practice is to number the pages and not the leaves of books.

FORM/S – in the early literature of letter design and typefounding, used vaguely of the shapes, patterns or moulds from which characters were replicated. (The spelling "forms" has been kept for the German *Formen* wherever early documents are unspecific.)

FORME/S – type matter and blocks assembled into pages and locked up in a chase or frame ready for printing.

FOUNT – complete set of metal type characters of the same design and size. (*Font* describes a film or digitised typeface irrespective of size.)

FRANCISCANS – Brothers of the order founded by St Francis of Assisi, also known as barefoot friars or minorities, who followed the early Christian ideal of poverty.

FRISKET – a rectangular iron frame covered with vellum, hinged to the *tympan* of a hand-press, and used to hold the sheet of paper in place and lift it clear after printing; the vellum is cut away to fit the printing area, the remainder protecting the margins from accidental soiling.

GALLEY – a metal tray, open at one end, on which set-up type-matter is placed, proofed, corrected and made-up into pages.

GOTHIC – of typefaces of this period: these are variously defined in the text as Gothic bastarda, Gothic cursive, Gothic rotunda, etc. The typeface used for the main title in this present book is based on a black letter from William Caslon's specimens, which was recut by the Stempel Foundry as "Caslon-Gotisch" (Kapr, 1993: 108).

GUILDS – medieval associations within trades and crafts, having economic and political objectives.

GULDEN – most important monetary unit in medieval Germany. (1 Rhenish gold gulden = 24 schillings = 1 silver pound + 4 schillings = 1 Strasbourg denare + 4 schillings: an ox ready for slaughter cost 6–8 gulden.)

HAND-MOULD – adjustable casting-box enabling identical single types to be produced in adequate quantities.

HEIGHT-TO-PAPER – overall height of types and woodblocks in letterpress printing (standard for Anglo-American mechanical composition at 0.918 in. from feet to face), has never fluctuated wildly from this ergonomic norm.

HELLER – smallest monetary unit in medieval Germany (1 heller = 1/2 pfennig: 5 eggs cost 1 heller).

HOURS, BOOK OF – book of personal prayers for use by the laity, related to the calender and canonical hours.

HOURS, CANONICAL – portions of the day set apart for prayer and devotion, thus: matins, lauds, prime, terce, sext, none, vespers, compline.

ILLUMINATION – decoration added by a book artist or miniaturist to a manuscript or incunabulum in colours and gold or silver leaf, and usually incorporating ornamental initials or illustrations.

INCIPIT – the Latin for "it begins", used with its converse, *explicit*, to identify MSS and also incunabula before the introduction of the title-page.

INCUNABULUM/INCUNABULA – printing from Gutenberg's invention to 1500. Printed book or fragment from the "cradle-days" of printing. Ger. *Wiegendruck*.

INDULGENCE – written or printed letter, sold by a "pardoner" for the remission of the punishment still due for a sin after absolution by the Church.

INITIAL – opening capital of a text, distinguished by size or ornamentation.

INKING BALLS – pair of wooden-handled, mushroom-shaped pads, covered in soft leather, used for distributing ink evenly before the much later introduction of rollers.

INTAGLIO PRINTING – copper engraving, etching, or related printmaking from the incised or etched surface of a metal plate. The whole plate is inked, the surface wiped clean, and the image transferred from the inked recessions to dampened paper when it is passed through the press with layers of felt. The process developed more or less contemporaneously with Gutenberg's invention and the earliest book to have illustrations produced by an intaglio process was Antonio Bettini's *Monte santo di Dio*, Florence, 1477.

INTERDICT – excommunication of a district or country, as a punishment imposed by the Church, and which excludes all inhabitants from mass, baptism and Church festivals.

JET – mouthpiece of the hand-mould.

JOBBING PRINTING – official, commercial and ephemeral printing other than books and periodicals.

JUSTIFICATION – causing text to be composed in lines of equal length through adjusting the spaces between all words to a like degree within each individual line, so that both left and right margins are straight. In B42 and at the Humbrechthof works, the ideal was to achieve optically straight margins whilst at the same time maintaining a virtually standard word spacing, and this was achieved through the use of an extended fount with many abbreviations, ligatures and word-breaks; see also *ragged setting*.

KERN – any part of the face of a type which overhangs its body.

LEADING – strips of metal or paper used to increase the space between lines of typesetting.

LECTIONARY – liturgical book containing the scriptural lessons, those from the sermons of ecclesiastical writers and those from expositions of the day's gospel.

LEGENDA OR LEGENDARY – book of scriptural selections and stories from the lives of the saints read at divine service.

LETTERPRESS OR RELIEF PRINTING – printing from a raised surface, such as the earlier woodblock, or Gutenberg's system of movable metal types.

LIGATURE – joined letters cast as a single type; as fi, ffl, etc.

MAJUSCULE – letter from the upper case or capital alphabet.

MATRIX (pl. matrices) – small rectangular metal plate (usually of copper), in which a right-reading character is deeply impressed from a punch, and from which type is cast.

MINUSCULE – letter from the lower-case alphabet.

MISSAL – liturgical book, containing the antiphons and lessons as well as the prayers proper to the various days of the ecclesiastical year, together with the fixed canon of the mass.

MONASTIC FOUNDATION (*Stift/Stifter*) – in consequence of the accumulation of bequests and privileges throughout the Middle Ages, vast religious complexes arose, complete with administrative buildings and dependencies, although these foundations were originally monastic in intent.

MORTICED CHARACTERS – cutting or filing away metal from the non-printing area at the sides of types to permit closer setting.

NEUMES – medieval system of music notation.

NICK – a regular indentation to the fore edge of types, enabling compositor to align them correctly by touch.

PALLIUM – archbishop's vestment, which was conferred on him by the pope after election and on payment of an assessed "pallium fee".

PAPAL PARTY – grouping in Church politics which placed papal supremacy above that of any council, and vigorously opposed ecclesiastical reform.

PIE – printing accident where lines of setting fall apart into a jumble of single types.

PLATEN – flat and heavy plate, lowered and pressed against horizontal printing surface on bed of early press.

POINT SYSTEM – standard unit of modern typographical measurement: 72 points = 1 inch; sizes were sometimes named earlier after types of books for which they were considered appropriate; as primer, brevier, large- or small-canon, etc.; see also *body*.

PRELATE – in medieval usage the term might be applied to almost any person having ecclesiastical authority; certainly to priors and superiors, priests in charge of monastic schools, correspondence and choirs, and all senior priests within an order.

PSALTER – liturgical book containing the 150 psalms used in choral prayer.

PSALTER-TYPES – those of the *Mainz Psalter*, and in general, large types that could be seen by several singers sharing one psalter.

PUNCH – master for a type character engraved in hard metal, tempered and used as die to strike matrices, from which in turn type is cast.

QUARTO (4to) – book size resulted from folding a sheet with two folds at right-angles, thus giving pages one-quarter the size of the original sheet. Further folds yield the 8vo, 16mo, and 32mo formats; and folding the longer edge in thirds gives rise to the duodecimo or 12mo, and 24mo series, etc.

QUINTERNION – 20–page section; made up of five sheets, each printed with two pages on each side, and inserted one within the other and folded to yield 20 consecutive pages ready for sewing.

RAGGED SETTING – even word spacing and a ragged right-hand edge occur naturally in manuscript, and are also found in the small-scale work produced at the Gutenberghof; see also *justification*.

RECTO – right-hand page; see also *verso* and *folio*.

REGISTER – exact correspondence in position of the printed area on the two sides of a leaf; also the precise fit of colour printings.

REGLET – strip of oil-soaked wood used as inter-linear spacing material; the term "leading", to denote increments of space between lines of type, came about when metal strips were substituted for this purpose.

RITUAL – liturgical book which sets out the exact observation of the routine of worship for the celebrants.

ROTUNDA – round Gothic script of the fifteenth century, with Romanesque origins, and also favoured in Italy and Spain.

RUBRICATION – work of a scribe in adding initials, headings and other functional details, mostly in red (*rubrica, -ae* = red ochre) to MSS. or printed books.

SAND-CASTING – short-lived and laborious method by which types may have been cast in various cultures before the arrival of the typefounder's hand-mould.

SCHILLING – medieval monetary unit (1 schilling = 12 heller or 6 pfennigs).

SCHISM – state of divided spiritual allegiance resulting from a disputed election to the papacy.

SCRIPTORIUM – monastic or secular workshop for the copying and embellishment of manuscripts by hand.

SLUG – casting from the face of a line of type (or two lines, in the case of Needham's *Catholicon* theory) as an indissoluble unit.

SORTS – individual types or characters comprising a fount; special sorts being the less common ones not held in case.

SPACES – non-printing material in compositor's case for separating words and filling line endings.

SPECULUM – mirror, also signifying the book title: *Speculum humanae salvationis*, or *-nostrae salutis* (*The Mirror of Human Salvation*).

SPINDLE – the screw of a handpress, which transmits the impression.

STATIONER (Lat. *stationarius*) – bookseller, who conducted the production and trade in books on behalf of a university.

STEREOTYPING – making a duplicate metal cast of a printing surface from sand, plaster-of-paris or papier-mâché (technically feasible in incunabula period, but not harnessed industrially until later).

STRIKE – see *matrix*.

TABULA RUBRICARUM – list to show scribe what to insert in spaces left blank in printed text.

TENACLE – wooden copy-holder, an aid in setting from manuscript.

TEXTURA – contemporary northern black-letter hand, narrow, tall and spiky, which was taken as the model for the DK-, B42, and psalter-types.

TILL – a wedged, transverse board in the construction of a hand-press, through which the *spindle* passes.

TRINITARIANS – members of a monastic order, who had appointed to themselves the task of ransoming Christian slaves.

TYMPAN – support where a sheet of paper about to be printed is positioned, so that the pressure from the *platen* of a hand-press is evenly distributed; see also *frisket*.

TYPES OR CHARACTERS – metal letters, which may each be cast with the identical face in large numbers, and used repeatedly for setting and printing.

TYPEFOUNDING – manufacturing supplies of type (through cutting *punches*, striking and adjusting *matrices*, and casting with a *hand-mould*), a preliminary hurdle for the first printers, but soon to become established as a separate branch of supply.

TYPOGRAPHY – the whole art of printing; and design for the same as practised by an exceptional printer, publisher or industrial designer.

UNCIALS – Manuscript hand flourishing between the fourth and sixth centuries, in which lower-case characteristics continue to evolve from Roman capitals. Book artists still added initials of uncial or Lombardic design to MSS and printed books, purely as decorative survivals.

VELLUM – writing material prepared from animal skins, and used by Gutenberg and other printers in parallel with paper for certain copies of many editions.

VERSO – left-hand page; see also *recto*.

WALDENSIANS – heretical sect, fiercely persecuted by the Catholic Church.

WALPODE – titular official responsible to the archbishop of Mainz for public order.

WATERMARK – design made of wire sewn onto the mould, and impressed whilst making paper; consequently a source for dating or provenance.

WOODCUT – design cut in relief with knife on plank (as distinct from wood engraving with burin on end-grain).

"WORK OF THE BOOKS" – presumed to mean: "the printing works for producing books"; used of the printing house of the Gutenberg and Fust partnership.

X-HEIGHT – height of lower-case letters without ascenders or descenders; as x, m, n, u.

XYLOGRAPHY – printing from woodcut, as in blockbooks.

Index

Note
Italic numerals indicate pages on which illustrations appear.
Early names are indexed by forename wherever this is customary.
A handful of technical topics under possible discussion in early accounts appear under their modern headings; i.e. "form" or "alphabet" or "mould" are indexed under "matrix" where this is one hypothesized interpretation.
Passim has been reserved for those extended page sequences where confusion could occur; minor discontinuities are to be expected elsewhere.